Women and American Socialism, 1870–1920

Glucophage 500 mg 3X

Cimetidine 400 mg 2X

Jennifer Swian

MARI JO BUHLE

Women
and American Socialism,
1870–1920

UNIVERSITY OF ILLINOIS PRESS

Urbana   Chicago   London

Illini Books edition, 1983

Library of Congress Cataloging in Publication Data

Buhle, Mari Jo, 1943–
   Women and American socialism, 1870–1920.

   (The Working class in American history)
   Includes index.
   1. Feminism—United States—History.   2. Women and
socialism—United States—History.   3. United States—
History—1865–1921.   I. Title.   II. Series: Working
class in American history.
HQ1426.B82   305.4′2′0973   81–719
ISBN 0–252–00873–1 (cloth)   AACR2
ISBN 0–252–01045–0 (paper)

To my parents,
Joseph and Wanda Kupski

Acknowledgments

I owe my largest debt to the many librarians who aided my research. Dorothy Swanson of Tamiment Library, New York University, and Josephine Harper and the staff of the State Historical Society of Wisconsin—the proprietors of the richest collections of American radical history—responded generously to my many requests for assistance. Eva Mosely and Barbara Haber of the Arthur and Elizabeth Schlesinger Library of the History of Women in America, Radcliffe College, guided me through invaluable collections. Eugene De Gruson, Haldeman-Julius Collection, Pittsburg State University Library, brought to life the Kansas materials. I would like to thank as well the staffs of the William R. Perkins Library of Duke University, Kansas State Historical Society, Chicago Historical Society Library, Newberry Library, Milwaukee County Historical Society, Houghton Library of Harvard University, Sterling Library of Yale University, Labadie Collection of the University of Michigan Library, Illinois State Historical Survey of the University of Illinois Library, Boston Public Library, New York Public Library, and the Sophia Smith Collection of Smith College Library.

Friends and colleagues contributed in many ways. Neil Basen, Karen Blair, Linda Gordon, Burton Rosen, Ralph E. Shaffer, and Meredith Tax shared their own research with me and supplied an abundance of tips and anecdotes. My colleagues at Brown University, especially Naomi Lamoreaux, William McLoughlin, James Patterson, Joan Wallach Scott, and Gordon Wood, read early drafts of chapters and offered precise and meaningful criticisms. Dolores Hayden, Nancy Schrom Dye, James R. Green, Judith E. Smith, Ellen C. DuBois, Ann D. Gordon, Carol Poore, Hartmut Keil, Susan Porter Benson, and Blanche Wiesen Cook read selected chapters and offered expert advice; I am especially grateful for their comradely assistance and encouragement. Paul Buhle translated the bulk of foreign-language materials, while Edith Hoshino Altbach and Walter Conser checked several crucial translations from German.

The Louis M. Rabinowitz Foundation kindly provided financial assistance at a critical phase of my research.

My editors at the University of Illinois Press helped lessen the agonies of the final stages of production: Richard L. Wentworth and Elizabeth Dulany responded speedily to my many requests and inquiries; Bonnie Depp caught many errors and inconsistencies in the final copy. Herbert Gutman offered invaluable advice for improving the final draft and, most important, lifted my sagging spirits by showing an unbounded faith in the project. But, then, Professor Gutman has indirectly guided this work from its inception.

Finally, I wish to acknowledge the comradeship of Paul Buhle, which has sustained me in all my work.

Contents

Introduction   xi

1 German-American Socialists and the Woman Question   1

2 The Woman's Movement and Socialism, 1870–1900   49

3 Grass-Roots Origins, 1900–1908   104

4 The Woman's National Committee, 1908–13   145

5 Women's Labor   176

6 Woman Suffrage   214

7 Sexual Emancipation   246

8 Autumn Song   288

Heritage Lost and Regained   318

Index   329

Introduction

This book traces the evolution of the American Socialist women's movement over several generations. The major theme concerns the interplay of two parallel traditions, immigrant and native-born, with wholly different modes of organization and world views. The story begins in the 1870s and peaks in the first decades of the twentieth century, when Socialist women partially reconciled major differences, articulated a roughly synthetic political philosophy, and created a national movement under a common leadership. The narrative follows Socialist women into their principal campaigns of labor, suffrage, and sexual reform and ends with the precipitous decline of their movement during World War I.

In the largest sense, this book is also an observation of the intersection of class and gender politics at a turning point in American history, the consolidation of corporate capitalism. It examines the various ways groups of women related this major event to their own understanding of women's fate, how a common identification of the capitalist enemy as Moloch brought discrete sectors of women toward a similar political outlook and at the same time different solutions. The class-conscious response of immigrant Socialists thus stands in sharp contrast to a militant and independent sisterhood advocated by native-born women activists and supplies the dynamic of the unfolding story.

The Socialist women's movement was not a function of some other, more objective tendency but was, as Edward Thompson has written about the British working class, "present at its own making."[1] This point is important for both political and conceptual reasons. The blinding assumption that the women's movement served merely as a waystation for activists moving on to "real" class-conscious struggles has been wholly abandoned and implicitly disproved. I have not fashioned a saga from the biographies of leftist heroes like Lucy Parsons, Emma Goldman, "Mother" Jones, or Elizabeth Gurley Flynn. My story focuses instead on women's own institutions, with the tens of thousands of rank-and-file women who formed the Socialist women's movement, and with the policies established largely upon their own initiatives. To write their history is to rewrite the history of American Socialism; if that task is beyond the scope of this book, it is emphatically suggested by the main thread of interpretation.

An early, precursive event offers an illustration of this hidden history. During the late 1860s the New York branch of the International Workingmen's Association, the "First International," drew native-born radicals alongside immigrant German revolutionaries. The two groups shared an undoubted dedication to the emancipation of the working class, but the "Americans" alone expressed an equal commitment to women's freedom. The American sections attracted an unusually large number of women, including the most renowned publicist of woman suffrage, Victoria C. Woodhull, who published her own newspaper urging the International to support the advancement of women. German-American trade unionists, the increasingly embittered opposition, judged the American members a pollution of the movement's class purity. Inevitably, the two groups came to open conflict. After a series of maneuvers by both sides, Karl Marx himself recommended the expulsion of the American sections on the ground that they gave "precedence to the women's question over the question of labor." Refusing the voice of authority, the American representative countered in classic form: "The labor question is also a women's question, and the emancipation of woman must precede that of the workers."[2] No later development drew the lines any clearer or served better to introduce the main antagonists in the nineteenth-century Socialist movement.

Yet historians of American Socialism, almost until the present day, have seen only one side of the battle lines. Friedrich Sorge, Marx's chief lieutenant in the First International fray, might have been properly expected to dismiss the women activists as middle-class adventurists. British historian of the International R. W. Postgate similarly intended to vindicate orthodoxy when he charged Woodhull and friends with "destroying the proletarian character" of the American section by forcing its attention on the woman question. Scholars with more reason for an independent viewpoint have not reached far beyond these simple-minded charges. American Socialist leader Morris Hillquit, himself a refugee from German-American sectarianism, could only repeat in his *History of Socialism in the United States* (1903) that the women Internationalists had been "especially troublesome."[3] Hillquit's successors have continued to turn a blind eye on the source of women's militancy and have consequently denied an important claim to legitimacy. Recent scholars have not redressed these sins of commission; Victoria Woodhull still awaits her vindication.

This book begins with the premise that the conflict within the First International was not a quirk of history but, rather, a harbinger of future developments. Native-born women, who made their own demands in the name of the "good time coming," envisioned Socialism as both a cooperative and an egalitarian society. Thus the admonition "Make way, ye law makers and capitalists, make way for the coming cortege of the laborer and his bride" was not the raving of a Woodhull but the honest expectation of an ordinary suffrage activist.[4] Others asked: how could Socialists seek to transform the existing system without the self-confident participation of those most trampled underfoot by economic arrangements? Where could the vision of a better society be gained if not from an understanding of the home along with the factory?

Historians of American women have recently provided a conceptual framework for assessing the significance of these exhortations. By documenting distinctive forms of nineteenth-century social relations between the sexes, they have rooted the pervasive doctrine of spheres within its specific cultural context. Nancy F. Cott in *The Bonds of Womanhood* (1977) offered a valuable insight. Despite the tendency of industrialism to move production outside the household, Cott wrote, "the persistence of married women's occupation there, demanded by their obligation of housekeeping and child care, provided the material basis for separating the qualities of *women as a sex* from those of men." Cott concluded that because women shared a special destiny they viewed one another as "peers par excellence." Carroll Smith-Rosenberg also attributed a strong tendency toward female association to a rigid system of gender-role identification within the nineteenth-century family and society. She described extensive supportive networks emanating from the intimate friendships women reserved for themselves. She identified as well a highly complex set of rituals and conventions that brought women together and at the same time restricted the occasions for intimacy between men and women. Whereas relations between even husband and wife were stiff and formal, sisterly bonds and life-long friendships supplied the emotional core of nineteenth-century women's lives; they provided women with their principal sources of identity and vigor and formed the basis of a distinctive cultural experience.[5]

It is my contention that this specific cultural experience shaped women's political activities through the Gilded Age into the first decade of the twentieth century. Through their specialized role and separate institutions, native-born women achieved a collective consciousness that took on an explicitly political dimension. The link between "womanhood" and "sisterhood" thus formed quite naturally as women gathered into associations open only to members of their sex. The woman's movement, which formed after the Civil War, replicated in philosophy, patterns of organization, and ritual its cultural underpinnings and enlarged the concept of womanhood to its ultimate political limits.[6]

Other historians have suggested ways to appreciate the process by which groups remold popular ideology to express such grand political claims. Herbert Gutman has uncovered a variety of forms of resistance to the consolidation of corporate capitalism that included a defense of traditional values against those of the rising order. He has shown, for example, how trade unionists regularly used Christian imagery to express their political grievances, describing capitalists as latter-day pharaohs or money-changers in the temple and the working class as the children of Israel. Gutman interpreted this adaptation of popular moral concepts as a logical process of legitimation, as similar to the practice of demanding a truly cooperative society as the culmination of American republicanism. Radical activists, in other words, routinely drew upon indigenous traditions to strike out against injustice and to create a vision of a harmonious social system.[7]

Women activists employed the same means to express their own political grievances. True to expectation, they transmuted Christian piety into moral politics and, like other radicals of their day, gained a strong sanction in the adaptation of popular values. Enlarging the contemporary concept of womanhood, they asserted an active role for themselves in shaping the social order. Indeed, their faith in woman's agency—so firm in the Gilded Age and by contrast so alien to our modern sensibility—served to bolster their demands.

Native-born Socialist women, in the First International and after, inherited a distinct female culture rich in political potential. The majority of women within the Socialist movement, native-born women elucidated a distinctive philosophy of Socialism and outlined women's essential part in its creation. They clearly drew on deep-rooted traditions of sisterhood and maintained a spirit of separation from the male mainstream of the Socialist movement.

As the incident in the First International also suggests, a second group of Socialists possessed historic roots no less deep and tenacious. Turning to the nineteenth century, we find immigrant women performing an analogous adaptation of Old World values to the struggle for a better life in the new. Here again Gutman has underlined the power and perseverance of specific cultural forms among the foreign-born.[8] Strong enough to endure the trials of xenophobia and repression, immigrant Socialists proved equally obdurate in their commitment to family solidarity and most emphatically women's traditional role. The first groups of foreign-born Socialist women, the German-Americans of the 1870s, organized themselves as an auxiliary to the major Socialist organizations and prepared the way for Jews, Slavs, and other new immigrant women in later decades. Work in party schools, among the children, and in the kitchens of ethnic halls might be judged demeaning by twentieth-century observers, but foreign-born women took pride in their contributions. They aimed to ensure family cohesiveness within the radical community and, like native-born women, they placed their stamp upon Socialist practice. And they abjured the strident, independent activities of their native-born contemporaries.

The interplay between these two traditions, native- and foreign-born, also sets the American apart from the contemporary European Socialist women's movement. Only in Germany did the Socialist party boast a significant number of women, about the same proportion of 15 to 20 percent of the membership as in the United States. By way of contrast, German Socialist women lacked an autonomous political experience, for the mainstream women's movement was small, elite, and contributed only marginally, primarily at the leadership level, to the ranks of the party. The stellar activists and strategists in Germany addressed a range of issues similar to those discussed by their American counterparts. But the distance between formidable figures like Clara Zetkin and the average comrade kept the woman question at a relatively abstract theoretical plane in Germany, while women in the United States engaged in almost continuous, rough-and-tumble debates with experimentation and argument at nearly every level of the movement.[9]

If the Socialist women's movement in the United States lacked the size and sophistication of its German counterpart, it contributed vital insights to astute activists in its own country. First, American Socialist women insisted upon a more complex program than one designed to neutralize women's allegedly conservative instincts. They also sought to mobilize women under banners of sex no less than working-class emancipation. Second, the awakening of women from age-old bondage gave the American Socialist movement a moral depth and commitment to fundamental change in social relations in the coming order. Native- and foreign-born women, in their various ways, demonstrated that the prospect for a new civilization rested upon broader principles than class struggle.

Although I have avoided the vocabulary of sociology, I have intended this study as a contribution to the understanding of the formative generations of Socialist women and their particular aspirations. I hope to demonstrate that their movement was as much cultural as political, and that it developed over the course of a lengthy historical period. *Women and American Socialism* traces that development from its earliest expression in the 1870s, to its flowering at the turn of the century, to its demise by 1919. It follows several sectors of American women over this crucial half-century and relates their dreams of bringing into existence a cooperative and egalitarian social order. In a subtle fashion, this book also asserts the significance of women's presence to the shaping of the American radical tradition.

The first part concerns the key decades of the late nineteenth century, when women gained their initial experiences within parallel political movements. Chapter 1 discusses women's role within the German-dominated Socialist organizations of the 1870s and 1880s, the evolution of a distinctive perspective on the woman question, and the genesis of special types of women's societies within the fraternal wing of the Socialist movement. Chapter 2 examines the work of native-born activists within the mainstream woman's movement of the Gilded Age, especially its two major elements, the urban-based institutions and the Woman's Christian Temperance Union. It traces a key constituency into the major protest movements of the late 1880s and early 1890s and assesses their contributions. Together these chapters outline the contours of opposing conceptions of women's economic and political emancipation.

The next major section builds upon the nineteenth-century foundations. The eventful formation of the Socialist Party of America in 1901 inaugurated a new era by gathering a variety of radicals under its large and flexible umbrella.

For several years women veterans of the late nineteenth-century movements carried their traditions to the doorstep of the Socialist party, established a network of organizations, and sorted out their attitudes toward one another and toward the Socialist leadership itself. By 1907 a second generation of women ascended within the ranks of a maturing Socialist movement. Chapters 3 and 4 discuss attempts to mediate between major groups, the problems associated with the development of a national movement, and the personalities of a new generation of leaders.

The next three chapters follow Socialist women into their political work. Especially in the major urban areas, Socialist women intervened, sometimes decisively, in the great campaigns of the Progressive era. They asked hard questions about the work they undertook and repeatedly assessed the value of each accomplishment. They attempted also to relate political theory, which they studied assiduously, to practice; they argued the nature of their position with regard to mainstream women's groups. Chapter 5 takes up the most fundamental concern of Socialist women, women's right to labor. It outlines the theoretical premises that guided activists in the major strikes of wage-earning women, 1909–13, and outlines their contribution to these landmark labor events. Chapter 6 addresses a historic demand, woman suffrage, and examines Socialists' role in the climactic campaigns of the 1910s and their attitudes toward "bourgeois" suffragists. Chapter 7 turns to a more controversial issue, sexual emancipation. This chapter contrasts differing interpretations as suggested by the two major campaigns, the antiprostitution propaganda of the century's first decade and the birth control agitation of the second. It also relates contemporary discussions of sexuality to yet another important generational shift in the Socialist movement, the emergence of young men and women who broke the intellectual barriers of formalism to take on the colorful and heterodox garb of modernism. Chapter 7 thus represents the end in a progression of political perspectives and agitations.

Chapter 8 concludes this story by unraveling the Socialist women's movement into its constituent parts and describing its demise by 1919.

More than a quarter-century ago Daniel Bell claimed that Socialists failed because they were *in* but not *of* their world. He described Socialists as dreamers who could never find their moorings in American society.[10] Like other early scholars, Bell delved only deep enough into the history of the Socialist movement to discover its formal ideology, which he judged both superficial and alien to the prevailing pragmatic outlook shared by most Americans. Recently, historians have begun to investigate aspects of the Socialist movement besides its theoretical pronouncements. They have looked instead into the collective biographies and ritual practices of the participants, the defeated and now forgotten warriors against triumphant capitalism. *Women and American Socialism* is a contribution to the restoration of their history.

NOTES

1. E. P. Thompson, *The Making of the English Working Class* (New York, 1963), 9.
2. *The First International: Minutes of the Hague Congress of 1872*, ed. and trans. Hans Gerth (Madison, Wis., 1958), 195.
3. Friedrich A. Sorge, "Die Arbeiterbewegung in den Vereinigten Staaten, 1866–1876," *Die Neue Zeit*, 10 (1891–92), 394–95; Morris Hillquit, *The History of Socialism in the United States* (New York, 1903), 179; R. W. Postgate, *The Workers' International* (London, 1920), 77.
4. E. L. G. Willard, "The Labor Question," *Woman's Advocate* (Dayton, Ohio), Aug. 21, 1869, reprinted from *The Agitator*.
5. Nancy F. Cott, *The Bonds of Womanhood: "Woman's Sphere" in New England, 1780–1835* (New Haven, Conn., 1977), 188; Carroll Smith-Rosenberg, "The Female World of Love and Ritual: Relations between Women in Nineteenth-Century America," *Signs*, 1 (Autumn, 1975), 1–30.
6. For an insightful analysis of the woman's movement, see Estelle Freedman, "Separatism as Strategy: Female Institution Building and American Feminism, 1870–1930," *Feminist Studies*, 5 (Fall, 1979), 512–29. See also my essay in "Politics and Culture in Women's History: A Symposium," *ibid.*, 6 (Spring, 1980), 36–42. Since the completion of this manuscript, two important books on the Gilded Age woman's movement have appeared: Karen J. Blair, *The Clubwoman as Feminist: True Womanhood Redefined, 1868–1914* (New York, 1980), and Ruth Bordin, *Woman and Temperance: The Quest for Power and Liberty, 1873–1920* (Philadelphia, 1981).
7. Herbert Gutman, "Protestantism and the American Labor Movement: The Christian Spirit in the Gilded Age," In *Work, Culture and Society in Industrializing America* (New York, 1977), 79–117.
8. Gutman, *Work, Culture and Society.*
9. Research on European Socialist women has only recently appeared in print. Werner Thönnessen, *The Emancipation of Women: The Rise and Decline of the Women's Movement in German Social Democracy, 1863–1933*, was first published in Frankfurt in 1969; it was translated and reissued in London by Pluto Press in 1973. An anthology of essays, *Socialist Women: European Socialist Feminism in the Nineteenth and Early Twentieth Centuries*, ed. Marilyn J. Boxer and Jean H. Quataert (New York, 1978), suggests several lines of comparison. The fullest treatment to date is Jean H. Quataert's *Reluctant Feminists in German Social Democracy, 1885–1917* (Princeton, N.J., 1978). Quataert discusses the social context of the Socialist women's movement as well as the prevailing ideology of womanhood; she focuses, however, on the leadership rather than rank-and-file participants and discusses their political behavior as a function of the philosophical tensions between feminism and Socialism. Karen Honeycutt, "Socialism and Feminism in Imperial Germany," *Signs*, 5 (Autumn, 1979), 30–41, also centers on the ideological proclivities of the leaders.
10. Daniel Bell, "The Background and Development of Marxian Socialism in the United States," in Donald Drew Egbert and Stowe Persons, eds., *Socialism and American Life*, 2 vols. (Princeton, N.J., 1952), 1, 213–405.

1 German-American Socialists and the Woman Question

> The bourgeoisie has absolutely no interest in women's emancipation. On the contrary, only where there are slaves can the bourgeoisie prosper, and a proper bourgeois does not even want to make his own wife equal, let alone the entire female sex. The Social Democrats, on the contrary, must bend their entire will and effort, whether it is for the accomplishment of their own immediate purposes or not, to lend support to women's strivings for freedom. And although the woman question stands entirely upon its own principles, in the future when the two parties oppose women's emancipation, the Social Democratic party here in America must—if it is to be a true socialist movement—place in its program a short but meaningful paragraph: COMPLETE EQUALITY OF WOMEN WITH MEN.
>
> Augusta Lilienthal
> *New Yorker Volkszeitung*
> February 16, 1879

Delivered to an assembly of German-American intellectuals in New York, these eloquent phrases captured a sublime vision of American woman's rights merged with European Socialism. What constituency held such an unlikely view? The audience almost certainly comprised veteran reformers—aged Forty-eighters who had been pioneers of free thought, abolitionism, and trade unionism—sprinkled with woman suffrage advocates, younger bohemian workers, and petty merchants. It was a pugnacious if small group, heterodox even among the most radical. Lacking the means to effect such a grand reconciliation, its members nevertheless shared the speaker's aspiration. Woman's rights, a representative American reform, wedded to Old World proletarian militance promised a child surpassing both parents in raw power and adaptive vigor. Yet this vision, so carefully phrased by speaker Augusta Lilienthal, appeared decades before most Socialists entertained the possibility.

Augusta Lilienthal could understand woman's plight. Like many of her political colleagues, she had been born to a middle class in flux, a situation exacerbated in her case by the insecure status of women. Growing up during the 1840s in a village outside Berlin, Augusta enjoyed the privileges and relatively high social standing of a craftsman's family, actually touching royalty when her grandfather was summoned to repair the palace organ and she frolicked in the king's gardens. Such happiness and security proved only temporary. At the premature death of her father she was married off while still in her teens to a man three times her age. Bitterly unhappy in marriage, she survived her husband's early death a young and lonely widow.

Fortunes changed again, as Augusta drew close to circles of political reformers. At age nineteen she fell in love with an idealistic Jewish physician and in 1861 sailed with him to America. Saddened by the departure from her native land, Augusta found new joy sharing her husband's passionate interest in contemporary American events. The Lilienthals, abolitionist in spirit, devoted themselves to Lincoln and the Civil War effort until a typhoid epidemic quelled their activities. They were briefly thrown into a fight for personal survival, as Augusta tried to support the household on whatever wages she could earn as a needlewoman. With the war's end and the family's renewed health, Augusta and her husband were drawn again into reform circles. Labor unrest, the revival of the woman's rights movement, and the heightened political climate enticed the Lilienthals to take a prominent role in the contemporary radical movements. By the end of the decade Augusta Lilienthal had emerged from private life an ardent propagandist for woman's emancipation.[1]

Lilienthal located a politically congenial milieu among New York City's freethinkers. The first radical German-Americans, refugees from Germany's failed 1848 revolutions, had spread the doctrines of liberalism among their fellow emigrés. This generation fulfilled its historic mission by creating distinctive cultural-political institutions, like the *Turnvereine*, gymnastic and debating societies which supplied battalions of immigrants for the northern army during the Civil War. These intellectuals, many self-taught artisans or petty shopkeepers, had shared with native-born radicals an Enlightenment-inspired faith in free inquiry and advocated political freedom for all, including—at least some prominent German-Americans would insist—women. The most radical, like Mathilde Anneke, also espoused the postwar causes of Socialism and woman's rights.[2]

Lilienthal gained a platform for her views in the free-thought journal *Die Neue Zeit*, published in New York City. Determined to create a voice for women within the German-American community, its editors had set their sights upon a "perfect republic" wherein "man and woman must be equally considered by the laws." Lilienthal and other *Die Neue Zeit* writers praised the American woman's rights movement and sought to build upon its accomplishments. Its leaders they termed "born republicans," instinctively attuned to "their own political significance and grasping their coming opportunity" for freedom. They passionately defended the militant suffragists, even outspoken free lover Victoria Woodhull, as maligned champions destined to advance their sex and in the process all humanity. Thus *Die Neue Zeit* editors joined the contemporaneous American Woman Suffrage Association, Association for the Advancement of Women, and the first organizations for international peace formed by women. They might blanch at the Protestant piety endemic in woman suffrage circles and write blistering editorials against the tyranny of institutionalized religion over women in particular, but they nevertheless admired the moral fervor of indigenous radicals.[3]

By ties of language, heritage, and political commitment, Lilienthal and her colleagues were drawn as strongly to the German-American Socialist movement. They noted the dynamic influence of Socialists within the ethnic community and shared their devotion to workers' struggles. *Die Neue Zeit* editors demonstrated their sympathy by publishing reports of the International Workingmen's Association and by carrying popular essays on Karl Marx's recently published first volume of *Das Kapital*. Lilienthal and her friends also noted that these more recent immigrants, unlike the Forty-eighters, looked upon Socialism as their sole *raison d'être* and seemed to lack the necessary reverence for individual freedoms. Most important, German-American Socialists exhibited little enthusiasm for woman's rights. *Die Neue Zeit* editors could not compromise on this score and refused to sacrifice woman's cause to a movement blind to any struggle save that of the proletariat.

This unique stand placed its adherents in an ideological limbo. The masthead of *Die Neue Zeit* depicted conversational combatants over cups of steaming liquid, a scene that could have been drawn from life at some coffee bistro in Manhattan's Yorktown wherein the talk was enlivening but insufficient in itself to alter society. Rarely, such as during a peace rally at the height of the Franco-Prussian War, *Die Neue Zeit* editors played a pivotal role in the combined protest of native- and foreign-born radicals. The magazine's influence was, however, short-lived, as many of its respectable supporters opted for the patriotic cause of German nationalism following Bismarck's victory. *Die Neue Zeit* folded in 1871. Its core group fought on, taking advantage of whatever opportunities arose. Decades later Lilienthal described the "little circle of friends," hardly large enough to fill a parlor, launching a German-American woman suffrage society. In 1872 they had orchestrated a public meeting so remarkable that it purportedly stirred a new zeal for woman suffrage in the homeland. Addressing the crowd, Lilienthal reportedly won the heart of a doubting audience.[4] Although she rose to prominence after this event, she, like her comrades, lacked a stable constituency and could never utilize the full range of her talents and energy.

Lilienthal and the freethinkers did play a crucial role within the German-American Socialist movement. Freethinkers became outstanding intellectuals, pedagogues, and editors of the Socialist press. Although they sometimes restrained their enthusiasm for woman's rights to maintain their positions, they nevertheless preserved their dedication to universal reform. They helped to moderate the often narrow and sectarian spirit of the movement and kept the door open to a reconciliation with native-born activists. Lilienthal, unwilling to soften her own opinions, continued to crusade for woman's rights. With the help of friends, she forced the emerging Socialist leadership to articulate its position on the woman question.[5]

During the quarter-century of their prime, from the early 1870s until the late 1890s, German-American Socialists elaborated their formulations on the woman question into a distinct theoretical perspective and tactical program. Their own cultural traditions, fealty to the homeland Socialist movement, and aversion to the strains of indigenous American radicalism remained fundamental to their world view. Nevertheless, their perspective underwent a definite evolution, especially as their movement encompassed women determined to carry through programs similar to those proposed earlier by Augusta Lilienthal. German-American Socialist women did not create a coherent movement of their own. But they did set standards for women's participation within the larger Socialist movement and raised a banner that would float over a large segment of radical women for decades to come.

WOMANHOOD AND THE QUEST FOR SOCIALIST IDENTITY IN THE NEW LAND

In the 1870s German-American Socialists shaped a perspective on women's emancipation fully consonant with their desire for ideological purity. They looked askance at native-born radicals and sought to define themselves against all indigenous aberrations. Essentially romantics, they acted as redeemers of this alien land and set themselves to building trade unions and a political party first within their own ethnic working-class communities. Their attitude toward woman and her plight flowed directly from these predilections. Only the free-thinkers at their margins kept German-American Socialists from acting conclusively on their instincts and disavowing entirely two key issues of the day, woman's right to labor and woman suffrage.

German-American Socialism came of age at a portentous moment in national life. While Americans reveled in the gala centennial celebration of 1876, the radical community reached the nadir of its prestige and influence. Its descent from the glory of abolitionism had been swift and brutal, as corrupt politicians and entrepreneurs stole the fruits of the grand moral crusade which had culminated in the Civil War. Ostentatious wealth, uncontrolled cupidity, and unapologetic exploitation served as credo for an emerging elite, while the public seemed too apathetic to offer heartfelt resistance. Erstwhile prophets of American democracy, like Walt Whitman, were driven to silence. The great orators and journalists of the 1850s and 1860s—Wendell Phillips, Elizabeth Cady Stanton, Frederick Douglass, William Lloyd Garrison—had been reduced to the status of *eminence grise,* honored but no longer heard. Worse, their movements suffered incalculable losses. Groups of blacks, women, and labor now worked at cross-purposes rather than as the unified progressive force once envisioned, each becoming more narrowly self-interested. In short, the imagination, political verve, and unbounded philosophical outlook which had once marked the American radical spirit had dissipated, and radicals themselves seemed exhausted.[6]

Fatefully, most German-American Socialists immigrated just as the radical community fell into disarray, so that they had not even a bittersweet memory of the glory days. Then, too, the shibboleths of the 1870s—temperance and cheap money—seemed to workers trained in Germanic Socialism a ludicrous sham, "die amerikanishe Wirren" (American craziness). Devasted by unemployment following the Panic of 1873 and stung by nativist prejudice, German-American Socialists had little cause to adopt the democratic rhetoric of their new home. They came instead to view native-born radicals of nearly every variety as mountebanks proclaiming false principles and detracting from the serious tasks of proletarian mobilization.

Against the American grain, German-American Socialists predicted the inevitability of class conflict despite all fair-minded efforts at rational persuasion. The citizen, that basic unit of indigenous radicalism, they deemed an outmoded category, virtually irrelevant in the system of social classes under capitalism. Not a morally conscious, politically enlightened citizenry, they insisted, but the working class anticipating the future society in the forced socialization of their factory labor would be humanity's emancipator. If German-American Socialists saw themselves less as philosophers than as footsoldiers for the workers' revolution, they articulated a distinctive political philosophy nonetheless.[7]

Because indigenous radicals failed to appreciate the symmetry and beauty of their world view, German-American Socialists often described themselves as wandering prophets cast by destiny into a strange and hostile environment. They claimed a cultural heritage second to none, rich in genuine idealism yet rooted in the common people's struggle for existence. They embodied the race memory of the proletariat, a memory of continuous, collective life reaching back through centuries of oppression to olden times. Creative work had given them the strength to survive, while the struggle for a better existence had imparted a heroic consciousness:

> Away, my jumble of darkest thoughts
> Away, my mind to more beautiful times!
> In struggle have I become a man
> As a man I will struggle on.

> You working people, you alone
> Have all my thoughts, all that is me!
> Look to the struggle, past sorrow and pain
> To better days where the red glows plain
> Then—may you bury me in peace.[8]

Holding back their crusade was a selfishness now personified by the capitalist class. Through power over economic, social, and intellectual life, capitalists had disguised their Midas love for gold and in the name of "progress" had forced their culture upon humanity. "The so-called godly world-order," editor and novelist August Otto-Walster reflected, "now recommended and praised, is seen in its true light as a hateful and gluttonous monster."[9] Against Moloch, Socialists set themselves, outnumbered but destined to win. If they felt the sting of temporary disfavor, slandered in the capitalist press as near-criminal rabble and treated to a justice as corrupt as the bourgeoisie itself—"a caricature of a republic, that we [suffer] in a parody of a free land"—the end would come.[10] As the proletariat grew more perceptive, as the bonds of class began to cross ethnic and national boundaries, workers everywhere would join what Lenin later termed the "festival of the oppressed":

> O brothers from East, from South and West
> Still for a moment your expectant calls.
> Let us celebrate our festival
> And the days ahead of harmony for all.
> O! That the world would be a temple
> Humanity at last made free
> To sink wage-slavery once for all
> That I wish—may it be![11]

Consistent with their faith, Socialists pinned their highest hopes upon the mobilization of the working class into trade unions and their own political party. In many places where German-American workers gathered, their industrial skills and organizational abilities allowed them to create successful trade unions and enjoy an influence disproportionate to their numbers. The brewing industry in St. Louis, Milwaukee, Chicago, New York, and other cities thus prompted one of the earliest industrial union movements in the United States. Woodworking of all kinds, particularly the more skilled sectors of carpentry, piano construction, and cabinetmaking, similarly offered important labor opportunities. Through a range of occupations, from cigarmaking to textile and shoe production, German-American Socialists gained confidence from their superior mechanical knowledge and capacity for union leadership.[12] They hoped to use their relatively strong position in the shop to create the principal mechanism for advancement: the revolutionary political party. The *Communist Manifesto* of 1848 had designated the party as the major instrument of political representation, and most Socialists envisioned the party as a unifying force, center for clarifying theory, arbiter of revolutionary strategy. Perhaps that party could broaden itself into a vast political movement, contest elections, and finally seize the state from the bourgeoisie; or perhaps, for an interim at least, it would more modestly guide the economic struggle and protect the proletarian movement from ideological dilution. In either case, the chief responsibility of Socialists was to maintain and develop the political organization. Composed of regional branches, usually subdivided by neighborhood or ethnic group, and presided over nationally by an executive committee, the party presumed to function as a democracy unto itself, a model for the ultimate democracy that was Socialism. [13]

A strong network of cultural institutions on the Old World model under-pinned the economic and political organizations, gave them vitality and staying power. Like most other German-Americans, Socialists clustered in ethnic neighborhoods wherever possible to defend their distinct style of life and to enhance their material well-being. As soon as Socialists formed trade unions and party branches, they moved to create an array of social clubs and sick-and-death benefit societies. Greater New York, New Jersey's Hudson County, Bal-timore, Buffalo, Detroit, Cincinnati, Chicago, Philadelphia, Milwaukee, St. Louis, and San Francisco along with the smaller settlements like Allegheny City, Pennsylvania, Evansville, Indiana, Manchester, New Hampshire, West Meriden, Connecticut, Menomenee, Wisconsin, Grand Rapids, Michigan, and Burlington, Iowa, could boast a cultural flowering suffused with socialistic principles. Through this institutional web Socialists extended their influence far beyond the actual party membership, which fluctuated between a few hundred and a few thousand. Often rootless and alienated outside their com-munities, Socialists built upon their strengths within, eager always for the better day ahead. [14]

Socialists struggled against heavy odds to maintain their ethnic-qua-political identity. Not merely did Socialism not arrive as scheduled, but the precious resources German-Americans carried in their hearts faced the threat of anni-hilation. Old World holidays did not fit the American calendar. The sense of craftsmanship already fragile in Germany now faced severe threats from accel-erating technological change. Far more than in Europe, the catchpenny mer-chant seemed to advance over the honest worker, creating a German-American petty bourgeoisie anxious to abandon old faiths for scraps from the capitalist's table. The ethnic neighborhood, barely established, was subject to disintegra-tion as sons and daughters moved away and new immigrant groups crowded the most impoverished sections. German-American radicals tasted the bitterness of their new life, punned their adopted land "Malhürica"—misfortune, country of broken dreams. [15]

Still, German-American Socialists were politically resilient and transcended these sorrows. They succeeded for decades because new German immigration reinforced their communities, and because their transplanted culture was vital enough to sustain the immigrants at least for their own lifetimes. Through their trade union and social clubs more than through their party, in their dreams of gathering proletarian battalions more than in their actual experiences with American workers, they kept alive a vision formed during their youth. The costs of this unyielding will were borne out in an emotional rejection of the very American society they sought to transform. However ostensibily interna- tional in purpose, German-American Socialists could not risk assimilation without the threat of losing themselves.

This dedication to ideological integrity affected the manner in which Social- ists handled the critical issues of women's emancipation. They might phrase their interpretations in philosophical terms culled from the approved European texts, but beneath the rhetoric lay the same qualities that endowed their move- ment with its unique and unyielding character. Socialists believed in the sanc- tity of separate spheres for men and women and enshrined women's role as guardian of the proletarian family. No less romantic about womanhood than the proletariat, they sought to preserve feminine virtue against all threats, be they capitalism or a pernicious woman's rights influence.

According to a sympathetic observer, Germans brought with them to the new country "two great virtues": reverence for woman and devotion to family life. Most German-Americans immigrated as families and tried to recreate as far as possible Old World customs. As the husband slaved to secure his home, the *Hausfrau* served as his companion and guardian of the precious family circle. "Depth of sentiment," "warmth of heart," "strength of feeling"—German- Americans commonly employed such phrases to describe women's unique contributions to the family spirit. Even more than their nonradical compatriots, Socialists believed in the strength and beauty of the proletarian family, for they envisioned it as the basis of a new civilization. [16]

Economic arrangements tightened these bonds of sentiment. As craft or semiskilled workers, many German-American men enjoyed sufficient incomes, at least in good times, to maintain the family's welfare. Few married women worked outside their homes, although many supplemented the household budget in various ways, such as by keeping boarders, performing home needle- work, or joining the factory force temporarily as seasonal laborers. Like most of their ethnic neighbors, Socialists defended the principle of the family wage, with the man the chief and preferably only breadwinner. Most wage labor by women and children they viewed as anathema, abhorrent in itself and a leading cause of economic distress. They relegated woman to a distinctly different— although not inherently inferior—station from man's. Wage earner and help- meet, factory worker and guardian of the household, husband and wife were congruent elements in the proletarian family. [17]

Socialists anxiously repelled the tendencies in American life that seemingly threatened this harmonious division of responsibilities. Itinerant journalists, scholars, and social critics from at least the time of the Civil War into the early twentieth century thus described American "peculiarities" not infrequently as the chief sources of a malaise that deprived second- and third-generation immigrants of their cultural heritage. Adolf Douai, soon to become a leading Socialist intellectual, wrote in 1864 that the Yankee family was incapable of true harmony, torn by the antagonism between the sexes. Less joy existed among husband, wife, and children; the entire mien of the American household was "too distant and cold" for Old World tastes. Worse, the precious link between generations had snapped. "Growing children often leave the parental home never to return, . . . daughters marry without consultation, without even knowledge of the parents. . . ." No wonder women sought absolute equality in this strange country, dressed sometimes in bloomers, and praised an individualistic Manchester-liberal economics that Socialists despised.[18]

German-American Socialists therefore saw it their duty to bolster the working-class family and especially to protect woman's domestic role. Like Marx and Engels before them, they mourned the "action of Modern Industry [wherein] all family ties among the proletarian are torn asunder, and their children transformed into simple articles of commerce and instruments of labor. . . ."[19] Adolf Douai wrote in 1878 that "one of the most beautiful aims" of Socialism was the restoration of family unity.[20] Thus Socialists transmuted "scientific" principles into a reaffirmation of woman's traditional role.

The roots of this sentiment were, however, deeper than the *Communist Manifesto* and could be traced through the powerful literary romanticism of German culture. Like their ethnic counterparts, Socialists admired Friedrich Schiller, whose historical drama had popularized the romantic archetype, the heroic figure driven by inner feeling to overcome the strictures of existing society. In this poetic vision, honor, love, and bravery counted more than rationality, and the protagonist sought the objects of his imagination through a bittersweet struggle for destiny. At the center of the drama was Woman, all-embracing symbol of life. Because she signified nature, woman possessed a messianic fate above the commonplace affairs of men. Only through woman could humanity realize its potential, escape its sorrowful condition to find eternal happiness.[21] In their own minds Socialists, of course, were the heroic figures, the revolutionary struggle their "poetry of life." With little difficulty they translated the Romantic paradigm into proletarian terms: the rebel as worker; the woman as proletarian sweetheart, wife, and mother; restrictive reality as American bourgeois society. While the original romanticism sought to recapture the unspoiled folkish beauty of peasant life and to promote a sense of national culture, the Socialist "romantics" apotheosized the worker and his family, the microcosm of a universal people's culture about to realize age-old aspirations in the coming events.

German-American Socialist literature, itself a vibrant testament to the power of the romantic mood, reinforced the vision of woman as timeless inspiration. The early movement's most talented writer and prestigious journalist, August Otto-Walster, thus devoted his literary energies to refashioning the medieval romance. In his stories of the youthful artisan and his beloved maiden, centuries fell away and the eternal traits—physical beauty, vigor, the will to resist tyranny—predominated. The quality of pure womanhood, perhaps perceived more readily in a less complex era, had essentially endured and was, in the mid-nineteenth century, ever capable of inspiring man to reach toward his destiny. German-American poets, following the young Heine, Freiligrath, and others in the old country, likewise gave heroic treatment to womanhood. They typically depicted proletarian misery, the working class's struggle for redemption, and gave woman a central place in the dramatic narrative. [22] Domestic life was imperiled by low wages, woman abused and dishonored by her lot, the family suffering terribly:

> The man cries for labor, the child for bread
> The wife appeals for better health from her sick bed
> But satisfaction in the hovel is only for the dead! [23]

Woman the victim but also woman the carrier of freedom were complementary images. An eyewitness to the bitter Lawrence, Massachusetts, textile strike of 1877 captured this imagery of woman as inspirational figure:

> O, Bride of Freedom the hour draws nigh
> Lead us into struggle, to Victory
> Resound 'Equality' as slogan of the Hour
> And end the Rulers' bloody War.
> And if not Freedom, then call us back
> The spirit of vengeance shall not lack. [24]

Literary giant, Socialist-anarchist Robert Reitzel, spun romantic images of womanhood into a radical philosophy. "What would paradise be without Love?" asked Reitzel rhetorically as if to challenge mundane material aspirations. For it was Love that in the first instance stirred the revolutionary consciousness. The romantic rebel's vision of paradise, perhaps not to be realized in his lifetime, was nurtured at every stage of life by woman's presence. From childhood under mother's guiding hand through the aching joy of first love, on to maturity's tangled paths, the image of woman—as mother, sweetheart, and wife—remained always the guiding star. No revolutionary could think otherwise. "If I did not already have a wife whom I love with an ideal glorification, the legacy of mother's love in man's heart," Reitzel testified, "I would still have to love in order to attain that heroic portion that grows from the struggle for liberation to Revolution." [25]

The importance of this lyric sensibility can hardly be overestimated. If woman herself often represented little more than an abstraction, hardly a shadow compared to the subjectivity of the male protagonist locked in joy and agony over life's choices, the depiction of her suffering pushed the romantic imperative to revolutionary ends. Just as the rebellious spirit found its surest enemy in the capitalist class, so woman found her savior in Socialism. The Socialist mission thus called for the realization of ancient ties among working people, a return to the precapitalist cooperative spirit now armed with the productive apparatus capitalism had done so much to create. Woman would indeed be emancipated under Socialism, free to live and love as she chose. But there was little doubt that she would retreat from the workaday world, resist the appeal of individualism inherent in the woman's rights campaign, and regain her "natural" relationship with man at the hearth, realizing herself in the family life now impossible under capitalism. Precisely how woman might add her virtue to the energy of the male proletariat nevertheless remained somewhat a mystery.

Given their strong attachment to romantic conceptions of womanhood, German-American Socialists were not inclined to promote women's advancement into civil society. They certainly had no qualms about attacking the woman's rights campaign as a danger to woman's destiny as well as a major distraction from the class struggle. Left to themselves, German-American Socialists might have dismissed the woman question as one more example of American eccentricity. The freethinkers within their ranks, however, denied such an easy resolution, and at their most important meetings of the 1870s German-American Socialists articulated a rudimentary position on the role of women in the revolutionary struggle.

For doctrinal guidance the immigrant cadre turned to Europe. By the mid-1870s the German Social Democracy had advanced a general position. Especially instrumental in shaping this view were the followers of Ferdinand Lassalle, who had popularized Socialism during the 1860s through a program of universal male suffrage, workers' cooperatives, and the attainment of a "People's State." Marx's followers had regarded such schemes as utopian and suspiciously nationalist, but they could hardly dispute the popular appeal that far outstripped their own program. Despite Marx's objections, the historic unification congress at Gotha in 1875 grafted considerable Lassallean notions upon the world's most prestigious Socialist movement. The Lassallean praise for the "coziness" and "poetry of domestic life," its disdain for women's wage labor, was not made explicit in the Gotha program, but its logic imbedded itself in the fundamental Socialist world view of the 1870s.[26] Woman suffrage gained even less acceptance. Marx himself had privately treated the subject with derision, writing to a friend in the late 1860s that "German women should have begun by driving their men to self-emancipation" rather than "seeking emancipation for themselves directly." The vast majority of German Socialists looked upon woman suffrage as a secondary issue at best, likely to be used by capitalists to retard the class struggle. [27] German-American Socialists, many former followers of Lassalle, had scant reason to question this position. "Die Frauenfrage wird nur mit der allgemeinen sozialen Fragen ihre Lösung finden"—"the woman question will find its solution only with the entire social question"—phrased a dozen different ways, became the dominant logic. [28]

• German-American Socialists replicated this logic in the United States. As far back as the 1850s German-American typographers had struck to ban women from their trade, and by the mid-1870s several party leaders were ready to join a renewed craft union call for the restriction of women's labor. Although some Socialists had sought in various times and places to organize women workers, the majority leaned toward some form of exclusion, gaining sympathy from those who granted the abstract principle of women's right to labor under ideal conditions but who feared for their welfare under capitalist production. In 1875 Socialists moved to amend the party platform to include a statutory restriction of women's labor, demanding the elimination of all work by mothers with children under fourteen, the banning of women workers from nightwork, over-time, and Sunday employment, and a limitation of their hours to eight per day. [29] Socialists proved even more obdurate on the issue of woman suffrage. A key New York section in the early 1870s had passed a resolution stating, "In recognition, that universal suffrage cannot free humanity from slavery. . . . The gaining of the vote by women is not in the best interests of the workers." In the mid-1870s this opinion still prevailed. Movement propagandists wrote that the existing woman suffrage movement had nothing to do with women's emanci-pation, that the current agitation was led by "bad" wives who "don't know or don't want to know that marriage is a relationship which depends upon women performing their duties," or, again, "the woman of true spiritual and heartful nature, feels that . . . active participation in public affairs is . . . not in her best interest." [30]

At precisely this point Augusta Lilienthal and her friends played a crucial role in forcing Socialists to reflect upon the implications of their actions. Shortly before the publication of the proposed plank to restrict women's labor, the New York freethinkers called a meeting to discuss the pertinent issues. At this gath-ering two prominent party functionaries, leading newspaper editor Gustav Lyser and union champion Adolph Strasser, offered a picture of unrelieved misery, the simultaneous lowering of men's wages and the increase in prostitution, a degradation so fierce and comprehensive that it practically unsexed the race. They summoned up images almost too frightening to contemplate, of wives emerging from German ironworks drunk with brandy and covered with soot, of British women coal miners half-naked yet laboring alongside men. Opposing speakers, outstanding intellectual Alexander Jonas and Augusta Lilienthal, were unshaken by these portraits. Jonas pointed out that the proposed call for banning women's labor would utterly discredit the Socialist movement before the American radical community. Lilienthal declared it barbaric to deny poor women the right to work for the bread they and their families needed. For a party which sought to diminish women's few existing rights, she added, one could only say as Bismarck did to the pope, "Pfui!" The responsible alternative, Jonas averred, was for Socialists to demand equal wages for equal work and to proclaim women's enfranchisement a potential boon, an opportunity to utilize women's exceptional abilities and hence a contribution to the movement as a whole.[31]

Over the protests of the freethinkers, led by Jonas and Lilienthal, the restrictive program passed the first regular party congress in 1875, along with a demand for equal wages for equal work. But the issue would not rest. A prominent party journalist appealed the same year to the authority of European masters and warned that the persistent discussion of woman's rights had led to dangerous "arguments and splits" in the ranks.[32]

Drawing together several regional groups and remnants of the First International, the historic conference of 1876 promised to bury old controversies in the spirit of unity. Although the renamed Workingmen's party existed only a year, the meeting did mark the inauguration of a permanent Socialist movement. Delegates rebuffed a demand by the only surviving women's section of the First International for an outright pledge to women's equality.[33] They rendered instead what they believed to be the definitive Socialist statement on women's economic and political status:

> The emancipation of Labor is a social problem, a problem concerning the whole human race and embracing both sexes. The emancipation of women will be accomplished with the emancipation of *men*, and the so-called woman's rights question will be solved with the labor question. All evils and wrongs of the present society can be abolished only when economical freedom is conquered for men as well as for women.
>
> It is the duty therefore of the wives and daughters of workingmen to organize themselves and take their places within the ranks of struggling labor. To aid and support them in this work is the duty of the *men*. By uniting their efforts they will succeed in breaking the economic fetters, and a new and free race of men and women will arise recognizing each other as peers.
>
> We acknowledge the perfect equality of rights of both sexes and in the Workingmen's Party of the United States this equality of rights is a principle and is strictly observed.[34]

Between these lines read the whole pathos of the movement. To achieve their presumed destiny in the United States, Socialists would have to adapt their faith; yet their very staying power seemingly depended upon a fidelity to a world view only immigrants possessed. Because woman's rights had come to symbolize the adaptation at once sought and shunned, German-American Socialists developed a unique perspective. They outlined a position fully consistent with their fidelity to the class struggle and, equally important, with their conception of women's primary responsibility to the working-class family. This resolution left an indelible mark upon the Socialist movement. It not only suggested the forms of women's mobilization in the 1870s but set the tone for all future discussions of the woman question and Socialism.

WOMEN'S ORGANIZATIONS IN THE 1870S

"Working women! Wives and daughters of German workers," the first official German-American Socialist newspaper intoned in 1873, "Everything which is said in this paper for the worker . . . applies to you also!"[35] This appeal was not, however, a literal command for women to assume a place alongside men in the unions and the party. Rather, women's evident talent for managing domestic affairs suggested a subpolitical mobilization essentially educational and fraternal in character. Organically bound to the party through personal loyalty, family ties, and administrative obligations, the women's sector was to transmute domestic skills into organizational excellence.

The auxiliary form fitted this purpose and became the organizational staple of generations of immigrant Socialist women. The German Social Democracy had pioneered this form, and as one correspondent noted with pride (if also considerable exaggeration), in Germany "one hears now . . . that no maiden will have a husband who is a [political] sleepy-head. . . ."[36] So it was to be in the United States. German-American *Hausfrauen* and their daughters found ways to participate comfortably, to feel essential to the revolutionary struggle while fulfilling their duties to the family and to the larger family circle of the Socialist movement. Gathered in auxiliaries, women provided a host of social services and, party leaders conceded candidly, were safe from the influence of woman's rights agitators.

The Socialist milieu, ostensibly political, also operated as a spiritual home, a relief corps, a marriage brokerage, a recreational center, and in the last instance as a burial service for the loyal member. Like an ideal community or all-consuming lodge, the Socialist movement meant everything for the revolutionary wanderer who had come so far in search of home and work as well as political destiny. And this essential inner social life of the movement did in fact depend on women for its perpetuation. In turn it was the social activities, appealing to women's sense of devotion to family and faith, that kept wives and daughters within the fold. As a Newark correspondent averred, these affairs encouraged women to pour their benevolent energies into the movement rather than elsewhere. Various charity leagues, choral groups, nurseries, and purely recreational programs established by the churches and businesses in the German-American communities inevitably exerted a strong, conservative pull on women. Only a Socialist network of parallel institutions and activities could draw women into the movement and retain their loyalty over the course of a lifetime.[37]

Here, in what is usually termed the fraternal network, women participated avidly and enjoyed a leverage they never gained in the party proper. To suggest that the participants merely found a harmless substitute for political activity would be an oversimplification. Along with Socialist men, women discovered ways to preserve their inherited culture and language and to educate their children to appreciate what they considered the positive aspects of the Old World traditions. Through their contributions women also gave order and meaning to their new lives in America. Social activities such as community bake fests or musical performances offered women an opportunity to enjoy along with their husbands and children a break from the workaday routine and, perhaps most important, to escape the isolation of household work. In the fraternal network women met others of similar sensibilities and formed enduring friendships. Women also gained a feeling of self-worth, for their expertise, denied in politics, was here widely granted. If some women found the service role intolerable, many created a place for themselves at the heart of the movement.

Women took responsibility for planning many entertainments and party fests. On a Saturday evening in New York, for example, a women's group (sometimes called *Frauenkränzchen*—literally, "hen parties") might sponsor an event held at the Socialist-owned Germania Hall in the Bowery. As the reporter customarily noted, the arrangements provided by the women "left nothing to be desired." Earnest and humorous readings by prominent women, their husbands, and children drew rousing applause, prefacing hours of song and dance lasting well into the early morning. At the close of the evening comrades joined in singing an honored revolutionary ballad and toasted the women for their good work. Thoroughly enjoyable, such an event was a mark of the party's standing in the community.[38]

Socialist women placed special emphasis upon children's participation in these events, especially where a ceremonial character allowed for recitations and pageantry. In St. Louis, where the local women's circle held its first ball in late 1876, the program began with a reading of the declamation "Freedom, Truth, and Love" by a twelve-year-old girl, followed by showering applause and the recitation of an exhortative poem, "Forward!" by a fourteen-year-old girl. In later years the organization of children's performances became major projects, and thousands of youngsters received their first voice or instrument lessons in Socialist ranks. Likewise as the movement grew, costumes became more ornate, pageants more elaborate to celebrate the Socialist spirit.[39]

Women also helped lay the foundation for the Socialist theater during these years, as the readings of declamations and poems turned into serious dramatic presentations. Thus Newark women in late 1876 sponsored a program featuring not only readings and musical solos but a tableau, "The Socialist Society," based on a story in a German Socialist newspaper, and a performance of folk humor.[40] Women usually did not direct such theatricals and often took secondary acting roles to male leaders. But their participation was essential. Their enthusiasm and skill helped foster the expansion of German-American Socialist theater and pageantry into a marked movement by the 1880s.

Women also joined in the holiday celebrations that played a crucial role in sustaining Socialist organization. As a historian of the movement has recorded, the Yankee penchant for unrelieved labor had sheered off the bulk of traditional Old World holidays enjoyed by Germans "on the other side." The ability of Socialists, therefore, to sponsor their own commemorative and celebrative events in America—Winterfests (instead of Christmas), Paris Commune meetings in February, even masked balls similar to those staged by their bourgeois ethnic counterparts—validated the movement's standing as a social force. During the warm summer months Socialists deftly grasped the opportunities afforded by the American Sabbitarian laws, which practically forced Germans into the countryside on Sunday to drink beer in peace and to find a momentary escape from the oppression of crowded city life. Providing campgrounds, speakers, and entertainments in the fresh air and sunshine, Socialists transformed the day's excursion into a mixture of organized leisure and radical propaganda, a high point in the round of annual events. As a hard-pressed Cincinnati section reported in 1877, the success of such events was itself a "moral victory" for the movement. Women could rightfully take pride in their indispensable contributions to the coalescence of the community and working class under the Socialist banner.[41]

By the close of the 1870s Socialists had launched the other major program which would occupy foreign-born radical women for generations: the Socialist school. Adolf Douai, author and pioneering activist in the kindergarten and progressive primary school movement, helped blaze the path for women comrades, many of whom were also experienced educational reformers. Here again, less in administration, which usually remained in men's hands, than as the staff of such schools, women played indispensable roles. A Socialist branch in Paterson, New Jersey, for example, in 1878 characteristically dedicated a new "free" school to the sainted Lassalle, the holy "Red Flag of Universal Brotherhood," and the future generations of Socialist revolutionaries. From the major urban settlements to the small industrial towns, Socialists introduced wherever feasible their own schools, a link in language and literature to the Old World, in free thought to the future society.[42]

Finally, Socialist women organized the solicitation of funds for party coffers.

Theatrical performances, musical entertainments large and small, gatherings of all kinds ended almost invariably in a fund appeal. And these public acts represented only a few of the many ways whereby women raised money to cover the party's expenses, for example, of the press and agitational campaigns. Not only did women plan the programs and provide the refreshments for such events, but they helped solicit strike donations and worked endlessly to raise necessary cash for the party's debt-ridden English-language newspapers. Women undoubtedly dug into their own meager household budgets to supplement these efforts. They provided baked goods and fancy works for raffles and bazaars, but they also made the fund-raising activity into something less than drudgery, the sacrifices required for the movement's survival other than self-denial. [43]

From their first appearances at public meetings, German-American women thus began to create a variety of means to demonstrate their loyalty to the cause, means suggesting the subtle strength of their role within the Socialist movement. Their modest goal of providing a "good red flag—without flaws," and often with elaborate needlework design, could imply a larger intent. Observers who perceived the flag as an empty ideological mechanism rather than the soul-stirring symbol it had become for European radical movements, or who judged the fraternal apparatus as a mere appendage to a political movement rather than a world unto itself, could scarcely appreciate the sincerity of women participants, the sense of self-worth they derived from their chosen tasks, their image of themselves as important Socialist activists. [44]

The same cultural bonds which gave German-American women distinct organizational duties also mitigated against any more sophisticated political orientation. Modest efforts at formal organization and education, supported by notable party leaders, nevertheless met with apathy and even resistance. The issues of women's collective participation on a higher level in the movement could be avoided, but only at a cost.

In January, 1875, a committee of New York Socialist women, including the wives of prominent party editors and organizers, issued a call to daughters and wives of local workingmen "to stand up for a great idea and to show the men that [women] also understood the full meaning of Socialism." [45] Soon after a similar call went out in Philadelphia, and party papers relayed the message to Socialist readers across the nation. Groups dubbed the *Frauenverein* (women's club), *Frauenversammlung* (women's organization), and *Frauensection* (women's section) sprang up in these two cities, Newark, and St. Louis, while the Milwaukee women's section of the International simply transferred to the new organization. Admittedly few in number, these women nevertheless felt their calling. "We have all the more burden to bear than the men . . . so we have the urgent duty . . . to organize ourselves on the side of . . . our loved ones in the holy battle to free suffering humanity," Philadelphia women declared. [46] Only Socialists among women's groups in the United States could so unequivocally affirm, "Our fatherland the whole world, Our religion the social democracy, Our nation all humanity," and quote with revolutionary fervor:

> Therefore without rest or quiet
> Until humanity has thrown off its burden
> The great work continues
> The robbers' den to vanquish
> And freedom, freedom shall blaze![47]

In the first instance *Frauenvereine* were intended to serve as educational societies for women learning the rudiments of Socialist doctrine. While the press emphasized the importance of reaching unconverted women, to counter their alleged conservative tendencies and to tap their emotional energies for the cause, *Frauenvereine* essentially provided a lecture series for the faithful. Speakers regularly explored "women's issues" such as the misery of destitute women or the plentitude of marital unhappiness caused by poverty, along with a variety of standard labor and political topics. The didactic message of these lectures, eliciting women's loyalty to the Socialist movement, had the predictability of day following night. Local party leaders frequently appeared, paying tribute to their own and comrades' wives seated in the audience. A handful of women speakers, usually the same wives of prominent organizers, repeated the familiar messages. Well-intended but uninspiring, *Frauenverein* programs offered busy women party loyalists extra responsibility without the compensation of real prestige or power in the movement.[48]

The indifference of the *Frauenvereine* to contemporary woman's rights struggles followed from the clubs' origins and composition. *Frauenverein* leaders, the most politically advanced women in the Socialist milieu, took no apparent interest in Augusta Lilienthal's plea for the recognition of women's interests distinct from their duties as proletarian helpmeets. They likely could not comprehend Lilienthal's charge that Socialist women who opposed the political advancement of their sex were their own worst enemies. Naturally, *Frauenverein* members failed to join the freethinkers' campaign to defeat the party's plank on the exclusion of all women from wage labor, or the parallel effort to contest the Socialist opposition to woman suffrage. *Frauenverein* activists stood closer to their friend Gustav Lyser, who simultaneously praised the value of women's fraternal organizations and cursed woman's wage labor as the shame of the nineteenth century. They accepted without protest the prediction that women would make unreliable voters, more likely "a new strength for priests and enemies of the proletariat" (in the words of one party leader) than a boon to the cause. The self-avowed "second line" to the Socialist offensive, women loyalists disdained to claim more.[49]

This perspective raised doubts about the viability of any organized activities for women distinct from their fraternal functions. Socialist editors devoted at most a few back columns of their newspapers to women's organizational discussions, and party conventions took no official action to encourage such ventures. By the end of 1876 Philadelphia women began to voice discontent with the status of women's organizations in the party proper. Disturbed by what they perceived as a growing "jealousy" toward women's own organizations, they could not understand why male comrades should resent women's small but hard-won successes. How could political men be so unmindful, they asked aloud, as to fail to recognize that social conditions necessitated a special approach to reach women? The fondest hope of these women, that their own organizations be endowed with official status and all due consideration, remained for this era unrealized.[50]

Most disappointing was their failure to develop the *Frauenverein* network into a distinct sector of the Socialist movement. Philadelphia women called for the formation of a national Socialist women's federation, an endeavor which might ease the pangs of geographical isolation while providing a forum for the exchange of ideas and skills. But as the party underwent a membership crisis in the late 1870s, the women's clubs virtually disappeared. Where *Frauenverein* members continued to gather to listen to now-familiar messages about the danger of woman suffrage activity alongside entreaties to aid their menfolk, about the equality of women in an abstract physiognomic sense alongside warnings that the woman's rights movement was a bourgeois trick designed to lure them away from Socialism, the mixture of signals proved confusing and ultimately a hindrance for those desiring to develop organizational self-confidence. Imploring women to cleave to a movement which had taken so few steps to recruit them held scant promise in hard times even for the faithful. To the end of the decade individual organizers testified that Socialist women were often as learned and as politically vigorous as their husbands and fathers, capable of far-reaching agitation. The *Frauenvereine*, however, could not build organizationally on this fact, and no form offered itself as a viable alternative. Political education, political mobilization, of women thus remained a tenuous phenomenon. Women's activities retreated to the solid, unpresumptuous tasks within the fraternal fold.[51]

The party itself formally concurred. Delegates to the Newark congress of 1877 reaffirmed the movement's unity and provided a name which it would use for decades, the SLP, Socialist Labor party (*Sozialistische Arbeiter Partei*); they also fixed the doctrinal status of the woman question. Confirming the position formulated at the previous year's meeting, Socialists refuted any notion of women's autonomy from the class struggle, reviling both what they referred to as "the so-called woman's rights question" and the native-born movement carrying its banner. Delegates admonished that absolute equality be observed within party ranks but urged the comrades to encourage women to participate in the fraternal organizations. Hereafter, speakers would commonly refer to the Newark resolution as having established the grounds for women's role in the Socialist movement from a "realistic standpoint."[52]

The plank was actually inconclusive, even in orthodox terms. It failed to reconcile the goal of women's emancipation, and the claim of equality among the Socialist vanguard, with a political strategy that could draw women into the Socialist struggle in the process of their own liberation. The contrast with the party's principal strategy directed essentially toward a male proletariat was painfully evident: factory workers possessed a natural path through the trade union to class consciousness; women absorbed by childcare and housework, their lives fragmented by intermittent wage labor, had no equivalent road.

Still, if the *Frauenvereine* failed to advance the demands for women's emancipation within the party framework or to erect a permanent Socialist women's organization, women themselves had established an important precedent. Finnish, Slav, Hungarian, Italian, and most of all Jewish immigrant women would for the next three-quarters of a century build upon the model German-Americans had pioneered in the 1870s. Socialist and Communist movements spawned schools, summer camps, festivals, children's orchestras, and a myriad of related activities—none far removed from the essential building blocks of family networks in service to the cause. The radical movements simply could not have survived as warm and compelling human institutions without these forms of participation; in truth, the English-language movement remained thinner for their absence. The 1870s experience with all its limitations offered a model for social (and not merely political) organization. In the next decade, when German-American Socialists made their greatest bid for national influence, they understood better the significance of women's activity at the movement's center.

A REVEALING INTERLUDE

The ultimate success of their movement, German-American Socialists recognized, depended upon recruitment among the English-language populace. Spirits were therefore high in the late 1870s when the party began to reach national proportions. Certainly this upsurge, they inferred, would draw real workers impelled by class consciousness and unencumbered by middle-class prejudices. The newly formed "American" sections nevertheless carried into the movement the traditions of indigenous radicalism. Briefly, the woman question re-emerged as a symbolic test of faith. Although the party soon receded before overwhelming pressures, the interlude had important long-range effects upon American Socialism: unyielding in their perspective, the German-Americans had promoted a native-born client tendency more rigid even than its mentors.

Beginning with the unity conference of 1876, Socialists had sensed a modest political turn in their favor. The great railroad strike of the following year accelerated this tendency. In the aftermath of massive rioting and a widespread public disaffection with the conduct of government and business, Socialists foresaw a new era of political awareness among the American populace. Within a year a handful of weekly and daily newspapers appeared in German, Bohemian, and English, espousing Socialism from such diverse locations as Indianapolis, Chicago, Cleveland, Philadelphia, Detroit, and New York City. By 1878 Socialists had elected a number of state and local officials, rolling up especially impressive tallies in Chicago's working-class wards. Although membership rolls peaked at scarcely 7,000, the party's greater prestige and the stream of English-language enthusiasts provoked German-American Socialists to predict a rosy future. [53]

As Socialists readily perceived, these recruits represented the basis for further developments. But the German-American leadership exerted little control over the formation of party sections in neighborhoods and cities where they lacked an ethnic cadre. And they were slow, and no doubt unwilling, to perceive the importance of the woman question to many native-born activists and allies. Rather suddenly, they discovered in their midst ardent advocates of views they had so strenuously repelled.

Despite the absence of any specific appeal to their interests, a number of women moved into positions of authority within the English-language branches. Alice Hyneman Rhine, later a prominent labor journalist, recalled that the well-publicized New York state party convention of 1879 attracted a sizable female gallery, only the most visible manifestation of an important trend. Women and their allies swept into newly created groups from New York and Chicago to smaller industrial cities like Fall River and Providence. A few recruits attained prominence, such as one "Miss LeCompte" who became secretary of Manhattan's "American" branch and later acted as assistant editor of the Socialists' English-language paper, the *Labor Standard*. Most women served more quietly; a sympathetic comrade remarked that they "are falling in line in the Socialist ranks . . . doing the cause efficient and noble service that is worthy of all commendation. . . ." If partly flattery, this remark suggested that for the first time since Woodhull's departure English-language women were present to bolster the freethinkers' position on the woman question. [54]

The prevailing prejudice against women's direct political participation seemed to many of the new recruits unsocialistic and almost unbelievable. As they accommodated themselves to party work, they launched a modest campaign for rectification. "What! Claim to be a Socialist and do not believe in the fundamental principles of Socialism—the principles of justice, equal rights, and equality to all?" expostulated an outraged Kansas correspondent to an English-language party paper in 1879: "Then, brother Socialists, go study your doctrines anew. . . . If it will injure the party to do right and to have the truth plainly spoken, then it is time it *was* injured and forever overthrown and a new and better one substituted in its place. Put a plain and direct plank in our platform in favor of woman suffrage, and it will gain us thousands of votes and the aid and support of some of the best women in our land, and whose services we need."[55] The same year an SLP section in strike-torn Lawrence, Massachusetts, called upon the party to cut the Gordian knot and to take up the struggle for woman's vote.[56] Chicagoan John McAuliffe, the most prominent native-born labor agitator in the movement, similarly charged his brother Socialists with lacking the "manliness" to insert a woman suffrage plank in the party platform, and advised women to refuse even to "dance at balls with men, nor grace festivals with their enobling presence until [Socialist men] learn to treat them as equals."[57]

English-language Socialists also challenged the movement's complacency on issues of women's wage labor. Ignoring the German-Americans' dudgeon against female wage earning, far-sighted activists gravitated toward the Socialist movement precisely to use its resources for organizing working women. Prominent New England labor reformers thus joined the SLP in 1878 to form the International Labor Union (ILU), the first organization pledged to unionize the unskilled along with the skilled across sex, ethnic, and racial lines. This development had particular salience for workingwomen because the ILU, aiming strategically at the largest agglomeration of the unskilled, attacked a textile industry where women constituted fully 40 percent of the work force. Drawing the *Labor Standard* from New York to Fall River, the "Little Lancashire" of British immigrant textile workers, Socialist activists conducted a remarkable propaganda campaign in favor of unionization while providing logistic support for strikes and political momentum for legislative reform.[58] In Chicago English-language Socialists concurrently helped to create a Working Women's Union that allied factory workers and housekeepers, native- and foreign-born. The union formed originally as an educational society, to encourage workingwomen to advance themselves politically and to alert middle-class women of their duty to their sisters. The Chicago Socialist movement, then at its apex, steered this educational movement in a radical direction. At an 1879 lecture the union's president, Alzina Parsons Stevens, discarded her notes for a prepared lecture on "What part of the Labor question Socialism does not include" and announced to a surprised audience that her study had led her to Socialism "as the only means of salvation from the horrors of our present social and industrial system!"[59]

Despite these hopeful signs, the movement nationally did very little to encourage women's participation. "We know," one recruit complained, "sections are formed in nearly every city, but we have failed to see [in the Socialist press] anything relative to the women having their names enrolled as members of those Sections, or to their taking a part in the affairs of the meetings, holding offices, etc. Neither do we find any woman's name on the list of 'agitators or lecturers'."[60] Where women had not taken part in the formation and leadership of the newer sections or helped establish the political mood, they found participation often personally difficult. Few English-language proletarian comrades so much as invited their wives into the male clubhouse, and when they did, the bar-room surroundings, "the air reeking with tobacco smoke, beer, whiskey, and profanity invariably drove away who came."[61]

By dint of circumstances and the bold initiatives of a minority, the movement nevertheless seemed to near a crossroads on the woman question. A few English-language Socialists went so far as to predict that if the party were sufficiently dedicated to advancing women's status in the work force, it might compel unions to abandon their exclusionary craft orientation and thereby prompt the genuine class consciousness Socialists impatiently awaited. More realistic, others believed a flexible policy toward workingwomen might foreshadow the emergence of German-American radicalism from the darkness of the ethnic ghetto to the brightness of the American day.[62] From the viewpoint of 1878-79, this expectation was not altogether improbable. Had the party jelled around industrial unionism and electoral politics, the influx of English-language Socialists would have balanced the Germanic contribution with a distinctly indigenous radical sensibility, heir to the woman's rights traditions. Indeed, the entire subsequent history of American Socialism might have been markedly different.

Events obliterated the prospects for a fortuitous reconciliation. Socialist economic and political advances met with shattering defeat in a few years and left a reduced and embittered rank-and-file to assess the implications. During their initial bursts of enthusiasm, activists had unknowingly strained their resources to the limit and had trusted naively in the vagaries of American politics. Elections were stolen through political trickery, local Democrats and new reform parties moved in to absorb the protest vote, popular interest in Socialism fell away and with it most of the recently founded Socialist newspapers.[63] Worse, the ILU could not withstand the millowners' offensive and free use of police power against workers and their leaders. Native-born labor reformers simultaneously separated themselves from the SLP so as to take up low-profile legislative and labor-education campaigns guarded from local red-baiting and from ideological complications. The Chicago Working Women's Union and scattered women's labor institutions in other cities, faced with the same overwhelming forces, faded from sight, the Socialist influence they represented eroded or wiped out.[64]

Such reverses would have a familiar ring to later generations of American radicals. While in Europe the literal class character of politics maintained a solid cadre of Socialist members who voted for their candidates even in times

of defeat, Socialists in the United States repeatedly suffered a calamitous decline
after a few years' promising advance and therefore never achieved permanent
status as an important minority party. Similarly, European Socialists built and
for the most part directed the official labor movements, while American labor
activities tended to draw the talented militant away from political commitments. Those comrades who held fast exhibited a loyalty that such complications and disappointments could not batter down.

Essentially, SLP loyalists returned to the milieux they knew and trusted, the
ethnic ghetto and craft union, now both in periods of expansion. Itself reduced
to 1,500 members by the early 1880s, the party could hardly exert much
influence outside its immediate circles anyway. This tendency proved doubly
isolating as native-born activists recovered from their own defeats and entered
a new phase of heightened agitation. As it moved onto the national scene, the
Knights of Labor took over the field the ILU had once claimed, while new
coalitions of agrarian, labor, and temperance reformers moved toward the elec-
torial insurgencies of 1886–96. Only occasionally and at the local level could
Socialists manifest the leadership their upsurge of the late 1870s had seemed
to promise, and they exerted little influence indeed upon the volatile western
agrarian sectors. Never in the short history of the Socialist movement had the
gap between the leadership and the presumed constituencies been so wide;
never had Socialists been so blind to their own limitations. [65]

At the nadir of their retrenchment ethnic Socialists exhibited the symptoms
of bitterness through renewed hostilities toward such indigenous reforms as
woman's rights. Those German-Americans destined to become major figures
in the congealing craft unions espoused more strongly than before a protec-
tionist defense of their trades and viewed workingwomen primarily as competitors in the labor force. Socialists who retained primary loyalty to political work
watched the departure of the women members from their ranks with more spite
than regret. The handful of English-language recruits who stayed with the
movement did so because they shared the Germanic proclivities and merged
their feelings of disappointment into the prejudices of the immigrants.

Renditions of Socialism for the native-born during these times had the literary texture of translated German such that even the dilution of class analysis
could not alter the basic framework. A chief product of this mood, Laurence
Gronlund's *The Coöperative Commonwealth* (1884), undertook to make Socialism more palatable to the native-born by excluding basic concepts indigenous radicals had most distinctly developed. Perhaps unwittingly, Gronlund
actually fed the ethnic backlash by issuing a forceful defense of the family
against women's emancipation.

The Coöperative Commonwealth flatly denied the legitimacy of the woman's
rights tradition. Gronlund wrote that in the happy Socialist future woman

would be placed on *"an equal footing* with man, *economically,* that is all." He emphasized that this conception of economic equality differed sharply from the ideas of "equal rights champions" who argued for woman's unrestricted access to the labor market. "Now *we* can say that the worst that can befall both sexes," Gronlund wrote, "is for woman to *compete with man in man's work."* Woman was in fact unsuited for wage labor. "Certain notorious physiological facts" required of her *"a periodic rest,"* and she usually performed her work in an unsatisfactory and slovenly manner. Under the future order those women who might choose to work would therefore be restricted to vocations such as the care of young children, which would afford women the opportunity to exercise their "peculiar natural gifts." But nothing would compel most women to "neglect their domestic affairs." Gronlund predicted that under Socialism men would retain their rightful place as heads of the household, while women labored happily in their domestic roles. Marriage would be secured on a firm financial basis, for it was a major goal *"to enable every man and woman to form a happy family."* Moreover, because the road to Socialism was so bumpy, women's formal participation in the electoral process could not be risked. Gronlund supposed that under the cooperative order, women might gain the ballot and enjoy full political rights. But meanwhile their enfranchisement would only delay the transition. By nature "conservative, even reactionary," women could not be trusted in the capitalist political arena. Nor could Gronlund suggest any other means by which women might organize their own ranks. [66]

A popular reading of *The Coöperative Commonwealth* might have helped doom Socialism to additional years as an "alien" ideology. Actually, the book had slight sales and little measurable impact, especially as English-language branches had all but disappeared by the time of its publication. As the single major English-language popularization of Socialism, the book nevertheless conveyed to its scattered readers a characteristic German-American message. [67] In rendering Socialism respectable for the middle classes and simple for the proletarians, Gronlund had made grand humanitarian gestures at woman's expense. Gronlund had reasoned from the European class analysis to the American faith in moral suasion but had bypassed the presumed vessels of ethical values.

The Coöperative Commonwealth aptly symbolized the dilemma into which German-Americans had fallen. In their correspondence Marx and Engels had rained fire upon the SLP for its inability to lead the mass movements of the 1880s and charged Socialists with a failure of nerve. [68] The problem was deeper than the masters of theory could grasp at such a geographical distance. The whole history of Germanic Socialism in the United States during the 1870s had led toward a *cul de sac.* Predisposed to distrust the instincts of the native-born population and hard-pressed to break out of their comfortable ethnic enclaves, Socialists read each setback as proof positive of a self-fulfilling prophecy. The events of the late 1870s served ultimately to reinforce their siege mentality, and the German-Americans withdrew forcefully into their own communities. Under these circumstances, the sources for a major change in outlook lay outside the United States entirely.

THE EMERGENCE OF THE *Frauenfrage*

The single most important fact about the German-American Socialist movement of the 1880s could be found in the immigration statistics. By the first years of the decade Germans were arriving at record levels of a quarter-million annually. Fleeing Bismarck's anti-Socialist laws of 1878, a vital minority brought with them the kind of political experience and sophistication denied earlier arrivals. Whereas the first waves of the 1860s had carried a rather primitive Lassallean perspective, this final major immigration brought Socialists shaped by Marxism and the activities of a maturing German Social Democracy. Subtly but decisively the generation of the 1880s reconstructed the German-American movement from within and built no mere workers' vanguard but a wide-ranging cultural apparatus with an all-encompassing philosophy strategically versatile and theoretically rich. The American movement would never come up to the Old World standard in theory or practice. But under the pressure of authority the new immigrants could impel the movement to mend old wounds in the name of a higher political unity. With their ascendancy the patterns of the 1870s became so much history.

During the 1880s the party's stand on the woman question changed significantly, especially with regard to women's role in the class struggle. As refugees from major urban centers like Hamburg and Berlin, where women constituted upward of 30 percent of the work force by 1880, many new immigrants appeared acclimated to the reality of women's participation in wage labor. German Socialists had not lost all their romantic inclinations, but they had adapted the poetic vision of woman's salvation to her industrial presence. They carried this unique consciousness to German-American communities undergoing dramatic alterations in women's economic roles. Through a curious international circulation of ideas, the German Social Democracy which earlier had provided its emigrant cadre with restrictive notions toward women now offered an antidote—indeed, a call for their emancipation.[69]

The homeland's greatest contribution on the woman question was *Die Frau und der Sozialismus* (1883) by August Bebel. Bebel warred against the contemporary bourgeois schools of history characterized by von Ranke's "wie es eigentlich gewesen ist" and by the religious or "great man" approaches and affirmed that humanity made its own history if not in its own manner of choosing. This history constituted freedom unfolding through countless generations of sorrow, disappointment, and apparent reverses. Most important, Bebel made explicit what Marx had rarely articulated since his youthful philosophical days: the progress of humanity could be measured by women's condition. Bebel also took an important step beyond the romantic paradigm by endowing womanhood with historical subjectivity.

"Woman and workingman have, since old, had this in common—oppression."[70] This premise, Bebel's opening statement, underlay the entirety of his analysis. Bebel began his narrative by showing how woman's subjugation and the division of society into opposing classes had common historical roots. He postulated the existence of a prehistorical "Golden Age" of primitive communism wherein humanity had known peace and harmony under a matriarchal social system. As society became more complex economically, as the onset of private property destroyed the original collectivity by dividing the community into classes, the "first human being to come into bondage" was woman. Private property thus became an Archimedean lever for the ultimate erection of the whole edifice of class and sex exploitation. Bebel continued his historical narrative and demonstrated how, at each major juncture in the evolution of modern society, changes in class structure affected woman's position. He explained how the development of commercial and, later, industrial capitalism brought moral decadence to the ruling classes while forcing poor women into prostitution and making them fodder for machines of manufacture. Just as the immiseration of the proletariat increased with each further advance of class society, Bebel explained, so too did the oppression of woman intensify.[71]

Although the historical section was short relative to the length of the full text, it laid the foundation for Bebel's entire analysis. Bebel thus examined woman's lowly status in contemporary Wilhelmine society primarily as a function of cumulative development. On the impact of her recent advance into wage labor, he wrote: "Unquestionably, with the extension of female labor, the family life of the working class goes ever more to pieces, the dissolution of marriage and the family is a natural result, an immorality, demoralization, degeneration, diseases of all nature and child mortality increase at a shocking pace." Yet, unlike his predecessors, Bebel did not invoke domesticity as woman's salvation. Rather, the trend of our social life, he wrote, "is not to banish woman back to the house and hearth as our 'domestic life' fanatics prescribe . . . but is to lead woman out of the narrow sphere of strictly domestic life to a full participation in the public life of the people." In effecting a historical analysis of women's condition, Bebel thus implicitly rejected the romantic propensity to view woman as timeless symbol. Woman's entry into wage labor, despite the accompanying hardships, was merely a natural component of economic development and preparation for the final reconciliation. Forced to become part of the industrial classes, woman now readied herself for the class war and the vast reconstruction ahead. Destined by the historical process, woman arm-in-arm with her brother sufferers would re-establish the harmony of the Golden Age.[72]

Bebel not only had juxtaposed the sufferings of the working class and woman across history but had framed a definite theory of woman's emancipation. Everything in his analysis suggested moreover that woman would attain her freedom only insofar as she struggled to overthrow capitalism. Because it was private property which had historically determined her subjugation, woman now had to join her proletarian allies who sought to destroy this oppressive system. Bebel thus appealed to woman "not to remain behind in this struggle in which her redemption and emancipation are at stake"—indeed, afforded her the grand opportunity to take her stand—but to "prove that she had comprehended her true place in the Movement and in the struggles of the present for a better future."[73]

At first glance, Bebel's analysis seems too vivid for a Socialist movement heretofore ambiguous or unyielding on the woman question. Bebel acknowledged the inevitability of woman's entry into wage labor and even asked Socialists to support her enfranchisement. Yet it was Bebel's genius to set the goal of woman's emancipation clearly within the purview of Socialism and, really, nowhere else. Whereas other political writers had already discredited bourgeois abstractions about government as the product of idealism, now Socialists could argue with authority that woman's freedom rested upon an economic system long since destroyed and upon an ethical sensibility possible only when that economic system "returned" as Socialism. In between, woman was inevitably bound, to a greater or lesser degree, to man's whims. She was able to move toward freedom only through a class struggle wherein, because of her low status, she undoubtedly must be consigned to a secondary role. Indeed, Bebel's whole schema allotted woman no historical significance distinct from that of the proletariat. It followed logically that her duty remained as it had for decades: to support the working class in its (hence her own) struggle for liberation. For many Socialists, *Die Frau und der Sozialismus* stood as the authoritative statement forbidding any politically autonomous role for women.

Whatever its philosophical limitations or shortcomings in originality, Bebel's treatise placed the woman question nearer the center of Socialist doctrine than it had heretofore reached. *Die Frau und der Sozialismus* became after Marx's *Kapital* the single most important full-sized Socialist text. Sold under the less controversial name of *Die Frau in der Vergangenheit, Gegenwart und Zukunft* (1879) during the anti-Socialist period in Germany, the book went through seven editions by 1890, achieved numerous translations, and circulated among Socialists worldwide. In combining science with sentiment, rational persuasion with a glint of transhistoric mysticism, Bebel was able to attract a wide variety of readers. As numerous Socialist women later testified, *Die Frau* had been their open-sesame to Marx while simultaneously serving to bolster their demands for special strategic programs for women. Women's centrality to the whole social matrix and to the promise of Socialism had been taken out of the realm of abstractions at last and blessed with a theoretical analysis unimpeachable for the *Frauenvereine* faithful.[74]

The influence of this major theoretical development was apparent in the weekend supplements of German-American newspapers of the 1880s in the form of a historical literature on the woman question. The most important papers had survived the political drought, and through the sage editorial management of the *New Yorker Volkszeitung* and *Chicagoer Arbeiter Zeitung* a lively journalism sprang up, reaching German-American working- and middle-class readers far outside the immediate political orbit. Again America followed Europe. A German *Die Neue Zeit*, theoretical bellwether of the international movement until World War I, published its first volume in 1883, the year of Marx's death, and younger writers such as Paul Lafargue, Karl Kautsky, Eduard Bernstein, and Georg Plekhanov appeared on the scene to popularize and elaborate key notions. The American journals were a pale reflection of the European model, not least because potential scholars constituted but a handful strapped with running the newspapers and schools, lecturing, and handling the many bothersome technical chores of their small movement. German-American editors nevertheless kept abreast of European developments, mixing reprints from Germany, translations of other continental authors, and original contributions by German-Americans on women's issues. Essays on such topics as "The Position of Women in Ancient German Society," "Women in Roman Dynasties," "Amazons and Heroines," and "Wives of the Sultans" graced the Sunday literary supplements. Offering an enticing exoticism touched by sexual titilation, articles such as these hinted also at an important shift in Socialist doctrine. Woman's well-known plight, the shame of humanity, might have not only a distinct historical trajectory but an inner logic even Bebel had failed to unravel fully.[75]

Engaging and promising as these historical excursions might be, they did not address the strategic revolution Bebel had effected upon Socialist theory. Bebel's refutation of the earlier prejudice against women's wage labor demanded a dramatic shift in the movement's general perspective. Unevenly, perhaps a bit grudgingly, German-American Socialists came to this recognition. Following Bebel, they applied their "scientific" training to an examination of industrial capitalism in the United States and noted a remarkable increase in the numbers of workingwomen, especially within ethnic communities. Through short essays in their press, Socialists began to develop their own revised materialist analysis of the woman question.

German-American Socialists carefully observed the consolidation of a female labor force amidst the frantic economic growth of the 1880s. Railroad expansion in the previous decade, ensuring the national market, helped advance the factory system from a tendency to a central fact of production. "In America everything is made by machine, while we make everything by hand here," a Socialist correspondent could write from the Old World with only modest exaggeration. The rate of capital investment doubled between 1880 and 1890, causing an unprecedented shift in the ratio of machine to hand labor. As a result of these and other major changes in production, a new labor force, substantially foreign-born and unskilled, came into its own. Although accurate statistical indicators are lacking, one might trace a parallel increase in women's employment such that by the 1880s the woman factory worker was a common sight in most urban manufacturing centers.[76]

Previously guarded from wage labor, German-American women now joined the ranks. A growing demand of the nascent middle class for housekeepers and cooks drew thousands of German-American "girls" into domestic and personal service in the 1880s. But undoubtedly the most trenchant shift in custom accompanied the revolutionary expansion of the clothing industry. Between 1860 and 1880, immigrant tailors from Germany were the mainstay of the rapidly growing men's wear trade. Many wives and daughters worked alongside their menfolk during the early era, for the tailoring establishments were so small they bore the traces of a cottage industry. Around 1885, as considerable capital investment and power machinery became the requisites of successful enterprise, the shop system virtually displaced the family system of production. Although recently immigrated Jewish men soon supplanted women in New York's garment trade, fluctuations in other areas of the country were less extreme. Through the 1880s in cities like Chicago, St. Louis, Cincinnati, and Rochester, many young German-American women maintained their places in the trade only by becoming factory workers, wage earners in the modern sense. A German-American female proletariat, long feared by Socialists, had become a fact of life.[77]

True to Bebel's outline and their own perceptions, German-American Socialist editors paid increasingly close attention to the details of women's wage labor. They gleaned statistics from various government reports on labor conditions and emphasized the degradation of workingwomen. Adolf Douai, testifying before a congressional hearing in 1882, argued that the heartless exploitation of women and children endangered the health of future generations; in the same vein the *New Yorker Volkszeitung* in the early 1880s devoted a special series to the frightful conditions of tenement-house cigar workers, German and Bohemian women laboring in dank, lightless cellars for less than a living wage. Every recession, every further shift in the character of production, Socialists lamented, seemed to increase the misery of those least capable of fighting back.[78]

Reviewing these circumstances, Socialists called for the mobilization of workingwomen into the ranks of the proletariat. Many Socialists continued to appeal for workingwomen's salvation most strongly on moral grounds, as in the furious essay penned by the movement's beloved theoretician, Joseph Dietzgen, who on the morning of his death assailed the exploitation of German-American servant girls; the old literary contrast between youthful purity and the vampire-like desires of the bourgeoisie still excited protective instincts.[79] The most insightful leaders countered these lingering sentiments. They no longer implored men to resist the temptation of increasing the family wage by sending their wives and daughters to work but admonished the reader to view women as potentially class-conscious workers. If undertaken with a heavy heart, the task proposed by Bebel now seemed inevitable.

The Socialist movement had, at least in words, come to its maturity. The new perspective on women displaced conceptions that had been passed down from pre-industrial times, revised and formulated politically by the Lassallean and Marxist German Social Democratic tendencies. So long as Socialism might be imagined as a denial of Capitalism, a return to craft guilds at a higher stage of production, domestic bliss remained woman's only possible destiny. Socialists lost a great deal, to be sure, when they accepted the finality of much that industrial society had wrought. Nothing would ever be so simple or so clear again. But they gained a sharp understanding that the revolutionary potential rested upon immanent factors in the present order, however discomfiting. Through wage labor women linked their destiny to that of the proletariat; they were by implication no mere aids or benefactors but rather an essential part of the revolutionary process itself.

It remained for Socialist women to transform this abstract commitment to workingwomen into a positive strategy and to reaffirm that the intergration of women into the proletariat carried the mark of revolutionary destiny. The party compromise of 1876 demanding the banishment of women from factories where men worked they called a throwback to Lassalleanism. A few quoted Marx's *Das Kapital* chapter and verse to explain the inevitability of women's entry into the labor force. Drawing directly upon the long view of history popularized by Bebel, women suggested that the very division between home and factory had been of recent origin, women's exclusion from wage labor only a passing phase in human history now at an end. Women themselves would have to clear the path for such a realistic appraisal of the *Frauenfrage*; to do so required a march through the accessible institutions of the party to a higher form of political organization.[80]

THE EMERGENCE OF THE *Frauenbund*

Women's activities began to consolidate on new terms amidst the German-American Socialist movement's finest hour. During the political upsurge of the

1880s the woman question became for the first time integral to Socialist programs while women's organizations appeared an organic element in the strategic arsenal. Shifts in the labor market, a greater interest in women's affairs evinced by a few male leaders, and most of all the initiative of Socialist women themselves made this advance possible. The coming-of-age of the German-American Socialist women's movement soon revealed its own, distinctive contours, neither those of the service-minded *Frauenvereine* of the 1870s nor those of the native-born woman's movement. However limited by circumstances, a precedent for an active women's role in the modern Socialist movement had been set by the close of the decade.

The fraternal organization of women advanced from the weakened networks of the late 1870s to a principal sector blessed by the party leadership. Nowhere was this change so marked as in the movement's attentiveness to its youth. Here lay the future of the movement, an editorialist argued in calling upon women to play a decisive role in shaping the young mind.[81] Pioneer progressive educators and early pediatricians offered their expertise to parents. Augusta Lilienthal's physician-husband drew enthusiastic audiences to his lectures on childrearing, and offered his listeners the emancipatory message that in the future men would share with their wives the crucial decisions of children's upbringing.[82] This faith might be undercut by the daily life of working-class families, but the movement's most powerful thinkers exhorted women to prepare for brighter days ahead. "The greatest lesson we can provide," Adolf Douai thus reflected, "is our example."[83] New York women took this lesson to heart and helped initiate in 1880 what became the nation's most extensive Socialist school system. "Based on liberty, equality and fraternity," the system grew to some 255 students within five years. Socialists in other cities were rarely able to maintain distinct party-run schools but cooperated with free-thought and other liberal groups in the operation of "free" daily or Sunday classes which blended German-language training with a nonreligious, politically open curriculum. To a lesser extent, Socialists sought to integrate women into the politically potent *Turnvereine* by appealing to adolescent girls to search for a healthful beauty and by occasionally promoting an outstanding Socialist woman to *Turnverein* leadership.[84]

In the expanding web of fraternal activities, women similarly strengthened other positions held since the 1870s. Chicago offers a vivid example because its large numbers of new German immigrants fed into an exceptionally vital local movement. Where one Socialist women's section had flickered briefly in the mid-1870s, three clubs appeared a decade later, hailed by the local press as a center of the entire urban movement. Women's groups conducted regular and frequent social programs, raised sums of money large for that time and place, and offered lavish entertainments, providing for events like *Männerchor* concerts everything from refreshments to symbolic flags. On huge weekend picnics held in Ogden's Grove, women costumed as "Truth" and "Justice" took part in staging dramatic tableaux—"living pictures"—set on revolving platforms. On a smaller scale during the winter they gave recitations, took part along with their male comrades in comic playlets, and naturally coached the much-loved children's performances. If such activity did not allow women to enhance their political status significantly, it afforded them an opportunity to express themselves. For new immigrants from Germany the activity may well have simply continued their Old World traditions; for veterans of the German-American movement it surely signified a new and brighter day.[85]

Politically, the way was being prepared for a new stage of Socialist women's activities. The rebirth of the fraternal *Frauenverein* and *Frauenversammlung* did not so much retard this development as provide an accepted milieu from which women's self-assertion might further emerge. The true beginning of a second wave of women's organizations was marked by the creation of the *Frauenbund* (women's federation) in greater New York around 1883–84. Less an extension of their familial roles and more an expression of women's own interests, the *Frauenbund* could be properly designated the first political, rather than primarily social, women's sector of the German-American Socialist movement.

The *Frauenbünde* gained their initial impetus from the labor offensive cresting at mid-decade. Still deeply suspicious of indigenous reform politics, the Socialists could nevertheless appreciate the importance of strike activity, whatever its rhetorical concomitant. Beginning with the Great Southwestern railroad strike of 1883 and climaxing in the eight-hour campaigns of early 1886, Socialists strained every nerve to advise and prepare their own ranks for action. Rather suddenly, the potential influence of women came to be regarded as crucial to labor and Socialist success. *Frauenbund* activists, party spokesmen argued, could best explain to workers' wives how the eight-hour victory would benefit the whole family. They could inform their sisters how shorter hours, higher wages, and improved conditions would mean better fathers and husbands, healthier children, and a brighter future for the next generation. Through educational efforts, conversations with friends, and public meetings, Socialist women might rally the whole neighborhood to the cause. If there were a hundred women in the New York area who completely understood Socialism and could explain it fully, a leading comrade argued in 1886, "our movement would be greatly advanced."[86] Lecturers took pains to encourage the formation of such women's organizations in other parts of the country. Paul Grottkau, the most prominent recent political exile from Germany, thus traveled to Baltimore to urge women's mobilization. Another leader visited New Bedford, Massachusetts, and inspired the creation of the first *Frauenbund* outside New York. In parts as distant as Bloomington, Illinois, lectures on "Woman and Socialism" could be heard as a prelude to a call for organization. If party leaders failed to give *Frauenbünde* priority attention, they had at least ceased viewing women's organizations as troubling phenomena and gave them their political blessing.[87]

During the peak of labor unrest in 1885–87 *Frauenbünde* also became directly involved with workers outside Socialist ranks. Whereas the *Frauenvereine* of the 1870s had never strayed beyond party environs, the *Frauenbünde* aimed to assist young women in their economic struggles and to bring them into the Socialist fold. Several sections in New York reorganized as *Arbeiter Frauen und Mädchenbund* (organization for workingwomen and girls) and *Arbeiterinnen Versammlung* (workingwomen's organization) to develop programs to forward the eight-hour movement among younger workingwomen. German-dominated unions of seamstresses and servants also appeared in New York. A newly formed *Frauenbund* in Chicago dedicated itself to agitation among workingwomen. From the far corners of German immigrant life, such as Omaha, Nebraska, Socialist household servants proclaimed their bitter resentment at being treated as less than human, their determination to build fighting organizations for dignity and for better conditions.[88]

Within a short time the *Frauenbünde* had established themselves as a militant wing of the Socialist movement. Like their predecessors in the fraternal clubs, women activists still heard speakers praise woman's humanitarian instincts and her special ability to love. But now there was an important difference in the message: women were asked to care for their loved ones but also for themselves as an increasingly self-conscious group; not only to prepare the road for Socialists to travel, but to travel it themselves and to a certain degree in their own ways.

Soon *Frauenbund* leaders began to criticize the party for its tardiness in addressing women's issues. A few women activists articulated what many others must have believed. So long as women remained outside the factory, one admitted, the "passive attitude of our party" toward women "was perhaps justified." But as the rapid expansion of industry drew thousands of young women into the factory, life had presented the party a *fait accompli*. Women in the heart of manufacturing "instinctively place a challenge, more clearly and further than previously. . . . Here it is not enough, for a few political clubs or a few sections of our party to approach the women . . ., as it was in the beginning [of their emergence into industry]. . . . Now we must reach out to women, as they advance their struggles, to help them grasp the implications. . . ."[89] Women activists thus chided the party for its failures to institute a distinct agitational program for women workers and demanded that one be created immediately to supplement the *Frauenbünde*'s own efforts along these lines.

At the party's 1885 congress, the most important meeting since the Newark assemblage, the New York *Frauenbund* offered a formal statement underlining this sentiment. Its representatives traveled to Chicago to appeal for special consideration of women's issues. "When now our comrades see that we women have also begun to think about the social question, you could aid us with our striving in thought and deed to advance, and to offer us a little of your advice and interest. . . ."[90] The women freely admitted that the *Frauenbünde* could not make a great contribution to the agitational campaign among the native-born working class, or to the creation of an English-language press, which the party perennially viewed as a strategic necessity. But women could pursue a two-pronged program aimed at both the home and factory lives of their sisters.

Frauenbund activists outlined the basic planks of such a program. "Male society," they averred, had placed their sex in a "false social position," ascribing to them only the characteristics of weakness and frailty. Socialist women, more effectively than any other group, could work to eradicate this false belief. They must advance the cry of equal wages for equal work, a goal which would eliminate job competition between men and women and ultimately strike the chains off the female worker. They must simultaneously help women discover Socialism as the gateway to a more wholesome domestic life. Class-conscious mothers could best envision children enjoying the "sunshine of their youth" rather than slaving away in the dark factory because they, more than their ignorant working-class sisters, could see the promise of the new society within the old. Socialist women, inspired by programs currently popular in Germany, also envisioned women brushing aside the presumptuous and expensive male physician and learning to care for their family's medical needs. Politically organized women, in short, would bring other women to the realization of their destiny. Socialist women expressed their vision as the emergence of a "world household," the extension of woman's sphere throughout the whole society. However traditional in phraseology, this appeal demanded a shift in Socialist attitudes toward women's role, called upon Socialists to accept women advancing under their own weight and joining their male collaborators as comrades rather than as helpmeets.[91]

Socialist women in less well-organized parts of the country took up the call for party responsibility. The St. Paul, Minnesota, local thus unanimously passed the following year a series of resolutions offered by women:

> In recognition that Section St. Paul, as all sections of the SLP, has a great need in propagandistic as in practical tasks, for women to become active members, and

> In recognition that the Socialist Labor Party is the only party which upholds . . . equality for half of humanity, women who in present society are slaves to capitalist production . . .

> Therefore be it resolved that we, Section St. Paul of the SLP, request the means and ways to open up the path for organizing women.

> Resolved, that the procedure will be reorganized to promote singing and declamatory family entertainments, so as to include women and children's participation in body and spirit. . . .

Resolved, that when we call ourselves Socialists, we are not only theoretical but practical and wish to be still more practical, in order to bring this resolution into reality![92]

/ The last point was particularly salient. The distance between fine words and significant deeds might be great indeed, the popularization of Bebel in the newspapers and by a few party lecturers a matter apart from the regular allocation of party resources or a concerted intellectual energy devoted to woman's cause. Although *Frauenbund* leaders were proud of their efforts to remove the fraternal yoke from women's organizations, they nevertheless realized that as late as 1886 their movement had made only a ripple in party life. The crowds of women reported at meetings did not provoke the party to institute a special program to recruit women. News of women's activities escaped the "*Vereine und Versammlungen*" columns of the press only when *Frauenbund* leaders denounced "bourgeois" women's reformism. And, as in the 1870s, party lecturers and officials remained almost exclusively male; women still lacked their own voice in the party's leading councils and on the lecture circuit. At this critical juncture they received a champion of their own: Johanna Greie.[93]

Johanna Greie was easily one of the more remarkable figures to burst upon the German-American political scene. Born of middle-class parents in industrial Dresden in 1864, she had attenuated her formal education after primary school to enter a sales business. But she met and married Emile Greie, a lathe-turner devoted to the free-thought and Social Democratic movements. A friend of her new husband and editor of a Magdeburg newspaper discovered her literary talents and urged her to write for his paper. Had Johanna Greie stayed in Germany, she might have become a well-known journalist. Instead, she sailed to the United States with her husband to seek a new life and to find new grounds for her developing talents. Greie had come to share her husband's political convictions and, once in the United States, she flowered virtually overnight into a leading Socialist writer and lecturer. She became a persuasive editorialist in *Der Sozialist*, the party's weekly national newspaper, and discussed subjects ranging from child labor to the relationship of art and Socialism. She also conducted a lecture tour which called down praise from locals across the eastern states and the Midwest. And she wrote and spoke with a command heretofore lacking in any German-American Socialist intellectual, save Augusta Lilienthal, on her favorite subject—women's emancipation.[94]

Greie's viewpoint, well rooted in her German experience, complemented the sentiments espoused by her *Frauenbund* audiences. Her major essay on the subject, "Is It Necessary for Women to Organize Themselves?," was published in early 1888 in *Der Sozialist* and was soon reprinted as the first (and for many years the only) major political treatise on women's organization from within the German-American Socialist movement. Greie put the subject into stark perspective. The necessity for women's organization, she wrote, had become urgent with the rise of modern industrial society. Women could no longer fulfill their traditional responsibilities at the family hearth; nor could they resist degradation caused by worsening economic conditions. Thus women's exclusion from the ranks of revolutionary proletarian fighters not only endangered the entire struggle for Socialism but jeopardized their own positions as well. "If human activity is not to be a sisyphean labor," she wrote, "woman should and must take her place in human society," a new place to be carved out by her own actions as well as with the cooperation of progressive men. Yet women in the main seemed paralyzed by "indifference," by apathy, Greie thought, perhaps because their husbands forbade them any initiative.[95]

At this point in her analysis Greie advanced beyond the position taken by most *Frauenbund* activists. "Unfortunately, men are generally the enemy of women's emancipation," she wrote. "It is peculiar the way they act when they hear about the 'equalization of women.' They want to learn absolutely nothing about it and express partly their egotism, partly their indolence, partly their ignorance."[96]

These phrases offered by a Socialist woman barely twenty-three years old marked a minor revolution in German-American thought. Greie had not attacked the concept of women's emancipation as an expression of "bourgeois" women, had not lambasted the suffrage movement as a diversion from the proletarian struggle. "Emancipation is the goal of an oppressed group, [it means] material and spiritual freedom. . . . The goal of Woman's Emancipation is: the economic and political equality of women with men." Greie modified her complaint against Socialist men by affirming Bebel's maxim that to understand was woman's right, to explain man's duty. But she clearly aimed at something which German-American Socialists had not yet created, and which could not be created by even the best-intended men: a fighting, united women's movement for Socialism and for their own emancipation.[97]

The creation of a movement fully capable of advancing these grand purposes would be no simple matter. To make woman more than a sympathetic *Frau* or *Mädchen*, to make her a *Bundesgenossin* (female organizational comrade), required a central women's organization with national coordination. As of 1887 German-American Socialist men were still struggling to pull their own scattered locals toward that end. But optimistic observers believed that Greie might attain her ambitious goals.[98]

The political tide did seem to be shifting in Greie's favor. In the brief history of American Socialism thus far, 1886 had proved the most perplexing but also the most promising year. The eight-hour movement climaxing in mass May Day parades across the nation mirrored the consolidation of craft unions and the rise of mostly unskilled workers in the Knights of Labor, then a half-million strong. The Haymarket incident, which precipitated a forceful wave of anti-radicalism, dampened overly optimistic spirits. But if the tempo of labor activity lagged, political energies swelled considerably. The Knights, craft unionists, and their allies staged an unprecedented revolt against the two-party system in the fall of 1886; they elected only a handful of local officials but cast enough votes to lay the basis for a definite political realignment. In some areas, such as New York City, the shift was particularly dramatic, as Socialists were able to ally themselves with Irish-Americans, social reformers, and other friends of labor. Rather suddenly, the Socialist Labor party saw its membership rolls grow more substantially than during the 1878–79 upsurge, and apparently upon a more solid basis of trade unionism and party politics.[99]

Socialist women, like their brother comrades, foresaw the consolidation of the movement. They were also inclined to believe women would play a pre-cipitating role in this consolidation. In January, 1888, the New York *Arbeiter Frauen und Mädchenbund*, with Greie its principal leader, announced its determination to unite the existing Socialist women's clubs across the land into a single, permanent body. Asking local *Frauenbünde* to join this effort, the New York women in turn promised to dispatch a lecturer to assist in the great task of national coordination. The gem of the movement, Johanna Greie, thus set out on her triumphal tour.[100]

During the next nine months, and again for brief periods in 1889, Greie reached out directly to her constituency. The press reported that she had "spoken to the heart" of her listeners, male and female, wherever she traveled. Certainly she elicited a remarkably favorable response on the woman question. A large turnout of women in points as geographically and politically distant as New Bedford and Holyoke, Massachusetts, Baltimore, Cincinnati, and Chicago suggested that the existing *Frauenbünde* had merely tapped a wellspring of interest. In Holyoke, for instance, her audience passed without opposition a resolution "supporting the ideas of the speaker and their consistency with the positions of the Social Democracy."[101] Baltimore Socialists presented Greie as "the true spokeswoman of the struggle for women's emancipation." In Chicago Greie offered political direction to the socially dynamic women's groups, and the *Arbeiter Zeitung* reinforced the message by publishing several of her lengthy addresses in its editorial columns. Perhaps the typical response of the locals she visited could be summed up by the Cincinnati correspondent who grieved that her listeners, swept away by her clarity and eloquence, only rarely enjoyed such an uplifting experience.[102]

Greie's popularity was due to her ability to appeal to women as a distinct sector yet always to link the possibility of their advancement to the class struggle. A bourgeois Baltimore paper referred to her lecture as "A meeting of Unattractive Women and Scared Men" and called Greie a "Pretty Anarchist," presenting a caricature of her work reminiscent of the days of Victoria Woodhull—justly in a sense, for Greie was heir to the free-thought tradition which had made Augusta Lilienthal's pronouncements on woman's rights anathema to most

Socialists of the 1870s. Yet Greie had substantially modified the older arguments by stating that women could advance insofar as they strengthened their position within the Socialist movement.[103] "Seldom, very seldom," could a marriage of equality be found today, she warned, but the shared comradeship of woman and man would foreshadow the new society within the old. No one, she told her women listeners, had greater reason or more profound opportunity to unite the working class from within for domestic joy and industrial cooperation.[104] Encouraging women's nascent desires for self-expression yet always channeling their unleashed energies into the Socialist movement, Greie established herself as a model of what the determined woman might do, in her small way, at the local level.

For a moment Greie's plans for a Socialist women's national federation seemed to move forward. Her appearances in Holyoke and Baltimore sparked the formation of new local *Frauenbünde*. Women from communities she did not visit traveled to gain the inspiration and organizational tips they needed for local agitation. Everywhere she went Greie encouraged the often well-organized women in the fraternal network to take up political questions more aggressively. From the strong centers of New York, Hudson County, New Jersey, the New England industrial towns, and Chicago the framework for consolidation had at last been put into place. Brother comrades shared a stake in her success, as *Chicagoer Arbeiter Zeitung* editorialists reflected, because the maturation of the movement necessitated the participation of everyone, entire families and whole communities: "There is little hope, until [women] themselves become Socialists and also make many men Socialists, as only they can." Had the party held onto its gains at the end of the 1880s and continued to support women's organization, Greie would likely have found herself at the center of a dynamic and confident Socialist women's movement.[105]

Just at this moment the erratic pattern of nineteenth-century Socialist activity undercut the promise of women's organization. The political upsurge following the strike wave, which had seemed so promising, proved fleeting. By 1888 the Knights of Labor stood as a shadow of its former self, and mainstream politicians made new, often successful bids for workingmen's votes. Defeat hung like a pall over the movement. As fair-weather friends drifted away and party factions in desperation turned against one another, the Socialist movement underwent a major internal realignment. Johanna Greie, who had emerged as a national leader only to preside over the movement's decline, loyally accepted the National Executive Committee's destruction of *Der Sozialist*, the paper which had offered her a national forum for her views. She even accepted the party's decision that plans for the federation of the *Frauenbünde* be scrapped.[106]

From the vantage point of fourteen years later, Johanna Greie described this historic moment as one of lost opportunity. Left to their own devices, *Frauenbund* sections would have suffered, but a nucleus might well have survived.

The leadership's decision to tighten ranks by asking women to dissolve their special organizations thus determined women's fate in the Socialist movement. The most confident and experienced women like Greie herself could easily make the transition from the *Frauenbund* to the regular party organization. But the average members, unaccustomed to working alongside men, chose not to transfer their allegiance; deprived of the few women leaders available, they lost a lifeline to politics. As Greie later recalled, a scattering of women entered the party after the dissolution of the *Frauenbünde*, but "it was not long before they left, some here, some there, until only a few remained."[107]

Yet the brief life of the *Frauenbünde* represented a significant shift in women's status within the Socialist movement. Although the majority of loyal wives would continue to serve the fraternal network, a militant minority could claim the right to organize women as a distinct political sector—as long as that sector appealed exclusively to working-class women and remained within the jurisdiction of the party. The solution to the *Frauenfrage*, Socialists affirmed, lay in the class struggle.

CONCLUSION

In 1879 Augusta Lilienthal had sought to offer the movement a unique strategy for solving the woman question. In the speech given to New York freethinkers and reprinted by her friend Alexander Jonas in the *New Yorker Volkszeitung*, Lilienthal argued that the relation between Socialists and woman's rights activists had been wholly misconceived by party chieftains. She offered a bold alternative analysis. Like the proletariat, woman was stateless, lacking in rights, and unable to defend herself legally against repression. Although the existing woman's rights movement advocated only women's political rights, and although its adherents naively hoped to address the Social Question (i.e. the class struggle) *after* having gained their rights as citizens, the struggle tended inevitably toward Social Democratic ends. Just as the wives of northern Democrats before the Civil War had defied their husbands to become abolitionists, so the most advanced advocates of woman's rights would defy their Republican and Democratic husbands to join Socialists in the genuine struggle for human emancipation. But Socialists had to bring this potential alliance into being. By instituting the complete equality of the sexes as a major plank in the party platform, and by acting in every way to make the sincerity of this intention evident, Socialists could seize the golden opportunity before them.[108]

As the long-run trajectory of American radicalism would reveal, Lilienthal's projection was not as outlandish as her Socialist contemporaries must have concluded. Lilienthal had, almost singularly among her peers, been close enough to both American radical circles and the German-American Socialist movement to have divined a common purpose, and to have identified a common romantic approach toward life and politics. She perceived, too, that the chances for coalescence depended upon a reconciliation of the opposing strategies that seemed to hold radicalism in the United States perpetually at the crossroads—the individual search for freedom and the task of collective mobilization. Yet in her time Lilienthal's message could not be comprehended, let alone acted upon. Despite the similarities Lilienthal was able to perceive, the German and native-born radicals performed their tasks in wholly different ways, even thought in vernaculars as distinct as the languages they used to express themselves. The day of reconciliation had not yet arrived and would not for this generation of immigrant and indigenous idealists.

The actual accomplishments of German-American Socialist women must have been as incomprehensible to their indigenous radical sisters as the pre-industrial German calendar of workers' holidays was to American laborers. By their own lights ethnic women had achieved significant goals. They had, most importantly, created enduring forms of organization. They had made politics into a family affair, a training ground for the young and a retirement community for the old, a part of daily life rather than a lonely commitment. If the daughters and sons of this community would find the atmosphere too intense and flee, their elders had scant reason to seek an easy assimilation into American life. They not only represented, after all, the most prestigious Social Democratic movement in the world—however vicarious their actual role—but stood, they believed, at the brink of the historic moment when Americans would fall into line with their European brothers and sisters, take up the red flag, and finish off world capitalism. For women scarcely less than for men, strength lay in modifying rather than abandoning the old ways.

Within this context the ascendancy of the *Frauenfrage* in the 1880s had a significance all its own. The evolution of women's organizations from *Frauenvereine* to *Frauenbünde*, invisible to the world outside the German-American community, signified a growing sense of political confidence among Socialist women. Similarly the party leadership now recognized women's prerogatives, a move capped by Johanna Greie's political manifesto and cross-country crusade which nearly succeeded in creating a miniature version of the Social Democratic women's movement achieved in Germany by the turn of the century. Albeit without much fanfare, the Socialist Labor party amended its platform to include the principle of woman suffrage heretofore scorned.[109] Toward the end of the decade Socialists took positive if minor steps toward recognizing the fact of women's labor and began to consider women factory workers in their strategic calculations. The theoretical counterpart of this activity, August Bebel's historical-analytical treatment of woman, laid the foundation for modern Socialist thought on the woman question. Less than twenty years after the break with Victoria Woodhull, Socialists had derived their own strategic and theoretical orientation toward an issue they had once sought to bury.

To be sure, German-American Socialists understood the woman question only within their own frame of reference. They could no more imagine Socialist women participating in a political organization or reform movement separate from the party than they could imagine a history of women outside the class struggle. Whatever Socialists might do to aid workingwomen in their struggle for bread, the measure of success would have been the integration of working-class women into the party machinery. Had suffrage been incorporated into a fighting program, a similar pattern would have emerged. For as Bebel had set forth, woman was to be lifted up by the proletariat under the direction of the party; only as woman rose (or fell) into the proletarian ranks could she join the struggle as an equal participant and shape her own destiny.

At the same time the German-American Socialists were forced to relinquish their position in the larger radical movement without forsaking their ideals. Socialist *Deutschthum*, hit by the disappointments of the late 1880s and sectarian disorganization in the 1890s, looked with relief (if perhaps also with some ideological misgiving) at the rise of indigenous Socialist tendencies along with Jews and other new immigrants. The German era of American Socialism closed in a reversal of its beginning: political explosions and a slow drift toward fraternalism as the dominant aspect of a once-heroic tendency.

At the turn of the century the aging movement sought to pass the baton with dignity and flourish to a movement it recognized as different but sentimentally attached to its own. In the ceremony of an 1897 St. Louis meeting Germans and Bohemians crowned Eugene V. Debs an idol greater than their own movement had ever known. In so doing they accepted elements of the Americanism they had long disdained:

> The stage presented a magnificent view. Splendidly decorated with flowers and shrubs and flags, in the center a large picture of Karl Marx and Ferdinand Lassalle, with large and fine pictures of Washington, Jefferson, Lincoln and John Brown at both sides, the stage made an indelibly agreeable impression on the audience. The Socialist singing societies, "Vorwaerts" and "Herwegh," attended in a body, about seventy strong, and their songs were enthusiastically applauded. The Bohemian Ladies' Singing Society, "Vlasta," and the Bohemian Male Chorus, "Hlahol," also harvested cheering applause for their masterly songs, and the Social Democracy of St. Louis will never forget the great service of the Bohemian singer, Miss Mary Hrdiloka, [who] sang the splendid solo, "Deart Heart," and the ovation tendered her by the grateful audience must have filled the young lady's heart with noble pride and joy. . . .

At the climax of the ceremonies

> the woman to the left [of Debs] with the red phrygian cap, and with long red silk ribbons and sashes beautifully arranged to her dress, raises her hand, pointing to the red banner she is holding in the other, and in clear and

penetrating voice, she—Mrs. Ada Shattinger is the comrade's name—she began to speak of Socialism, right and justice and love, of love for justice and right, of right to life, liberty and the pursuit of happiness. In the name of the Social Democratic women of St. Louis she presented the banner to Comrade Eugene V. Debs, who graciously accepted it, and who, at this occasion, delivered one of the finest little addresses we have ever heard before, appealing to the comrades to stand by their banner, by their cause, in peace, in war, in joy and sorrow, in victory and temporary defeat. . . .[110]

The costumes, the choirs, the sentimental overlay for revolutionary values found a point of reconciliation, after all, with the oncoming of pluralistic Socialism. Debs, who would epitomize not only the proletarian content but also the deep commitment to woman's emancipation in the indigenous radical sector, made the synthesis of ethnic and native values the hallmark of Socialist organizational success across the United States.

But the synthesis had become possible because of the drift of radical currents outside—even in opposition to—Germanic Socialism. Reformers found their own way to the Socialist movement, and they created a vision of the Cooperative Commonwealth far more popular than that generated by the German-Americans. Women played no small part in this process.

Not so different from Augusta Lilienthal's prediction, women activists began in the late 1880s to espouse Socialism—but under their own banners. They shared with their ethnic counterparts a faith in human solidarity, a desire for community, a sentimental love of honest labor and perfected domesticity. But they were nevertheless closer to abolitionist traditions than to European Socialist practice, and they devised a strategy utterly alien to the German-Americans as the Germanic Socialist was to American-born radicals. Thus a second force for Socialism, no less vital than the first, sprang from sources the immigrants had least expected.

NOTES

1. Meta Lilienthal, *Dear Remembered World* (New York, 1947), 25–32, an autobiographical reminiscence by Augusta's daughter.
2. Carl Wittke, *Refugees of Revolution* (Philadelphia, 1952), 122–23, 150–57, 164–65; L. Vern Rippley, *The German-Americans* (New York, 1976), 75–76, 79–83. Most impressive, perhaps, is the pro–woman suffrage essays by prominent intellectual Adolf Douai in the first German-American workers' daily paper, *Die Arbeiter Union* (New York), which he edited in 1869–70. See, for example, *Die Arbeiter Union*, Jan. 9, 1869.
3. *Die Neue Zeit* (New York), Feb. 18, 25, 1871. See also reports in *The Revolution* (New York), May 27, June 3, 24, Oct. 7, 1869, and *Die Arbeiter Union*, Jan. 9, 1869.
4. *Die Neue Zeit*, Nov. 26, 1870. For reminiscences and discussion by Augusta Lilienthal, her daughter, and others, see *New Yorker Volkszeitung*, Apr. 28, 1879, Feb. 27, 1910, Feb. 26, 1911, Feb. 25, 1912.

5. See Hermann Schlüter, *Die Internationale in Amerika; Ein Beitrag zur Geschichte der Arbeiter-Bewegung in den Vereinigten Staaten* (Chicago, 1918), 98–101, on Adolf Douai as an outstanding example of this group.

6. William Appleman Williams, *Contours of American History* (Cleveland, 1961), 313–17; George M. Fredrickson, *The Inner Civil War: Northern Intellectuals and the Crisis of the Union* (New York, 1965), Ch. XII.

7. See, for example, *Vorbote* (Chicago), Sept. 29, 1877; *Arbeiter-Stimme* (New York), Nov. 19, Dec. 17, 1876, Mar. 4, 1887.

8. *Arbeiter-Stimme*, Dec. 17, 1876.

9. *Ibid.*, Feb. 4, 1877.

10. *Ibid.*, Aug. 12, 1877.

11. *Ibid.*, July 29, 1877.

12. Schlüter, *Die Internationale in Amerika*, 487–511; Selig Perlman, "Upheaval and Reorganization," in John R. Commons, *History of Labor in the United States*, 2 vols. (New York, 1966 ed.), I, 223–27.

13. David N. Lyons, "The World of P. J. McGuire: A Study of the American Labor Movement, 1870–1890" (Ph.D. dissertation, University of Minnesota, 1972), Chs. I-II.

14. See, for example, "Anzeigen. Arbeiterpartei der Ver. Staaten," and "Correspondenzen," columns in *Arbeiter-Stimme*, 1877.

15. The actual quotation is from Daniel DeLeon in *Daily People* (New York), Aug. 8, 1908. DeLeon had cause to see the German experience unsympathetically, but the nineteenth-century sources are ridden with painfully revealing commentaries upon Socialist alienation from American life and fear of the disintegration of their own communities. See, for example, *Chicagoer Arbeiter Zeitung*, Oct. 10, 1880, for reflections upon the advance of machine over hand labor in the United States, and *Vorbote*, Feb. 18, 1882, on "Americanism."

16. Georg von Bosse, *Das Deutsche Element in den Vereinigten Staaten* (Stuttgart, 1908), 346–47.

17. See, for example, *Arbeiter-Stimme*, Oct. 29, Dec. 23, 1876, Apr. 29, 1877; *Volks Stimme des Westens* (St. Louis), Sept. 5, 1877; *Social-Demokrat* (New York), Mar. 28, 1875, Apr. 21, 1876; *Ohio Volkszeitung* (Cincinnati), Dec. 23, 1877; *Vorbote*, Dec. 18, 1875.

18. Adolf Douai, *Land und Leute in der Union* (Berlin, 1864), 151, 147.

19. Karl Marx and Frederick Engels, *The Communist Manifesto* (New York, 1961 ed.), 40.

20. *New Yorker Volkszeitung*, Feb. 9, 1878.

21. Margarette Susman, *Frauen der Romantik* (Jena, 1929), 3–26. For general background, see Solomon Liptzin, *Studies in German Social Poetry* (New York, 1928), and F. W. Kaufmann, *Schiller: Poet of Philosophical Idealism* (Oberlin, Ohio, 1942).

22. August Otto-Walster, *Leben and Werk: Eine Auswahl mit unveröffentlichten Briefen an Karl Marx* (Berlin, 1966). See also *Arbeiter-Stimme*, 1876–77, and *Volks Stimme des Westens*, 1877–78, for his stories.

23. *Volks Stimme des Westens*, Dec. 6, 1877.

24. *Arbeiter-Stimme*, June 17, 1877.

25. Robert Reitzel, "Das Weib Spricht," in *Des Armen Teufel: Gesammelte Schriften*, I (Detroit, 1913), 319. For biographical data on Reitzel, see Max Baginski, "Zur Einführung," in *ibid.*, 9–34.

26. Noted in Werner Thönnessen, *The Emancipation of Women* (London, 1973), 21–22. For Lassalle's Hegelian reconciliation of his romantic free-love views

with his socially conservative attitudes toward women, see Sholomo Na'aman, *Lassalle* (Hanover, 1970), 362–66.

27. Marx to Kugelmann, Dec. 5, 1868, in *Letters to Kugelmann*, ed. Clement Dutt and trans. Jane Tabrisky (New York, 1934), 82; Thönnessen, *Emancipation of Women*, 20–21, 32–33.

28. *Vorbote*, Dec. 18, 1875.

29. *Social-Demokrat*, Feb. 7, 1875.

30. The statement by the IWA was quoted in a historical retrospective in the jubilee issue of the *New Yorker Volkszeitung*, Feb. 21, 1903. The two quotations from the mid-1870s appeared respectively in *Vorbote*, Dec. 11, 1875, and in *Arbeiter-Stimme*, Oct. 29, 1876.

31. *Social-Demokrat*, Jan. 17, 1875. Augusta Lilienthal made another outstanding public appeal for woman's rights at a meeting in 1874 protesting police violence against demonstrators at Tompkins' Square Park; see *Arbeiter-Zeitung* (New York), Feb. 21, 1874. For the text of a typical pro-suffrage speech by Jonas, see the *Woman's Journal* (Boston), Jan. 17, 1874. Jonas remained, for the rest of the century and after, the German-American movement's most prominent leader supporting women's emancipation; see the eulogistic description of his important role in *New Yorker Volkszeitung*, Feb. 4, 1912.

32. *Social-Demokrat*, Feb. 7, 1875.

33. Schlüter, *Die Internationale in Amerika*, 306; Philip S. Foner, "Introduction" to *The Formation of the Workingmen's Party of the United States* (New York, 1976), 6.

34. "Declaration of Principles of the Workingmen's Party of the United States," in Foner, ed., *Formation of the Workingmen's Party*, 34. Diehard members of the International could not likely accept such a compromise and probably for this among other reasons faded from view as a coherent force. Embittered at their isolation, a year or so earlier they actually denounced the German Social Democracy for its guarded references to women's ultimate emancipation under Socialism; see Schlüter, *Die Internationale in Amerika*, 335.

35. *Arbeiter-Zeitung*, Feb. 8, 1873.

36. *Social-Demokrat*, Dec. 27, 1874.

37. *Ibid.*, Apr. 16, 1876. The German Social Democratic model from which the German-American organizational structure was taken is described best (albeit for a rather later period) in Peter Nettl, "The German Social Democratic Party 1890–1914 as a Political Model," *Past and Present*, 30 (Apr., 1965), 65–95.

38. *Social-Demokrat*, Mar. 7, 1875.

39. *Vorbote*, Jan. 18, 1877.

40. *Arbeiter-Stimme*, Nov. 12, 1876.

41. *Friedrich A. Sorge's The Labor Movement in America*, ed. Philip S. Foner and Brewster Chamberlin and trans. Brewster Chamberlin (Westport, Conn., 1977), 176; *Vorbote*, Jan. 18, 1877.

42. *The Socialist* (New York), June 28, 1879. Douai had extensive pedagogical training in Germany, directed German-American schools in Boston, New York, and Paterson, N.J., and wrote one of the outstanding tracts on the value of "free education"; see *Das Pionier Volks-Kälendar*, 1886, 47–49.

43. Toward the end of the decade, at least the New York group actually became known as the woman's service group (*Frauen Unterstützungsverein*); see *New Yorker Volkszeitung*, Mar. 4, 1879. See also, e.g., *Social-Demokrat*, Feb. 7, May 30, 1875.

44. *Social-Demokrat*, Feb. 7, Apr. 4, 1875.

45. *Ibid.*, Jan. 31, 1875.
46. *Vorbote*, Sept. 16, 1876. German and Scandinavian women's sections appeared also in Chicago by 1878; see *The Socialist* (Detroit), Jan. 12, 1878.
47. *Social-Demokrat*, Apr. 4, 1875; *Vorbote*, Dec. 2, 1876.
48. *Social-Demokrat*, Feb. 7, May 2, 9, 1875; *Arbeiter-Stimme*, Oct. 22, 1876; *Der Sozialist* (Milwaukee), Feb. 4, 11, Mar. 1, 4, 29, Sept. 15, Oct. 27, 1876. The major exception to this rule was the women's sections, especially the Milwaukee affiliate with its own tradition of political organization. Here, at least lip service was paid to the principle of woman suffrage, although the leading local male intellectuals still appeared as luminaries at women's meetings, and the general discussion of American woman's reform activity remained negative.
49. *Vorbote*, June 22, 1878; *Social-Demokrat*, May 2, 1875; *Der Sozialist*, Jan. 29, Feb. 4, 1876.
50. *Social-Demokrat*, Dec. 3, 1876.
51. *Ibid.*, Oct. 22, Dec. 3, 1876; *New Yorker Volkszeitung*, Nov. 23, 1878, Aug. 26, 1879; *Volks Stimme des Westens*, July 8, 1878.
52. *New Yorker Volkszeitung*, Mar. 4, 1879.
53. Commons, *History of Labor*, II, 277–78; *New Yorker Volkszeitung*, Jan. 15, 1879; Lyons, "The World of P. J. McGuire," Ch. III.
54. Alice Hyneman Rhine, "Reminiscences of Charles Sotheran as Pioneer American Socialist," In Charles Sotheran, *Horace Greeley and Other Pioneers of American Socialism* (New York, 1915 ed.), iv; *Socialist* (Detroit and Chicago), May 24, Apr. 5, 1879.
55. *Socialist*, May 24, 1879.
56. *Vorbote*, Sept. 20, 27, 1879; *Socialist*, May 3, 1879.
57. *Socialist*, Mar. 1, 1879.
58. Commons, *History of Labor*, II, 302–4.
59. Lizzie J. Holmes, "Women Workers of Chicago," *American Federationist*, 12 (Aug., 1905), 507–10; Lizzie J. Holmes, "The Days of Our Infancy: A Reminiscence," *Progressive Woman*, 5 (Aug., 1911), 7; *Socialist*, Apr. 19, June 21, 1879.
60. Mrs. J. C. Garner, Long Lane, Mo., in *Socialist*, Jan. 25, 1879.
61. "Bon Accord," St. Louis, Mo., in *ibid.*, Jan. 4, 1879.
62. *Socialist*, June 21, 1879. As late as 1881 in Providence, R.I. a correspondent could boast that "weekly meetings are attended by quite a number of ladies" interested in labor reform and the Rochdale cooperative system for establishing public utilities; see *Labor Review* (Detroit), Aug., 1881.
63. Perlman in Commons, *History of Labor*, II, 284–90. This disappointment drove a key segment of Chicago Socialists, including several important organizers and sympathizers of workingwomen, toward anarchism or "Social Revolution." For the next half-dozen years anarchists dominated German-American radicalism in Chicago and a number of other cities, throwing political Socialists on the defensive and further reducing the ranks of the SLP.
64. Perlman in Commons, *History of Labor*, II, 305–6; Carolyn Ashbaugh, *Lucy Parsons, American Revolutionary* (Chicago, 1976), 34–35; Robert Howard, "Progress in the Textile Trades," in George E. McNeill, ed., *The Labor Movement: The Problem of To-Day* (New York, 1887), 226–36.
65. Perlman in Commons, *History of Labor*, II, 290–91; "History of the Knights of Labor," in McNeill, ed., *The Labor Movement*, 414–28. See also *New Yorker*

Volkszeitung, Oct. 10, 1883. For a doleful reflection on "Americanization" and the tragic-comic aphorisms, see *Die Fackel* (Chicago), Apr. 1, 1883.

66. Laurence Gronlund, *The Coöperative Commonwealth in Its Outlines; An Exposition of Modern Socialism* (New York, 1884), 194–205.
67. *Workman's Advocate* (New Haven, Conn.), Aug. 22–Sept. 19, 1886, ran a serialized edition of *The Coöperative Commonwealth*.
68. Karl Marx and Frederick Engels, *Marx and Engels: Letters to Americans, 1848–1895*, trans. Leonard Mins (New York, 1953), 162–64, 166–67, 169, 178–79, 190, 220, 224.
69. *Friedrich Sorge's The Labor Movement in the United States*, 203. *Vorbote*, May 15–June 1, 1887, has its own history of the Chicago movement's shift during the early 1880s, under pressure of the new immigration. See also the histories of the movement's development in the *New Yorker Volkszeitung's* twenty-fifth anniversary jubilee issue, Feb. 21, 1903.
70. August Bebel, *Die Frau in der Vergangeheit, Gegenwart und Zukunft* (Hottingen-Zurich, 1884), 5. Bebel had taken up the subject while incarcerated on political charges, writing what he described as "the first thing ever written by a man of our party on the position of women from the socialist point of view"—as an appendix to a study of French Utopianism; see August Bebel, *My Life* (New York, 1973 ed.), 259. Translations in the text are from the Daniel DeLeon edition, *Woman under Socialism* (New York, 1971 ed.), cross-checked with the original manuscript. See also the recent discussions of the importance of the book in Florence Herve, "Zum 100. Jahrestag des Erscheinens von 'Die Frau und der Sozialismus,' " *Marxistische Blätter*, Feb., 1979.
71. Bebel, *Die Frau*, 5–35.
72. *Ibid.*, 93, 99, 23, 96–97, 220.
73. *Ibid.*, 219–20.
74. Thönnessen, *Emancipation of Women*, 37.
75. *Die Fackel*, Dec. 12, 1880, May 23, 1883, May 11, 1884; *New Yorker Volkszeitung*, Nov. 19, 1882, Jan. 25, 1883, July 25, 1886; *Vorbote*, Mar. 14, 1888.
76. U.S. Bureau of Labor, *Fourth Annual Report* on "Working Women in Large Cities" (Washington, D.C., 1888); *Die Fackel*, Oct. 10, 1880.
77. U.S. Senate, Doc. 645, *Report on the Condition of Women and Child Wage Earners in the United States*, vol. II, *Men's Ready-Made Clothing* (Washington, D.C., 1911); Mabel Hurd Willet, *The Employment of Women in the Clothing Trade* (New York, 1902).
78. George Stiebeling, *Die Wirtschaftliche Entwickelung der Vereinigten Staaten in dem Jahrzehnt 1870 bis 1880* (New York, 1886); *New Yorker Volkszeitung*, Mar. 21, May 2, 1883; *Chicagoer Arbeiter Zeitung*, Sept. 27, 1883.
79. *Chicagoer Arbeiter Zeitung*, Apr. 17, 1888.
80. *New Yorker Volkszeitung*, Aug. 21, Sept. 1, 1886, Sept. 9, 1886; *Der Sozialist*, Jan. 5, 12, 1889.
81. *New Yorker Volkszeitung*, Nov. 20, 1884, June 18, 1885.
82. *Ibid.*, Feb. 26, 1885. By the early 1880s the expanded Socialist journalism dwelt in considerable length on the housewife's role in protecting family health. See, e.g., *Die Fackel*, Feb. 26, 1882, Oct. 19, 1884.
83. *New Yorker Volkszeitung*, Nov. 20, 1884.
84. *Ibid.*, July 27, 1885; see also the party resolution on schools at its 1885 congress in *ibid.*, Oct. 26, 1886, and a general commentary in *Der Sozialist*, Apr. 6, 1889.

85. *Die Fackel*, June 12, 1881; *Vorbote*, Sept. 16, 1885; *New Yorker Volkszeitung*, Sept. 9, 1886; *Chicagoer Arbeiter Zeitung*, Apr. 25, 1887.
   Concomitant with this activity, the Socialist press published its first columns directed explicitly at women, in general sentimental messages to win over a woman's heart but also reminders of the difficulty of material life under capitalism; see "Kleine Frauen-Zeitung" in *Die Fackel*, e.g., Oct. 2, 30, 1881.
86. *New Yorker Volkszeitung*, Sept. 17, 1885; see also Nov. 20, 1884, Dec. 18, 1885.
87. *Der Sozialist*, June 26, July 10, 1886, Aug. 27, 1887.
88. *New Yorker Volkszeitung*, Apr. 8, Sept. 9, 1886; *Vorbote*, Sept. 15, 1886.
89. *New Yorker Volkszeitung*, Sept. 9, 1886. Signed "Eine Sozialistin," this series of essays was probably written by the most outspoken figure of the *Frauenbünde*, one Frau Garthausen. Regrettably, nothing biographical is known about this important political figure.
90. *Ibid.*, Oct. 7, 1885.
91. *Ibid.*
92. *Der Sozialist*, Jan. 30, 1886.
93. See, for instance, reports of substantial women's attendance in Bridgeport, stirred by the Knights of Labor, in *Der Sozialist*, Apr. 3, 1886, and *New Yorker Volkszeitung*, Oct. 22, 1885.
94. Greie's biography is sketched in the *New Yorker Volkszeitung*, Feb. 26, 1911; see *Der Sozialist*, 1887–88, for her major contemporary essays.
95. *Der Sozialist*, Jan. 14, 1888.
96. *Ibid.*
97. *Ibid.*
98. See, for example, *Chicagoer Arbeiter Zeitung*, Sept. 18, 1888.
99. Perlman in Commons, *History of Labor*, II, 384–94, 439–54.
100. *Der Sozialist*, Jan. 14, 1888.
101. *Ibid.*, Oct. 7, 1888; see also *ibid.*, Jan. 1, Sept. 15, Oct. 10, 20, Mar. 9, 1888, May 4, 1889; *Providence* (R.I.) *Anzeiger*, Feb. 23, 1889.
102. *Chicagoer Arbeiter Zeitung*, Mar. 8, Aug. 25, Sept. 19, 1888; *Der Sozialist*, Mar. 17, Oct. 20, 1888.
103. *Der Sozialist*, Jan. 4, 1888.
104. *Chicagoer Arbeiter Zeitung*, Sept. 18, 1888.
105. *Ibid.*, Nov. 23, 1888.
106. Perlman in Commons, *History of Labor*, II, 413–23. Editors of the *Volkszeitung* essentially reorganized the National Executive Committee, purging those deemed insufficiently sympathetic to unionism, and ending *Der Sozialist*. See the charges by dissidents against Greie as member of the ruling clique in *Workman's Advocate*, Oct. 28, 1889.
107. *New Yorker Volkszeitung*, Jan. 23, 1902, is Greie's keenest memoir. See also her reminiscence of the few brave women who stood by women's organization, *ibid.*, Mar. 2, 1902, and a rank-and-file memory of the dissolution from a Newark *Frauenverein* member, *ibid.*, March 9, 1902.
108. *New Yorker Volkszeitung*, Feb. 16, 1879.
109. *Labor Review*, Feb., 1882.
110. *Social Democratic Herald* (Chicago), Dec. 16, 1897

2 The Woman's Movement and Socialism, 1870–1900

> A movement for the higher education of women was
> inaugurated. Colleges, universities, and professional
> schools were opening their doors to women. Industries,
> trades, and remunerative vocations, which hitherto had
> ignored them, now invited their coöperation, and
> women were becoming self-supporting members of the
> community. Hard and unjust laws which had grievously
> hindered them were repealed, and others affording larger
> protection and opportunity were enacted. Great organi-
> zations of women for missionary work were formed, and
> managed solely by themselves. Women by the hundred
> thousand wheeled into line for temperance work.
> Women's clubs sprang into being,—clubs for social
> enjoyment and mutual instruction and help. Woman
> Suffrage Leagues multiplied. Everywhere there was a call
> for women to be up and doing, with voice and pen, with
> hand and head and heart.
>
> Mary A. Livermore
> *The Story of My Life* (1899)

Mary Rice Livermore frequently recalled women's achievements since the Civil War, for she perceived the outline of her own life in this history. Born in 1820, Livermore had been reared to accept woman's special vocation as wife and mother. Marriage to an idealistic Universalist minister and temperance reformer seemed to seal this fate. She might help her husband publish a religious newspaper, even pen an occasional tract on the evils of alcohol, but she devoted herself to the care of her growing family. Livermore abstained from the woman's rights agitation of the 1850s, although late in the decade, after moving from New England to Chicago, she served on the board of directors of a newly opened home for destitute women and children; this latter involvement she interpreted as an extension of her maternal role. Just a decade later Livermore gained a national reputation. Her stature continued to grow as the century moved toward a close. An ardent suffragist, one of the most prominent lecturers in the country, successful writer, luminary on the membership lists of dozens of organizations, Mary Livermore enjoyed her last years as a leading advocate of women's emancipation and Christian Socialism.

Livermore named the Civil War the turning point in her life. Appointed to the Sanitary Commission in Illinois, she hired a governess to care for her children and devoted herself full time to this position. During the course of the war she delivered hundreds of public addresses, raised money for relief operations, fostered the organization of over 3,000 soldiers' aid societies, produced a monthly bulletin and several circulars on relief activities, and oversaw innumerable other projects. In October, 1863, she reaped the rewards of hard work as the sanitary fair which she helped organize raised more than $70,000 for the Sanitary Commission and became the model for dozens of local fairs nationwide. Overseeing a multitude of relief operations, Livermore gained a wealth of management skills. Most important, she emerged from under the weight of these responsibilities a new woman.

Livermore attested that her wartime experiences dramatically altered her conception of woman's duty. The ballot, she now readily perceived, was a necessary implement if women were to carry out their philanthropic programs speedily and effectively. Extricating herself from war relief work, Livermore called the first woman suffrage convention held in Illinois and soon thereafter rose to prominence in the newly formed American Woman Suffrage Association. Now wholeheartedly devoted to women's advancement, Livermore embarked on a full-time career as lecturer and writer. She took to the platform and spoke on subjects ranging from classical literature to women's history. Over the next twenty-three years she gave over 150 performances annually and financially sustained her family. Mary Livermore would appear, in middle life, the Advanced Woman incarnate, proving by her example that members of her sex were ready to share a greater portion of life's demands. [1]

In her many public pronouncements Livermore perpetuated a legend about women's awakening during the Civil War. Whereas woman's rights advocates traced their origins to Seneca Falls and claimed Lucretia Mott and Lucy Stone as patron saints, Livermore located her roots in the war emergency and eulogized her compatriots Louisa May Alcott, Clara Barton, and Anna Dickenson. These latter heroes had forced through their wartime dedication a wholly new conception of womanhood. Hundreds of thousands of middle-class women had similarly taken up volunteer work in hospital or relief agencies, often filling positions of leadership vacated by men involved in political or military operations. Their less fortunate sisters, facing previously unknown financial hardships with their male breadwinners gone, meanwhile found employment to care for their families. Although experiences varied among different social classes, the results were similar: women learned the techniques of organization and mobilization; they gained a sense of self-reliance and spiritual depth through their common triumphs and sorrows. As the horrors and tragedy of war receded, such women determined to preserve the feeling of independence they had gained during the emergency. However apocryphal, Livermore's interpretation signaled a new consciousness of woman's fate in American society.

The war, however, represented only the first step in this maturation. What wartime pressures had fostered, Livermore explained, the expanding industrial economy rendered permanent and full-blown. Here Livermore hit upon a theme that her contemporaries would gradually develop into a comprehensive philosophy of women's advancement. The myth that "all men support all women," long known to be false, Livermore opined, now shattered before economic realities. In the postwar society women regularly participated in the marketplace, gained their own sources of support, and broke once and for all with humiliating forms of financial dependency upon men. Women were finally realizing their latent capabilities and forcing their male rulers to "awake to the consciousness that there were in women possibilities and potencies of which they had never dreamed."[2] This was Livermore's own life, writ large.

Hundreds of thousands of women shared Livermore's estimation of female destiny. Like Livermore, the most prominent figures were middle-aged and focused a subjective eye on the exigencies of history. They, too, were old enough to know the attraction of small-town life and the virtue of domesticity. When they gazed upon the great cities filling up with immigrants, or when they witnessed the degradation of women at the hands of unscrupulous employers or worse, they could not suppress a twinge of nostalgia for the clean, neat towns of their childhoods and the sense of community they believed had existed there. They were shocked by the squalor of the slums and the failure of civic institutions to provide for that growing class of citizens, the poor, especially the underpaid women forced to labor under unhealthy conditions. The society emerging from the ruins of the Civil War thus forbode an auspicious future: woman's advancement or her ruination.

This uncertainty about woman's fate—what became known as the woman question—informed a perspective unique to Livermore's generation. Because of their advanced age, leading ideologues chose their political weapons from the traditions of a gender-conscious culture harkening back to their youth. They addressed the prevailing inequities and typically attributed the injustice to the absence of women from the ruling councils. Just as women protected their families and instilled them with moral virtue, so too they must guide the state along a righteous course. Woman's advancement, far from destroying womanly virtue, would ultimately serve to make that virtue a public resource destined to save the civilization.

If German-American Socialists had continually asserted a romantic view of womanhood, their indigenous antagonists demonstrated that romanticism could cut two ways. Woman's special qualities could prompt a sense of shame, indignity, and fervor for revolution in the heart of her alleged male protector;

the same qualities interpreted differently could give over to women themselves the potential power to render their principles a universal standard, their altruistic qualities the Golden Rule of all human experience. Women mobilized for this purpose might lack the "scientific" claims that European Socialists made to predictive omniscience. But they possessed a definite, thoroughgoing sensibility suited both morally and historically to the prospects of an American democratic renaissance.

This faith of Livermore and her collaborators assumed a very great role in the coalescing woman's movement. Between 1870 and 1890 thousands upon thousands of women organized along gender-specific lines. They formed their own associations, rural and urban, as an expression of sisterly concern and as a combination against the customs of male preferment. Although they could not single-handedly change society to suit their needs, they could through organization foster female solidarity and thereby make their voices heard. Compared to the single-minded agitation conducted by German-American Socialists, the woman's movement seemed to lack strategic coherence, but its leaders articulated the basic principles of women's economic prerogatives and organizational independence.

In the late 1880s, when the call went forth for a new crusade to restore national purpose, the leaders of the woman's movement were prepared. Seeking allies among the most progressive sectors of the mobilization, they determined to preserve their autonomy from male-dominated institutions. Indeed, women gained a great degree of prominence within the indigenous movements conducive to women's participation. They helped shape the character of English-language pockets of the Socialist Labor party, the Bellamy Nationalist movement, and Christian Socialism, as well as the sweeping agrarian movements culminating in Populism. Most important, they built upon their traditions in the woman's movement and made decisive contributions to the final grand campaign conducted in the name of republicanism, the last-ditch effort to ward off the consolidation of corporate capitalism.

When the Socialist movement emerged full blown at the turn of the century, it owed more to these pioneering women activists than could be easily comprehended. Livermore and her collaborators had failed to bring their followers en masse into the radical camp, but they established basic principles of women's role in American Socialism. They had contributed, as German-American women had, a distinctive style of organization in the form of independent women's clubs and societies. They also offered a unique assessment of their bequest. They had established woman's right to labor as the cardinal tenet of her liberation, woman suffrage as a means to participate in the political process of the revolution. They also promised the fulfillment of womanly virtue in a new moral standard for the Socialist civilization. Their own movement's trajectory, its symbols and rituals, found a new life in the Socialist Party of America.

No more than Augusta Lilienthal did Mary Livermore survive to see her dreams requited. But she traveled a great distance from the politically modest wife of a small-town minister to the renowned and enthusiastic advocate of Socialism at the end of her span. She lacked Lilienthal's European-trained mentors. But she possessed the enormous advantage of a sisterly constituency that praised and upheld her principles, moved in considerable numbers to assist the awakening of their sex, and took up the sword of righteousness against Mammon as against all indignities in a social system ruled by man alone.

THE WOMAN'S MOVEMENT

The Gilded Age woman's movement did not provide a massive constituency for the later Socialist movement, but it did set the standards for those native-born women who would participate. While German-American Socialists named the proletariat the agent of history and the Socialist Labor party its political vanguard, leaders of the woman's movement put forth an alternative paradigm. They endowed womanhood with a comparable power and named women's own institutions a motive force for social change; for the hallowed class consciousness they substituted an alternative sensibility, gender conscious-ness or a faith in a collective sisterhood. As the woman suffrage campaign grew only slowly into a genuine mass movement,[3] women poured into a multiplicity of urban clubs and institutions and rural temperance societies. By the late 1880s this assembly stood as a major political force in American society, sym-bolized by the creation of the International Council of Women, which acted as an umbrella for hundreds of local organizations. These clubs and societies, urban and rural, also served as the training ground for a core of women leaders who would make the first claims upon Socialism as the arena for women's emancipation.

The urban sector of the woman's movement which formed at the close of the Civil War made several lasting contributions. Its leaders identified a key political issue, namely woman's right to labor. They also instituted a form of organization radical for the time, the independent women's club or society. Together both elements served in a developing strategy of women's advancement.

The right to labor became by the late 1880s a cardinal principle of women's advancement. On one level this development paralleled other sectors of the radical community, for the shift in orientation from chattel slavery to wage slavery, forecast as early as the 1850s, was now complete, and the great questions of the day focused on the seemingly precarious relationship of capital and labor.

Many citizens evinced an understandable concern for the postwar drift of American society, its increasingly stratified character and the potential despoliation of the republican dream.[4] The women's leaders shared this sensibility yet added a unique touch. Aware of the incomparable hardships of their less fortunate sisters, they recognized nevertheless that all women regardless of social position endured a common economic injustice, be it expressed as discrimination in the marketplace or as a humiliating form of personal dependency. The physical injury of poverty and exploitation or the spiritual poisoning of idleness and dissipation—this was women's dual inheritance. Thus the labor question, no longer identified entirely by issues of class, took on a special dimension informed by problems peculiar to their sex.

The right of women to sell their labor at a "just price" had surfaced as a distinct issue before the war. In the 1830s New England workingwomen had begun to assert collectively the necessity of securing identical wage rates for male and female laborers and defended women's place in industry as a fundamental right, the right to be self-supporting and independent citizens of the republic. Likewise many middle-class women organized benevolent societies to aid their poorer sisters and perceived early on that destitute or "fallen" women's greatest obstacle was not moral but economic, that women simply could not sustain themselves and their families on the meager wages they typically received for their labors. With increasing industrialization, especially the mechanization of several key trades, the growing numbers of workingwomen in urban areas generated yet more interest. Several moral reform societies formed earlier to care for "fallen" women reconstituted themselves in the 1840s and 1850s to offer practical assistance such as temporary lodgings and day nurseries while women looked for "respectable" employment; their actions were a harbinger of future mobilizations.[5]

The Civil War provided women leaders with their ultimate insight. The rapid and erratic expansion of the needle trades and light manufacturing and the unforeseen necessity of self-support had combined to imperil the fates of thousands of women. The public response to their plight was swift and diverse. Religious women gained a wider range in their benevolent activities, and within the decade nearly every major parish in New York City sponsored sewing societies, emergency relief programs, and employment referral services. At the war's midpoint New York philanthropists created the Working Women's Protective Union, a model enterprise rendering relief and legal assistance to women cheated by unscrupulous employers. Elizabeth Cady Stanton and Susan B. Anthony joined this campaign; they officiated over the Working Women's Society, a self-help organization devoted to sisterly cooperation and affiliated briefly with the National Labor Union. Workingwomen in other cities, often with the aid of middle-class women, organized similar societies; by 1869 Boston alone claimed nine such organizations and, along with New York, hosted major conventions of workingwomen that year and the next. At the war's end even the conservative press had endorsed the principle of equal pay for equal work. The "stringent conservators of 'woman's sphere,' " one observer thus remarked, had conceded woman's rights "as an intonement, it would seem, for ages of injustice or as a bribe to pacify the restive spirit of said injustice into a fresh contentment with the spirit of her bondage."[6] Concession or bribe, newspaper publicity indicated that the problems women faced in wage labor had come into public light at last.

In the midst of these discussions a few prescient women began to shape an analysis that would guide activists over the following decades. Virginia Penny in *Employments of Women* (1863) had named a major problem: women were ignorant of their options in the marketplace. The war, Penny averred, had thrown more women on their own resources than at any previous time in the history of the nation and thereby dramatized the necessity for women to secure a variety of employments. She feared most women believed that household industries represented the full range of possibilities. Faced with financial distress, too many had instinctively picked up their needles, overcrowding the market and lowering wages already notoriously poor. Despite decades of philanthropic work by church and benevolent societies, despite the expansion of production during wartime, conditions in the needle trades were unstable; the introduction of the sewing machine, invented a decade earlier, completed the ruination of women's characteristic hand labor, their mainstay in times of crisis. The postwar future yawned menacingly ahead unless women could take up occupations heretofore reserved for man or not yet in existence but open to female bidding. The fateful choice—integration into the expanding market or segregation into marginal and precarious positions—seemingly hung in the balance. Women must respond assertively, Penny insisted, and seek both to protect themselves from the worst possibilities and to demand their right to equal opportunity. If women could capitalize on the new opportunities, Penny promised "a complete revolution . . . wrought in the social and political standing of women," the inauguration of a new era in the history of their sex, and ultimately their emancipation.[7]

The faith in women's advancement through wage labor marked this era of women's political history. To redeem this promise, women drew first upon their most precious resource: sisterly solidarity. An emphasis upon gender thus served to mute the differences between social classes and allowed activists to pursue a distinctive mission. Only by coming together —" 'in bonds as bound,' " as Caroline Dall had argued a decade earlier—could women create the mechanisms to advance their cause.[8]

To foster women's advancement, activists chose forms deceptively genteel. Women's clubs and unions, established by a minority of talented and relatively leisured women, might appear a manifestation of noblesse oblige. Their true purpose, the founders stated, was the abolition of polite society and its oppressive decorum that denied middle-class women the fulfillment only meaningful labor could provide and lower-class women the dignity and welfare only a just wage could ensure.

Was it possible, asked prominent author Jane Cunningham Croly, that women "have a life of their own, may learn to know and honor each other, may find solace in companionship, and lose sight of small troubles in larger aims?" Croly founded New York's premier women's club in 1868 to furnish a positive answer. Its typical constituent in her estimation was the "new woman" of the nineteenth century, a transitional figure on her way from the domestic confinement of an earlier era to the full social and economic life promised in the period ahead." By providing a common space outside the household, Croly and her associates hoped to create an environment wherein women might share their new experiences and push forward with sisterly solidarity into the larger civil society.

Most women's clubs founded in the 1870s had a dual purpose: to foster the advancement of white, middle-class women into the economic mainstream; and to serve as centers for various political and reform endeavors, especially to assist lower-class women who were searching for work. Popular opinion notwithstanding, club activities were not limited to literary pursuits or other dilettantish erudition. Most club members reported cultural affairs the least successful of the various programs sponsored by the clubs. Meaningful club activities, in their minds, had definite practical applications. For although the members were well educated and leisured by contemporary standards, they felt deprived of serious social intercourse. Many were representatives of the first generation of American women to experience a new dimension in life, a period not relegated to childbearing and childrearing. Often in their forties or fifties and with children grown, these women had the time, the desire, and often the necessity to take up useful labors outside their households. [10]

Clubwomen aspiring to remunerative employment had not far to look for lessons in frustration and disappointment. The rosters of the first women's clubs formed in Boston, New York, and Chicago included some of the most prominent professional women of their communities. Old and young, these women commonly expressed vexation at the male monopoly upon well-paying occupations, limiting women's ability to support themselves or to serve as financial heads of their households. Club founder Jane Croly was herself prototypical. A regular news columnist for many years, she had published several well-received collections under the pen-name "Jennie June." As a young mother Croly had also managed to combine her domestic and professional responsibilities by clearing away household work each morning and then laboring steadily for the next ten or twelve hours in her downtown offices. Now in middle age, she supported her ailing husband. Highly respected in the field of journalism, Croly nevertheless shared little camaraderie with her male peers and felt cheated of the full social and financial rewards. Turned away from a New York Press Club dinner honoring Charles Dickens, an imposing event in the journalistic world, she and other women writers had in response formed Sorosis.[11] Clubs to them meant not merely entertainment or abstract enlightenment but professional contacts and mutual encouragement.

From its first days Sorosis encompassed broader purposes than aid to a handful of aspiring women professionals. All workingwomen, the leaders believed, shared a common grievance and a common need for organization. Similarly in Boston, the New England Women's Club initiated the opening of the state's horticultural school to female applicants and the Boston school board to women representatives, founded the Girls' Latin School, and sponsored the New England Hospital for Women and Children. Such acts carried no philanthropic intentions. Breaking sharply and self-consciously with the Calvinist attitude toward charity, these reformers had faith only in self-help projects free of sectarian or ministerial reins and under the direction of women whenever possible. Julia Ward Howe, famed author of the "Battle Hymn of the Republic" and poet laureate of the New England Women's Club, could without hypocrisy speak of the "universal sisterhood" whose "sacred claims our whole life must more and more acknowledge."[12] For Howe, who like Croly had only recently taken up the support of her household, this sisterhood was not merely a worthy goal but a necessity of her own survival.

The departure from philanthropic tradition stirred up a minor tempest. "Had the club members started to *do* any one thing" along familiar lines, the movement's historian later reflected, "from building an asylum for the aged and 'indigent' females to supplying the natives of Timbuctoo with pocket handkerchiefs, it would have found a public ready made." The alternative emphasis upon sorority for its own sake provoked, in her words, "much abusive criticism."[13]

Speaking in the name of a universal sisterhood, club leaders hoped to leap social barriers and welcome working-class women on their own terms. Many described wage-earning women as morally superior to their leisured sisters. Unlike wealthy women who had succumbed to idleness and dissipation, wage-earning women maintained a strength of character only those who labored possess; truly virtuous, they preserved the republican heritage from those who sought to introduce the trappings of European decadence.[14] And if these humble specimens of womanhood suffered, ate badly, and dressed in rags, they had anyone but themselves to blame. Club leaders of Sorosis and the New England Women's Club responded by sponsoring an investigation of the actual conditions of workingwomen in their cities. The New England report on needlewomen gained the reputation of a landmark investigation when it appeared in

1869. This report provided the inspiration for a large-scale investigation several years later by Carroll D. Wright, renowned Massachusetts commissioner of labor statistics, who hired several of the original investigators to assist his enterprise.[15] By the late 1870s the NEWC prepared to embark on yet grander schemes and develop its "most cherished plan," which began a model institution for women's clubs across the urban landscape.

The Women's Educational and Industrial Union, organized by club members in 1877, embodied as much as possible the entire philosophy of women's advancement. Not "purse to purse or talent to talent or acquirement to acquirement, but heart to heart," the new organization's members came together, popular children's author and the WEIU's second president, Abby Morton Diaz, reflected. The "common ground of humanity" would serve as the guiding principle of the most ambitious women's urban reform effort to date.[16]

The WEIU's program had several main facets. First, it could be described as a downtown center for women's improvement, leisure, and entertainment. A lunchroom, reading room, and parlor provided all interested women safe, comfortable surroundings to pass a few minutes or hours. A series of classes were conducted to improve women's opportunities in the business world. Similar to the NEWC, the WEIU sponsored lectures on all aspects of the woman question, offered entertainments and festivals, and sustained a series of classroom courses on such topics as literature, religion, political and legal rights, social purity, physical hygiene, and especially domestic economy and practical trades. Instructors trained younger women to run an efficient household, as WEIU leaders believed that women frequently left their parental homes for the factory before learning the necessary domestic skill at their mothers' apron strings. Married women, even those with servants, gained instruction on how to manage their household affairs given limited finances or time. Efficient home management, far from converting women into total homemakers, would free time for other activities, so it was believed. These programs underway, the WEIU moved to consider the problems of women's employment in general.

The labor market itself served to focus reformers' energies. The WEIU's Protective Committee, personally directed by Diaz, became a notable institution within a few years after its formation in 1878 and concentrated on specific problems of women wage earners. Committee members often functioned as an investigative team, visiting local shops and department stores and noting the facilities for female employees, such as washrooms and seats for long stints of labor. It advised women on securing positions in various places, warning them against known unscrupulous employers and informing them of the conditions in certain stores and factories. It also secured legal services for women who had been cheated of wages and counseled them on how to draw up binding wage contracts with their employers to reduce the likelihood of this common occurrence. It published a list of reputable establishments and boarding houses in the city, and maintained referral services for unskilled factory workers, domestics, department store clerks, and professional women as well. For those women still encumbered by homemaking responsibilities or too reserved to break tradition by venturing into public employment, the WEIU operated a cooperative exchange whereby women could earn money from domestic skills by selling foodstuffs or fancy goods. The monetary gains would be modest and irregular, but even homemakers, the club leaders believed, required at least a modicum of financial independence from their husbands.[17]

The WEIU stood as a model institution for women reformers across the country. In at least thirteen other cities, including Buffalo, Providence, San Francisco, and Cleveland, women reformers sponsored a multitude of programs which offered similar assistance to workingwomen. Many such organizations attracted a sizable membership; the Boston WEIU claimed more than 1,200 members in 1890. The hundreds of smaller societies of the mid-1880s indicated a pervasive concern for woman's fate in industrial America.

Despite their dedication, sympathetic women lacked the financial and political power to alter significantly the condition of wage-earning women. Many of their programs failed, such as the NEWC's Friendly Evening Association, a short-lived plan to open club rooms to workingwomen. Class differences often proved insuperable, and many dreams of a universal sisterhood went unfulfilled. The programs designed to assist middle-class women in their wage-earning pursuits succeeded more frequently, and club members themselves undoubtedly benefited from camaraderie and mutual encouragement. But sisterly cooperation alone could not overcome the larger obstacles to women's advancement.

Whatever their shortcomings, these institutions made a decisive ideological impact upon the woman's movement. Within a decade of their inception, women's clubs and societies had projected through their programs a clear vision of women's advancement into civil society. WEIU activists and their sisters elsewhere encouraged a growing sensibility that women had other roles than wife and mother. "The cruel kindness of the old doctrine," wrote Julia Ward Howe in 1891, "that women should be worked for and should not work, that their influence should be felt, but not recognized, that they should hear and see but neither appear nor speak," had been exposed as a sham and pummelled into retreat. "The new activities sap the foundation of vicious and degraded life," she enthused, by bringing women together around a common philosophical outlook.[18]

In a survey of almost 1,300 clubs conducted in the 1890s by the U.S. Department of Labor, a reporter concluded that club members believed "the science of economics is at the bottom of nearly all their problems."[19] For decades their leaders had been speaking forcefully for woman's right to labor in dignity and naming her acquisition of an independent livelihood as the key to her emancipation. Whatever the future held for their institutions, women activists self-consciously built upon this foundation.

While an awareness of changing labor patterns and familial roles inspired urban activists to urge woman's advancement into civil society and to insist upon her right to meaningful labor, a growing dissatisfaction felt intensely in rural and small-town America called legions of women to attention. Industrial and urban growth might offer women either new opportunities or hardships, and activists sought to meet both contingencies. But the relative decline of the countryside in economic power and political prestige seemingly threatened to plunge the republic into chaos and to eclipse the progress of their sex at the very center of American civilization. Following the Panic of 1873, which fell heavily on small towns and rural areas, women found their own distinctive form of mobilization—the temperance crusade.

For thousands of women temperance as a fighting slogan gave coherence to long-standing grievances. By lashing out at symbols of men's abuse of power such as public drunkenness and political corruption stemming from the saloons, women helped to create a climate for a massive protest movement in the western states. Small-town and rural women also delineated a social critique and prescription for reform congruent with that of their urban sisters: to free themselves and to save the nation, women required the power only economic and political equality could bestow; to attain that power, women required a far-reaching sisterhood capable of overcoming all obstacles. Here especially the call for woman suffrage gained a new constituency and a new purpose. Not for abstractions alone did rural women demand the ballot but in order to bring womanly authority to bear upon a wicked world.

The western woman's movement grew from an outbreak of temperance evangelism beginning in the late 1860s and escalating significantly during the hard winter of 1873 and 1874. Through songs, prayers, scripture readings, and mass assemblies, women closed saloons in town after town across the Midwest. Within a year temperance agitation had spread so quickly, the pace of women's activities so dramatically, that the cause became known as the woman's revolution. In November, 1874, over 200 women representing organizations in seventeen states met to form the National Woman's Christian Temperance Union.[20]

Much like the urban activists, the most prescient leaders of the WCTU addressed from their first moment of involvement questions of women's social and political status. Because they perceived the saloon as a direct challenge to the sanctity of women's domain, the home, they reasoned that women must be enabled to protect their sacred trust by participating freely in civic life. Thus a resolution passed at the first WCTU convention stated boldly that "much of the evil by which this country is cursed comes from the fact that men in power

whose duty is to make and administer the laws" had failed.[21] Among the ranks
the seeds of protest had already fallen upon fertile ground. As one self-styled
"Private Dalzell" of the temperance army announced in 1874, "the seal of
silence is removed from Woman's lips by this crusade, and can never be
replaced."[22]

Other women came to this conclusion more gradually, as the experience of
collective activity outside the home pushed them in the direction of political
aspirations. Zerelda Wallace, who would later head the union's suffrage department, recalled that she had shown little interest in reform causes prior to
1874, although as wife of Indiana's governor she was no stranger to politics or
the machinations of political power. But only the woman's crusade had touched
deeply enough to impel her to action. Through it, Wallace, nearly sixty years
of age, found at last the opportunity to achieve distinction in her own right.
Representing her local union, Wallace had presented a temperance petition to
the state legislature, only to realize that the assemblymen tolerated her presence
because they found the situation amusing. At precisely that moment of hu-
miliation, Wallace concluded that women could not force men to take their
ideas seriously until they possessed commensurate political power. At the second National WCTU convention Wallace introduced a resolution stating:
"Resolved, That since women are among the greatest sufferers from the liquor
traffic, and realizing that it is to be ultimately suppressed by means of the ballot,
we the Christian women of this land, in convention assembled, do pray Al-
mighty God, and all good and true men, that the question of the prohibition
of the liquor traffic should be submitted to all adult citizens, irrespective of
race, color, or sex. . . ." Wallace had taken the first step in requesting the
"temperance ballot" alone. Soon thereafter she helped organize the Indianapolis Equal Suffrage League, destined to become the state's leading suffrage
organization. By example and through exhortation Wallace urged her temperance sisters to join the fight for full political rights.[23]

From the beginning of the woman's crusade, others besides Wallace had
pointed toward a natural conjunction with the suffrage agitation. One WCTU
organizer asserted that her co-workers were "doing more for Woman Suffrage
than any of you [suffragists] dream," and predicted "whether the terrible curse
of intemperance will ever be driven from our land or not, those who live to see
the end of these crusades will see women ready for the ballot."[24] Fearful that
the flamboyant tactics of the crusade might discredit local suffrage activities or
drain off needed energies, suffragists nevertheless acknowledged the importance
of such sympathy, the *Woman's Journal* saluting their sister reformers as a
"powerful auxiliary to the direct movement for Woman's Enfranchisement."[25]

Yet, in the shadow of the Beecher-Tilton scandal and the public outcry over
Susan Anthony's illegal voting attempts, many temperance leaders were cautious about making overt political demands. They had willingly risked public

censure for their militant acts but were not eager to commit themselves to more comprehensive reform programs, especially the problematical demand for woman suffrage. Moreover, these early temperance leaders, prominent citizens of their small towns mostly in the Ohio River Valley, lacked the means to reach sympathetic women of different classes and geographical regions.

The WCTU would take a wider gauge only as its contituents transformed the movement from within. Leaders of the urban-based woman's movement played an important role in this regard. Mary Livermore, for example, served for ten years as president of the Massachusetts WCTU and reigned nationally as the leading temperance orator of the era. Within a decade of the inception of the WCTU, Livermore would measure its success not in terms of its achievements in the field of temperance reform but according to its impact on women's lives. The crusade, she wrote, had managed to lift women to a "higher level of womanhood."[26] Not surprisingly, Livermore and her associates endorsed woman suffrage as a necessary corollary to temperance agitation.

The crusade found its most militant participants not in the cities but in the small towns and rural areas of the nation's heartland, among those women who proudly identified themselves as wives of farmers or skilled workers. These western women brought the WCTU to its pinnacle of influence and also provided the mass following for the century's most influential and revered American woman, Frances Willard. Having been reared on a Wisconsin farm, Willard recognized the strength of women's position among the western and rural constituencies. Paraphrasing an old adage, she proclaimed, " 'the silver sails are all out in the West.' "[27]

Willard, who in her short life became "Saint Frances" and "Woman of the Century," had an uncanny talent for organizational leadership. She saw in the vast multitude gathered under the temperance banner the makings of a far grander movement than women had yet known. She joined the crusade at its beginning, becoming the first secretary of the Illinois state society and corresponding secretary of the National WCTU. Within a year she was working full time for the organization. At the 1878 National WCTU convention Willard closed in on her goal; the next year she was elected president; and within a decade of making her commitment, Willard had transformed the organization from a holy crusade against drink into a social movement with far-reaching aspirations.[28]

Willard accomplished this goal by appealing to the WCTU's most progressive sectors, those women deeply committed to the principle of temperance but not so fanatical as to shun other possibilities. She cultivated carefully the western interests by sending out speakers armed with literature to promote her cause, and she went into the new territories herself to push her programs. Willard then reorganized the structure of the WCTU on a paid membership basis, so that delegates to the national conventions were apportioned according to a local membership figure; by this move, she strengthened further the representation and power of the large western blocs, her most militant allies. Within a few years of taking office, Willard had recharted the union's strategic map.[29]

Willard's first triumph was wedding the WCTU to the principle of unrestricted woman suffrage. An early attempt in the 1870s had proven premature, but Willard had, in fact, captured her own state. As its president she secured the names of over 100,000 women on a massive "Home Protection" petition which she presented to the Illinois state legislature in March, 1879.[30] Although this petition made little legal headway, Willard had demonstrated to temperance workers the popularity of her position. She had also identified her allies, for she was greatly aided by loyal friends in the Illinois Patrons of Husbandry and received considerable support from the state WCTUs which were likewise deeply involved in suffrage agitation. In Iowa, Indiana, Nebraska, Colorado, and especially Kansas suffrage proponents virtually filled the ranks of the WCTU. Willard thus appealed to these sectors to battle the lingering conservative opposition, and with their encouragement set out simultaneously to increase the movement's appeal to women not primarily concerned with the liquor question. By 1882 woman suffrage had become a cardinal tenet of the WCTU.[31]

Willard proceeded to rebuild the structure of the WCTU to encompass a variety of reform programs. She began by augmenting its treasured organizational staple, the parlor meeting. From its first days the WCTU had responded to the needs of a constituency relatively inexperienced with public agitation by gathering women in their most familiar surroundings. Women met in the comfort and privacy of their homes to plan local strategy, and there they found political comrades among their trusted friends. The parlor meeting continued to serve the WCTU well because it acted effectively as a waystation for women leaving their domestic spheres for broader participation in public affairs. But there were just so many plans a parlor-sized assembly of thirty or forty women could handle by itself, no matter how many committees were created. Willard, fully cognizant of the importance of the parlor meeting at the local level, planned to supplement its activity by expanding the union's organizational map. She thus proposed in the name of efficiency to establish a complex of departments, each headed by a national coordinator and devoted to a particular aspect of reform. The 1881 convention granted approval to Willard's "do-everything policy," which eventually grew to encompass some thirty-nine departments ranging from social purity, prison reform, labor organization, peace and arbitration, work among railroaders, lumbermen, and miners, to a host of other social welfare and moral uplift activities. Organized along district levels in each state, Willard's policy offered additional options for work beyond temperance agitation and thereby enlarged the categories of women's public involvements.[32]

Willard outlined her plans for the organization in *Women and Temperance,* which she published in 1883 ostensibly as a massive catalogue of the WCTU's accomplishments. "The W.C.T.U. stands as the exponent, not alone of that return to physical sanity which will follow the downfall of the drink habit," Willard wrote, "but of the reign of a religion of the body when for the first time in history shall correlate with Christ's wholesome, practical yet blessedly spiritual religion of the soul." Willard explained that all social institutions would become purified through women's work in the WCTU. Women would make society more Christ-like, beginning first with the redemption of the individual drunkard and then spreading rapidly to the home, church, community, and government, to the whole of American society. Temperance agitation would, she insisted, reach further into "circle after circle of human endeavor and achievement," until the kingdom of God was brought to earth. "[T]o help forward the coming of Christ into all departments of life," Willard proclaimed, "is, in its last analysis, the purpose and aim of the W.C.T.U."[33]

Willard's was no postmillennial promise of human virtue inducing Judgment Day but a worldly, almost materialistic vision of heaven on earth achieved through women's initiative. At one stroke Willard had redefined the Christian mission by her own lights, had articulated a New Testament–based promise of redemption but evoked secular means to achieve this end, and had given women the central role. She had made the very conquest of the old society a holy purpose contingent upon women's progress. In reconciling the Enlightenment idealism of the first woman's rights advocates with the missionary mentality of rural Protestant women, Willard placed both within an all-encompassing tradition. She had, in other words, made the existing values gain new, almost revolutionary content. To her following, she loomed as the Social Gospel theologian of the age.

Willard showed every sign of being as tactically aware as her radical view demanded. Compared to the grand resolution—Christ's reign on earth—the WCTU's purported purpose of ending the liquor traffic seemed unusually anticlimactic. Certainly the WCTU could not bring about such a monumental change by itself. But it might serve as a training group and headquarters for women learning how to expand their activities upward and outward, a place where they could learn "how to use the weapons with which the future is certain to equip them," and where they might gain "well-seasoned experience," learn how to "show power, for power is always respected whether it comes in the form of a cyclone or dewdrop. . . ."[34] According to Willard's plans, temperance agitation could only constitute one means among many for extending women's influence, and she therefore took the prerogatives of organizational leadership step by step as she eased the WCTU into a broad reform movement.

During the mid-1880s Willard moved deftly to utilize her influence and prestige by seeking alliances with compatible reform organizations. She formed organizational ties between the WCTU and the Patrons of Husbandry, the

Prohibition party, and the Knights of Labor.[35] With the weight of nearly 200,000 members and thousands more sympathizers behind her, Willard took bold steps—sometimes making very personal overtures toward the reform giants of the day—to fix a course that only political catastrophe could divert.

Strengthening the bonds between the WCTU and the inchoate urban-based woman's movement was, however, first on Willard's agenda. Although devoted wholly to the WCTU, Willard always felt a spiritual kinship with other women's organizations, the concept of woman's advancement having been early implanted in her consciousness. When she entered reform circles in the early 1870s, she had been estranged from militant suffragists but drew close to the New England leaders. She became a member of Sorosis and a prominent officer of the Association for the Advancement of Women, and gained a wide variety of contacts outside the WCTU who would prove useful in later years. In the mid-1880s Willard reached out among her allies to create a stronger association. In urban areas the WCTU programs often replicated or extended the activities pioneered by the women's clubs, and in a number of cities, such as Chicago, the two movements had joined forces on many occasions. In some places, like Boston, the association was almost organic. It was not difficult for Willard to find acceptance for her plans to create a unified movement.

"Were I to define in a sentence, the thought and purpose of the Woman's Christian Temperance Union," Willard reflected at the peak of her influence, "I would reply: *It is to make the whole world HOMELIKE.*" Woman had already shown her ability to civilize some sectors of society. She "came into college and humanized it, into literature and hallowed it, into the business world and enobled it. She will come into government and purify it, into politics and cleanse [it] . . . for woman will make home-like every place she enters, and she will enter every place on this round earth."[36] If such a perspective revealed a profound naivete about woman's powers, it nevertheless carried a mighty weight of tradition. Willard could not have spoken, perhaps, or even have known more intimately the problems of power without uprooting her own expectations and simple faith that gave her such a fiercely devoted following among America's Protestant women.

The political vision Willard propounded brought together the largest aspiration of the woman's movement in urban areas with the grass-roots insurgency of contemporary rural America. Through her, the old commitment to natural rights and the newer dedication to women's economic enfranchisement became congruent parts in a holistic program of woman's reform—a consciousness in the broadest sense of woman's role in civilization.

The magnitude of this achievement could not be easily measured. Willard had in effect formulated a principle by which women were to play an independent and self-organized role in the grand political events of the nation, not merely because they possessed the moral rectitude but because their own development had a validity irrespective of the emergence of the agrarian and labor protest movements. Willard more than any other single figure had struck out at the relegation of women to an ancillary role, the notion that women could be considered only a secondary factor in the processes of social evolution.

It remained for women reformers to assemble themselves and to set out a thoroughgoing program. Not even the most powerful individual leader, like Willard, could lead the troops faster than they were willing to go. But women from ostensibly different movements could join hands, point to the reconciliation of every cause and small purpose. The International Council of Women, assembled at the peak of the woman's movement, was both symbol and substance of this desired unity.

For eight days in March, 1888, representatives of fifty-three women's organizations from ten nations met in Washington, D.C., to have an "interchange of opinions" on the great questions of the day and to give women everywhere "a realizing sense of the power of combination." All-inclusive by design, the council nevertheless possessed a definite quasi-political character. As the call read:

> However the governments, religions, laws, and customs of nations may differ, all are agreed on one point, namely, man's sovereignty in the State, in the Church, and in the Home. In an International Council women may hope to devise new and more effective methods for securing the equality and justice which they have so long and so earnestly sought. Such a Council will impress the important lesson that the position of women anywhere affects their position everywhere. Much is said of a universal brotherhood, but, for weal or for woe, more subtle and more binding is universal sisterhood.[37]

The ramifications of this sisterhood as expressed in the call were larger and more socially significant than anyone unfamiliar with the woman's movement would likely have suspected.

The idea of an international gathering originated with Elizabeth Cady Stanton, who had met with British suffragettes in 1883 to lay the foundations for an International Woman Suffrage Association. Susan Anthony worked through the National Woman Suffrage Association to design the agenda and make the necessary arrangements, which included the publication of over 650,000 pages of advertisement alone.[38] Whatever the intentions of the suffrage pioneers, their allies planning the worldwide meeting broadened the scope of the program and subtly shifted its purposes.

The meeting took the form of a ritual celebration commemorating the fortieth anniversary of the first woman's rights convention at Seneca Falls and marking the progress of women over the four decades since. Women from all parts of the country attended, aided by the railroads' policy of reduced fares for delegates and visitors to the council. The gathering virtually dominated life at the capital during those eight days, as the press played upon the public's fascination with feminine pageantry. Formal meetings were supplemented by gala social events, including overcrowded dinner parties, a reception at the White House, and a hearing at a Senate committee. Amidst this excitement an inner tranquility reigned. As one delegate recalled, Washington's newest opera house became a scene of genteel beauty and calm utterly unlike raucous political meetings conducted by men: "The platform was fragrant with evergreens and flowers, brilliant with rich furniture, crowded with distinguished women, while soft music, with its universal language, attuned all hearts to harmony. The beautiful portrait of the sainted Lucretia Mott, surrounded with smilax and lilies of the valley, seemed to sanctify the whole scene and to give a touch of pathos to all proceedings."[39]

To the public, the conference appeared merely as a celebration of women's achievements. To its own constituents, it marked a symbolic change of the guard that had already taken place within the movement's leadership. Stanton, who along with Lucretia Mott had called the Seneca Falls meeting, gave the formal opening address welcoming delegates to the commemoration of "the greatest movement for human liberty recorded on the pages of history." It was now time for the elder generation, knowing its holy mission would not fail, to relinquish its position. "Those who, like children of Israel, have been wandering in the wilderness of prejudice and ridicule for forty years," Stanton reflected, "must feel a peculiar tenderness for the young women on whose shoulders we are about to leave our burdens." Grizzled veterans Lucy Stone, Frederick Douglass, and Robert Purvis gave witness to this event, as relative latecomers Julia Ward Howe, Clara Barton, and Frances Willard affirmed the wisdom of this transition, while sometimes expressing guilt for not having played a part in the first woman's rights campaigns.[40]

Behind the verbal bouquets an important shift was taking place, one more political in substance than purely generational. Many leaders of the postbellum woman's movement, like Livermore and Howe, were contemporaries of Stanton and Anthony but had simply bypassed the first rounds of agitation. If they came to endorse suffrage, it was because they recognized the ballot as a means to their own larger ends. The council itself, while naming "equal wages for equal work" its cardinal tenet, failed to include woman suffrage in its "catechism" of goals. Indeed, the major elements of the woman's movement, such as the ubiquitous women's clubs and temperance societies, had formed not at all to aid the woman's rights campaigns but to address different issues entirely. Council notables who hailed Stanton and Anthony as their precursors did so because the suffrage activists had taken a bold and unpopular stand in the early days. Rhetoric notwithstanding, the new leaders were not carrying out the political mission of the woman's rights campaigners.

The convention proceedings likewise reflected the change of guard. While Anthony presided formally over the council, the WCTU supplied its president, Frances Willard, along with a quarter of all speakers on the program. The high-spirited mood of the gathering had little in common with the perfunctory, hard-nosed suffrage conventions of recent years, and was more reminiscent of the pioneering agitations of the 1850s and the conclaves of temperance advocates in the 1870s. The woman suffrage movement appeared reconciled with the existing political order, Anthony herself finding allies within the increasingly staid Republican party, whereas Willard upheld the reformers' vision of old. She spoke to the delegates of "the new America, the good time coming . . . when He shall rule in our hearts and lives, not outwardly, but by His spirit. . . ." These were strong words characteristic of the Social Gospel temper of the day. Speaking no less than five times, Willard had ample opportunity to impart her message to the delegates.[41]

Willard's temperance co-worker and ardent ally, "Mother" Zerelda Wallace, summed up best the sentiments of the new leadership. "We hear a great deal about the growth of civilization," Wallace mused at the close of the session. "Dear friends, what is civilization? . . . Does it consist in your marble palaces? In your railroads; your electric lights; your telephones and telegraphs?" Men might be deceived by such materialistic accouterments and overlook the cor-ruption that had accompanied society's industrial advance. The heritage of women's reform since the onslaught of the Civil War had taught the delegates otherwise, and the women seated before Wallace had, she hoped, no such il-lusions. Their reform efforts had struck out at a male-fostered materialism, the poverty, waste, debauchery, and degradation leading society toward a Sodom-and-Gomorrah condition. As Wallace had reminded her audiences on many occasions, "You shall hate evil was said to women and evil shall hate you. There shall go forth from you a force that shall ultimately exterminate it."[42] For Wal-lace, Livermore, and Willard especially and for a handful of other dignitaries, to propound such visionary aims and to create the mechanisms by which women might garner strength to besiege entrenched evil were the true purposes of the council.

As outlined in Wallace's address, the woman's movement had a dual purpose, for women had organized "to plead for freedom for themselves in the name of and for the good of humanity."[43] Forty years earlier women had asserted their equality and demanded their natural rights as citizens; they had hailed the Constitution as a grand document lacking only in details of universal citizen-ship, and whose exceptions in regard to race and sex could now be struck out. By contrast, the highest leader of the Gilded Age woman's movement proposed to create

> within the national government, as carried on by men, a republic of women, duly organized and officered, in no wise antagonistic to men, but conducted

as much in their interest as in that of women. It would promote mutual fellowship among women, and establish solidarity of sentiment and purpose throughout the nation of women workers. It would put a premium on organized as against isolated efforts for human betterment. It would train women for the next great step in the evolution of humanity, when women shall sit side by side in government, and the nations shall learn war no more.[44]

The vision of a Fifth Estate composed exclusively of women had an indisputably romantic air but also the soundness of tested principles. The International Council of Women in itself created nothing, but its leaders had named women's contribution to civilization as separate and unique and had identified women as the chief protagonists of justice at the climax of social evolution. In so doing, they articulated the philosophical world view developed by women activists over the previous decades. Women had begun with only piety and dimly understood aspirations; by the close of the 1880s they possessed the confidence to make claims for themselves comparable to those which orthodox Socialists made on behalf of the proletariat. Neither Socialists nor women activisits had demonstrated a capacity to make good their claims, although women enjoyed an advantage of numbers and relatively favorable public opinion. Each could avow the evolution of society according to its own principles; "scientific" observation apparently rested in the eyes of the beholder.

The most far-sighted participants recognized that the whole of virtue rested neither with the Socialists nor with women alone. If Socialists failed to encompass the possibilities of womanhood, organized women turned a blind eye to potential and necessary allies. Alice Hyneman Rhine, a sympathizer with both movements, thus declared with her sisters the revolutionary kernel of women's activities, their promise "to bring about in so many ways a universal sisterhood of women, a reign of peace and happiness to all on earth." Yet Rhine perceived an important limitation in women's activities: their failure "to take in the caste most in need of their labors . . . the proletariat." If women would embrace the cause of the proletarian revolution, Rhine contended, women would triumph and finally institute the millennial beliefs they upheld.[45]

WOMEN LEADERS EMBRACE SOCIALISM

The reformist aspirations of the leading representatives of the International Council of Women coincided with a general revival of indigenous protest movements from their low point in the mid-1870s. The rapid postwar development of industrial capitalism, the increasing disparity between rich and poor, became targets for a last-ditch defense of the republic against ruination. By the mid-1880s an organizationally diffuse but powerful reform tendency had set out to transform American society along cooperative lines. Farmers, workers, and middle-class reformers, Social Gospel protestants alongside Irish Catholics, suffrage and temperance advocates, Populist politicians and union leaders, and significant numbers of English-language Socialists for the first time commonly opposed the existing economic and political elites. They shared also a certain confidence that the worsening exploitation of plain folk would ultimately call into existence a victorious antimonopoly crusade. They had reason to be expectant. In a few years' time they had seen the rise of the most extensive protest movement since antebellum days. The ascent of the Knights of Labor and massive eight-hour educational campaign, an urban labor political constituency mirrored by Populist electoral and cooperative activity in the South and Southwest, the birth of a middle-class Christian Socialism with Bellamy Nationalism in its lead, and a renaissance of suffrage and temperance offensives—all seemed on the verge of coalescing into a grand reform army.

Above all, the various movements restored to American radicalism the moral vigor lost since Reconstruction. Old-time crusaders, still revered for their contributions to abolitionism, reappeared from obscurity to make a final statement. They blessed the younger generation of activists for keeping alive the ideals of the American Revolution. Wendell Phillips, in a celebrated message, suggested that the movement in formation summed up within itself the entire radical heritage, and that the social transformation it promised would be the logical consequence of American democratic promise.[46] In contrast, the corruptors—monopolists, liquor salesmen, speculators, and party politicians—were symptoms of all that ailed the republic.

If radical activists hoped to rouse the citizenry for a last democratic crusade, they could not remain blind to the lessons of the woman's movement. More single-handedly than other sectors, organized women had adopted the moral imperative and given unique expression to it: womanly virtue against marketplace capitalism, cooperation overcoming competition, social reconstruction rather than class warfare. Shaded by a certain naivete, this assertion of womanhood as agency of social change marked a potential revolution in political strategy.

Women leaders rallied their constituents and asked them to infuse the emerging protest movements with the sentiments women cherished. Women's contribution might prove crucial at this historic juncture, perhaps decisive in shaping the content of the impending crusade. At the minimum, women's leadership could impart a distinct political sensibility to the major radical development of the era: to a sector of the Socialist Labor party in the process of "Americanization," to the Bellamy Nationalist movement and its Christian Socialist following, and most fatefully to the Farmers' Alliance bound toward Populism.

The German-dominated Socialist movement, given its heritage, seemed the least likely of radical forces to absorb women's collective energies. Socialists had granted no concessions to the woman's movement, issued no invitation to its constituents. Native-born women moved toward the SLP rather as a logical consequence of their own political development. They forced their attentions upon Socialists, swept into corners of the party otherwise lacking a political dynamism, and succeeded at least to a limited extent in making over a portion of the Socialist organization in their own image.

This pattern showed itself most clearly in Chicago, where women activists joined hands with Socialists to improve the situation of the city's working-women and children. As early as 1879 clubwomen had participated in the Socialist-influenced Working Women's Union, and had in the mid-1880s supported the Knights of Labor mobilization among Chicago's workingwomen. In June, 1888, a small group began the most ambitious project to date by organizing the Ladies' Federal Labor Union No. 2703, a mixed assembly chartered by the American Federation of Labor. The organizers reported that between 1870 and 1880 the number of women workers had increased by 64 percent and the number of children workers by 59 percent, while conditions of employment and wages remained typically poor. They stated, "Without organization for self-protection, with the many disadvantages of sex, and the helplessness of child-hood, the female and child-workers are the victims of every avaricious, unscrupulous and immoral employer. The Ladies' Federal Labor Union has been organized to prevent, to some extent, the moral, physical and mental degradation of women and children employed as wage workers in this city." The LFLU enlisted working girls and women, at 5¢ per week dues, and sought the aid of other labor organizations and women's groups. The LFLU acted, in its own words, as a protective society and conducted investigations, received complaints, sponsored legislation and agitated for the enforcement of existing laws, and provided emergency relief to individual workers, "intellectual improvement," and "social enjoyment" to all. [47]

The LFLU was founded and led by two Socialist women who combined the principles of the labor movement and the woman's movement. Elizabeth Morgan, born in Birmingham, England, to impoverished factory operatives, abandoned formal education to begin working at age eleven. Married young to Thomas J. Morgan, she set out with her husband for America in 1869 and made her way to Chicago, where they both became active in the Socialist and labor movements. While Thomas Morgan became the English-language leader of the SLP and local Trades and Labor Assembly, Elizabeth became one of the first women in the Chicago Knights of Labor. [48] From her position of prestige among men and women workers, she became the key liaison between the LFLU and the labor movement. Corinne Stubbs Brown, daughter of a Chicago craft worker, rose to an early respectability as teacher and principal in the Chicago public school system and married a prominent banker with whom she moved to a fashionable south-side neighborhood. She nevertheless was prompted by the Haymarket tragedy to advance beyond an eclectic moral concern for the poor to Socialism.[49] A leader of the women's club movement, Brown sought to integrate the service activity carried on by women into labor radicalism.

Along with their supporters, Morgan and Brown set reform precedents for the nation. In the summer of 1888 a local newspaper ran a series of articles on Chicago's sweatshops, and Morgan responded by organizing a committee of the LFLU to judge the validity of the reports on "Gotham's White Slaves." Convinced of the accuracy of the exposé, Brown and Morgan then sought the cooperation of the Trades and Labor Assembly and various women's groups and inaugurated a large-scale campaign to ameliorate conditions. In November, 1888, members of the prestigious Chicago Women's Club and some twenty-five other women's organizations ranging from the flower clubs, the WCTU, physiological societies, and various church-affiliated women's relief associations combined with the Trades and Labor Assembly to form the Illinois Woman's Alliance.[50]

The IWA, which promised to foster "nothing . . . that all good men and women can not agree upon," directed a major campaign for factory investigation and compulsory education legislation. Under IWA pressure the Illinois state legislature made significant changes in its educational laws, and the Chicago school board was restructured so as to include more women representatives. By the early 1890s IWA activities further proliferated into clothing drives, new schools for the poor, and public bath houses. But its most important and noteworthy venture was an all-out attack upon the sweating system. Morgan herself wrote an investigative report eliciting a great response from a conscience-stricken public; she hosted the official congressional investigation of the sweating system, and led the IWA into a successful fight to limit the hours of women "sweaters." In cooperation with the Trades and Labor Assembly and Hull House residents, the IWA saw its work realized in the landmark Illinois Factory Inspection Act of 1893, only to see the measure struck down later in court. In perhaps its noblest hour the IWA took up the cause of prostitutes, seeking to protect their legal rights and to spare them from police harassment.[51]

During its brief life the IWA stood as a model institution of cooperation between the local woman's movement and the Socialist-influenced Trades and Labor Assembly and received nationwide recognition for its activities. Major journals of both sectors carried reports of its exploits, owing in part to Corinne Brown's diligence as corresponding secretary. Its leaders wore their Socialist colors proudly, and in turn labor officials, notably Thomas Morgan, issued statements in behalf of woman suffrage, certainly a rare move among SLP chieftains. Even local German-American Socialists, usually cynical about women reformers' intentions, could not help praising the IWA as a true friend of the proletarian woman. [52] Women activists had succeeded in finding political space for their sentiments and programs within a corner of the English-language Socialist movement.

The Chicago experiment, however, did not find many imitators. In other cities the distance between women activists and Socialists proved too great, or perhaps the political dynamic that inspired the IWA was simply missing. In New York City, for instance, a Working Women's Society similarly called for sweatshop investigations, but shopworkers called to testify before a municipal panel were summarily dismissed from their jobs. Although the SLP extended a helping hand toward the Working Women's Society, the organization fell into disarray and decline. Its most prestigious leader, Ida Van Etten, emerged in the SLP's "American" branch and served as foremost party speaker on women's labor at the 1890 American Federation of Labor convention. Along with a number of other eminent women reformers and journalists, such as Alice Hyneman Rhine, Van Etten soon attempted to launch an organizing drive akin to the Ladies' Federal Labor Union in Chicago. The Central Labor Federation and the Socialist-influenced Knights of Labor pledged their support, as did settlement-house workers and sympathetic clubwomen. A sharp economic downturn and growing differences among Socialists, labor activists, and reformers doomed the effort. As in many other communities, elements of the IWA experiment had been present, but they remained incompletely assembled. [53]

For lack of a conducive milieu, women activists in several cities tended to work as individuals within the Socialist movement proper. At best, in New England and in California, they succeeded in converting some of their own political sentiments into Socialist coin and prepared the SLP for a more receptive welcome toward indigenous radicals. The moral shock of Haymarket prosecutions and the rise of the Knights of Labor propelled a scattering of women into the SLP's fledgling "American" sections. In textile-heavy Rhode Island, for instance, where women had vigorously organized themselves into the Knights of Labor, veteran reformer Ellen M. Bolles emerged as a leading columnist of a Providence socialistic labor weekly. Her Christian piety and ardent support of women's advancement appealed to both temperance-minded unionists and local women activists, while her moralistic Socialist faith bespoke a new version of the millennial promise. In Waltham, Massachusetts, the widow of a noted labor economist and herself the direct descendant of a Minute Man, launched a local SLP section in 1888 after some fifty women had signed a petition protesting the outrages of the Russian czar. In Boston a group of blue-blooded Yankee women reformers became a vital section of the party. By the early 1890s these women had made their mark upon the character of the New England Socialist movement. [54]

An outstanding orator and intellectual of the 1890s, Martha Moore Avery, illustrated the curious form that the fusion of Yankee reform, gender consciousness, and Socialism could take. Born to a respectable family and well educated in Maine, Martha Moore married and moved to Boston when her husband became a traveling salesman. Like so many other reformers of her day, she dabbled in mysticism, studying "Cosmic Law" for more than a decade. In the meantime she awakened also to a social purpose and joined the Socialist Labor party. Described by contemporaries as a "woman of splendid physique" and rare oratorical abilities, Avery rapidly became known as the English-language Socialists' most spellbinding lecturer. Women of all social classes found Avery especially impressive, perhaps because they saw in her both a guiding spirit and an admirably strong public figure. Even German-American Socialists hailed Avery, despite the weirdly eclectic nature of her ideas. According to Socialist legend, she judged herself a modern Hypatia, venturing on the Boston docks in Grecian robes and addressing workers as "Units of the Future Civilization." (One longshoreman was said to have queried another about her meaning, and the second thought she was describing a castrate.) To some she may have provided comic relief to somber Socialists, but she unquestionably also possessed a palpable mystery and excitement usually lacking among English-language hangers-on to the German-American Socialist movement. [55]

In California women activists similarly accommodated themselves to a notoriously undoctrinaire corner of the Socialist movement. Veterans like sandlot spellbinder Anna Ferry Smith recruited many women and joined a younger generation, including the now-renowned lecturer Charlotte Perkins Stetson (later Gilman). Local women organized party sections, ran in school board elections under new municipal laws, and in general helped to impart a unique spirit to the state movement. Indeed, one of the most successful public meetings California Socialists held in the 1890s featured a program on "white slavery" and its roots in capitalism, prepared and publicized by Bay Area Socialist women. [56]

Such signs of women's progress in Socialist ranks, although scattered across the country, appeared promising for the future. A short-lived Kansas Socialist newspaper portraying Martha Moore Avery as a reform goddess and urging fraternal support of the WCTU; a mass turn-out for Socialist women speakers from Boston to Holyoke, Massachusetts, Providence, Rhode Island, to Oneida, New York; early electoral triumphs, as in the case of the Oakland woman who ran so far head of the ticket as to almost guarantee Socialists a place on the county ballot—these boded well for an amalgamation of women's reform and Socialist traditions. Relatively few as they were in numbers, Socialist women of the 1890s spoke with an authority their predecessors in the SLP's English-language sectors had lacked a decade earlier. [57]

The advance of women in the SLP paled before a broader movement more avowedly pietistic. While the SLP doctrine lent itself to a millenarian interpretation, and the party made marked steps toward "Americanizing" its public image in the late 1880s, the hard-and-fast principle of class struggle and its tenacious foreign character posed certain limitations for women's participation. Not "scientific" Socialism but something more in the American grain captured the attention of mainstream women activists and allowed itself, to an extent never possible within the SLP, to become a Socialist vision amenable to women's political instincts.

Perhaps it was only natural for women to play a major role in the greatest American reform movement launched by a novel. In an age when low-priced reading matter constituted the heart of popular culture, and women's senti-mental fiction led the field, the aspiring writer would necessarily be sensitive to the potential audience. Since Harriet Beecher Stowe's *Uncle Tom's Cabin*, reformers recognized the power of persuasive fiction. But only in the mid-1880s, with the revival of the protest spirit, did the literary offensive again assume significant political proportions. Women reformers contributed several outstanding visionary novels, often character studies of well-to-do and poor women who discovered in each other the sisterly fortitude to struggle against their common disadvantage in man's world. In a handful of novels written by men the depiction of womanly virtue became a central motif, and several best-sellers found an avid readership among women activists themselves. Through this popular medium the qualities women leaders urged, although often ex-aggerated and sometimes warped, became common passwords for masses of Americans. From the printed page, in turn, women drew the intellectual ammunition they needed for their next fusillades against an oppressive order. [58]

Edward Bellamy's *Looking Backward* (1888), one of the century's three best-selling novels, appeared as a virtual mirror image of women activists' own, decidedly sex-conscious dream of a just society. Its success was immediate, and it served, many readers were to testify, as foremost inspiration for the thousands of native-born Americans who came forward for Socialism over the next two decades. [59] Women, of course, responded to the same programmatic appeal of *Looking Backward* that other readers found so attractive, its blueprint revealing how all citizens could share equally in the benefits of collectivized production and distribution and participate fully in a universal political democracy. But many women were attracted primarily by Bellamy's consideration of women's place in the future order. [60] Through the Nationalist movement prompted by the publication of *Looking Backward*, hundreds of women took their first steps in becoming a motive force for Socialism.

Looking Backward is the story of a Boston gentleman, Julian West, who fell asleep in 1887 while under a hypnotic spell and awakes in the year 2000 to find himself in an entirely different civilization. The main plot describes the effort of Dr. Leete and his daughter Edith to quell West's fears and end his confusion. Together the Leetes explain in detail the organization of their society and how and why it was brought about. West learns how the concentration of wealth and the tendency toward monopolization—problems which had stymied the great thinkers of his own time—had actually laid the basis for a harmonious social order. Through a collectivization of the old capitalist enterprises, brought about by the electoral processes and without a bloody class struggle, the new society emerged from the ruins of the old, preserving its best qualities while eradicating its divisive tendencies. There were no parasitic rich with propensities toward decadence and ostentation, no poor degraded and humiliated by their condition—only virtuous, industrious citizens, contributing fully to the economic and political systems while enjoying an elevating intellectual culture. Heralding the beauty of technology and efficient management, the citizens of the Nationalist state joined in a common effort while each person lived a full and useful life.[61]

Unlike Laurence Gronlund, who had been utterly unwilling to treat women's advancement as a facet of progress, Bellamy granted women a prominent role in his utopia. The industrial army of *Looking Backward*'s earthly paradise pooled the labor of all citizens between the ages of twenty-one and forty-six, male and female alike. Only during periods of maternity did women forsake their chosen occupations; at such times they received full support from the state (rather than from their mates) and guaranteed rest to bear healthy children and to preserve their own physical well-being. A year or so after childbirth women would return to work, never to sacrifice their talents to the demands of domestic drudgery or childrearing. Public kitchens and dining rooms adapted to an individual's preference for privacy or for company, nurseries and dayschools for children, all managed by the state, released women for other activities. "That any person should be dependent for the means of support upon another would be shocking to the moral sense as well as indefensible on any rational social theory," Dr. Leete explained. Women, of course, would have full political rights. Having achieved independence, they could partake freely in the social and cultural life of the nation, improve its quality by investing it with their unique sensibilities, and move the race toward its full potential. Women, Dr. Leete averred, would be the "wardens of the world to come, to whose keeping the keys of the future are confided."[62]

Bellamy thus became the first popular novelist in the English language to delineate the economic basis of women's freedom and to assert women's prerogative in maintaining the classless society of the Cooperative Commonwealth. Although some contemporary reviewers accused Bellamy of appropriating such ideas from August Bebel's *Woman under Socialism*, contextual evidence suggests a stronger inspiration from American writers and activists, especially those involved in the urban-based woman's movement.[63] Bellamy was certainly familiar with their endeavors. A longtime political journalist, he had covered various meetings such as those of the Association for the Advancement of

Women and local suffrage events. More careful observer and brilliant popularizer than original thinker, Bellamy essentially demonstrated his understanding of the woman's movement and his concordance with its goals. [64]

If Bellamy had successfully captured the *mentalité* of women leaders, enthusiastic readers of *Looking Backward* created a political movement complementary to the structure of the contemporary woman's movement. Forming a network of clubs, Bellamy's followers adopted at first a nonpartisan, educational format. Voteless women, who would have necessarily found electoral campaigns somewhat alien, were familiar with this type of organization and fit in well. By 1890–91 over 160 clubs had been formed, and commentators noted from the onset the exceptionally large proportion of women among the members and their prominence within the local leadership. Executive positions of the most influential clubs in Boston, New York, and California were filled by women, and several clubs adopted bylaws guaranteeing women's representation on all committees. [65] In Chicago, for example, women had been instrumental in organizing the first club and within a year its membership had grown so large that another club had to be formed. This second Chicago Nationalist Club was officiated entirely by women and presided over by the inimitable Corinne Brown. [66] It was clear that in its first years of activity the Nationalist movement would find, if not vast numbers, efficient workers among the ranks of the woman's movement. Editors of Nationalist publications thus urged women to join; they demonstrated their sincerity by endorsing woman suffrage and by providing space to women writers. Such editors intimated occasionally that women might indeed prove a greater asset than their brethren. [67]

The affinity between the woman's movement and Nationalism showed itself vividly in the home city, Boston. More than an outlet for their considerable reform energies, Nationalism provided an important meeting ground for women activists and their male allies. Julia Ward Howe and her daughter, Maud Howe Elliot, were only the most eminent recruits from the local woman's movement. Leading reformers and professional women joined housewives and workingwomen to help swell the movement's ranks, which peaked at 5,000. From Boston a Nationalist Woman's Alliance was launched, promising to educate women in particular to the cause. [68]

Women also played a major role in California, the second principal center of Nationalism. With a membership of about 3,000 in 1890, state clubs concentrated in the Bay Area and greater Los Angeles and attracted a sizable portion and remarkable diversity of women activists. More than in Boston, Californian women were catalysts. They actually founded the first Los Angeles club and inscribed upon the northern California constitution proportional representation of the sexes. [69] Woman's movement veterans, New Englanders transplanted into the still-pioneer West, accounted for much of this vigor. Caroline Severance, founder of the New England Women's Club, served as proselytizer for

Christian Socialism in Los Angeles after having prepared the way by launching a local women's club movement.[70] Addie Ballou, dynamic president of the state's banner club in San Francisco, saw in Nationalism the culmination of a long search for a universal reform movement. Speaking to Nationalist audiences, Ballou recalled her father's part in the underground railroad, her own work with the wounded during the Civil War, the call she signed for Victoria Woodhull's Equal Rights party in 1872, her stints as a spiritualist and suffrage lecturer. Nationalism inspired in her, she averred, a deeper dedication than all previous ventures. It represented the opening fire of a "war against a detestable social system" that perpetuated a slavery "more prevalent and more destructive than even that of the negro."[71] Aging giants like Severance and Ballou imparted more than respectability or continuity; they infused the California Nationalist movement with ideals expressive of women's political aspirations.

A large sector of California women responded primarily to the ethical appeal of Nationalism. Although a scattering of Mary Baker Eddy's followers drew close to the Nationalist movement, they were outnumbered by the more aggressive advocates of Theosophy. Like other contemporary mystical religions, Theosophy recruited largely among women evidently dissatisfied with men's earthly rule. Its founder, Madame Blavatsky, proclaimed female virtue an agent of God's will on earth and encouraged her followers to join Nationalist clubs. Popular among many Boston Nationalists (and conspicuously among members of Bellamy's immediate family), Theosophy supplied an important organizational impetus in southern California.[72] Blavatsky's second-in-command, Katherine Tingley, a one-time urban reformer and former leader of the Do-Good Mission of New York City, became the exalted founder of a Theosophist-Nationalist utopian colony in Point Loma, outside San Diego.[73] Most Theosophists soon drifted away, but religious mysticism had proved—as had spiritualism among many women participants in the First International—a touchstone for Nationalist (and later Socialist) women throughout the state.[74]

The claims of *Looking Backward* in behalf of women, the conducive structure of the movement, and its strong ethical appeal all encouraged women activists to see in Nationalism a synthesis of their own aspirations for women's emancipation and the necessity of a grand transformation of American society along collectivist lines. "If man represents the head of humanity," one local activist opined, "woman represents the heart. . . . Civilization after civilization that man has tried to run alone has failed. Already this civilization is toppling to its fall," and the "one hopeful sign" could be found in woman's ascendancy in the protest movement. Certainly the Nationalist movement did not always live up to its high principles, but it had formally "declared our minority at an end." Through its portals women from all walks of life passed to "discuss plans and concentrate and utilize the influence they are universally acknowledged to possess in moral, religious, and even political reforms."[75]

Lucy Stone, Jane Cunningham Croly, Imogene Fales, and Zerelda Wallace, previously repelled by a proletarian or "foreign" Socialist movement, fell into line, while other prominent converts articulated the first open expression of a socialistic philosophy framed from the distinct point of view of women. Together these women presented the means by which the new idea offered a visionary possibility and became a living doctrine for an important sector of the woman's movement.

Mary Livermore acted forcefully to relate the complementary goals of Nationalism and the woman's movement. She became a vice-president of both the Boston Nationalist Club and the Society of Christian Socialists, which had formed concurrently. The bestowal of such honor was an acknowledgment of not only her fame as a lecturer but her important contributions to the Boston reform community since the 1870s. Her commitments besides temperance work included the New England Women's Club, the Women's Educational and Industrial Union, the Association for the Advancement of Women, and a virtual multitude of other local institutions. So beloved among the reform community was she that her portrait hung on the living room wall of Boffin's Bower, the chief settlement house for Boston's workingwomen. Despite these many fulfilling associations, Livermore claimed to find in Nationalism an all-inclusive program surpassing any one of her other involvements. Nationalism provided her with a coherent intellectual framework for creating a comprehensive solution to the woman question by substituting social transformation for mere amelioration or even for sisterly self-help.[76]

Other women activists, one at the end of her career, the other just beginning, were similarly influential in shaping a holistic philosophy of collectivism and women's emancipation. Abby Morton Diaz, longtime president of the WEIU, called *Looking Backward* "the book of the century" and Nationalism the "noblest and greatest [cause] in which lovers of humanity can engage." After forty years of reform Diaz hailed the movement as humanity's greatest hope, not so much revolutionary as "Applied Christianity . . . the truest political economy." Diaz gathered during an extended lecture tour for the movement the material for *Only a Flock of Women* (1893), the only Nationalist tract written entirely from the perspective of the woman's movement.[77] The rising intellectual star Charlotte Perkins Gilman, a generation younger than her reform sisters, found in the Nationalist movement the road to fame. Recovering from the personal collapse she suffered in the 1880s, Gilman became in the early 1890s a prominent Nationalist lecturer in California, where she rehearsed many of the arguments she later outlined in *Women and Economics* (1898). Bellamy she considered the "prophet who made us understand and believe."[78] Gilman remained substantially true to the collectivist faith of Nationalism throughout her rich and fruitful career as a leading proselytizer of women's emancipation.

Of all the women to make Nationalism's cause her own, none was more enthusiastic or instrumental in spreading its ideas among other women than Frances Willard. Willard read *Looking Backward* on the advice of Laurence Gronlund, who had recommended it over his own "dry" book. Willard found *Looking Backward* more than a "wonderful" story with "a spice of romance."[79] She proclaimed it "a revelation" and an "Evangel." Having never heard of Bellamy before, Willard wrote to her personal secretary that "Edward Bellamy must be *Edwardina*," because only "a great-hearted, big-brained woman" could have written such a sensitive book. She aspired to meet the author, curious to know what kind of person he really was.[80] After spending time with him, she was more enthusiastic than ever. She wrote that Bellamy had confided to her that "when he felt the touch of his little girl's hand upon his cheek the exclamation of Luther, 'This is a hard world for girls,' came to his lips." Moved by Bellamy's deep empathy for woman's plight, Willard became a prime agitator for his movement.[81]

Willard was especially drawn to the collectivist principles outlined in *Looking Backward*. She frequently lectured to groups of women on the marvelous possibilities of socialized housekeeping, such as public laundries or mass catering services.[82] *Looking Backward* gave substance to her dreams of such a future. But she also appreciated Bellamy's strategy for bringing the future into existence, "how the tyranny of the 'Trusts' may perhaps be as yet transformed to the boon of brotherhood." She agreed: "If men would say, 'Let us have no enmity, let us have no outrage, . . . let us have cooperation instead of the wage system,' " a better world would see the light of day.[83] Because Bellamy had shown how this grand transformation could be accomplished peacefully through the electoral process, by love rather than by bloodshed, he further ingratiated himself to Willard.

Willard became a devoted evangelist for Nationalism within the temperance movement. It was she who persuaded her WCTU colleague Livermore to affiliate with the Boston Nationalist Club. Within WCTU circles Willard used her office to agitate on behalf of the cause. In 1888, at the first national convention held after the publication of *Looking Backward*, Willard outlined her plans to unite the three great questions which "to-day enlist the nation's heart": temperance, labor, and women's emancipation.[84] At the next annual meeting Willard once again addressed this theme: "the colossal Labor Question looms up more and more; its correlation with the Temperance Question is being candidly considered, and as the two armies approach nearer to each other, they discover that uniform and weapon are curiously alike." Willard urged her followers to study the Nationalist program, which she printed in the convention proceedings. She asked them to join Nationalist clubs. As monopolies continue to multiply, she predicted, "humanity will in some future age be very likely to declare itself just one huge monopoly, and that will be

Humanity itself. We shall then have simply swung around to the New Testament basis, and reached the day when all men's weal is made to be each man's care, *by the very construction of society and constitution of government.*"[85] It was therefore of the utmost importance, she insisted, that WCTU workers understand that "in every Christian there exists a socialist; and in every Socialist a Christian."[86]

Although Willard failed to convert the WCTU membership to Nationalism, she enjoyed a small, receptive audience for her teachings. The editor of the *Union Signal*, the official publication of the WCTU, extended a friendly hand to Bellamy's followers,[87] and the WCTU leadership encouraged Socialists to play more active roles in the organization. The national superintendent of the National WCTU department of labor and capital, Anna S. Cairns, advocated cooperation in industry and in 1890 called for an alliance of the WCTU, the Knights of Labor, and agrarian radicals.[88] Especially in the Midwest and in California, many temperance workers shared Willard's sympathies.

As president of the National Council of Women, Willard broadcast her faith to the entire woman's movement. She devoted her address to the 1891 meeting of the council to the labor question and "cooperative happiness." She proclaimed Nationalism "the way out of the wilderness for women, and through her mankind." Because "labor will doubtless . . . be the only potentate" in the era to come, Willard explained, women's emancipation will "come first of all, along industrial lines." Willard thanked Bellamy for demonstrating the centrality of woman's industrial freedom to the transformation of society: "she must, in her skilled head and hands, represent financial values. Today the standard is gold; tomorrow it will be gifts; the next day, character. But, in the slow, systematic process of evolution it is only through financial freedom that [woman] will rise to that truer freedom which is the measure of all her faculties in trained, harmonious, and helpful exercise." This, she explained, was the ultimate appeal of Nationalism. It promised women their economic independence and their self-realization through productive labor, and it predicted that the classless society would be attained through a moral revitalization conducted by women. Nationalism was the "Socialism of Christ, the Golden Rule in action." Although Willard understood that the "Woman's Council, as such does not accept the theories herein set forth," she nevertheless hoped some prescient women might see a glimmer of truth, that Nationalism would eclipse the "most ancient form of bondage"—female subjugation—and institute a new era of peace and harmony.[89]

Willard was unable to convert the woman's movement at large to the principles of Nationalism. The best she could do was to recruit some of her most loyal co-workers. She was, however, too astute to be thwarted by the failure of Nationalism to grow into a mass movement of women activists. She knew her constituency too well to be disheartened at this early date. Willard observed women in the small towns and rural areas of the West gathering their forces for an even greater agitation, and she therefore lost no time encouraging women to add their weight and unique sensibility to the rising agrarian movement, Populism.

Women's position in Populism had been prepared by decades of participation in agrarian movements, particularly the Patrons of Husbandry. Organized in the late 1860s as a secret society devoted to cooperation, the Grange invested womanhood with a mystical significance rooted in ancient lore. The founders described the Eleusinian mysteries wherein male and female cult members worshipped the goddess of agriculture, Ceres. Modern-day Grangers continued to revere women. "Like a bright star in the dark pathway of life," as a Minnesota Worthy Master said to a Grange convention in 1879, woman guided human existence, her "purity, tenderness and delicacy" an inspiration for the Patrons of Husbandry. Support for her cause "more than all else," he added, was destined to "make our Order live forever."[90]

On a more mundane level, Grangers considered women a necessary element in rural association. Because the Grange emphasized the unity of the family, women served jointly with their husbands. A local assembly, for example, could acquire a charter only by demonstrating that at least four women as well as nine men were ready to enroll. Women possessed full voting rights, had access to any office, and enjoyed special posts created for women's affairs. In a majority of assemblies the lecturer who directed its programs was female, as were the leading officials of several state organizations. At picnics, processions, banquets, concerts, and other social events, women took the more familiar role of preparing refreshments and caring for children. Often relegated to positions of nominal equality, especially in southern assemblies, women gained at the minimum a sense of participation comparable to that of German-American women in the Socialist fraternal network. But in many midwestern Grange chapters women shaped the social character of local institutions along more egalitarian lines and won support for both temperance and woman suffrage campaigns.[91]

In its first years the Grange served to strengthen the western woman's movement. By the mid-1870s, when the organization had grown to nearly 25,000 chapters and three-quarters of a million members, its geographical center was the Ohio River Valley and adjoining states where the WCTU gained its first ground. The temperance crusade profited directly as the Patrons of Husbandry placed itself squarely on the side of the WCTU. The Grange required a vow of abstinence for admission and included temperance instruction in its ritual. In Ohio, home of the woman's crusade, the first links between the Grange and the WCTU were established. While the state Grange met in Xenia, woman's crusaders struck at a local tavern and forced the owner of the "Shades of Death" to empty his kegs. The Grange voted unanimously to join the ceremony, the State Master delivering a temperance speech atop the empty whiskey barrel. The sentiment spread rapidly among Grangers, pushed to such an extreme that the Illinois order officially condemned the use of tobacco as well as spirits. WCTU activists could find among their Grange friends across the Midwest and Plains states ready listeners and collaborators in their sacred vigil. [92]

The Grange also became a force for woman suffrage. As early as 1876 one Granger predicted that their assemblies would "prove a more powerful organization for the inauguration of Woman Suffrage than even the Woman Suffrage organizations themselves." [93] In western Kansas some of the ablest lecturers routinely presented woman suffrage arguments; one claimed that the "nation's safety lies in the political advancement of Woman." [94] The southern sector obstructed any uniform position until 1885, when at a national convention the Patrons of Husbandry finally passed a resolution recognizing the equality of the sexes as one of the order's cardinal principles. Grangers avowed they were "therefore prepared to hail with delight, any advancement of the legal status of woman, which may give to her the full rights of the ballot box, and an equal condition of citizenship." [95] Grangers subsequently reaffirmed this policy, blessed the WCTU for its salvational roles, and established a special committee to accelerate programs on women's behalf. Admittedly the southern delegates continued to harbor more conservative opinions, and committee work often relegated women to traditional pastimes, such as kitchen duty. Despite these limitations, many women used their Grange experiences to prepare for wider political roles. Some rank-and-file women actually became locally notorious in the 1880s when they initiated the first discussions of the forbidden political issues. During the severe rural recession of 1887–88, when the political taboo became impossible to enforce, women in states ranging from Texas to Michigan, Minnesota, and Nebraska to Colorado and California rallied to the banner of Populism. [96]

Although the most militant sector of the Populist movement at large originated among farmers in the South and Southwest, it was not surprising that women organized as a distinct force where they had struck the deepest roots. True to its woman's rights heritage stretching back to the bloody strife of the 1850s, the historic woman suffrage campaign of 1867, and the early temperance victories, Kansas became the organizational epicenter for Populist women. Residents of the state's growing commercial centers, urban women likewise found an opportunity to participate in a far-flung movement not merely agrarian—contrary to belief common at the time and since—but profoundly radical.

The most prominent Populist women—Fanny Randolph Vickery, Marion Todd, Sarah Emery, Mary E. Lease, and Annie Diggs—had gained their spurs in a variety of antimonopolist movements foreshadowing Populism. Significantly, none had been a lifelong resident of a farm. Mary E. Lease, for example, before calling upon farmers to raise less corn and more hell, lived as a housewife in Wichita, where she cared for her family, handled the usual household chores, and took in laundry to supplement the family budget; her first political act upon moving to Wichita had been the organization of a women's discussion club. Women like Lease displayed an acute awareness of the plight of the urban working class, particularly its female component. They typically had helped organize institutions for workingwomen and often joined the Knights of Labor in recognition of its pledge to equal wages for equal work. Observing the intensification of urban woes most especially among women fresh off the farm, these experienced activists felt a strong kinship with their rural sisters and served as their voice within the movement's leadership.[97]

Populist women in cities or on farms shared a common aspiration. Transcending all differences was foremost a universal commitment to women's enfranchisement that found its ideological and organizational base for women of varying backgrounds within the WCTU. Annie Diggs, for example, had begun her career in Lawrence, Kansas, as a pollwatcher in a prohibitionist campaign, later to become vice-president of the state suffrage organization. Sarah Emery, known as the "Elizabeth Cady Stanton of the Michigan Home Crusade," served as national superintendent of the WCTU's department on temperance and labor. Mary E. Lease claimed a half-million "white-ribboners" in the Populist ranks, and WCTU officials reciprocated, blessing the Farmers' Alliance as a major temperance ally in the struggle to abolish the liquor traffic and unearned wealth.[98] This sense of shared perceptions created an ideological continuity, from the WCTU to Populism, almost precisely parallel to that between the urban-based woman's movement and Nationalism. Women had moved in their own ways from self-interested causes to broader radical concerns.

Populist ideology reflected vividly the sentiments put forth by the WCTU, especially as thousands of alliance women helped revive the struggle for temperance and woman suffrage in the late 1880s. But even more as symbols, temperance and woman suffrage conveyed the special signficance the WCTU had invested in the concept of womanhood. The rhetoric of Populism alone was testimony to this fact. Womanhood embodied, as Grangers had likewise insisted, the moral imperative against evil.

If Nationalist women found their desires expressed in *Looking Backward*, Populist women located their own literary idol in master politician Ignatius Donnelly, whose sequel to the famous *Caesar's Column* (1890) tells the story of the reconstruction of a new order along feminine lines. *The Golden Bottle* (1892) incorporated the popular faith in the power of womanhood to purify the civilization and to guide the entire process of reconstruction. The great struggle is led in unison by two characters, Ephraim Benezet and his wife, Sophie. Ephraim, a Plains state lad who discovers a liquid that turns base metals into gold, uses his rapidly accumulating fortune to secure a place for himself as reform demagogue, finally to become president of the United States. From his position Ephraim directs a worldwide revolution. In weaving this tale, Donnelly suggests only a faint blueprint of the future political order but provides massive details on how the revolutionary struggle is to be waged. He exalts the concept of womanhood as symbol of morality and political wisdom.

In many respects it is not Ephraim but Sophie who emerges as the major protagonist. After a close call with the ultimate degradation brought about by a forced move to the city, Sophie is awakened at a tender age to the reality of women's powerlessness and sagely turns to political action. She first organizes the women of Omaha into a grand sisterhood. She speaks to the middle-class women and explains the horrible plight of farm families, the desperation which allowed farm parents to send their daughters off to the cities in search of work. The family, Sophie explains, was being destroyed, "crushed under the rolling rock, the Sisyphine weight of interests, of taxes, of monopolized markets, of cruel trusts, of every form of human selfishness and cunning." The poor country girl is thus driven into the "great wicked city" to find work or to perish. But even if she does find work, it is usually of some unhealthy type paying only starvation wages. This girl, Sophie explains further, "becomes a merciless hunter of men, armed with the poison darts of disease and death" as she turns to the only good-paying occupation available. Having moved her audience to tears, Sophie pleads with these women to recognize their duty to their sisters and to aid them in some substantial way.[99]

The women of Omaha form the Woman's Cooperative Association, a self-help society gathering both middle- and working-class women and spreading to every ward of the city. The association erects a splendid building to house workingwomen, to provide fine reading and music rooms as well as large halls for dancing and lectures. These establishments were, Sophie remarks, "little paradises on earth."[100] The project succeeds so well that the workingwomen are uplifted from their abject misery and the entire city is transformed into a pure and moral place.

Sophie then builds upon her initial success and forms a national society, the Woman's League of America, which pledges to buy no goods made by women except from women themselves. Then the "race rose with the elevation of the *matrix* of the race; for the river of humanity cannot ascend above the level of its fountain—woman. . . . The earth became beautiful, peaceful, happy, hopeful; full of all kindness and goodness." Rich women were released from enforced idleness and dissipation and walked hand in hand with their "sisters of one blood." The solution was "Not charity, but justice. Not stealing from the poor and giving them back part of it, with many airs and flourishes and ostentation; but stopping the stealing, and *permitting industry to keep the fruits of its own toil*."[101]

As the quintessential Populist novel of social reconstruction, *The Golden Bottle* focuses clearly on woman's role in transforming the industrial order into the Cooperative Commonwealth. There is, notably, no nostalgia for the pre-industrial past, no backward glance at domesticity. Rather, the inequities and degradation of modern life are met head on, their eradication premised upon a collective solution to economic problems with women taking a major part in the effort. At the conclusion of the novel, a grand finale indeed, the readers follow Sophie's triumph as, mounted on a white horse, she gallops across the Russian steppes leading the masses out from under czarist oppression and darkness, completing the last chapter in the revolutionary purification of the world.

Behind the gripping action of Donnelly's tale, his depiction of womanhood has a ring of familiarity. Like Bellamy, he drew on the sentiments of his milieu and rendered them a literary device of far-reaching significance. As in the case of *Looking Backward*, *The Golden Bottle* owed much of its popularity to the seedwork of the woman's movement in creating a female audience eager to accept its political message. At rank-and-file levels the positive images of womanhood which women leaders put forward and Donnelly converted into a literary metaphor became Populist icons.

This praise of women's role could prove deceptive in certain respects, for women did not share leadership or gain a consistent leverage region by region. The Farmers' Alliance and its electoral arm, the People's party, did not provide women with as much organizational space as did the Grange. Whereas the Grange viewed itself as a cooperative and fraternal order, Populism spread like wildfire as a protest movement. Cooperative marketing, widespread agitation, and electoral activity directed against the railroads and other monopolies launched the agrarian movement almost overnight as a major regional political force. By 1890 the alliance appeared to many observers to lack only urban allies in its campaign to take control of American society. But a price had been paid, better understood by women than by their brother comrades. The family-based and socially oriented activities familiar to the Grange had given way to an apparatus more like that of a traditional political movement. Populists abandoned the dual representation of men and women in its internal offices, jettisoned much of the elaborate ceremony that ensured women's centrality, and relegated voteless women to an ancillary role.[102]

Yet women re-emerged near the movement's center by virtue of their energy and self-organization, the authority they wielded as wives and mothers, and the ideological position they gained in the Populist articles of faith. At the local level especially, individual women participated as chapter secretaries, stump speakers, newspaper writers, and editors. As groups they inevitably took in hand the social services that kept the movement alive and thriving. Like the German-American Socialists' summer outings but larger and more dramatic, massive tent meetings reached across the southern and western states in the late 1880s, adapted both from the educational Chautauqua meetings and from the revivalist gatherings common to the region. Through their own initiatives in the national organization and with the hope of forging a far-reaching political alliance, Populist women pushed the movement to its limits.

Especially in states where women were well organized, Populist agitators could turn their demands for the ballot and equal wages into a wider program. Writers in the local and regional press thus hammered away at the fact that woman's sphere was not, properly speaking, the home. The movement's female base was, of course, the "farmer's wife," and the primary description of the home still reigned as the "sacred refuge of our life."[103] But essayists frequently addressed the largest fact of rural domestic existence: drudgery. They commonly implored women to resist the temptation of excessive cleanliness and order, to let their household chores slip by the wayside if necessary, and to make more time for themselves and their loved ones. Ordinary Populist women developed their own strategy along lines paralleling the cooperative politics of the Grange and the Farmers' Alliance: the cooperative household. With home care shared systematically by all family members, they argued, women would be freed from their bonds and capable of doing anything they chose. As one woman wrote, "Some people think it is acutely funny if a woman anywhere is not devotedly attached to making biscuits and darning socks. And yet men have been known who preferred other occupations to plowing and cleaning sewers, and no one seemed to think they were monstrosities."[104]

Years of devotion in the WCTU had, necessarily, instilled in Populist women a great respect for women's traditional roles, but they affirmed the goodness of woman innate to herself rather than to her current drudgery. The fate of civilization rested in the hands of those who had gained moral sensibility as guardians of the family, they believed. But to exercise that power, women had to be more than dutiful housewives. Thus Bettie Gay gave a Populist gloss to the sentiment the WCTU had done so much to make popular:

> What we need, above all things else, is a better womanhood, a womanhood with the courage of conviction, armed with intelligence and the greatest virtues of her sex, acknowledging no master and accepting no compromise. When her enemies shall have laid down their arms, and her proper position in society is recognized, she will be prepared to take upon herself the responsibilities of life, and civilization will be advanced to that point where intellect instead of brute force will rule the world. When this work is accomplished, avarice, greed, and passion will cease to control the minds of the people, and we can proclaim, "Peace on earth, good will toward men."[105]

Much like their sisters in other sectors of the woman's movement, Populist women named men's political hegemony as a major cause of civilization's decline. Only as women assumed their rights would the republic return to its proper course.

So well entrenched in the philosophy of the woman's movement and committed to women's prerogatives, Populist women sought alliances with other women reformers. They dispatched delegates to suffrage conventions, to WCTU meetings, and to the National and International Councils of Women. In 1890 a group of Topeka, Kansas, women took a portentous step further. They established a newspaper with the expressed purpose of fostering a new, national women's reform coalition. The monthly *Farmer's Wife*, emblazoned with the time-tested motto "Equal Rights to All, Special Privileges to None," urged women to communicate with one another and to promote the "natural unity" of temperance, suffrage, labor, and agrarian radicalism.

In September, 1891, Populist women founded the National Woman's Alliance with presiding officers Fannie McCormick, a Kansas "foreman" in the Knights of Labor, and Emma D. Pack, *Farmer's Wife* editor and honored women's club leader in Topeka. Women in twenty-six states served as vice-presidents, and the adopted charter carried the signatures of Annie Diggs, Mary E. Lease, Sarah Emery, Marion Todd, and other leading Populist women. The "Declaration of Purposes," a representative document of Gilded Age woman's reform, read:

> In view of the great social, industrial, and financial revolution now dawning upon the civilized world, and the universal demand of all classes of our American citizens for equal rights and privileges in every vocation of human life, we, the industrial women of America, declare our purposes in the formation of this organization as follows, viz.:
>
> 1st. To study all questions relating to the structure of human society, in the full light of modern invention, discovery and thought.
>
> 2d. To carry out into practical life the precepts of the golden rule.
>
> 3d. To recognize the full political equality of the sexes.
>
> 4th. To aid in carrying out the principle of co-operation in every department of human life to its fullest extent.
>
> 5th. To secure the utmost harmony and unity of action among the Sisterhood, in all sections of our country.
>
> 6th. To teach the principles of international arbitration, and if possible, to prevent war.
>
> 7th. To discourage in every way possible the use of all alcoholic liquors as a beverage, or the habitual use of tobacco or other narcotics injurious to the human system.[106]

The thirst for enlightenment, the demand for equal political rights, and the faith in women's regenerative power rendered the Woman's Alliance the logical successor to the WCTU and women's clubs. Far from the rural paranoia often attributed to Populists, the *Farmer's Wife*, as official organ of the National Woman's Alliance, carried column upon column of news and encouragement from countryside and urban areas alike. The federated plan of organization accommodated various possible models, from the Illinois Woman's Alliance that the paper publicized, to the Woman's Christian Alliance of Lufkin, Texas, which was launched after an alliance organizer toured the area.[107]

The success of the National Woman's Alliance would depend upon a favorable response from allies in the urban woman's movement and from the Populist leadership itself. Organizers therefore asked Populist politicians to lend their official endorsement to woman suffrage and to women's rights as laborers. They asked, too, for statements of encouragement. Pungent epigrams in the *Farmer's Wife* expressed better than any theoretical treatise the weight Populist women placed upon a positive response:

> Give our women encouragement and victory is yours.
> Be as true to the women as they are to you.
> Don't give us taffy; we are too old for that.
> Give the women a suffrage plank: you may have the rest.
> Rule the women out and the reform movement is a dead letter.
> Put 1000 women lecturers in the field and revolution is here.[108]

This buoyant sentiment fed expectations of cataclysmic change, no less for women than for men. The Populist political momentum, gaining steadily since the late 1880s, seemed to need only an urban counterpart to become the major force in the nation. That necessity required in turn the kind of alliance women prided themselves in having pioneered and which could evidently become whole only through their participation.

The women who rose to prominence in the major radical movements of the late 1880s and early 1890s—in the "Americanized" sections of the Socialist Labor party, Bellamy Nationalism, and the Farmers' Alliance—carried with them certain articles of faith from earlier involvements. They clung to a romantic notion of womanhood expansive enough to encompass a vision of women organized as the ultimate force against corruption. As principal organizers, renowned orators, or activists of regional standing, women began to seek alliances with various elements of the nascent protest movement, and they endowed this new endeavor with distinctive qualities transferred from their own organizations. Decades of preparation in the independent woman's movement had firmed their faith. As Mary E. Lease announced at the peak of the People's party campaign in 1892: "Thank God we women are blameless for this political muddle you men have dragged us into. . . . Ours is a grand and holy mission, a mission as high and holy as ever inspired the heart, fired the brain, or nerved the sinew . . . ours the mission to drive from our land and forever abolish the triune monopoly of land, monopoly, and transportation. Ours is the mission to place the mothers of this nation on an equality with the fathers. . . ."[109] Women's accession to political and economic power was, in this perspective, not merely a desirable goal but the prerequisite for the establishment of the Cooperative Commonwealth.

CONCLUSION

Helen Campbell, distinguished New York reformer and author, had as early as 1886 captured a vision of native-born women activists and Germanic Socialists moving side by side toward a common goal. In writing *Mrs. Herndon's Income,* Campbell utilized a Dickensian mode to express this fantasy and created two alter-ego protagonists to represent womanhood at the distant ends of the social scale. Margaret Herndon is wealthy, well educated, and sensitive but lacks direction in life; her opposite number, Meg, is the archetypal female victim of economic distress. Despite their contrasting positions in society, both women share the dour consequences of woman's lot. Married, they are similarly financially dependent upon and therefore subject to the men of their respective classes. The intemperate working-class husband physically abuses his wife, whereas the middle-class husband ignores his wife and sexually betrays her trust. In either case the woman must suffer. Fatefully abandoned by their mates, one by death, the other by desertion, the two women draw upon their shared plight to effect an alliance of strength. Thus joined, they come to a mutual political awakening, a realization that Margaret's class privileges are indirectly responsible for the hardships borne by Meg. In seeking to alleviate Meg's condition and to find meaning in her own life, Margaret moves beyond philanthropy to discover the cause in capitalism itself. A happy ending finds each heroine wedded to the Socialism appropriate for her background and station, Margaret married to a middle-class Christian Socialist, Meg to a proletarian German-American revolutionary.[110]

Beyond resolving her plot in sentimental fashion, Campbell had made an important point. The drastically different historical development and temper of the two movements foretold the impossibility of a simple merger; rather, native- and foreign-born radicals would move step by step toward a reconciliation—all had harmonized well with the sensibilities of the woman's movement. But too often woman found her greatest role as mere symbol—wronged and betrayed daughter of the masses, goddess of the reform Armageddon. Without a trace of cynicism orators and propagandists like Donnelly and Bellamy could trade off imagery with fabulous results while rarely considering the actual status of women within their ranks. To the expectant women leaders, the sentiments eventually proved hollow, the promise illusory.

As various reformers moved toward forming a grand political coalition, Willard decided to test the good faith of their leaders. She convened a "private meeting" of prominent reformers in January, 1892, and assisted in the formulation of a tentative platform that rhetorically condemned the liquor traffic and demanded no more than a limited municipal franchise for women. This *quid pro quo*, the group believed, ventured as far as possible toward compromise without forsaking basic principles. Even this partial concession, however, proved too bold at this important juncture.

Willard and her co-workers faced their ultimate disappointment at the St. Louis Industrial Conference of February, 1892, that ushered in the People's party. Whereas Populist women might take consolation in the substitute resolution supported by Annie Diggs and Mary E. Lease and passed by the convention without dissent, the recommendation to encourage suffrage referenda in the state and territorial legislatures did not satisfy those who had hoped for an official endorsement of temperance and the woman's ballot. Feeling abandoned on several fronts, Willard accused Populist and labor leaders of forsaking women's cause for the "craft of the liquor wing and the conservatism of our southern brethren in the People's Party." Master politician Donnelly, who had drafted the original platform at the Chicago meeting, acknowledged that the "moral" issues of temperance and suffrage had died at the hands of German and Irish antiprohibitionists and southern opponents of woman suffrage. Willard might reign in the titular office of vice-president of the convention, but a perceptive woman journalist noted that the real strains of Populism had been struck by an orchestra that played "The Girl I Left Behind Me."[111]

Populists did not find victory in concessions, and the coalition Willard had spent years helping to piece together fell into final disarray. As if doomed by its origins, the People's party failed to break through to an urban working-class constituency; its subsequent turn toward regionalism ended in the silver issue and the William Jennings Bryan campaign of 1896, both delivered a smashing defeat by McKinley's presidential triumph. Willard meanwhile lost her grip upon prohibition forces, and the Knights of Labor toppled into oblivion. Nationalists continued to experiment with electoral politics, but without Populists mobilized behind them, their efforts of the mid-1890s flagged. The combined wreckage signaled the end of an era.

Nowhere were hopes crushed so completely as in the major metropolitan areas. The political confusion following 1892 left radical activists unprepared to meet the challenge of the devastating depression of 1893, the worst heretofore in the nation's history. Concurrently, they witnessed the influx of new immigrants from southern and eastern Europe and strained to welcome them to their ranks. Both the SLP in the process of "Americanization" and the urban woman's movement retreated politically under these trying conditions.

The disintegration of the Illinois Woman's Alliance might be taken as a case in point. The great Pullman strike of 1894 drew the class lines sharply in Chicago and shook the vision of a transclass sisterhood to the bones. The IWA stumbled into internal disorder and thereby weakened the links between Socialists and women activists of various types. Finally, in 1894 the IWA refused to sanction labor's candidate for a city appointment, and the Trades and Labor Assembly, including Elizabeth Morgan, severed relations with the IWA. Politically isolated, the IWA soon perished, a monument to heroic effort and misalliance.[112]

Meanwhile, SLP ideologues tightened their ranks. Increasingly convinced of the imminence of class war, national leaders unloosed a furious attack upon middle-class reformers and especially upon women activists who would not unequivocally take up the red flag. Criticisms of this policy brought forth a "burlesque reign of terror," which drove the most prominent women from the party and its peripheries.[113] Diatribes in the first substantial English-language SLP newspaper against reform "fakiresses" and "free lovers" could only widen the gap that should by all rights have been closed. The formation of an organizationally archaic "ladies' branch" pledged to "stand shoulder to shoulder with men in the SLP," where there had formerly been an independent women's sector of vitality and principle, foretold the future. Those women who remained in the SLP turned upon middle-class women; they called them agents of the capitalist class sent to dupe workingwomen by offering meaningless aid. To demonstrate their loyalty to the SLP, such women savaged the very movement that had allowed them to achieve a public voice.[114]

The SLP once more reached a dead end in its belabored attempt to adapt to the strains of indigenous radicalism. After nearly a generation the German-dominated Socialist movement had come, albeit reluctantly, to accept women as participants in the class struggle, although organized in a manner "suitable" to their situation. Socialists finally recognized the inevitability, at least under capitalism, of women's wage labor. Woman suffrage they endorsed quietly, choosing not to take up the struggle themselves. But they continued to scorn independent initiatives and gave not one essential inch on their original assessment of the woman's movement. Here their charges of class collaboration revealed a doubled standard. Socialists could bend easily to include their own petty shopkeepers and tavern owners, those of an earlier wave of immigration who had come up in the world. But they could not countenance an alliance of native-born women and their immigrant sisters; that still smelled of patronage and political corruption.

This dereliction revealed yet another shortcoming. German-American Socialists simply could not accommodate indigenous protest movements. More than any other, the woman's movement symbolized the Tiber that the revolutionary Caesars would have to cross. But to do so—and here they clearly understood the problem—raised the hazard of doctrinal infection. Immigrant Socialists and their native-born protégés once again decided to avoid this risk at all costs, and the SLP became for the last time a mere sect. The air of *Schadenfreude*, expressed toward women reformers in particular, thus disguised a pervasive self-hatred, as those who doubt their own intentions often turn toward ritual purification. Only the destruction of their movement would force such a realization.

The woman's movement itself experienced a similar fate in the 1890s. Elder leaders, steeped in a once-vibrant woman's culture forced to a political maturity during the Gilded Age, now faded from the scene, some disillusioned by the debacle of 1892, others too tired or too feeble to struggle under such unpromising conditions. In truth, the elders had outlived their usefulness as visionaries, for the interpretation they had given to the romantic values of womanhood meant far less to their successors. The next generation of leaders in the mainstream women's movement emerged during the 1890s more organizationally sophisticated but less inclined toward a millenarian optimism about the wholesale reconstruction of society. They continued to look forward to women's advancement but into society *as it existed*, an aspiration shared by increasing numbers of young women drawn to the movement. In size, the women's movement grew stronger than ever, but the survivors of its glory years could readily perceive a spiritual decline.

Despite the wholesale organizational wreckage and the oceans of bad blood discoloring the once-bright spirits of activists, future generations would salvage some very important building blocks. For one thing, local participants often outlasted conservative or sectarian national leaders. Pockets of faith in womanhood remained among Socialists, suffragists, and temperance advocates where local and state movements held their own counsel. Donnelly's *The Golden Bottle* had summed up a tenacious image of woman as purifying agent, fitted to act upon society's evils because she had been denied the temptations and corruptions of power accessible only to the more worldly male. If this assumption contained an ultimate logical fallacy and was steadily undercut by women's entrance into public life, it nevertheless continued to correspond to the life patterns and institutional practices of many women. Such women may have been denied Sophie's opportunity to redeem the world from horseback, but they lost little of their collective faith in woman's salvational powers.

Second, a modest renaissance along lines conducive to the cooperation of women and the Left developed steadily through the 1890s. Utopian settlements appeared in several parts of the country, with equality for women a central precept. In these colonization experiments indigenous radicals made new contacts with Christian Socialists, former Populists and Nationalists, disillusioned SLP members, and whole state branches formerly connected with the party. Despite the absence of their familiar leaders, many women who had been attached to the radical movements of the late 1880s and early 1890s looked again with hope for a common struggle and a "good time coming."[115] The re-emphasis upon political education and political action by an embryonic Socialist movement did not guarantee women's participation, but it placed the emerging Socialist consciousness squarely in line with traditions running back through temperance, woman suffrage, and abolitionism where women's sensibilities had infused the democratic cause.

Finally and most important, the congruence of woman's cause and labor's cause for the true course of Socialism had become, at least for a minority, more vivid than ever. The most optimistic looked upon the travail of the 1890s as a necessary baptism of fire. In the New England industrial center of Providence, Rhode Island, Socialist journalist Margaret Haile bore witness to this faith. Granted the first women's column in an official English-language Socialist publication, Haile argued for an independent dialogue, women's right to "talk about . . . things and explain them in our own way, and see how they affect us and what we are going to do about it." Aiding and advising workingwomen while encouraging those already active Socialists, Haile pulled the thread of the Gilded Age woman's movement into the next struggle for the Cooperative Commonwealth.[116]

Haile traced the roots of her dedication to Socialism to the pioneering work of Frances Willard and the WCTU. "From the home, as from a center, the movement started—nay, from the very hearts of wives and mothers, crushed by disappointed hopes and broken by the ruin and disgrace of their loved ones." The movement then grew as it formed a sisterhood across class lines and named the goal all women shared, their right to define themselves by honest, well-paid labor. To this analysis, familiar to anyone knowledgeable of the history of the woman's movement over the past thirty years, Haile added two sharp corollaries: the entrance of women into the proletarian sectors, where they could join the class struggle; and the social evolution of women into freer beings through every endeavor and circle of life.[117] Just as the male wage laborer learned his destiny by awakening to the secrets behind exploitation and surplus value, so woman evolved within capitalism to the precipice of a higher stage. The Woman of Tomorrow was "developing other sides of her nature than the wife and mother side; one who is attempting to become an all-round human being, instead of the one-sided individual she has hitherto been compelled to remain. She feels her individuality more than her sex. . . . Her intellect trained; her tastes educated; and all her mental and physical powers developed. She does not believe that life is over for her when she stands at the altar. . . . The new woman believes in being herself right down to the end of life, living out her own personal life. . . ."[118] Women were moving toward a destiny "we of this generation can perceive but dimly. . . ." Socialists, Haile warned, could ignore this force only at their own peril.[119]

NOTES

1. Biographical data on Mary Rice Livermore (1820–1905) are supplied by Robert
   E. Riegel in *Notable American Women*, ed. Edward T. James, Janet Wilson
   James, and Paul S. Boyer, 3 vols. (Cambridge, Mass., 1971), II, 410–14; Frances
   E. Willard and Mary A. Livermore, eds., *American Women: Fifteen Hundred
   Biographies*, 2 vols. (New York, 1897), II, 467–68. Livermore's autobiography,
   The Story of My Life (Hartford, Conn., 1899), which she allegedly wrote to
   finance her granddaughter's college education, contains unique perceptions
   about the place of the Civil War in the history of women's reform. Livermore
   describes her war experiences most fully in *My Story of the War* (Hartford,
   Conn., 1889), which sold over 60,000 copies.
2. Livermore repeated these lines on several occasions. Two of her best-known
   lectures, "Superfluous Women," printed in the Association for the Advancement
   of Women, *Papers and Letters of the Woman's Congress at Syracuse, New York,
   1875* (n.p., n.d.), and *What Shall We Do with Our Daughters* (Boston, 1883),
   contained this sentiment. Livermore again made this statement at the meeting
   of the International Council of Women in 1888, which is quoted in the council's
   Report assembled by the National Woman Suffrage Association (Washington,
   D.C., 1888), 131.
3. On the political orientation of the early woman's rights movement, Ellen Carol
   DuBois, *Feminism and Suffrage: The Emergence of an Independent Women's
   Movement in America, 1848–1869* (Ithaca, N.Y., 1978), provides a full and
   insightful analysis. See also Aileen S. Kraditor, *The Ideas of the Woman Suffrage
   Movement* (New York, 1965).
4. David Montgomery, *Beyond Equality: Labor and the Radical Republicans,
   1862–1872* (New York, 1967).
5. Norman Ware, *The Industrial Worker in America, 1840–1860* (Boston, 1924),
   records the early labor activities of women textile operatives, as does Thomas
   Dublin, *Women at Work* (New York, 1979). Barbara Berg, *The Remembered
   Gate: Origins of American Feminism* (New York, 1978), details the evolution
   of women's antebellum voluntary associations. An excellent specialized study
   is Susan Porter Benson, "Business Heads and Sympathizing Hearts: The Women
   of the Providence Employment Society, 1837–1858," *Journal of Social History*,
   12 (Winter, 1978), 302–12.
6. Ellen M. Harris in *The Revolution* (New York), Jan. 20, 1870. *The Revolution*
   contains much valuable information on woman's rights and workingwomen.
   See also Alma Lutz, "Susan B. Anthony for the Working Women," *Boston Public
   Library Quarterly*, 11 (Jan. 1959), 33–43; Israel Kugler, "The Trade Union
   Career of Susan B. Anthony," *Labor History*, 2 (Winter, 1961), 90–100; DuBois,
   Feminism and Suffrage, Ch. 5.
7. Virginia Penny, *Employments of Women* (Boston, 1863), vii.
8. Caroline Dall, *Woman's Right to Labor; Or, Low Wages and Hard Work* (Boston,
   1860), vii.
9. John Cunningham and others, *Memories of Jane Cunningham Croly, "Jenny
   June"* (New York, 1904), 124–26.
10. Jane Cunningham Croly, *History of the Woman's Club Movement in America*
    (New York, 1898), 79.
11. Biographical data on Jane Cunningham Croly (1829–1901) are provided by
    Elizabeth Bancroft Schlesinger in *Notable American Women*, I, 409–11, and
    in "The Nineteenth-Century Woman's Dilemma and Jennie June," *New York*

History, 59 (Oct., 1961), 351–79; Willard and Livermore, *American Women*, 216–17.

12. Quoted in "Record Book of the Weekly Social Meetings of the New England Women's Club," report of May 30, 1868 meeting, New England Women's Club Papers, Box 3, Schlesinger Library, Radcliffe College. Julia Ward Howe (1819–1910) records her club interests in *Reminiscences, 1819–1899* (Boston, 1900). See also Howe's essay, "How Can Women Best Associate?" printed in *Papers and Letters of the First Woman's Congress of the Association for the Advancement of Women* (New York, 1874), 5–10.

13. Croly, *History of the Woman's Club Movement*, 18.

14. Julia Ward Howe, *Modern Society* (Boston, 1880).

15. Carroll D. Wright, *Working Girls of Boston*, from the *15th Annual Report of the Massachusetts Bureau of Statistics of Labor for 1884* (Boston, 1889); New England Women's Club, *Report of the Committee on Needlewomen, April 12, 1869* (Boston, 1869).

16. Women's Educational and Industrial Union, *Annual Report* (Boston, 1881), 10. Biographical data on Abby Morton Diaz (1821–1904) were compiled by Jane Johnson Bernadette in *Notable American Women*, I, 471–73; Willard and Livermore, *American Women*, I, 240–41.

17. Diaz summarizes programs in "Woman's Educational and Industrial Union," a speech delivered to the first International Congress of Women, reprinted in its *Report* for 1888, 198–200. The bulk of WEIU papers are housed in the Schlesinger Library; several early minutes books and annual reports are still held by the WEIU in downtown Boston.

18. "Introduction" to Annie Nathan Meyer, ed., *Woman's Work in America* (New York, 1891), 1.

19. Ellen M. Henrotin, "The Attitude of Women's Clubs and Associations toward Social Economics," *Bulletin of the Department of Labor*, no. 23 (July, 1899), 504.

20. Annie Wittenmyer, the first president of the National WCTU, wrote one of its first histories: *History of the Woman's Temperance Crusade* (Philadelphia, 1878). Among the many histories written since Wittenmyer's publication, Norman Clark's *Deliver Us from Evil* (New York, 1976) offers the deepest analysis of the social origins and cultural significance of the crusade.

21. *Minutes of the First Convention of the National Woman's Christian Temperance Union*, held in Cleveland, Ohio, Nov. 17–19, 1874 (Chicago, 1889), 29.

22. *Woman's Journal*, May 16, 1874. Ruth Bordin, " 'A Baptism of Power and Liberty': The Women's Crusade of 1873–1874," *Ohio History*, 87 (Autumn, 1978), 393–404, examines the first years and demonstrates the importance of the crusade in bringing women into civic affairs.

23. *Minutes of the Second Convention of the National Woman's Christian Temperance Association*, held in Cincinnati, Ohio, Nov. 17–19, 1875 (Chicago, 1889), 61; also reported in *Woman's Journal*, Dec. 4, 1875. Wallace's temperance activities are recorded in Frances Willard, *Woman and Temperance* (Hartford, Conn., 1883), 476–85. For biographical data on Zerelda Wallace (1817–1901), see Paul S. Boyer's essay in *Notable American Women*, III, 535–36; Willard and Livermore, *American Women*, II, 742–43.

24. *Woman's Journal*, May 23, 1874.

25. *Ibid.*, Dec. 4, 1875.

26. *Union Signal* (Chicago), June 4, 1885.

27. Willard, *Woman and Temperance*, 47.

28. Mary Earhart, *Frances Willard; From Prayer to Politics* (Chicago, 1944), supplies the details of Willard's rise in the WCTU as well as the most perceptive analysis of her character to date. See also Frances Willard, *Glimpses of Fifty Years*, 1838–1889 (Chicago, 1889). For biographical data on Frances Willard (1839–1898), see Mary Earhart Dillon's essay in *Notable American Women*, III, 613–19; Willard and Livermore, *American Women*, II, 777–81.

29. Earhart, *Frances Willard*, 193–209. Willard's reorganization of the National WCTU as a dues-paying commitment is recorded in *Minutes of the Woman's National Christian Temperance Union at the 16th Annual Meeting* (Cleveland, 1879), 110–12.

30. *Woman's Journal*, July 24, 1875; *Minutes of the Woman's National Christian Temperance Union at the 16th Annual Meeting*, 45–46.

31. Earhart, *Frances Willard*, 157, 173.

32. *Ibid.*, 184. On the symbolic significance of the parlor as a place for women's meetings, see the report by Wendell Phillips in *Woman's Journal*, Feb. 18, 1871, wherein he describes the parlor as conveyor of "a high-toned delicate sense of private honor, [and] self respect." See also the annual reports of the National WTCU, sections on "parlor meetings." *Minutes* of the National WCTU, Nov. 14–18, 1890 (Chicago, 1890), 199–201, is especially informative.

33. Willard, *Woman and Temperance*, 42, 43.

34. *President's Address to the Annual Meetings of the National Woman's Christian Temperance Union*, 1892 (Chicago, n.d.), 6.

35. On the relationship between the WCTU and the Knights of Labor, see Earhart, *Frances Willard*, 245–59; Ronald Morris Benson, "American Workers and Temperance Reform, 1866–1933" (Ph.D. dissertation, University of Notre Dame, 1974). For relationships with the Patrons of Husbandry, see, for example, *Proceedings of the 21st Session of the National Granges of the Patrons of Husbandry* (Lansing, Mich., 1887), 80; *Proceedings of the 24th Session . . .* (Philadelphia, 1890), 80–81.

36. *Minutes of the National Woman's Christian Temperance Union at Its 11th Meeting* (Chicago, 1884), 50–51.

37. The call was issued in early June, 1887, and was reprinted in the *Report of the International Council of Women*, 1888, 10–11.

38. Ida Husted Harper, *Life and Work of Susan B. Anthony*, 2 vols. (Indianapolis, 1898), II, 632–45; Mary Lowe Dickenson, "The National Council of Women of the United States," *Arena*, 17 (Feb., 1899), 478–93.

39. *Report of the International Council of Women*, 1888, 30.

40. *Ibid.*, 36, 323–40.

41. *Ibid.*, 113; Earhart, *Frances Willard*, 273–86.

42. *Report of the International Council of Women*, 1888, 430.

43. *Ibid.*, 428.

44. Quoted by Mary A. Livermore, "Cooperative Womanhood in the State," *North American Review*, 153 (Sept., 1891), 295.

45. Alice Hyneman Rhine, "The Work of Women's Clubs," *Forum*, 12 (Dec., 1891), 519–28.

46. Phillips's speech reported by Jesse H. Jones in *Irish World* (New York), Feb. 24, 1884. For a comprehensive survey of these developments, see Howard H. Quint, *The Forging of American Socialism* (Indianapolis, 1953).

47. Undated newspaper clipping, Thomas J. Morgan Papers, Illinois Historical Survey, University of Illinois Library.

48. The Thomas J. Morgan Papers contain various newspaper clippings giving bi-

ographical data on Elizabeth Morgan. For an assessment of her labor activities, concerning the IWA in particular, see Ralph Scharnau, "Elizabeth Morgan, Crusader for Labor Reform," *Labor History*, 14 (Summer, 1973), 340–51.

49. Corrine Brown (1849–1914) received biographical attention in Willard and Livermore, *American Women*, I, 126. Gertrude Breslau Hunt also sketched Brown's political history in *Socialist Woman*, 1 (Feb., 1908), 2. Various women's groups in Chicago joined in a memorial service at her death, from which a pamphlet containing resolutions and letters was published.

50. The series began on July 30, 1888, in the *Chicago Times*, entitled "City Slave Girls," and was followed by John T. McEnnis, *The White Slaves of Free America, Being an Account of the Suffering, Privations, and Hardships of the Weary Toilers in Our Great Cities* (Chicago, 1888). Clippings on the founding of the IWA and its activities are located in the Thomas J. Morgan Papers.

51. Regular reports on the activities of the IWA are contained in the Trades and Labor Assembly of Chicago Minute Books, Chicago Historical Society, as well as in the local Chicago papers clipped in Morgan's papers. On the significance of the Illinois Factory Inspection Act, see Elizabeth Brandeis, "Labor Legislation," in John R. Commons, *History of Labour in the United States*, 4 vols. (New York, 1935–36), III, 465–66.

52. *Chicagoer Arbeiter Zeitung*, Nov. 15, 1890.

53. For a brief history of the Working Women's Society, see Maud Nathan, *Story of an Epoch Making Movement* (Garden City, N.Y., 1926), 15–32. Contemporary reports may be found in *Workman's Advocate* (New Haven, Conn.), Nov. 3, 1888; *Woman's Column* (Boston), Apr. 7, Sept. 1, 1888; *The People* (Providence, R.I.), Aug. 30, 1891. See also Ida Van Etten, *The Condition of Women Workers under the Present System* (Detroit, 1890), and the recollections of Alice Hyneman Rhine, "Reminiscences of Charles Sotheran as Pioneer American Socialist," in Charles Sotheran, *Horace Greeley and Other Pioneers of American Socialism* (New York, 1915 ed.), xix–xxii.

54. *Workman's Advocate*, Mar. 1, May 10, 17, June 7, 14, 1890; *The People*, July 7, 1888, Feb. 2, Apr. 27, 1889.

55. Biographical data on Martha Moore Avery (1851–1929) are provided by James P. Shenton in *Notable American Women*, I, 69–71. Her political activities are assessed by D. Owen Carrigan, "A Forgotten Marxist," *New England Quarterly*, 42 (Mar., 1969), 23–43. Descriptions of Avery may be found in August Claessens, *Didn't We Have Fun* (New York, 1953), 14; *The People* (New York), Mar. 5, 1893, Sept. 27, Oct. 6, 1896; *Paterson* (N.J.) *People*, July 7, 1894.

56. Note, for instance, *The Impress*, 1 (May, 1894), 2–3, and *The People* (New York), Jan. 15, 1893, Jan. 19, May 6, Sept. 24, 1894. Ralph Shaffer, "Radicalism in California, 1869–1924" (Ph.D. dissertation, University of California–Berkeley, 1964), contains much valuable information on women in the local Socialist movement.

57. *Lincoln* (Nebr.) *Socialist-Labor*, May 4, 11, June 29, 1895; *The People* (New York), Jan. 26, Aug. 23, 1896; *Vorwaerts* (New York), Mar. 3, 1894.

58. Walter Fuller Taylor, *The Economic Novel in America* (Chapel Hill, N.C., 1942). Elizabeth Stuart Phelps, *The Silent Partner* (Boston, 1871) and *Hedged In* (Boston, 1870), are two vivid examples of visionary novels written by a woman and from woman's perspective.

59. Taylor, *Economic Novel*, 184–213; Elizabeth Sadler, "One Book's Influence: Edward Bellamy's *Looking Backward*," *New England Quarterly*, 17 (Dec. 1944), 530–55.

60. As one woman remarked, one of the first things that struck her about *Looking Backward* "was the lofty position assigned to woman"; see *California Nationalist* (Los Angeles), Mar. 15, 1890.

61. Edward Bellamy, *Looking Backward* (New York, 1960 ed.).

62. Bellamy, *Looking Backward*, 176, 180.

63. Marie Shipley, "Bebel's Bricks or Bellamy?" *Liberty*, 7 (June 21, 1890). Sylvia E. Bowman, "Bellamy's Missing Chapter," *New England Quarterly*, 31 (Mar., 1958), 47–65, contends that Bellamy had a much more radical view of marriage and the family but tempered his opinions to ensure the popularity of his book. On Bellamy as a mainstream reformer, see Sondra Herman, "Loving Courtship or the Marriage Market? The Ideal and Its Critics, 1871–1911," *American Quarterly*, 25 (May, 1973), 235–54

64. Arthur Morgan, *Edward Bellamy* (New York, 1944), supplies biographical details and literary analysis.

65. John Hope Franklin, "Edward Bellamy and the Nationalist Movement," *New England Quarterly*, 11 (Dec., 1938), 754. On women's participation, Francis A. Walker, "Mr. Bellamy and the New Nationalist Party," *Atlantic Monthly*, 65 (Feb., 1890), 260, represents a contemporary observation.

66. A statement by Brown on women's position in the movement is recorded in *Nationalist*, 1 (July, 1889), 92.

67. "Editorial," *New Nation*, 1 (Aug. 8, 1891), 443.

68. For an assessment of the Boston Nationalist Club, see C. F. Willard in *Nationalist*, 2 (Dec., 1890), 37–40. For women's participation, see *Workmen's Advocate* (New York), July 7, 1890; Quint, *Forging of American Socialism*, 83; Morgan, *Edward Bellamy*, 251. On women's participation in neighboring Somerville, see *New Nation*, 1 (Feb. 21, 1891), 67. *The Second Nationalist Club of Boston, Massachusetts, U.S.A.* (Boston, 1889) contains an extensive listing of women members and their occupations. Report of the Nationalist Woman's Alliance may be located in the *New Nation*, 2 (Jan. 16, 1892), 40.

69. F. I. Vassault, "Nationalism in California," *Overland Monthly*, 15 (June, 1890), 659–61, offers a general description; an anonymous article, "History of Nationalism in Southern California and Los Angeles," *New Nation*, 1 (Feb. 14, 1891), 51, credits Anna F. Smith and Louise A. Off for calling the first meeting in the area. *California Nationalist*, Feb. 9, 15, 1890, contains similar information. It was the Oakland Nationalist constitution which guaranteed equal representation; see *Pennsylvania Nationalist* (Philadelphia), June 21, 1890. In its issue of July 26, 1890, this same paper published a directory of California Nationalist clubs with names of prominent women members. Reda Davis, *California Women: A Guide to Their Politics, 1885–1911* (San Francisco, 1967), supplies biographical information on local Nationalist women, as does Shaffer, "Radicalism in California."

70. Biographical data on Caroline Severance (1820–1914) are supplied by Joan M. Jensen, *Notable American Women*, III, 265–68; Willard and Livermore, *American Women*, II, 641. See also Ella Giles Ruddy, ed., *The Mother of Clubs* (Los Angeles, 1906).

71. Reported in Burnette Haskell's *The Commonwealth* (Kaweah, Calif.), Dec. 16, 1889. Ballou's narration of her reform history was reported in the *California Nationalist*, Apr. 10, 1890.

72. Helen Blavatsky, *Key to Theosophy* (New York, 1889), 44–45; Ernest T. Hargrove, "Progress of Theosophy in the United States," *North American Review*, 162 (June, 1896), 698–704; Robert Hine, *California's Utopian Colonies* (San Marino,

Calif., 1953), 40. C. F. Willard, an active Theosophist, also cited Madame Blavatsky's appeal among Nationalists in his unpublished autobiography (pp. 12–13)
in the Edward Bellamy Papers, Houghton Library, Harvard University. Morgan,
Edward Bellamy, 260–75, discusses Bellamy's reaction to Theosophists within the
movement.

73. A biographical sketch of Katherine Tingley (1847–1929) by Arthur H. Nethercott
appears in *Notable American Women*, III, 446–48.

74. A few spiritualists of socialistic inclinations drifted into the Nationalist movement. The *Pennsylvania Nationalist* contains reports of their activities; see especially Dec. 29, 1894.

75. Report of speeches given at the Los Angeles Nationalist Club in *California
Nationalist*, Mar. 15, 1890. For similar sentiments expressed in this publication,
see the following issues: Mar. 8, Apr. 19, 26, May 24, 1890. For sketches of
prominent women in the Nationalist movement, see *Workmen's Advocate*, July
7, 1890; see also *The People* (New York), May 3, 1891, for a list of prominent
women reformers including Jane Croly, Helen Campbell, Alice Hyneman
Rhine, and Florence Kelley, who converted to Socialism at this time.

76. *Workmen's Advocate*, July 7, 1890. See also Charles H. Hopkins, *The Rise of
the Social Gospel in American Protestantism, 1865–1915* (New Haven, Conn.,
1940), 171–83, 233–44. *The Dawn* (Boston), which Livermore served as an
editor, conducted a lively woman's department coordinated by Annie R. Weeks
of Chicago.

77. *Workmen's Advocate*, July 7, 1890, quotes Diaz on *Looking Backward*. Diaz's
comments are from a speech delivered to the twenty-second annual convention
of Free Religious Association, reported in the *New Ideal*, 2 (July, 1889), 127.
Only a Flock of Women (Boston, 1893), is drawn from lecture notes; for reports
of these tours, see, for example, *The Dawn* in the early 1890s. Diaz published
one of her most precise statements on the relationship of Women and Nationalism, "The Why and Wherefore," in *Nationalist*, 2 (Dec., 1889), 5–10.

78. Quoted from a lecture delivered to a memorial meeting for Bellamy and reprinted
in *American Fabian*, 4 (June, 1898), 2–3. Drafts of lectures delivered to various
Nationalist meetings are contained in the Charlotte Perkins Gilman Papers,
Boxes XIII and XIV, Schlesinger Library, Radcliffe College. Reports of lectures
may be found in the *New Nation*, 1 (Feb. 7, 1891), 34; 2 (Jan. 23, 1892), 58.
A tribute to Gilman for her work in the California labor movement is Eugene
Hough, "The Work and Influence of Charlotte Perkins Stetson in the Labor
Movement," *American Fabian*, 3 (Jan., 1897), 12.

79. Frances Willard, "The Coming Brotherhood," *Arena*, 6 (Aug., 1892), 321–22.

80. Frances Willard to Lilian, May 15 and June 4, 1888, in Edward Bellamy Papers,
Houghton Library, Harvard University.

81. "President's Address," *Transactions of the National Council of Women*, ed. Rachel
Foster Avery (Philadelphia, 1891), 40. See also Frances E. Willard, "An Inter-
view with Edward Bellamy," *Our Day*, 4 (Oct. 10, 1889), 539–42, and "Woman's
Cause Is Man's," *Arena*, 5 (May, 1892), 721.

82. See, for example, Willard's address to the Chicago Woman's League as reported
in the *Woman's Journal*, Oct. 13, 1888. Many women in the woman's movement
shared Willard's desire for collective solutions to the problems of housekeeping.
Mary A. Livermore, "Co-operative Experiment," *Nationalist*, 1 (Oct., 1889),
198–203, is a statement that housekeeping in the future must be cooperative.
See also Dolores Hayden, "Two Utopian Feminists and Their Campaigns for
Kitchenless Houses," *Signs*, 4 (Winter, 1978), 274–90.

83. "President's Address," *Minutes of the National Woman's Christian Temperance Union, 15th Annual Meeting, October 19–23, 1888* (Chicago, 1888), 53; Willard, "Coming Brotherhood," 321–22.
84. "President's Address" . . . *1888,* 52.
85. "President's Address," *Minutes of the National Woman's Christian Temperance Union, 16th Annual Meeting, November 8–13, 1889* (Chicago, 1889), 114, 117.
86. "President's Address," *Minutes of the National Woman's Christian Temperance Union, 20th Annual Meeting* (Chicago, 1893), 52.
87. "Nationalism," *Union Signal,* Aug. 15, 1889.
88. *Minutes of the National Woman's Christian Temperance Union, 17th Annual Meeting* (Chicago, 1890), 368.
89. "President's Address," *Transactions of the National Council of Women, 1891,* 23–57.
90. Worthy Master Samuel E. Adams, recorded in *Proceedings of the Thirteenth Session of the National Grange of the Patrons of Husbandry* (Philadelphia, 1879), 22–23. For a similar statement, see T. A. Thompson in *Proceedings of the Eighth Session* . . . (Claremont, N.H., 1875), 19. The symbolic role of women was suggested by O. H. Kelley in *Proceedings of the Ninth Session* . . . (Louisville, Ky., 1875), 16.
91. Grangers incorporated the principle of women's equality into their philosophy at their inception; the founder O. H. Kelley quotes personal correspondence on this matter dating to 1868 in *Origin and Progress of the Order of the Patrons of Husbandry in the United States* (Philadelphia, 1875), 71–75. See also James Dabney McCabe, *History of the Grange Movement; Or, the Farmers' War Against Monopolies* (Philadelphia, 1873), 450–61; Marie Howland (a member of the First International), "The Patrons of Husbandry," *Lippincott's,* 12 (Sept., 1873), 338–42. Kenyon L. Butterfield, "The Grange," *Forum,* 31 (Apr., 1901), 241, summarizes some of the duties and responsibilities women shared in the Grange. The most thoroughgoing description and analysis is Solon Justus Buck, *The Granger Movement* (Cambridge, Mass., 1913), 280–81. See also Sarah Margaret Stephenson, "The Social and Educational Aspects of the Grange, 1870–1934" (Master's thesis, University of Wisconsin-Madison, 1935), 16–43.
92. Buck, *Granger Movement,* 297–99; Wittenmyer, *History of the Woman's Temperance Crusade,* 258–63. On the regional and demographic character of the early Grange, see D. Sven Norden, *Rich Harvest* (Jackson, Miss., 1974), 25–31.
93. *Woman's Journal,* Sept. 23, 1876. See also *ibid.,* July 6, 1873, for a similar statement.
94. "A Granger," reporting in *Woman's Journal,* May 9, 1874. The *Woman's Journal* frequently reported news of women's organizations in the Grange during the early 1870s and recognized their activity as a complement to the woman suffrage movement.
95. "Minority Report of Committee on Woman Suffrage," *Proceedings of the Tenth Session of the National Grange of the Patrons of Husbandry* (Louisville, Ky., 1876), 169–71, indicates the early opposition. The endorsement of the suffrage resolution was achieved in 1885: *Proceedings of the 19th Session* . . . (Elmira, N.Y., 1885), 105. For a reaffirmation, see *Proceedings of the 25th Session* . . . (Philadelphia, 1891), 13. For a continuing southern opposition, see a report by Florence M. Adkinson in *Woman's Column,* Jan. 23, 1892.
96. Annie Diggs, "The Women in the Alliance," *Arena,* 6 (July, 1892), 167–79.
97. For biographical data on Marion Marsh Todd (1841–1913), see the essay by Paul

L. Murphy, *Notable American Women*, III, 469–71; on Sarah Van De Vort Emery (1838–95), the essay by Russell B. Nye, *ibid.*, I, 582–83; on Mary Elizabeth Clyens Lease (1850–1933), the essay by Ross E. Paulson, *ibid.*, II, 380–82; on Annie LePorte Diggs (1848–1916), the essay by Ross E. Paulson, *ibid.*; I, 481–82. See also Dorothy Rose Blumberg, "Mary E. Lease, Populist Orator: A Prolife," *Kansas History*, 1 (Spring, 1978), 3–15; Edward T. James, "More Corn, Less Hell: A Knights of Labor Glimpse of Mary Elizabeth Lease," *Labor History*, 16 (Summer, 1975), 408–9. On the complementary nature of Populist and labor ideology from women's viewpoint, see the poem "Toilers Unite, Organize and Educate Women" by Luna Kellie in *Farmer's Wife* (Topeka, Kans.), July, 1892; and "Luna E. Kellie and the Farmers' Alliance," *Nebraska History*, 50 (Summer, 1969), 184–205.

98. See, for example, Mrs. H. A. Hobart, president of the Minnesota State WCTU, "Thoughts after the Convention of the National Farmers' Alliance," *Proceedings of the 7th Annual Meeting* (Beatrice, Nebr., 1887), 4–6, wherein she discusses the complementary aims of the Farmers' Alliance and the WCTU. See also Mary E. Lease, "Women in the Farmers' Alliance," in *Transactions of the National Council of Women*, 1891, 159; Diggs, "Women in the Alliance." Diggs contributed the chapter on the woman suffrage movement in Kansas to Susan B. Anthony and Ida Husted Harper, eds., *History of Woman Suffrage*, 6 vols. (Rochester, N.Y., 1902), IV, 638–48. Marion Todd's *Prof. Goldwin Smith and His Satellites in Congress* (Battle Creek, Mich., 1890) was widely circulated among Populist suffragists.

99. Donnelly, *The Golden Bottle* (New York, 1892), 98. I would like to thank Kathryn Kish Sklar for first calling this book to my attention.

100. *Ibid.*, 102.

101. *Ibid.*, 104–6; emphasis in the original.

102. For an assessment of the complex position of women in the Southern Farmers' Alliance, see Julie Roy Jeffrey, "Women in the Southern Farmers' Alliance: A Reconstruction of the Role and Status of Women in the Late Nineteenth-Century South," *Feminist Studies*, 3 (Fall, 1975), 72–91. For a contemporary assessment of women's potential role in the alliance, see W. Scott Morgan's *History of the Wheel and Alliance* (Hardy, Ark., 1889), 253. Eva McDonald (Valesh), leading woman in the Minnesota Farmers' Alliance, encouraged women to play a larger role; see her address in *Proceedings of the National Farmers' Alliance* (Des Moines, Iowa, 1891) and Rhoda R. Gilman's essay, "Eva McDonald Valesh, Minnesota Populist," in *Women of Minnesota; Selected Biographical Essays*, ed. Barbara Stuhler and Gretchen Kreuter (St. Paul, 1977), 55–76. For a contemporary statement on women's role in the "Social Features of the Alliance," see *Proceedings of the National Farmers' Alliance* (Des Moines, 1893), n.p.

103. Jennie E. Dunning, "Home and Household," in *The Farmers' Alliance History and Agricultural Digest*, ed. N. A. Dunning (Washington, D.C., 1891), 618.

104. *Farmer's Wife*, Jan., 1892.

105. "The Influence of Women in the Alliance," in *Farmers' Alliance History and Agricultural Digest*, 312.

106. *Farmer's Wife*, Jan., 1892.

107. See, for example, *ibid.*, Apr., July, 1892. On the Woman's Christian Alliance, see *ibid.*, Feb., 1892.

108. *Ibid.*, Feb., 1892.

109. *Woman's Journal*, Sept. 3, 1892.
110. Helen Campbell, *Mrs. Herndon's Income* (Boston, 1886).
111. *Woman's Tribune* (Beatrice, Nebr.), Aug. 6, 1892; *Woman's Journal*, Feb. 27, 1892; *The Voice* (New York), Apr. 7, 1892; *Farmer's Wife*, Mar., Apr., 1892; *Woman's Column*, Feb. 27, 1892; *Union Signal*, Mar. 3, 24, 1892. See also Jack S. Blocker, Jr., "The Politics of Reform: Populists, Prohibition, and Woman Suffrage, 1891–92," *Historian*, 39 (Aug., 1972), 614–32. For a different assessment, see Earhart, *Frances Willard*, 227–44.
112. "Going to Pieces," unmarked clipping dated 1894, in Thomas J. Morgan Papers.
113. Alice Hyneman Rhine's exit from the party's fratricidal atmosphere is recorded in her "Reminiscences," xx–xxii. Ida Van Etten's departure, her attempt to help create a separate New York English-language Socialist group outside the SLP, and her obscure death in a Paris hotel are recorded in *The Socialist Labor Party in New York: A Criticism* (New York, 1892), and in *Di Arbeter-Tseitung* (Yiddish—New York), Mar. 16, 1894. Martha Moore Avery, who remained a party loyalist into the 1890s, ultimately broke to become one of the most famous anti-Socialist lecturers in the United States.
114. For an example of the Socialist Labor party women's attack upon reformers, see *Workers' Call* (Chicago), Oct. 14, 1899; for hostile commentary on Mary E. Lease, see *The People* (New York), May 5, 1893.
115. Quint, *Forging of American Socialism*, Chs. IX, X.
116. *Justice* (Providence, R.I.), May 12, 1894.
117. *Ibid.*, July 6, 1895.
118. *Ibid.*, June 1, 1895.
119. *Ibid.*, Oct. 6, 1894.

3   Grass-Roots Origins, 1900–1908

She came forth in the music and the
Rhythm of the Infinite. The passion
Of the soul-dream filled her heart,
And like the aura of the violet
Made rare the world in which she moved.
The upward looking of her eyes reflected
In their liquid depths the light from whence
She came. The numberless threads
Of gold and bronze that draped
Her shapely head, were worn with rarer grace,
Than queens or princesses wear crowns.
Her breath was like the morning when
The dew is on the rose. Her plastic brain,
Susceptible alone to tracings of the
Wise One, brought wisdom often to men
Old in years, and drew the veil of error
From their eyes, and showed the radiant
Light beyond. Each new expression of her
Mind bore in its note the dignity and
Fearlessness of truth. The keynote
Of her life was charity; and hate and
Petty jealousies were crowded from her
Heart by love's great depth and breadth
And height. All felt the womanhood
In her, and babes drew wisdom from her breast.
The morning found her with a note of praise
Upon her lips. The evening left her calm
And peaceful as the last rays of the
Setting sun. The mark of God was on
Her soul; she caught the meaning of
His word, and sailed a noble craft upon
The sea of life, undaunted by the waves
Of careless thought, the ideal of the
Infinite, the flower of human life,
A woman perfected.

Josephine Conger, "A Woman Perfected"
Appeal to Reason, April 4, 1903

Will you hear, noble women, what I have to say?
With no hesitation, not a moment's delay,
I speak my opinion, not at all to please
Those who cling to the old, tired ways.

Give me your attention! Not long will we wait,
We hear now the sounds of tomorrow's fate:
With sharp strokes the scythe cuts through the grain
And clears the fields of freedomland!

So Forward, Women, take up your rights,
Win your bouquet in the glare of the fight!
Show energy, courage, and boldest faith,
Forward always! No steps back!

And forget not your brothers, lend your respect
To the brave men who suffer, who do not forget
To give us the strength, from our yoke to be freed,
And Destiny gained, that is our Creed!

Emilie Hofmann, "Zur Arbeitsfrauen"
New Yorker Volkszeitung, March 16, 1902

At the founding meeting of the Socialist Party of America, the historic unity conference assembled at Indianapolis in July, 1901, only eight of the 128 delegates were women. None spoke on women's behalf. Margaret Haile, for example, participated actively in the heated discussions over key policies. Other women delegates, including Corinne Brown, Elizabeth H. Thomas, and Carrie Rand Herron, likewise took up matters solely related to the operational policies of the new organization. The question of women's status in this promising venture did not surface.

Not that the founders wholly ignored woman's rights as a political issue. In drawing up the party platform, delegates included a plank calling for "equal civil and political rights for men and women." Later proponents of sex equality would refer to this act as evidence that the Socialist party had taken a strong stand for woman's rights from its inception. In truth, the delegates adopted this plank without fanfare, as one in a long list of "immediate demands." After all, several minor parties, including the SLP and Populists, and a handful of local labor parties had endorsed the universal franchise since the 1890s, although only Prohibitionists demanded woman suffrage as a distinct principle. Not until 1908 would Socialists revise their constitution to incorporate a meaningful program for women's enfranchisement *per se*. In sum, the founders' advocacy of woman's rights was sincere but perfunctory. Only their failure to do so would have been noteworthy.

Although party leaders offered few inducements to women as such, the overwhelming success of the unity conference did stir interest within several sectors. Many women reformers had been seeking a viable national organization since the political collapse of the mid-1890s, and they now watched expectantly as a new Socialist movement took shape. Moreover, the Socialist Party of America had an appealing quality the earlier ethnic movement had lacked, a claim to legitimacy as it named itself successor to all earlier indigenous radical movements, from the American Revolution, through abolitionism, to the recent Populist insurgence. Although they blanched at the underrepresentation of women in the ranks, numerous veterans hoped the Socialist party might serve as a stronger beacon for the emancipation of their sex.

The experience of the 1890s, however, had tempered women's enthusiasm and affected their strategic approach. At the crest of the woman's movement in the 1880s, many activists had anticipated the formation of a grand political movement and had allied themselves with the radical insurgents. But the various political movements proved ultimately disappointing, not merely in their failure to stave off the emergence of corporate capitalism but in their unwillingness to grant women equal status or to fight their battles. The deadening collapse of the People's party in particular had provoked widespread disillusionment, leaving in its wake survivors determined to guard their principles more carefully should another major reform movement arise. Then, too, the Socialist Labor party of the late 1890s, with its heated sectarianism, its vitriolic hostility toward middle-class women reformers, and its undemocratic expulsion of dissidents, summed up the worst of male intolerance. The simultaneous turn to the right of the suffrage movement, women's clubs, and temperance organizations meanwhile provided a mirror image of a growing narrow-minded conservatism among the various women's reform forces. Elder leaders might well say with Marx that they had sowed dragon's teeth and reaped fleas. The women who enlisted in the Socialist party thus represented a hard core among the reduced ranks of the nineteenth century's great movements.

This choice contingent of mostly middle-aged veterans was faithful to its Socialist ideals but wary of weak commitments to women's emancipation. They therefore fostered the mobilization of women into clubs outside the official ranks of the Socialist party itself. Because the Socialist movement flourished in places where nineteenth-century traditions held fast—in the small towns of the nation's heartland and in the West—they enjoyed a favorable climate for their work. By 1904 they succeeded in establishing a small but solid network of Socialist women's clubs imprinted with familiar styles and organizationally autonomous.

The German-American women's auxiliaries had also reappeared with the formation of the Socialist party but remained politically quiescent until stimulated by a force new to the twentieth century, native-born women too young to have experienced the trials of previous decades and recently immigrated Jewish militants. These latter women were especially important because they joined the Socialist party with few preconceptions save their faith in the class struggle. Self-confident activists, they sought immediately to uplift "party wives" from their subordinate status in the auxiliaries so all women might participate fully within the regular party local. In several key cities like New York and Chicago, a novel alliance of ethnic matrons and determined youth thus presented itself as a second viable contingent of Socialist women.

This urban sector, more complex culturally and generationally than its rural counterpart, managed to take a firm position on matters of affiliation with the party and modes of organization. Although they admired the organizationally precocious women in the small towns and the West and shared their commitment to women's emancipation, the urban leaders were above all loyal to the party and suspicious of their sisters' adamant insistence on autonomy. Organizing more slowly and more fitfully, urban Socialist women thus became the prime supporters of a policy born earlier in the German-dominated movement and now updated by the prestigious Second International: allegiance to the party at all costs and disdain for activities associated with the "bourgeois" women's movement.

Rooted in a thirty-year history, fundamental differences apparently would not easily vanish. Basic ideological principles, methods, and forms of organization—indeed, the entire set of cultural assumptions about women's role—remained unsettled. The European-based Socialist leadership had originally assigned women a tertiary role in the class struggle and modified its policy in the 1880s not so much by granting concessions as by adjusting the existing framework to encompass issues of women's emancipation. Women's fraternal activities meanwhile bolstered the social life of the movement and reinforced these basic predilections. Not even the failure of the SLP and the partial assimilation of immigrants and their children could displace old practices. For their part, native-born veterans held fast to notions of womanhood that had not yet proven false. Only a mutual respect and a determination to avoid open conflict could smooth the way for a common effort.

As Socialist women took up the task of forging a national movement from such disparate tendencies, the nineteenth-century legacies played themselves out. Certain key questions concerning the precise relationship between the overthrow of capitalism and the liberation of women remained unsettled. Debates over such seemingly mundane matters as organizational style and affiliation thus became the context for major philosophical battles.

"IN THE BONDS OF (SOCIALIST) WOMANHOOD"

The Socialist women's movement grew during the first years of the twentieth century in parts of the country where nineteenth-century traditions remained relatively intact. As a result the movement's character was highly reminiscent of an earlier era. Socialist women in the small towns of the Midwest and Plains states and in California, the first to demonstrate their undying faith in Socialism as the key to women's emancipation, thus appeared somewhat anachronistic in the modern era. They were visionary, moralistic, and militantly Protestant as well as class-conscious revolutionaries. Old-fashioned in many ways, these aging comrades were nevertheless the moving force behind the creation of the Socialist woman's movement. Experience had taught them that women must be true to their sex regardless of their other political inclinations, and this article of faith continued to shape their relationship with the Socialist party. Primary loyalty to women, enduring from earlier times, was also the lifeblood of their distinctive endeavor.

Socialist women in the small towns of Kansas, Iowa, Nebraska, Missouri, Illinois, and Indiana shared with their male comrades a political world view indigenous to this region. Many had been converted to Socialism by *Looking Backward* or had feasted intellectually upon Donnelly's apocalyptic novels of capitalist self-destruction. Nearly all had placed their hopes in the Populist insurgence and faced disappointment with its collapse into the Bryan Democracy of 1896. They had later cheered Debs's efforts to found a Socialist city upon a hill; with him they had turned to the ballot box as the best means for redressing their grievances and setting America aright once more. Now as members of the Socialist party they read in the *Coming Nation* and the *Appeal to Reason* familiar denunciations of the usurpers who had vandalized the American heritage for the sake of uncontrolled wealth, and who had desecrated the memory of the revolution by suppressing strikes and by protecting railroad rate gouging. Men and women alike thus believed in the banishment of extreme riches and poverty, the attainment of national prosperity, and the realization of dreams of happiness kindled at the family hearth.

If one symbol could unite all the strains of compassion in small-town women, it was the legacy of Frances Willard. Her "beautiful life"[1] continued to provide inspiration for thousands of party members and sympathizers and reigned as the definitive proof that Socialism was neither immoral nor un-American but, on the contrary, the grandest expression of woman's instinct for moral perfection. Even Elizabeth Cady Stanton, champion of woman's rights also known for socialistic leanings, paled in reputation next to Willard.[2] One of the most popular propaganda leaflets, a staple of the midwestern Socialist press, was an excerpt from Willard's 1897 address to the National WCTU. In this last evocation before a national convention, Willard stated flatly that had she her life to live over she would devote it to Socialism. Socialists took great pride in this document. One editor captioned a reprint, "Frances Willard Preached the 'Debs Doctrine.' "[3] Socialists applauded Willard for understanding that intemperance was not the cause of poverty but the result, for setting out in her last years to improve the human condition through an unrelenting attack on the corruptor, Mammon. To be a Christian in the truest sense was to be a Socialist—this was Willard's admonition.[4]

Yet Willard's endorsement of Christian Socialism was only one of her lasting contributions to the twentieth-century movement. As had no other charismatic leader, Willard had demonstrated that women had a decisive—perhaps even determining—role to play in the coming of the Socialist millennium. First, however, women had to prepare by sharpening their own political tools; woman suffrage, social purity, and temperance were thus campaigns designed for this purpose. Clearly, Willard's methods were intertwined with her vision. In gaining leadership of the WCTU Willard had learned to harness enthusiasm to organization by appealing to women's special interests. She knew well her rural constituency, women who considered the home their chief material resource, a fount of authentic political and moral virtue. She tapped this feeling and encouraged women to raise it as their claim upon the national heritage. Although the slogan "For God and Home and Native Land" might seem a dubious doctrine for radicalism, Willard had interpreted it in such a way that the polluters and corruptors became not so much liquor salesmen and foreigners as money-bag capitalists who used weak men to poison all things pure. Willard had therefore asked women to stave off the destruction of their society by realizing the power of their combined strength. No woman who joined the WCTU need feel abandoned to man's world. The chains of friendship and sisterhood, blessed by republican beliefs but linked by female bonds far stronger, held together a great family of women.

Plains states Socialist women best demonstrated Willard's great reverence for womanhood. At the all-day or several-day Chautauqua-type meetings, for example, women were a major consideration, their part in the great struggle for Socialism taken seriously. From across the countryside families gathered in encampments to listen to the latest Socialist message. Wives, usually uninterested in the day-to-day wrangling typical of the Socialist local, joined these festivities and renewed their Socialist faith. While most tent-meeting programs combined spirit-raising sermons with short, exegetical orations on the fine points of theory, the woman question appeared centrally on the list of topics. Speakers pitched their deliveries to women in the audience. Eugene Debs, known for his touching soliloquies to motherhood—on occasion to his own mother—could be counted on, regardless of his designated topic, for a sentimental exhortation of woman's virtue and an appeal for political equality. Dozens of other Socialist stump speakers made their reputations on this circuit, in part because they could creatively mix tributes to womanhood with excoriations of the capitalist enemy. Women orators were among the favored celebrities; they seemed best able to combine the fire of demagogy with the delicacy of mother love. More than any male speaker, they approached the almost feminine appeal of Debs's simple love of children and the poor, his compassion

for the most hated criminals, his hatred for only the historical forces that
produced physical ruin and spiritual isolation.[5]

Kate Richards O'Hare, the compleat female orator, adopted this style and
served as a model for thousands of rural Socialist women. Trained in social
purity and temperance crusades, O'Hare delivered her first messages to a
Socialist audience in 1902. Soon after, she celebrated her marriage with a
lecture tour of Missouri towns, becoming the first of several prominent women
to share the intimacies of the honeymoon with devotion to the cause. She
described this act of abnegation, telling a Missouri audience, "I would much
prefer to be at home, but a sense of duty forces me to do something to improve
the conditions of women in the industrial struggle for existence."[6] She perpetuated this image of self-sacrifice over the years. She was, she insisted, a domes-
tic-minded woman like any other, who had willfully left the security of the
home for a political calling. She nevertheless ensured the affection of numerous
crowds by bringing her children upon the stage while she called for a vindication of motherhood. The Socialist press embellished advertisements of her
tours with a family portrait, just as a prize photograph of Debs showed the great
man with the little children of Girard, Kansas. O'Hare, like Debs, understood
her encampment audience.

It was in the towns and rural counties that such sentiments gained a fruitful
application. Whereas men and women gathered together at the encampments,
once home they seemed to follow Willard's advice, for they parted and formed
separate political societies. Each had a unique character. The regular party
local, officiated primarily by men, might establish study groups to review the
classic political texts, but served most often as the propagandistic or electoral
arm of the party. The women's club, in contrast, operated primarily as an
educational society. Often consisting of no more than a dozen active members,
these clubs trained women in the principles of Socialism and fostered their
commitment to women's emancipation. On occasion women joined men for
the party's big public events, such as dances and fairs that formed the cultural
substance of the local movement. For the most part, women preferred their
own company.

The preference for separate organizations, a carry-over from earlier times,
was politically salient. As individuals women might consider themselves loyal
members of the Socialist party; most paid dues and attended meetings regularly.
They nevertheless believed that women as a group could serve their special
needs only in separate organizations. Twentieth-century Socialist women thus
adopted the organizational forms that had for several decades served the
woman's movement so well.

The allegiance to old forms showed itself decisively in the ever-popular parlor
meeting usually convened in the afternoon, often on the Sabbath. Decades
before the founding of the Socialist party, women's club leaders had found it
difficult to attract women to an evening meeting. The supper dishes, the chil-

dren's bedtime, the priority given their husband's schedule, the unsafety of travel after dark—all proved insuperable. Women's club leaders had also discovered that a parlor provided the most conducive setting for discussions. Although men might meet in an office or in a saloon, women seemed more comfortable and self-confident in their own homes. As one popular writer explained, "Women like a little touch of froth in all their undertakings—that is, the average woman does. A parlor meeting with a light refreshment and a little gossip will be more effective as a rule, in interesting new members than a formal business meeting in a rented hall."[7] WCTU officials under Willard had tried to make even their formal meetings "homelike." At state and national conventions they filled their halls with shrubbery and flowers and arranged the platform to look like an inviting parlor, replete with overstuffed chairs, lace cloths on the tables, bowls of flowers, and so forth. Twenty years later Socialist women took similar pride in the "feminine" character of their settings. They explained that "the social intimacy of women" was necessary for carrying out the important work.

The agenda of parlor meetings also resembled the forms created by the WCTU and women's clubs. In Omaha, Nebraska, for example, the Woman's Socialist Union, an affiliate of the regular party local, self-consciously imitated standard ritual. The president described a typical meeting:

We open our meetings with Socialist songs and draw inspiration for greater effort from the thrilling words of the immortal Marseillaise, or the prophetic lines of William Morris. The [Socialist] hymns of Charles H. Kerr are full of vigor and bring us new hope. We could not do without the singing.

In answer to roll call, each member responds with a question from some inspired pen, or a thought of her own, on the subject of socialism.

We then proceed to the order of business. In this we encourage every member to take an active part, in accordance with parliamentary usage.

Then follows the lesson from "Merrie England," which is read a page about, and discussed in an informal way.

Time for adjournment comes all too soon, as we return to our family circles with warmer hearts and brighter visions of a better day than if the afternoon had been spent at a "quilting bee" or a "Kensinger tea."[8]

In the tradition of the late nineteenth-century woman's movement, these meetings were designed to train women for public roles, provide them with the rudiments of knowledge, and instill within them a sense of sisterhood and self-confidence. "Business" was abbreviated to allow ample time for educational programs, or was relegated to special committees. Topics and assigned readings were announced well in advance so that each woman could prepare sufficiently and participate freely. Rather than abstract knowledge alone, the arts of public speaking and parliamentary procedure were important to the ritual. It was assumed that the "scientific" terminology of Socialist texts would be unfamiliar to most women, but as a group they could master the difficult works and become proficient enough to carry the Socialist message to their friends. Once sufficiently equipped, Socialist women took to the public arena. Circulating libraries, debating clubs, Socialist Sunday schools, and children's choruses were their special charges. But as in all party locals, the spirit of solidarity and lasting comradeship was the most crucial product of their affairs. The parlor rather than the saloon, tea rather than beer, pleasant readings rather than factional wrangling, better matched women's sensibilities.

Socialist women's clubs seemed to form spontaneously wherever the Socialist movement struck roots. Burlington, Sioux City, and Dubuque, Iowa, Anderson, Indiana, Lawrence and Wichita, Kansas, and Omaha, Nebraska, became major centers of activity. Many small towns of the Plains states also claimed women's organizations. As the history of the nineteenth-century woman's movement indicated, the next logical step, given such promising signs, was the establishment of networks among these scattered societies. With luck and perseverance, the most dedicated organizers might locate the rudiments of a genuine Socialist women's *movement*.

Not surprisingly, more than a few of the most enterprising organizers were veterans of the WCTU. Of these none was so venerable as the one-time temperance leader, Marion Howard Dunham. She had joined the temperance campaign early, in 1877, and had quickly emerged as a prime mover in local Burlington, her home town, and in the Iowa state WCTU. She was an outstanding lecturer, a skillful organizer, and an outspoken militant. In the 1880s Dunham came to favor Willard's controversial "do-everything" policy, and she valiantly convinced a sector of the Iowa WCTU to follow the beloved leader into partisan politics. In the early 1890s internal dissension wracked the Iowa organization as Willard sought to fuse the National WCTU with the radical insurgents. Iowa's Republican women bolted, but Dunham stood firmly behind Willard and presided over a loyal sector of the WCTU. When tempers cooled later in the decade, rival factions reunited, and Dunham resumed her position as president of the entire state WCTU.

Dunham proved an important asset to the Socialist women's movement because she knew how to organize and to provide leadership. Within the WCTU Dunham had long insisted that women could wage an effective battle only if they gained training and knowledge for political citizenship. She had encouraged her temperance followers to broaden their interests by forming economic study clubs. She used to tease that she "had hardly been fair" to her temperance sisters because she rarely mentioned the liquor question at Socialist meetings but always offered socialistic messages to her WCTU following. Her annual addresses to the state WCTU through the 1890s became increasingly socialistic in tone. When Dunham joined the Socialist party at the turn of the century, she was sixty years old and possessed all the requisite skills for leadership. And with such deep roots in the regional woman's movement, she was a natural candidate for midwestern coordinator of Socialist women's clubs.[9]

From the ranks a few younger women appeared to build on the foundation of the early woman's movement. Luella Roberts Krehbiel was a prime representative of these grass-roots leaders. Known as the "Hypatia of modern times," she was both intelligent and passionate, said to possess a "dramatic temperament with a comprehensive brain to guide it." Krehbiel, who had grown up on a farm in Winfield, Kansas, was then in her mid-thirties. Her mother had been a suffrage lecturer for over thirty years, and Luella did the same for some six years. She dated her interest in radical causes to the late 1880s when the single-tax movement caught her attention. She took part in the Populist crusade, the Socialist Labor party for a brief while, and received a commission from Debs to organize for the Social Democracy. Once the Socialist party formed, she presented herself as candidate for Kansas state organizer and set as her special task the creation of women's clubs and their federation into a statewide and eventually national union. The party, she explained, might "work and struggle until the crack of doom but something never yet was born of nothing and the world will never be liberated until the women are aroused, justified, and developed." With this thought in mind Krehbiel formed women's clubs across Kansas, entertained a massive correspondence, and sought through every available means to break down the barrier that distance and lack of communication posed for the unity of Socialist women.[10]

Within a few years, with organizers like Dunham and Krehbiel in the field, a weak network of Socialist women's clubs emerged in the Plains states. Kansas, former bastion of Populist women, led all efforts. It seemed clear that if a movement were to be forged from these various outcroppings, it would stand, in the participants' own minds at least, as the legitimate expression of Frances Willard's dreams. Socialist women here had been indelibly marked by the nineteenth-century woman's movement, especially by its WCTU component. Organizers therefore planned to shape a Socialist movement in the mold they knew best and continued to value. Along with independent women's clubs, they created a philosophically distinct world view.

This sensibility showed itself vividly in the literature of the Socialist movement, particularly in the pages of the *Appeal to Reason*. The *Appeal*, published in Girard, Kansas, was the most popular Socialist newspaper in the United States and, for a time, the best-selling political weekly of any kind in the world. Through its massive subscription drives and its down-home language, the "little ole *Appeal*" ultimately achieved a weekly circulation of a half-million. Its success lay with the remarkable J. A. Wayland, small-town newspaper publisher, land speculator, self-styled political philosopher, and true believer in the superiority of the gentle sex. His paper pulled at the heartstrings of ordinary men and women. It condemned, even more than economic injustice, capitalism's moral failure.[11] In 1903, just as the scattered Socialist women's clubs were making their presence felt, Wayland located the ideal journalist to play upon their sentiments and to increase the *Appeal*'s female readership.

Josephine Conger, born in Centralia, Missouri, eventually became the leading editor of the Socialist women's movement. She retained much of the
nineteenth-century faith in womanhood. She described herself as having been
"one of those delicate and dreamy sort of children," never ambitious, but by
age sixteen enamored of literature, particularly the works of Emerson and
Carlyle. A little younger than her peers, she shared their tastes in poetry and
prose, and this dreamy character would last throughout her life. Her family
sent her to college at nearby Columbia, Missouri, where she was to cultivate
her musical talents. Journalism, however, became her first love. Conger took
a position in her brother's country newspaper office, where she learned to set
type, print, and handle the business end of publishing. She also submitted a
few pieces to various newspapers in the state. Then, drawn for reasons she later
could not remember, she spent the next two years at the radical Ruskin College
in Trenton, Missouri. There she picked up a great deal about scientific Socialism from a later translator of *Kapital*, Ernest Untermann. She left Ruskin
a Socialist journalist. For a short time she conducted a woman's department
for Walter Vrooman's *The Multitude*, but received her big break when she
obtained a place on the editorial staff of the *Appeal*. Conger moved to Girard
to edit a column initially called "Hints to the *Appeal's* Wise Woman," and
thereby commenced a lengthy career.[12]

Conger's column, like the rest of the *Appeal*, was intimate and inspirational
but served primarily to encourage women to show their colors. Conger published many of her own sentimental poems on the glory of womanhood, the
sweetness of children, the vitality of the class struggle, and a variety of related
subjects, usually phrased in mystical New Thought rhetoric. She kept her
readership closely informed on matters central to the contemporary suffrage
movement, reported National American Woman Suffrage Association conventions, and reprinted leaders' addresses. But her main subject was Socialism and
the creation of a coherent political force to win the final victory. With the same
aim in mind, the *Appeal* had already launched the most extraordinary movement of solicitor-agitators in recent American history. Like the "agents" of abolitionist newspapers, members of the *Appeal* army carried the message to their
communities; they hawked subscriptions and described in the *Appeal's* columns
the personal satisfaction they gained from this task. By 1903 the army had
nearly 200,000 names on its roster of subscribers and casual readers—nearly
all male. "Now Socialism," Conger objected, "isn't for men only." She recognized, however, that most women readers undoubtedly had little opportunity
or the audacity to sell subscriptions. She therefore asked her readers to form
their own "army." Conger designed a returnable coupon bearing only the simple
pledge, "I am interested in Socialism and the Emancipation of Women," and
asked her readers to demonstrate their commitment by signing their names and
mailing the form to the *Appeal* office.[13]

In partially transforming her column into a readers' forum, Conger contributed a collective portrait of a significant sector of the Socialist women's movement. Within a few months she received over a thousand letters. Although she soon abandoned the pledge form to save space in her column, Conger continued to solicit personal messages, which she edited selectively for publication. Many respondents reportedly attached photographs of themselves; all sought to explain why they were such ardent Socialists.

Conger's "army" had much in common with its nineteenth-century predecessor. Her readers tended to reside in places where the older woman's movement, especially the WCTU, had lasting influence, and they continued to espouse its goals. Most letters, Conger reported, came from the Middle and Far West, scarcely any from northeastern cities or states, and the greatest number from California and Kansas.[14] Most writers were housewives and advanced in years, professed veterans of both the woman's movement and various radical ventures of the 1880s and 1890s but still steadfast in their faith. Many lived on farms and expressed mixed feelings of loneliness and resilience. They wrote that they were comforted by the printed letters of other women like themselves who, faced with endless housework or childcare, found the occasional trip to town their only opportunity for agitation. Mrs. F. C. Cole of Elk City, Kansas, wrote to explain that she was "an old lady living in the country . . . but I cast in a might now and then. My heart is in the good work. I distribute all the papers and all the literature I can get." Other women had a more spiritual communion with their comrades. Annie Wilson, living outside Monmouth, Illinois, reported that although isolated she regularly came "into psychic touch with noble minded women whose souls are in a condition of spiritual activity on the plane of moral advancement of the race."[15] In various ways Conger's columns supplied these women with the reassuring knowledge that there were others like themselves who had kept the faith and were now ready to take up the struggle again.

The radical sentiments of women in these regions of the country, be they expressed through the rhetoric of temperance or of Populism, had been for decades the Social Gospel. Nor surprisingly, Josephine Conger and her readers, like the bulk of the *Appeal's* devoted following, continued this tradition. They proclaimed their faith Christian Socialism. Many still inclined, as did Conger herself, toward mystical religions. New Thought, an eclectic tendency that stressed the power of mind over matter, "applied" Christianity, and the righteousness of woman's cause, proved a popular successor to Theosophy.[16] The official organ of the Kansas state Socialist party, *Social Ethics*, for example, was a New Thought paper; its editor advised readers to associate spiritually with each other through regular evening meditations of mind projection.[17] The Anglo-Saxon women of Coffeyville, Kansas, Muscatine, Iowa, or the dozens of other towns that dotted the Plains states found such mystical doctrines quite compatible with their understanding of the New Testament and especially with their faith in woman's power to confront the evil embodied in the capitalist system. "The hand that rocks the cradle *does* rule the world" continued to be a popular aphorism among these constituents.[18] As late as 1914, the chairwoman of the Galena, Kansas, local, Georgia Scovell, was a dedicated Socialist who deserted her duties to the party only to conduct spiritualist revival meetings.[19]

Most of Conger's readers were, however, closer to the millennial Protestant tradition common to Populist and temperance circles of the late nineteenth century. Conger thus frequently evoked the wisdom of Frances Willard. She appealed to her readers to remember that prayer was "the reaching out of the soul for its needs" and that the "deepest prayers are often those that are not framed in words." She warned her readers not to accept the false notion some-times preached in church that " 'The Lord will take care of us; He knows our needs.' " Such sentiments were only a cowardly evasion of the true imperative to political activism. "If such women will listen closely and honestly to the voice of the Infinite within their souls, they will hear these words," Conger wrote: "INASMUCH AS YE HAVE DONE IT UNTO THE LEAST OF THESE WILL I DO IT UNTO YOU."[20] Rendered freely, this dictum interpreted Christian duty as the struggle for Socialism, Willard's message exactly.

Conger's readers also offered their own versions of Christian Socialism rem-iniscent of earlier times. One woman from Madden, Oklahoma, wrote, "I see in Socialism the possibility of a literal practice of the Golden Rule . . . and the possibility of living every day the highest life, the 'Christ life' as He taught it." In evangelical fashion other writers similarly addressed their sisters: "Women, let us march to the Kingdom God has prepared for us with the banner of Socialism floating over us." Very frequently these writers referred to the example set by the saintly Frances Willard and interpreted their own efforts as a contin-uation of her struggle against Mammon. Although they often recalled with lingering disappointment the time "when populism was dethroned," many shared the opinion of Mary Sharp from Woodward, Oklahoma: "I am fifty-one years of age but I am with the Socialists to help pull down Satan's ranks and build God's kingdom here on earth."[21]

Most characteristic of earlier times was a rendition of Christian Socialism as a faith based on the principle of woman's equality. Socialism must mean, in this view, not merely the brotherhood of man but the sisterhood of woman. Conger and her readers frequently espoused this faith and thereby gave a dis-tinctive cast to their messages. As one reader implored, "Let us go to work, sisters, and do something for ourselves and Christianity." Or, as another woman from a small town in Indiana explained, "First to me, [Socialism] is the only true religion, according to the teachings of the New Testament. Second, I am convinced that it is the only intelligent way out of the unjust and unequal conditions existing in the present time and last, but not least, it is the only thing that can or will strike the shackles from the feminine race and place her in a rightful sphere." Most readers might agree with everything in this explanation except the priorities; for them, faith in Socialism was derived foremost from its possibilities for woman's freedom. Writers often replicated the sentiments of Mrs. Mattie Barney of West Point, Oklahoma, who explained simply, "I am a Socialist if Socialism is in favor of women. I hope the day will come when we can vote for the laws that govern our lives. I am always a friend to my sex." Even more straightforwardly, another woman wrote that the "best thing about Socialism is that it advocates Woman's Rights."[22] Josephine Conger herself made this connection most explicitly. In a letter to Clara Colby, editor of the *Woman's Tribune*, Conger explained: "I am a Socialist, but I am one because I see through the Socialist platform the only possible emancipation of women and children from tyranny and superstition. I want the women educated to see themselves free and that is the work I am trying to do in my present capacity."[23]

If Conger and her readers embraced Socialism because it promised the liberation of women, they also believed that women were to be the principal agents in this great transformation. Like their forerunners in the WCTU, they invested their faith in woman's special role as protector of the family and the larger social family, the state. Conger thus characteristically lamented any infringement on women's domestic prerogatives, especially what she identified as a pernicious tendency toward "heterogenous rule" in the home.[24] Socialist women, of course, denied the charge that Socialism would destroy the family. Opponents merely made this accusation, Socialists explained, because they knew nothing was so sacred as a person's home, "no matter how poor or humble." As Margaret Haile countered in 1903, would anyone conclude that in declaring herself for Socialism Frances Willard was "ignorant and degraded"? "Do you think she would be in favor of breaking up the home?" Haile asked.[25] Such Socialist women still clung to the notion of the home as a traditional source of woman's power, domesticity as a special feminine preserve.

The home as the locus of woman's strength was, of course, a metaphor, much as it had been for political women in the late nineteenth century. "Home, to the earnest, wide-awake woman, means the center of all things," one Socialist explained, but "not the circumference. Home remains, as it has been, woman's pride and joy. But the circumference bounding the home has immeasurably widened."[26] Frances Willard had popularized the interpretation now commonplace: from her position as head of the household, woman could reach out to purify all aspects of the human condition, from the most intimate relationships between man and woman to such grand tasks as reforming government and ending wars. Ada K. Schell of Ponca, Nebraska, admitted that the Socialist party might not directly "touch on the domestic and private relation of the people," but if Socialism meant anything at all, it meant the "freedom of woman will be the ennoblement of man." The husband, purged of his masculine vices, would be able to share with his wife the consecration of the abode of human happiness and, once purified, would also be capable of moral political and economic acts. The home, therefore, "must be the environment of all that is pure and good before the nation can become entirely so." According to this interpretation, the dialectic of history was certain: the purified home as the necessary setting for Socialism, the imperative of womanhood the determining factor. Schell pleaded: "Mothers, then and there, in the sanctuary of your own love and freedom—will you not stand together and declare that a system under which it is impossible to work in harmony with God shall be overthrown?"[27] Mrs. J. N. Sample of Belknap, Montana, looked beyond the current travail to the imagined future: "I believe that Socialism will some sweet day express to the world the mother love of the Universe in all her Infinite revealings. . . ."[28]

Josephine Conger's readers, and most Socialist women active in the region, quite freely adapted sentiments nurtured during their youth in the woman's movement to the cause of Socialism. For many, the radical insurgence of the late 1880s and 1890s had provided a taste of a synthetic vision, but the new Socialist movement appeared even more promising, more comprehensive in securing both women's freedom and the end of capitalism. They eagerly professed their loyalty. But in their hearts they never relinquished a special faith in the power of womanhood, a tenet which remained central within their own movement. Thus they found in their independent societies, expressed in their old-fashioned rhetoric, an ideological kernel still capable of eliciting the interest of reform-minded women. Socialist women of this milieu were in essence the major progenitors of the distinct Socialist women's movement. In the first years of the twentieth century their voices, now cracked from age, resonated most clearly, their organizations however archaic appeared most spontaneously. They set the precedent.

A similar sensibility showed itself briefly among Socialist women in Boston. They formed a women's club to conduct discussions among themselves and to educate children in the "principles of social democracy," and they sponsored occasional public meetings at Paine Memorial Hall to attract new members. With over two-thirds of its members native-born, this club failed to grow, as the shrinking Protestant base of heavily immigrant, economically beset New England offered limited prospects. Along with many regional party locals, the Boston Socialist women's club declined.[29]

In California, where a number of former Boston residents had retired, conditions were more promising. Fabian Socialism in particular provided an important context, and magazines like the *Comrade* and *Wilshire's Magazine* enjoyed an avid readership among the progressive middle classes. In San Francisco women formed a William Morris Club, adopted the motto "We Strive to Build the Comrade World, in Freedom, Art and Fellowship," and aimed to develop in its members "a full expression of life." Across the bay in Oakland the Vida Scudder Club kept alive Fabian idealism. These clubs included seasoned activists from movements that had grown and collapsed in the 1890s, from the Farmers' Alliance, Bellamy Nationalism, and the Socialist Labor party. Across a remarkable spectrum of experience California women continued to share with their Plains states sisters a tenacious world view rooted in women's political traditions. [30]

Los Angeles remained the only major city in the nation where these traditions thrived among Socialist women, and it became their chief center of activity. A predominantly Anglo-Saxon area less culturally closed than the hide-bound East, southern California remained a natural setting for utopian fantasies—"Socialism among the Orange Groves," as one brochure depicted a potential colony. Southern California had also attracted scores of professional women nurturing a variety of Socialist schemes. In 1901, when party membership in Los Angeles was estimated at about 200, twenty-six women formed a local Woman's Socialist League. They issued a call destined for wide circulation, promising to create a "distinct movement to interest women in the principles of Socialism." The major speaker at the first organizational meeting clarified its goals: the WCTU should be taken as a proper model, and Socialist women must draw the proper conclusions from their experience and carry them through into their new activity. Independent women's clubs, they argued, provided the special training women needed to participate in the Socialist movement. Some organizers contended boldly that even fully prepared women might function better without men's presence or interference. Within a month additional details of the league were set, committees formed, and a slate of officers elected; within a year membership tripled. [31]

As in the Plains states, the pacemakers in Los Angeles were veterans of the late nineteenth-century woman's movement. Mary Alderman Garbutt was a prime example. Then in her late fifties, Garbutt was a veteran of abolitionism, woman suffrage, Bellamy Nationalism, and the Christian Socialist endeavor. Through all her forays into radical politics, she had retained her ties with the WCTU. She had, in fact, represented the WCTU at a People's party state convention in 1892, and was still a special correspondent to the *Union Signal*. Frances Willard had converted her to Socialism, and she likewise shared the great leader's devotion to women's organization. She said that her followers were "in hearty sympathy" with the Socialist party and appreciative of its efforts on behalf of woman's cause. Nevertheless, as women were just "awakening to the fact that they are persons," they needed "to arouse and deepen among themselves the consciousness of their own individuality." Men could not really understand the importance of this process because they had been trained since childhood to be self-confident; women, in contrast, especially as they entered upon a public phase, had to learn first how to think for themselves, how to express themselves, "in order that [they] may better cooperate with the comrades of the Socialist party, when it comes to that 'strong pull and pull altogether' that will bring in the new order of society." Garbutt thus concluded that men and women should organize separately and according to their own traditions. In separate clubs women would be able to reach others of their own sex, even if they had to bend a little on the "profoundly scientific" theories.[32]

Due in no small measure to their clarity of purpose, California women effected a statewide movement similar in kind to that in the Plains states. They promoted amiable relations with the existing woman's movement, such as mainstream women's clubs and suffrage societies, and affiliated with the state's umbrella organization, the Woman's Parliament. Simultaneously they strengthened their own organizational apparatus by uniting the various clubs. A tour conducted by former Populist Anna Ferry Smith laid the groundwork for a state convention of Socialist women's clubs, which convened in San Francisco in 1902. Any woman calling herself a Socialist, whether a party member or not, was invited to take part in the proceedings; no men except those admitted as honorary members could participate. Conventioneers exchanged notes on propaganda techniques, framed a state constitution, made nominations for offices and special committees, and planned to broadcast their success through the Socialist national press.[33]

Philosophically as well as organizationally, California women were the natural allies of their Plains states sisters. They, too, believed in women as the principal revolutionary agents. Whereas party regulars, especially in the ethnic sectors, complained about the conservative influence of women and the apathy of their wives, Mary Garbutt predicted self-confidently, "You may be sure that when women are soundly converted to Socialism, they will not rest until they have converted their fathers, and husbands, their brothers, and sweethearts. . . ."[34] California women were generally less apocalyptic and more genteelly sentimental, more often Unitarian than Methodist—in short, more comfortably middle class than their counterparts in the Midwest. But they shared a common heritage in Christian Socialism and found inspiration in the New Thought poems of Ella Wheeler Wilcox. They, too, hewed to older styles of moral reform and infused their Socialist activities with a self-consciously developed feminine ethos. They tended to be middle-aged or even older, veterans of the WCTU or women's clubs, and they hoped to continue their endeavor to prepare women for the great struggle ahead. They voiced the most persistent cries for a distinct and autonomous Socialist women's movement.

In one sense women in California and in the Middle West might be described as proponents of a radical interpretation, first of a distinct woman's culture, and second of Socialist politics as it gave theoretical coherence and direction to that culture. They summed up within themselves the latent possibilities of the late nineteenth-century woman's movement. Only a few individual women had been outright Socialists; now a distinct movement was in the process of organizing itself for women's contribution to the class struggle. Especially in the first years of the twentieth century, the influence of these women was paramount. The Middle West supplied the down-home women who gave life and meaning to the movement's vision. California supplied the experienced leaders who advanced the struggle for national organization. Both sectors could appreciate the significance of Mary Livermore's final testimony to her continuing faith in Socialism. Livermore wrote in 1903: "I believe most heartily in 'the good time coming' and while seeing 'distant gates of Eden gleam' I 'do not deem it all a dream.' "[35] Time was running out for this sector, but they were willing to fight to the end.

URBAN ETHNIC HERITAGE

Socialist women in the industrial centers, like New York, Chicago, Milwaukee, and St. Louis, were in many ways similar to their small-town and Californian sisters. The majority were married and understood fully the notion of woman's sphere. They, too, felt the sting of paternalism and twinges of self-doubt when asked to participate in the regular party local. But the differences between these two sectors—and, indeed, among the urban women themselves—proved crucial.

The urban sector of the Socialist party inevitably comprised a wide variety of elements. Inheriting the remnants of the nineteenth-century Socialist movement, the branches maintained a substantial ethnic component. But, as during other periods of advance, an assortment of English-speaking radicals joined, including a host of municipal reformers, a few former Populists, and a scattering of college-educated or independently wealthy intellectuals. These native-born radicals together with the German-American veterans of the SLP, many now second-generation Socialists, encouraged an "Americanization" of the urban movement previously lacking. The women's membership reflected this entire demographic spectrum, albeit in miniature.

This diversity had political significance. Socialist women in the urban areas confronted considerable problems in building a culturally cohesive force, and established themselves as a distinct sector years after their small-town and Californian sisters had created a rudimentary movement. They did, however, have certain advantages, such as the extremely close-knit ethnic neighborhoods. Perhaps most important, they shared a strong loyalty to the Socialist party which superseded other political commitments. Indeed, a common allegiance to the party eventually served to mute the differences among the various urban groups and became the major tenet of their political world view.

At the turn of the century the largest female constituency remained "party wives." Many now had memories reaching back to the SLP of the 1880–90s and had long served in auxiliary labors to the movement, whether organized for that purpose or not. Few had taken part in the mainstream woman's movement, alienated by its middle-class aura, especially its WASPish devotion to temperance and religious messianism. The ethnic majority was, in other words, essentially a variant of first- or second-generation immigrant homemakers who, despite their Socialist faith, accepted men's leadership in political affairs. In the class struggle, above all, they considered themselves secondary agents. Removed from the means of capitalist production, Socialist women had, they believed, other duties to perform for their families and for themselves.

In some specific instances women's party duties changed little in the twentieth century. The auxiliary, for example, continued to claim women's energies. The sick-and-benefit societies, choirs, union label leagues, and similar enterprises provided a social milieu for the new movement to draw to itself thousands of sympathizers. Indeed, one of the party's major tasks was to recruit those culturally active immigrants who had broken with the SLP and remained on the political sidelines, skeptical of any American-led movement. The revival of cultural activities and the re-establishment of the auxiliaries among many newly awakened immigrants proved of inestimable value for the membership and financial base of the urban party. As in the nineteenth century, women stood at the center of these activities. Not because they were elected officials but because they performed the essential services and kept the spirit alive, women were an indispensable element. Second-generation immigrant women and wives of assimilated immigrant workingmen continued to organize the bazaars and raffles and to produce the baked delicacies and fancy goods. They also supervised the major social events. May Day picnics, annual suppers, commemorative fetes, and group entertainments remained prerogatives of the "ladies."

Party leaders at first encouraged women to fill their traditional responsibilities. Occasionally to reward party wives for their loyal services, the local would sponsor a "ladies' night." For this affair men would prepare a simple program, which included what they designated a "low level" political discussion calculated to match the male comrades' estimation of their wives' intellectual attainments. Women rarely participated at such meetings. As in the nineteenth-century *Frauenvereine*, they listened politely while male functionaries tendered short speeches on historical materialism or more topical subjects. Many comrades tried to assuage women's alleged fears of their husbands' political activity, for even the husband grateful for his wife's auxiliary service often continued to consider her politically retrograde by nature. Thus even the praise bestowed upon women for their work had a certain patronizing tone, like the report of leading party pedagogue Algernon Lee on the Haverhill, Massachusetts, women's club. "[A] most useful auxiliary to Local Haverhill—especially on the financial side," Lee noted before adding: "Doubtless these ladies discuss hats and shirtwaists at their meetings, sometimes. That is said to be woman nature. But they do their work, anyhow, and do it well."[36] The fact that Haverhill had been a center of British rather than German radicalism and a unique addition to the English-language sectors of the 1890s SLP mattered less than its continuing observance of broad dichotomies between male and female roles within the Socialist movement.

Socialist women in the urban movement indeed clung to their traditional roles. As late as 1904 a native-born organizer toured the Chicago locals and observed that, despite a healthy attendance at branch meetings, no more than five or six women were present. After the meeting adjourned and the comrades turned to the more congenial aspects of ritual, the hall suddenly became crowded with women serving refreshments and beaming over the performance of the children's choir which they had so carefully trained. Visiting the kitchen, the organizer found the women genuinely interested in Socialism. Many told her that they regularly read the newspapers and were familiar with the party platform. Although not active participants at the business meetings, they nevertheless considered their own contributions essential to the cause.[37] Many women apparently still felt comfortable with the auxiliary form of organization.

Despite the tenacity of old ways, several new factors combined to enlarge women's role in the movement. Certainly the example of the independent Socialist women's clubs suggested a tempting alternative to the auxiliary. Indeed, a core group of German-American women had advanced politically, primarily in response, however, to shifts in the Second International which called for a more active role for women in the class struggle. Far more influential were the new recruits to the urban movement. Large numbers of recent immigrants and a second generation of native-born women had joined the party at the turn of the century and fostered a different form of women's contribution. They set aside the auxiliary model and demanded an equal status within the regular party local. The urban sector, comprising an assortment of radical women, mobilized slowly but eventually shaped its own organizational style and articulated a distinct interpretation of the woman question true to its European heritage.

The unique example of Jewish women provides an insight into the complexity of this development. Although Jewish Socialists had achieved a major breakthrough in the 1890s, women played a mixed role in the movement. There was a rich tradition of activism among Russian Jewish women in particular. Among the Old World middle classes, exceptional women had seized educational opportunities, become physicians or other professionals, and supplied numerous martyrs to the anti-czarist struggles of the 1880s and 1890s. Among the immigrant masses in the tenements and sweatshops of New York, a parallel tradition developed as Jewish workingwomen became renowned for their rebelliousness and radical proclivities. Such militancy, however, appeared characteristic of single women, for party wives made scarcely any headway within the movement. Here historic Jewish culture made its mark. Women had been by definition profane, denied the sacred Hebrew language, kept ignorant to such an extent that illiteracy among Jewish immigrant women was twice that of their menfolk and nearly 50 percent. Married women's position within the party proper remained weak, their familial status allowing few prerogatives.[38]

The organization of Jewish women proved painfully slow and complicated. Jewish activists at first sought to imitate their German sisters. A Women's Progressive Society (*Frauen Fortbildung Ferein*) appeared in New York and in Chicago in the 1890s with the usual trappings of the ladies' auxiliary. The society attracted an impressive body of speakers including the poet Morris Rosenfeld, the young Morris Hillquit, and Johanna Greie before it disappeared, victim perhaps to the heightened union struggles and to the catastrophic effect of the depression of 1893 upon Jewish life. For the duration of the 1890s Jewish women took little part even in the Socialist fraternal activities. When the Workman's Circle (*Arbeter Ring*), Jewish version of the German sick-and-death benefit society, first organized in 1892, its statutes formally permitted the participation of both sexes. But as the movement's official historian recorded, women were generally thought to belong at home with the children, and without any special encouragement few women participated. At the reorganization of the Workman's Circle in 1901, the first ladies' branches were recognized. By 1904 these bodies comprised some hundred women in mostly East coast cities. The sex-segregated branches ultimately flourished, but the character of their activities—essentially extensions of the close-knit networks among party wives—afforded few avenues for the most ambitious women and failed to integrate women into the party's mainstream.[39]

From the 1890s it was clear that Jewish women would achieve distinction primarily as individuals and not as a discernible sector of the Socialist party *per se*. Usually as trade unionists, sometimes as political leaders, they emerged as vigorous and combative activists. Such women bore their Jewish heritage proudly, and most continued their agitation among a predominantly Yiddish-speaking constituency. A far-sighted minority also probed alternative milieux, joining English-language branches as individuals, even founding Jewish affiliates of the German-American Socialist women's movement. Whatever their surroundings, they had ceased defining themselves according to patriarchal Jewish prescriptions, and demanded the right to equal standing in the movement. But only after 1910, when thousands of Jewish women fought successfully for union recognition, did their leaders and allies play a major part in the Socialist party.

The German-American constituency developed along a slightly different path. Like the Jews, these women first gained a new status within the fraternal network. The major sick-and-death benefit society, the *Allegemeine-Kranken und Sterbe-Kasse*, originally organized in 1886, reincorporated in 1896 and again in 1899, finally granted women equal status. Women's organizational life leaped forward, however, in 1897, after their European comrades entered a new political phase.[40]

German-American Socialist women organized primarily in response to shifts in Second International policy. During a major conference at Erfurt in 1891, Social Democrats for the first time incorporated into the party platform a demand for universal suffrage without distinction as to sex and resolved to establish special agitational committees for women. At the next year's conference the party created a system of women's representatives, which became a major educational arm. Then, at the party conference at Gotha in 1896, Clara Zetkin presented a major report on the woman question, and the delegates not only endorsed her report but adopted a lengthy resolution in its favor and passed an elaborate program designed to improve women's status. An official Socialist women's movement of Germany thus came into being.[41]

German-American women copied the Old World model by establishing a Social Democratic Women's Federation, which eventually received the blessing of the party. At first composed only of two branches in the New York area, it gained affiliates in Philadelphia, Cleveland, Chicago, and St. Louis. Nearly a decade late and now close to the political margins of the larger Socialist movement, German-American women achieved the status for which Johanna Greie had fought so hard.

The Social Democratic Women's Federation had an inestimable advantage over its predecessor, the *Frauenbund*: regular access to the party press. Never in the nineteenth century had women's activities received serious attention save in the "Vereine und Versammlungen" (clubs and assemblies) columns; the "women's page," which appeared sporadically as a feature in the weekend supplements of the daily German-American Socialist papers, contained primarily light propaganda and amusements, much in the fashion of the programs of "ladies' nights" at party locals. In its first years the Social Democratic Women's Federation gained only little more publicity. But in 1901 the *Volkszeitung* granted the unprecedented luxury of a permanent Sunday half-page (shared with children's materials), "Für Frauen," which reprinted serious essays from the Old World press, reports from sections, and discussions of controversial questions raised by women themselves. The precedent for this coverage may well have been the German *Die Gleichheit*, Clara Zetkin's magazine which first appeared in 1891 and was renowned for the high quality of its contents, or the existence of women's columns in the English-language press, such as the *Appeal to Reason*. Whatever its genesis, the *Volkszeitung's* women's page proved a major attraction, in the first place because the newspaper in general exuded a kind of Second Internationalist, European dignity that provided a distinguished context for women's journalism. The sense of informal give-and-take was also such that women could write in comparing their shopping budgets or asking questions—even about the existence of God—that their Socialist husbands had laughed off as either too difficult for women's comprehension or too trivial for men's attention. Most important, the *Volkszeitung* columns permitted the identification of a political leadership.[42]

Editing the "Für Frauen" column in its first years, Johanna Greie staged a remarkable comeback as an organizer. Now widowed and remarried, Greie-Cramer, as she called herself, tended toward ill-health but determined to make the most of the political opportunity. Armed with the example of the successful Old World Socialist women's movement, Greie argued forcefully against any simple attempt to organize women directly into the party on an individual basis or to confine their work to the auxiliaries. The Social Democratic Women's Federation, she insisted, had a unique perception of women's problems and a unique responsibility to mobilize women. Although the federation would not gain official recognition from the party until 1908, Greie-Cramer sought to give substance to the movement by engaging in one last, major lecture tour across the East and Midwest. Through backwoods farming areas of Wisconsin and coal-mining towns of southern Illinois, by horse and buggy outside the radius of the railroad during the bitter early spring, she carried her message. Greie-Cramer once more became a major figure among the now-aging but steadfast *Genossinnen*.[43]

Greie-Cramer eventually gained the collaboration of able colleagues who could broaden the base of the movement. No less willful or articulate, several young Jewish women leaped at the opportunity. They wrote for the *Volkszeitung* bcause no women's column appeared in the Yiddish press until 1916. And they tapped the *Volkszeitung* constituency for their own purposes. Theresa Malkiel, prestigious trade union leader of the 1890s and already a party functionary, became the most prominent Yiddish journalist to contribute her talents to the German-American women's movement. Anna Ingerman, a Russian emigré who had been one of the early women physicians to join the party, similarly had made her mark in the Yiddish sector by organizing an unprecedented demonstration of some 4,000 Jewish women for a New York May Day parade in 1895. Lecturer and writer for German-American women, Ingerman also became one of the first American women to attend as a delegate an international Socialist congress. Antoinette Konikow, neither Jewish nor German, was a Russian emigré educated in Europe. One of the first party journalists to write on questions of sex hygiene, Konikow was adamant about women's responsibility to themselves and to the future society. Like Greie-Cramer and the others, Konikow insisted that the responsibility manifest itself within the Socialist party, along the lines set out by the German Social Democrats.[44]

The human material available to these capable leaders was, however, constrained by age and by culture. Despite their determination to draw women away from the auxiliaries and into political activity, despite the *de facto* mandate

from the party leadership, despite frequent educational meetings, yearly conferences, and the visible emergence of a few prominent women in the regular
party branches, the Social Democratic Women's Federation became neither
large nor national in character. Membership increased from a handful in 1900
to nearly 600 in 1908, limited almost entirely to the East. Its strongest centers
lay in the working-class neighborhoods of greater New York and New Jersey—
Long Island City, Morrisania, Jersey City Heights, Elizabeth, Newark, and
Hudson County generally—where the combined proximity to urban sophistication and the intimate ethnic atmosphere created a remarkably close-knit
and political movement of German-American families. To the west, where
political questions had never been foremost in the women's sector, the women's
branches failed to revive. In the East as well, service activities predominated,
albeit under federation auspices. The participants were in all likelihood veterans
of the past movement. Even the younger local leaders, like Charlotte Schneppe
and Anna Stahl of New York, had virtually been raised in the nineteenth-
century Socialist milieu, educated by the *Volkszeitung* and lecturers like Adolf
Douai, married to working-class Socialists, and veterans of the various flag
clubs and press support organizations. They would remain loyal activists to the
end, but their style changed little over the years and had slight appeal to those
outside their shrinking circles.[45]

Ideological constrictions reinforced these limitations. Doctrinally, every advance toward an explicit analysis of women's position was undercut by deep,
historic fears of being associated with the "bourgeois" woman's movement.
Thus Anna Stahl, as foremost functionary, rarely missed an opportunity to
attack heterodox tendencies in the party or to stress that her sex would gain
emancipation "as people, not as women." The party fidelity and class-conscious
rhetoric of notables like Ingerman, Konikow, and Malkiel similarly tended to
overshadow their personal forcefulness as individuals and their determination
to enlighten women in the principles of Socialism. The modest claims made
by Johanna Greie-Cramer for relative autonomy, for the right of women to talk
among themselves and to work out their own tactics, proved to be as controversial in the twentieth century as in decades earlier. The shadows of the past
hung over the reawakening women's movement, never to be dispelled.[46]

The final eclipse of the German women's efforts was forecast by the assimilation of younger women into the English-language branches. In the large
metropolitan areas, where the party became ethnically mixed, new political
opportunities for women appeared. German-American daughters loyal to the
cause need no longer limit themselves to auxiliary work or be bound to ethnic
organizations like the women's federation. Not surprisingly, the membership
rolls of the American branches in Chicago and New York filled with German
and Jewish names. The party was a net gainer. Women geographically ill-placed
or temperamentally ill-suited to work exclusively within the ethnic sector could

extricate themselves socially without forsaking their political faith. The price extracted from the German-American women's movement proved the last the aging pioneers could offer up to their life-long dedication. But in truth its contribution was permanent, for the urban leadership of whatever ethnicity benefited enormously from the strategic patterns set in the nineteenth-century mold.

Meta Stern, Augusta Lilienthal's only daughter, was a case in point. Meta had grown up in a family suffused with the Socialist spirit. Her childhood memories included the exciting Henry George campaign of 1886, the visits of foreign dignitaries Wilhelm Liebknecht and August Bebel, and her own parents' valiant deeds. She received a conscientious education, her freethinking parents having secured private tutors to prepare their daughter in Latin, Greek, and higher mathematics. But like so many children, Meta did not share her parents' aspirations. She entered Barnard College only to drop out and to marry. A young woman, Meta seemed destined to forsake her political heritage and academic training for mere private life. Yet as the Socialist women's movement in both the German-American and indigenous camps gathered momentum, and once her babies were old enough to thrive without a mother's constant watchfulness, Meta reported that she experienced a great mental awakening. She discovered that she, too, had "an individuality . . . an unquenchable thirst for a broader life than one limited by the four walls of the home."

Meta had contributed literary sketches and poems to the Socialist press since the turn of the century under the pen-name "Hebe." She nevertheless studied the Socialist classics for one year before she joined a party local. Her appointment as associate editor of the *Volkszeitung*, succeeding Greie-Cramer as director of the "Frauenecke" (women's corner), combined literary and theoretical tasks into a signal journalistic endeavor lasting more than a decade.

Meta Stern was not fully entrenched in the German-American culture of the *Volkszeitung* readership, but she accepted the responsibility undoubtedly because no one else was suited for the task. Like her mother, she constantly took heterodox positions and urged her sisters to bid for greater autonomy. She strengthened her claim by establishing firm ties with the English-language sections, and contributed agitational articles to the *New York Worker* and the daily *New York Call* after its founding in 1909. She became one of the few persons to press for woman suffrage and women's organization in both German and English and still achieve leadership status. To the extent that the German-American Socialist women's movement came to appreciate the contributions of their native-born sisters, it was Stern's work more than any other that was responsible. Stern also helped other women of German ancestry span the two movements and to break with the orthodox manner of downplaying the woman question without forsaking Socialism.[47]

If Meta Stern chose to retain ties with the German ranks and to try to infuse them with "American" notions, most of the new ethnic recruits destined to achieve party prominence opted for political assimilation. Often born or reared in the United States, more comfortable with English than their parents' native tongue, they abandoned the old circles for the fight within the party mainstream.

Meta Schlichting Berger, in contrast to Stern, was a more characteristic example of assimilation, a "party wife" who eventually established her own place in the movement. When Meta was growing up in what she later described as a "so-called middle class neighborhood" of Milwaukee's South Side, her father, a local school commissioner, befriended a young teacher. In 1897 Meta married this teacher, her own former grammar-school German instructor. Victor Berger was thirteen years Meta's senior, and he set out during their courtship to remake her "according to the pattern he thought a wife should be," by Meta's account. Mostly, she later recalled, "it was difficult," and she remembered spending many "unhappy moments trying to understand and catch up." Victor demanded, for example, that his young fiancée attend various political meetings. She remembered the street corner rallies where she stood "in the shadow of a building or a tree," and the difficulty of discussions, most of which were conducted in German and "way above" her head. When she asked her future husband to explain, he reportedly just laughed " . . . and said, 'Du bist eine dumme Ganz' or he would with some irritation say, 'Das Verstchst Due [sic] nicht.' " After they married, Victor expected his wife to drop her own friends and interests and become his secretary, "adopt his political philosophy—even to become a writer of renown." Meta found it difficult to live up to her husband's expectations. She remembered that when comrades called at their home, she experienced "a secret mortification as talk invariably turned to politics, economics and the international situation." "All I sensed," she later recalled, "was that I was ignored and not of them." During these first years of marriage Meta remembered feeling "humiliated and frustrated" at her lack of political acumen.

In addition to the pressures to grow intellectually, Meta also accepted the responsibilities of a typical German *Hausfrau*. Victor, at this time publishing a weekly German-language Socialist newspaper, could barely make financial ends meet, and after three weeks of marriage he learned that he was a prospective father. Meta was overjoyed, hoping that with a new baby Victor might spend a little more time at home and show some concern for their domestic life. She was soon to be disappointed. Not only did Victor express some chagrin when the baby turned out to be a girl, but Meta realized that the entire care of the baby was to be heaped upon her other duties. All the more determined to achieve an equitable balance of responsibilities, she prodded Victor, only to discover that the master of "scientific" Socialism did not know the first thing about housework and could not even wipe the dishes properly!

Meta continued to forge ahead with her studies, not knowing if she was absorbing anything and worrying all the time "whether or not the baby's bottle was too hot or too cold." She wanted her marriage to be a "true partnership." Even if Victor neglected his portion of household tasks, she would share his commitment. Besides, she realized that her husband admired those women who were active in the Socialist party; wanting his "approval and admiration," she, too, would learn "to do what the courageous venturesome women did." A prominent figure in the movement, Victor attracted a following of "adoring women" who paid "glowing tribute," heaping "mushy compliments" upon him. Meta had several reasons to pursue her course.

Meta's first opportunity appeared when her husband was out of town. The Milwaukee Socialist party had nominated her for the board of education. With much trepidation, and only after receiving assurance that she would in all likelihood lose the election, did she accept the nomination. Much to her surprise, she won.

As a representative on the board of education, Meta Berger developed a political style which would serve her well. The post was especially suited to her talents, for before her marriage she had attended normal school and had worked as a school teacher. She knew the operations of the local school system and excelled as an administrator. After serving an initial six-year term, she was re-elected—a German-American and outspoken Socialist, victorious in the midst of world war patriotism—and eventually served as its president. She defended women's prerogatives from her first meeting, when the board considered a measure which, if adopted, would prohibit women from serving as department heads in Milwaukee high schools. Meta recalled that she forgot "everything except that [she] must defend women and their rights." Shortly thereafter Meta became the leading Socialist in the mainstream woman suffrage movement in Wisconsin.

Despite her commitment to woman's rights, Meta did not play an important role in encouraging women to join the Socialist party. She stated she had always preferred to work with men and therefore had found her political home within the regular party local rather than in the women's auxiliary or study club. Yet as a prominent wife of a prominent leader, she symbolized for many the ideal Socialist woman. Loyal to the party, she had overcome through her political commitment both the limitations of her housewifery and even the subservient role of the auxiliary. Meta Berger became an influential Socialist in her own right, certainly not as powerful within the party as her husband but nevertheless important in the state organization. "Socialism became a real cause to me as it had become to my husband," she later recalled. Because of that shared commitment, Meta and Victor Berger became, she added, "comrades in the real sense of the word and as a result . . . certainly were happy."[48]

Few party wives came close to attaining this ideal. As women left the ethnic sector for the party mainstream, most stood quietly along its periphery. They were ill-equipped to participate in trade unions or political campaigns, and felt uncomfortable at business meetings or during high-powered theoretical discussions. Time, too, was a big problem, for most party wives continued to oversee their households and to serve the party in their auxiliary associations. Few had the freedom Meta Berger acquired by hiring a housekeeper—or the connections with party leaders, or the formal education to pursue doctrinal texts. Yet, like Meta Berger, they sought their husbands' respect and desired to demonstrate their commitment to Socialism.

It was precisely at this point that a core of women organizers relatively new to the Socialist movement played a determining role by helping party wives make the transition from their auxiliaries to the regular local. Native-born sympathizers from the settlement houses, college-educated professionals, and militant Jewish activists, this generation had no taste for the service mentality of the auxiliaries and found the Social Democratic Women's Federation too culturally removed from their experiences. By drawing upon the daughters, literally and figuratively, of the old ethnic base, these exceptionally valuable recruits were instrumental in shaping an English-language women's contingent within the Socialist party.

These urban leaders also designated a distinct strategy. Certainly less gender-conscious than their small-town or Californian counterparts, they sought to arouse a female solidarity essentially as a means rather than an end in itself, as a temporary supplement to the preferred class consciousness. Believing that women should be integrated into the regular party local, they decided to lure women away from their auxiliaries and at the same time demand from the party the equal status promised in its platform.

As their first task, organizers often had to address Socialist men who were apathetic or opposed to their wives' participation. Husbands must come to understand, they implored, that married women bore overwhelming household responsibilities that precluded deep thinking about the great political questions of the day and that a husband's indifference merely exacerbated this situation. Organizers could cite such typical cases as the wife who related that during the "six years in which my husband has been a Socialist, he has a good deal of the time been interested in the local and in public meetings; and he has never yet asked me to attend any of them." A German-American organizer described a characteristic male attitude: "My wife belongs to no clubs. She stays at home, that's better."[49] Other organizers discovered that even sympathetic husbands were often condescending or counterproductive. One party wife explained that she had become "so disgusted with Socialism for breakfast, dinner and supper that I would not join the local for some time after I was converted. . . ." Even the most responsive wife could not bear to hear her husband "talk every day for four or five years, always on the same subject. . . ."[50]

Ultimately, organizers aimed to reach women directly. Nellie Zeh, a Chicago Socialist who never achieved more than regional fame, quickly came to this

conclusion. She remembered that when she filed her application for membership in the party, she was surprised to learn there were no other women in her
branch. She had anticipated a strong representation of women within a movement promising them both political and economic freedom. At first she was
perplexed but soon understood why so few women had joined: "In the first
place our men folks, like ourselves, still have the capitalist mind, and though
they may theorize, read Marx and Bebel, yet when it comes right down to
practice, they feel that the only place for women is in the home. Then, on the
other hand, the women are also held back by the same false teaching and feel
like criminals if they dare venture outside their traditional sphere."[51] Zeh refused
to be put off by this situation. Using the party's register of members and sympathizers, she set herself to locate party wives and became in a short time the
acknowledged master of the neighborhood canvass.

Zeh developed an effective technique as she tracked down party wives in
their homes. She would present herself at a doorstep:

> "Good Morning. Is this Mrs. Jones?"
> "Yes."
> "I am Mrs. Zeh, one of your neighbors."
> At this point I stop and wait expectantly for her to invite me in which she
> nearly always does.
> When seated, I begin by saying, "Mrs. Jones, I have called to talk with
> you regarding some of the evils of the present day civilization." I then adapt
> my talk to her special needs so far as I can judge them from her manner and
> surroundings. If there are children about we may discuss the child labor
> problems, etc.
> I do not use the word Socialism at first, but express the idea of Socialism
> in the terms commonly used by them, so if she knows anything of the subject
> at all she will soon recognize the trend of my talk. If she knows nothing of
> it I continue to talk and explain the existing evils until the ordinary objections
> to Socialism have been answered and then introduce the word by saying
> something like this. "Now I have told you of the great evils of our present
> day, have shown the injustice of the capitalist system, how our great working
> class of men and women and children are defrauded and ground up for
> profits; but I have not told you of the great army that is now forming to
> overthrow this system. There is such an army. It is the International Socialist
> party."

Unless vehemently opposed, Zeh claimed, the listener was now at the stage of
conversion—unless the agent herself was tactless or "does not understand the
philosophy of Socialism herself, or makes her explanation so ambiguous that
the hearer is confused rather than enlightened." The interested woman might
then receive a free leaflet or a nickel pamphlet to read at her leisure. Before

leaving, Zeh would ask the name of the woman's immediate neighbor, to gain an "entering wedge" into the next apartment.[52]

Once outside the door, Zeh recorded her impressions of the interview in a notebook so that she or another canvasser would know what points to seize upon or what arguments to confront during the next visit. If the woman seemed sympathetic but did not eventually fill out the party application Zeh left behind or show up at a branch meeting, Zeh would study the case to ascertain the reasons for such reticence. For example, Zeh told of

> Mrs. C., whose circumstances I can readily remember by referring to my little book. She is an intelligent woman, and her environment and tastes would lead one to think that she would have become a full-fledged Socialist and party member long ago. She attends the lectures of our best speakers and her husband has been a party member for many years. She is heartily in sympathy with the cause, yet it has never occurred to her to join the party. . . .
>
> The husband, somewhat remiss in his duty, I think, nevertheless a good Socialist, has not given any thought to the subject; besides, the wives of other members have not joined. And she feels certain that he would not approve of her going to the ward meetings unless there were other women present.

Zeh concluded that this woman could not be converted without her husband's encouragement. Zeh then approached him directly in order "to get right down to the root of the matter." She patiently explained that his neglect was hindering the progress of Socialism, and "being a reasonable man and a Socialist, he sees the point."[53]

Zeh's path was not always so smooth. At its worst, canvassing was not only wearisome but full of false leads and disappointments. Yet compared to previous neglect, Zeh's efforts were demonstrably successful. She trained other women in the same style and checked with them from time to time, comparing notes and weighing accomplishments. She claimed to be able to measure the impact of this agitation by regularly visiting the various party branches and counting the number of women present. Zeh considered each new recruit a personal victory and a political breakthrough. She recalled a chance meeting with one of her own converts and added, "I can assure you that the little talk we had gave me a greater uplift and more courage for my future work than anything that has happened for a long time. . . ." She advised other women to utilize the networks already existent in the Socialist community. "Just put a bundle of literature under your arm," she enjoined, "and go out among your neighbors."[54]

Urban organizers like Zeh developed a characteristic style unlike that of their small-town or Californian counterparts. Rather than relying upon women's institutions, such as clubs or temperance societies, they utilized the party's networks and worked within the larger Socialist community. Zeh's technique, which retained a hint of parlor talk, was qualitatively different from the after-noon gatherings common in other localities. The culture of woman's sphere did not inform their perspective.

The disparity between the two styles of organizing was not merely idiosyn-cratic but indicative of larger ideological and strategic differences between the two sectors. Unlike their small-town or rural counterparts, urban organizers had a low regard for the traditional source of women's power and prestige, the home. Although they often approached women as housewives, they did not envision the home as a potential site of political education but, rather, termed it the prison of timid women, a place to be shunted aside while women took their stands in civil society. In their propaganda urban organizers emphasized the oppressive aspects of woman's domestic role rather than its nobility. Such was the case of Marie Jayne's "Of Interest to Women" column published in the *Chicago Daily Socialist* in 1907–8. The editor advised women to reduce the amount of time devoted to household duties even if it meant abandoning the once-sacred parlor. [55] Other journalists displayed similar attitudes toward tra-ditional notions of womanhood. One writer insisted that the woman of today had less faith in "virtues that were once deemed distinctly womanly, but were in reality the virtues of the slave." Another explained that today's woman was "less a creature of sex," and she therefore disdained all signs of "over-femini-zation in her character." [56] As one writer phrased the urban consensus, an "un-derstanding of social consciousness" must arouse in each woman "a hatred for the narrow humiliating sphere in which she is compelled to live." [57]

This negative assessment of woman's sphere also showed itself in the forms of organization preferred by uban leaders. Where small-town organizers drew upon a female culture still vibrant in their locales and built a network of au-tonomous women's clubs, their urban counterparts aimed to integrate women directly into the regular party local. Often they faced resistance, for the majority of women could not imagine working alongside their husbands in a political endeavor. The urban leaders therefore compromised and advised the women's auxiliaries to prove their loyalty to the Socialist party by requesting formal affiliation. When the Chicago Ladies' Auxiliary became the "Ladies' Branch," the urban leaders thus rejoiced in a symbolic victory. [58] Failing to integrate women, urban organizers encouraged women to model their branches upon the mixed local. Compared to their small-town sisters, they downplayed self-help programs and concentrated instead on public agitational campaigns. They expected their ranks to be familiar with parliamentary procedure and prepared to devote themselves to the business affairs of the regular local. Above all, urban leaders encouraged members of the ladies' branch to attend meetings of the local, to participate as much as possible, and to look forward to the time when their separate organizations would become unnecessary.

from *New Yorker Volkszeitung*, Feb. 26, 1911

Johanna Greie Cramer

from *My Story of the War* (1889)

Mary A. Livermore

Frances Willard

Elizabeth J. Morgan

Populist Women

from *The Arena*, July, 1892

Mrs. S. E. V. Emery

Fannie Vickrey

Mrs. Bettie Gay

from *The Arena*, July, 1892

Marion Todd

State Historical Society of Wisconsin

Corinne S. Brown

KATE O'HARE

CHARLOTTE PERKINS STETSON.

FRANCES WILLARD.

LUELLA R. KRAYBILL.

MOTHER JONES.

MARION H. DUNHAM.

MRS. R.F. ORR.

WENONA STEVENS ABBOTT.

MAY WOOD SIMONS.

MISS AGNES WAKEFIELD.

Socialist Women Activists

Josephine Conger Kaneko at desk, *c.* 1909

Meta Stern Lilienthal   Meta Berger

The urban-based Socialist women's movement thus carried within it a distinct heritage of the nineteenth century. It gathered steam more slowly than its counterpart in the Plains states and in California because the task of forging a coherent sector of diverse elements proved exceedingly difficult. The older German-American *Genossinnen* and their partially assimilated daughters, the recently immigrated Jewish women, and a second generation of native-born sympathizers represented an unwieldy constituency. Cultural and generational differences constantly pulled the various elements apart. Despite this problem, urban Socialist women outlined a distinct policy reminiscent of their forebears' in the small nineteenth-century Socialist Labor party: loyalty to the party, suspicion of independent women's organizations, and the desire to integrate women into the Socialist mainstream. More firmly established than in previous decades and blessed by the prestigious Second International, Socialist women in the major cities set their own standards of Socialist womanhood.

THE WOMAN'S NATIONAL SOCIALIST UNION

Almost from the first days of the party's existence, as an ambitious few aimed to create a national Socialist women's movement, the major differences between the two sectors proved a strong obstacle. Veteran campaigners might wish to avoid the self-isolation caused by sectarianism. They might take genuine pride in the accomplishments of distant comrades. They might exchange greetings, correspond occasionally, or cluster together at various party functions. Most definitely, Socialist women regardless of predilection hoped to combat male prejudice and achieve equal status within the larger movement. And they recognized the benefit of taking a united stand. Despite good intentions, disagreements abounded over basic principles and especially over the all-important question of affiliation—the ultimate test of loyalty *qua* class consciousness, in the eyes of some.

The most successfully organized and independent-minded, Socialist women in the Plains states and in California issued the first call for national unity. In 1901 Los Angeles women promulgated a document which was reprinted widely in the party press. In it they appealed to all women "whose souls throb responsible to freedom and duty, all who seek to be loyal to God and humanity . . . to take part in this world struggle for the elevation of mankind and to enroll themselves as members of the Woman's National Socialist League."[59] A temporary committee, mostly veterans of the late nineteenth-century woman's movement, took up the familiar task of seeking all potential affiliates.

Although women in the urban-based locals responded to the call, they nevertheless did so on their own terms. Veteran Socialist women in New York and in Chicago issued their own statements concerning the strategic needs of women. Within a short time it was clear that cooperation among the various sectors would be achieved only with great difficulty.

Indeed, the ensuing conflicts mirrored, in almost uncanny fashion, the dual heritage of Socialist women. The two major protagonists of women's organization thus appeared as ghosts of movements past. Wenonah Stevens Abbott of California and Imogene C. Fales of New York, each with political histories reaching back to the 1880s, had followed different paths to Socialism. Fales had taken part in the woman's movement but had served primarily among male reformers. She had been a principal exponent of the Rochdale Cooperative plan, moved through the Bellamy Nationalist movement and into the Socialist Labor party and the short-lived Brotherhood of the Cooperative Commonwealth, and finally to the Social Democracy and the Socialist party. By the early years of the twentieth century she was well known among Socialists and sympathizers for her pamphlet on cooperation. Fales considered herself a leader among women in the principles of "scientific" Socialism.[60] Abbott, by contrast, traced her roots to the woman's movement. She described herself as an aristocrat by "ancestry and training" who, because of circumstances, had become "a class conscious working woman." Born into a prominent New England family, she had married well and, like so many middle-class women, had become interested in programs to aid workingwomen and to improve the conditions of their labor. The tables soon turned. At age twenty-two and with two small children to rear, she faced life as a self-supporting widow. She worked in a sweatshop, took up dressmaking for a time, and finally found a good income in writing. As the popular "Cricket" and "Sunshine," author of children's stories, Abbott re-entered the woman's movement and became a major activist in the WCTU. Under Willard's influence, she became a Christian Socialist and a prominent member of a local Los Angeles society. She joined the Socialist party at its inception.[61] Abbott and Fales thus represented the twains of Socialist women's political heritage.

In negotiating plans for the national organization, Fales and Abbott disagreed on most issues. Fales drafted a constitution that, according to the more club-oriented Abbott, gave too much power to the executive. Fales disliked Abbott's suggestion for the name of the prospective organization. Abbott complained that Fales's propaganda technique was "iconoclastic" rather than constructive. Fales charged Abbott with fearing real class conflict and with promoting a "timid conservative policy" that couched "all its utterances in terms of love." And so they quibbled incessantly.

The real bone of contention was the relationship between the prospective women's organization and the Socialist party itself. On this point the disagreement was significant. Abbott conceived of the Woman's National Socialist Union as an association outside the party's jurisdiction, as a mechanism to guarantee political autonomy to the women's sector. Fales rejected this position; she declared that in the "militant Socialist movement . . . there is room and work for women as well as for men, on perfectly equal footing. . . ." If Abbott's constituents would not affiliate with the party, Fales would ask her followers to withdraw from the venture. Both sides held their positions. Fales led New York City women in a formal protest against Abbott's wing; they charged the independent-minded women with empty sentimentalism and treason to the Socialist party.[62] Negotiations broke down.

The proponents of women's autonomy were not likely to yield to political bludgeoning. With their independent heritage and guarantee of party democracy in hand, they turned the charges against their accusers. Were women disloyal, they asked, or did men by practicing discrimination force women into separate societies? Previously discreet about such tensions within party life, some women now publicly cited instances of intolerable conditions. In San Francisco, one woman reported, the appointment of a woman to an *ad hoc* committee caused the resignation of a prominent male comrade who "refused to allow his name to stand with that of a woman." The response of the local was hardly encouraging; the comrades staged a debate, "Resolved, That Women Are an Important Factor in Socialism."[63] To women, this matter was not debatable. As the editor of the *Comrade* affirmed, such complaints only scratched the surface of a grim reality:

> At most [women] are treated with amused indulgence in much the same manner as children are treated. Open, frank, and equal comradeship is very rarely shown toward even the few women, who find their way into the party organization. If a woman is brave enough to face the ostracism of the rest of her sex and society generally to take the platform in the interest of Socialist propaganda, she is permitted—and even encouraged—to do so as a "drawing card." And when money raising schemes are set afoot women are welcome more heartily for the reason that they are "specially adapted" to some of the work, generally the most arduous and least pleasant, involved in such schemes. For the rest there is toleration rather than welcome for them. And, as a consequence of this, many women of enthusiasm and ability have given up the attempt to work within the regular party organization and establish separate organizations for themselves. . . .[64]

The Woman's National Socialist Union, then, took as its task the organization of women but not necessarily their recruitment into the regular party local. Even when women lost their inhibitions about public agitation, organizer Marion Dunham affirmed, they might stand apart. "[N]ot all men who call themselves Socialists," she explained, "are fully so where women are concerned. They do not hold to absolute equality of rights between men and women just as firmly as to equality among men. The old habit of considering [women] a dependent, if not inferior class, still clings to them. . . ."[65] Abbott's conviction, that women were constitutionally "fitted to work along original lines," also gained practical strategic implications.[66] Women needed their own associations and would continue to need them for the foreseeable future, or until such time when discrimination had no place in the Socialist party. The protocol of their WNSU affirmed women's distinctive task on still other grounds. Preaching the doctrine of "universal cooperation founded upon the Golden Rule of love and justice," Abbott and her friends hinted at a feminine vision of Socialism organically tied to women's reform heritage, allied with rather than submerged into the proletarian quest.[67]

WNSU leaders succeeded only in igniting a spark of national consciousness among their geographically scattered constituents. Abbott, slowed by ill-health, toured the Midwest under Marion Dunham's auspices. Through correspondence and personal contacts, local affiliates increased in 1902 and 1903, notably in California and in Kansas, where Luella Krehbiel directed an impressive statewide convention. Elsewhere the organization made little headway. Within party ranks, on the other hand, women had scarcely any presence at all. As Abbott and her co-workers warned, Socialist women had only begun their work.[68]

Armed with the initiative, the WNSU luminaries called a special meeting to be held at the time of the party's national convention.[69] At this first national meeting of Socialist women held in 1904, delegates once more reproduced the crucial differences separating the two major sectors. A resolution, "That the separate organization of women is conducive to the good of the Socialist cause, tends to upbuild the party organization, and must be done if the sex is not to be a drag when the Co-operative Commonwealth is initiated," provoked a heated discussion. The supporters of the motion included the champions of the nineteenth-century woman's movement. Corinne Brown, who chaired the session, upheld the vision of the WNSU; she wished "people would get rid of the idea that women are organizing to antagonize the male portion of the Socialist party." A surviving and venerable leader of the old spiritualist and social purity movements, Lucinda Chandler, also supported the union and credited it with having initiated a new wave of revolutionary activism. Against these aging giants gathered mostly younger urbanites who criticized the WNSU largely by paraphrasing the objections Fales had stated. The union, they said, discouraged women from joining the party and limited their activities to self-education when the necessity of public agitation loomed paramount.[70] The differences between the sectors could not be reconciled.

Party loyalists had time on their side. When Socialist women finally established a national movement, they did so according to procedures outlined by the nascent urban leaders. Party journalism played an important part in tipping the balance; after the 1904 meetings Socialist newspapers attacked independent women's clubs as bands of infidels. But the development of the Socialist party itself made the decisive difference. Located near the seats of party bureaucracy, urban organizers took advantage of the relatively rapid growth of membership in major cities. Guided by agitators like Nellie Zeh, they began to form strong women's branches around 1907 and recruited women to the regular mixed locals. A few women gained regular access to Socialist newspapers and issued a barrage of propaganda calling upon their unorganized sisters to join their ranks. In contrast, the independent Socialist women's clubs centered in the Plains states and in California had reached a stasis. Despite promising beginnings, they could not sustain the momentum. Most disappointing, their plans for an independent federation had clearly failed.

The quest for unity had taken an ironic turn. As many elderly defenders of women's autonomy either bowed to the popular mood or retired, party enthusiasts intensified their efforts to recruit women directly to the party locals. The traditions shaped by the nineteenth-century woman's movement, the initial source of solidarity, faded from view as a rising generation of women recast the movement in their own image.

Wenonah Stevens Abbott thereby remained the prophetic representative of an older movement lodged inside modern Socialism. In a sense this imagery is fitting, for Abbott had envisioned woman acting as a moral force upon humanity's best instincts. But as she made her last tours and retired infirm to a ranch in southern California, finally limited to editing a woman's department in the Christian Socialist *Vanguard* and writing "Chats for Young Folks" in the *Coming Nation*, she could not help expressing resentment against those Socialists who had misrepresented her purposes. Those who described her as "liberal" were not, she believed, referring so much to her faith in a peaceful transformation as to her commitment to work primarily among women and children. "When all children are born with adult brains, all women evolved to a knowledge that before they are women they are human souls," she explained, "I shall rest. Until then, I can not." How could women be reached? It was not a simple matter of "scientific" and "economic" propaganda alone:

> I want [women] to see the truth. If they can most master it by having it made amusing, so be it. If they must see the world's pain and search for truth in an effort to relieve it, well and good. If they are so self-centered that a personal appeal must be made, make that. If you can only reach the head by working through the heart, take that route; and if the path leads through the stomach, take advantage of that. WAKE THEM UP. After you accomplish that Herculean task, give them strong scientific food; but do not become discouraged when you find that intellectual babes can not digest meat. Try milk instead. If it is pure and wholesome, it will help them thrive and prepare them for your own diet.[71]

Abbott's lesson was enduring. Organizers would return to it repeatedly, not because women were incapable of intellectual effort but because each constituency had its distinctive, historic needs. Abbott had also touched, less in her words than in her deeds, upon a larger truth. The strength of her appeal lay in her easy relationship with her grass-roots constituency of women. No organizational sophistication could substitute for the organic bonds of sisterhood that she enjoyed there, just as no theoretical expertise could provide successful propaganda if alien to its intended audience. Still, it was possible that the Socialist women's movement might prosper given access to the party machinery and support of party officials and luminaries. But how far this path could be traveled, how much women could gain within the regular locals, depended upon factors too complex for Abbott to predict.

NOTES

1. Anna Gordon, *The Beautiful Life of Frances Willard* (Chicago, 1898).
2. The Socialist party published *Elizabeth Cady Stanton on Socialism* as an agitational leaflet; its circulation was never as great as Willard's 1897 address. Socialists did, however, claim Stanton as their own. Leonard D. Abbott, "A Tribute to Elizabeth Cady Stanton," *Comrade*, 2 (Dec., 1902), 58, wrote that in "economics Mrs. Stanton was quite definitely a Socialist. . . ."
3. Caroline Nelson, editor of the "Women's Department," in the *Oakland* (Calif.) *World*, Oct. 3, 1908.
4. For a vivid rendition of this interpretation, note Mrs. J. P. Roe's text "Socialism and Women," which she read to the Socialist Literary Club of Omaha, and her "If Christ Came to Omaha"; see *Nebraska Socialist* (Omaha), Dec. 15, 1900, and Jan. 5, 1901. See also "One Woman's Conviction," *Vanguard*, 2 (Nov., 1903), 6–7, which claimed that "Miss Willard's acceptance of Socialism was the most natural thing in the world. . . ." Mrs. Julia Smith Hobson, Sedan, Kans., wrote a letter to the *Socialist Woman*, 1 (Nov., 1907), 11, in which she claimed that she decided to work for Socialism when she "learned of the stand Frances Willard took shortly before her departure [death]."
5. For excellent descriptions of Socialist encampments, see *Coming Nation* (Girard, Kans.), Nov. 19, 1910, and Ida Crouch Hazlett's column in the *New York Call*, May 15, 1916. James R. Green, *Grass-Roots Socialism: Radical Movements in the Southwest 1895–1943* (Baton Rouge, La., 1978), describes this regional movement in rich detail. The funeral oration of Eugene Debs was reprinted in *St. Louis Labor*, May 12, 1906.
6. *Appeal to Reason* (Girard, Kans.), Mar. 22, 1902. A biographical sketch of O'Hare appears in *Socialist Woman*, 2 (Oct., 1908), 4, 5. O'Hare relates portions of her childhood in *The Sorrows of Cupid* (St. Louis, 1912). See Ch. 7 for a full analysis and description. Frank and Kate were married on Jan. 1, 1902, in the home of J. A. Wayland; the Reverend Walter Thomas Mills officiated; see *Appeal to Reason*, Jan. 4, 1902.
7. Josephine Conger in *Appeal to Reason*, May 9, 1903.
8. Mary Pierce Roe in *Los Angeles Socialist*, Oct. 18, 1902. See also similar reports of the Woman's Socialist Union of Fargo in *Common Sense* (Los Angeles), Mar. 18, 1905, and the Ladies Social Economy Club, Sioux City, Iowa, in *Iowa Socialist* (Dubuque), Dec. 18, 1902.

9. "President's Address," *Proceedings of the Third Annual Meeting of the WCTU of the State of Iowa, October, 1892* (Burlington, 1892), 14–30. A biographical sketch of Dunham appears in Frances E. Willard and Mary A. Livermore, eds., *A Woman of the Century* (New York, 1893), 263. Marion Howard was born in Ohio, Dec. 6, 1842, and spent her childhood on a farm. She began teaching school at age fifteen, and in 1873 married C. A. Dunham, an architect in Burlington, Iowa. On Dunham's suffrage advocacy within the WCTU, see, "The President's Message to Her Comrades," *Union Signal* (Chicago), Feb. 12, 1891; on her Socialist commitments, see *Los Angeles Socialist*, Oct. 25, 1902, and *Chicago Daily Socialist*, July 23, 1908.

10. Luella Roberts was born near Winfield, Kans., on Nov. 28, 1866. Biographical sketches appear in *Chicago Daily Socialist*, May 10, 1907, and *Socialist Woman*, 1 (July, 1907), 3. For Krehbiel's statement on the necessity of women joining the class struggle, see *Appeal to Reason*, Oct. 10, 1903, and "Woman, the World Is Waiting for You," *Socialist Woman*, 1 (May, 1907), 4. Krehbiel's organizing tours were reported throughout 1903 and 1904 in *Social Ethics, Appeal to Reason*, and *Iowa Socialist*.

11. J. A. Wayland, *Leaves of Life* (Girard, Kans., 1912), 232–33. For a description and history of the *Appeal*, see Paul M. Buhle's essay in Joseph Conlin, ed., *The Radical Press in the United States, 1890–1960*, 2 vols. (Westport, Conn., 1974), I, 50–59.

12. Josephine Conger's autobiographical sketch appeared in the *Chicago Daily Socialist*, May 20, 1907. See also *Woman's Who's Who in America, 1914–1915*, ed. John W. Leonard (New York, 1914), 444.

13. *Appeal to Reason*, Apr. 18, 1903 and Apr. 25, 1903. Wayland called for a Women's Legion, apparently without success, in the Dec. 22, 1902, issue of the *Appeal*. For a description of the *Appeal* army, see James R. Green, "The 'Salesmen-Soldiers' of the *Appeal* Army: A Profile of Rank-and-File Socialist Agitators," in Bruce Stave, ed., *Socialism and the Cities* (Port Washington, N.Y., 1975), 13–40.

14. Conger reported having received 1,157 names of women, and a few from men who professed a special interest in this phase of the movement. She did not include men's names because she preferred to keep her effort "a purely feminine proposition"; see *Appeal to Reason*, Oct. 10, 1903.

15. *Appeal to Reason*, May 2, 30, 1903.

16. For example, *New Life* (Lewiston, Okla.), Oct., 1904, contained a column on the relationship of New Thought and Socialism and stressed in subsequent issues its implications for women's advancement. Addie Ballou still promoted woman's cause in the spiritualist, progressive sheet *Forward Movement*, published in Los Angeles at the turn of the century. For a scholarly interpretation of New Thought, Gail Thain Parker, *Mind Cure in New England* (Hanover, N.H., 1973), is informative but limited to the leading intellectuals. For a geographically more comprehensive treatment, see Charles S. Braden, *Spirits in Rebellion* (Dallas, 1963). Most loyal to the contemporary spirit, advocate-historian Horatio W. Dresser, *History of the New Thought Movement* (New York, 1919), is the most revealing.

17. See especially *Social Ethics* (Enterprise and Wichita, Kans.), Jan. 29, Feb. 14, Mar. 28, 1903, Aug. 18, 1904. For a recent study of this paper's colorful editor, see Ina Turner Gray and Phillip E. Chastain, "Granville Lowther—Heretic or Herald," *Kansas History*, 1 (Aug., 1978), 177–82.

18. *Social Ethics*, Feb. 14, 1903.

19. *The Echo* (Galena, Kans.), Mar. 19, 1914.
20. *Appeal to Reason*, Oct. 24, 1903.
21. *Ibid.*, May 9, 16, 23, 30, 1903, May 4, 1904.
22. *Ibid.*, May 2, 9, 23, 30, 1903.
23. Josephine Conger, "Practical Suggestions," *Woman's Tribune* (Washington, D.C.), Oct. 24, 1903. Clary Colby, however, did not believe that women should ally with any party until they had won their political rights. She felt that, once enfranchised, women would have a "quieting and conservative influence" on the Socialist party; see "Socialism and Suffrage," *Woman's Tribune*, Dec. 26, 1903. Colby did on occasion give guest lectures before Socialist women's meetings; see *Challenge* (Los Angeles), July 24, 1901. Susan B. Anthony also warned Conger against putting "trust in men's party promises"; Conger published Anthony's letter in *Appeal to Reason*, May 30, 1903.
24. *Appeal to Reason*, Oct. 24, 1903.
25. "Objections to Socialism, 2. 'Socialism Will Break Up the Home,' " *Vanguard*, 1 (Feb., 1903), 14–15.
26. Lula McClure-Clark, Edith, Colo., writing in *Appeal to Reason*, Aug. 15, 1903.
27. Ada K. Schell in *Iowa Socialist*, Oct. 24, 1903; *Appeal to Reason*, Apr. 30, 1904.
28. *Appeal to Reason*, May 2, 1903.
29. B. O. Flower, "Topic of the Times," *Arena*, 30 (July, 1903), 100; Agnes Wakefield, Souvenir Program, Fifth Annual Picnic of the Socialist Party of Boston, July 4, 1903.
30. Reports of activities in *Los Angeles Socialist*, Oct. 31, 1903, Apr. 2, 1904; *Appeal to Reason*, Mar. 5, 1904.
31. Reports on early organization in *Los Angeles Socialist*, Nov. 23, 30, Dec. 21, 1901. See also *The Worker* (New York), Aug. 31, 1902. On the Los Angeles Socialist party generally, Grace Heilman Stimson, *Rise of the Labor Movement in Los Angeles* (Berkeley, Calif., 1955), 255, provides some information. On the Los Angeles woman's movement, Reda Davis, *California Women: A Guide to Their Politics, 1885–1911* (San Francisco, 1967), 11, 118, supplies information about Socialists.
32. *Los Angeles Socialist*, Dec. 21, 1901. Biographical data on Garbutt may be found in *American Woman's Who's Who, 1914–1915*, 315, and in *Socialist Woman*, 2 (June, 1908), 2. Mary Alderman was born in Salem, N.J., in 1844. She began teaching school at age eighteen and continued for the next twenty-five years. In 1867 she married Frank Clarkson Garbutt, a mining engineer and manufacturer; in 1882 she moved to Los Angeles. Garbutt worked devotedly for the WCTU for over twenty-five years. Her Populist activities were recorded in the *Woman's Journal* (Boston), Oct. 22, 1891. For details of her husband's career, see *Who's Who in Pacific Southwest* (Los Angeles, 1913), 151–52.
33. *Los Angeles Socialist*, Aug. 23, Oct. 4, 1902.
34. *Ibid.*, Dec. 21, 1901. Various reports of local activity in San Jose, Pasadena, and San Diego appear in *Los Angeles Socialist* throughout 1903 and 1904.
35. Letter from Mary Livermore, dated Jan. 30, 1903, was published in *Comrade*, 2 (June, 1903), 216.
36. Algernon Lee in *Haverhill* (Mass.) *Social Democrat*, Dec. 15, 1900.
37. Josephine Conger's report in *Appeal to Reason*, Feb. 24, 1904. May Wood Simons, reporting in the *Workers' Call* (Chicago), Apr. 13, 1901, estimated that

of the 1,200 Socialist party members in Chicago at that time, no more than fifty were women.

38. Charlotte Baum, Paula Hyman, and Sonya Michel, *Jewish Woman in America* (New York, 1975), Ch. 3 and 4.
39. *Di Arbeter-Tseitung* (Yiddish—New York), Nov. 28, Dec. 5, 10, 1890, Jan. 2, 18, Mar. 13, May 22, July 3, Aug. 14, 28, 1891, Sept. 18, 1891; A. S. Sachs, *Di Geshikhte fun Arbeiter Ring 1892–1925*, 2 vols. (Yiddish—New York, 1925), I, 213–15, 253–58.
40. *New Yorker Volkszeitung*, Feb. 8, 15, 1903.
41. Werner Thönnessen, *The Emancipation of Women* (London, 1973), 52–54; Jean Quataert, *Reluctant Feminists in German Social Democracy, 1885–1917* (Princeton, N.J., 1979), 140–46, describes the independent organization of women as a function of the legal bans on women's political participation then existing in Germany. For documents on women's organization, see *Dokumente der revolutionaeren deutschen Arbeiterbewegung zur Frauenfrage, 1848–1974* (Leipzig, 1975), 32–34, 36–38.
42. *New Yorker Volkszeitung*, Jan. 19, 26, Mar. 22, June 15, 1902.
43. *Ibid.*, Dec. 1, 8, 1901.
44. For a full treatment of Antoinette Konikow, see Ch. 7. On Ingerman, see *Der Abend Blatt* (Yiddish—New York), May 2, 1895. Eulogistic clippings about Anna Amitin Ingerman (1865–1931) are found in the Sergie Ingerman Papers, Tamiment Library, New York University: *New Yorker Volkszeitung, Jewish Daily Forward*, and *New York Times*, all for May 21, 1931.
45. *New Yorker Volkszeitung*, Feb. 26, 1911.
46. *Ibid.*, Dec. 29, 1901, Oct. 13, 1902, Feb. 22, 1903. Similar comments, such as attacks on women's clubs and appeals to "proletarian" women, appeared in the *Workers' Call*; see, for example, articles by Myra Strawn, Sept. 23, Dec. 3, 1899.
47. "Hebe" [Meta Stern], "How I Became a Socialist," *Socialist Woman*, 1 (Jan., 1908), 4–5. Meta Lilienthal, *Dear Remembered World* (New York, 1947), concerns New York City life as the author recalls her childhood.
48. Unpublished autobiography (typescript), Meta Berger Papers, State Historical Society of Wisconsin.
49. Frank Hubschmitt in *New York Call*, Nov. 21, 1909; Kiichi Kaneko, "Where Is Your Wife?" *Socialist Woman*, 1 (Aug., 1907), 6; *New Yorker Volkszeitung*, Nov. 1, 1911.
50. *National Socialist* (Washington, D.C.), Mar. 5, 1913.
51. *Chicago Daily Socialist*, Feb. 27, 1909.
52. *Ibid.*, Aug. 24, 1908.
53. *Ibid.*, June 27, 1908.
54. *Ibid.*, June 13, 1908.
55. *Ibid.*, May 25, 27, 1907.
56. "Hebe" in *New York Call*, Mar. 1, 1909.
57. Helen Untermann, "The Man and the Woman," *Progressive Woman*, 5 (Aug., 1911), 13.
58. *Chicago Daily Socialist*, Feb. 15, 1907.
59. *Appeal to Reason*, Nov. 23, 1901.
60. Reports of Fales's Nationalist activity appeared in the *California Nationalist* (Los Angeles), Feb. 22, 1890, and the *New Nation*, 1 (June 4, 1891), 370. On

Fales's later political inclinations, see her article on women and the Social Democracy in the *Social Democrat* (Chicago), May 5, 1898.

61. See the biographical sketch of Abbott by Mary Garbutt in *Socialist Woman*, 2 (Jan., 1909), 2.

62. *Los Angeles Socialist*, Jan. 11, Feb. 1, 15, Mar. 8, 1902; *The Worker*, Jan. 19, 1902.

63. *California Socialist* (San Francisco), Aug. 22, 1903.

64. *Comrade*, 3 (Oct., 1903), 12.

65. *Vanguard*, 2 (Nov., 1903), 19.

66. Wenonah Stevens Abbott, "Women's Department," *Vanguard*, 2 (Jan., 1904), 16; letter to *Wilshire's Magazine*, Sept., 1902, 68-69. See also Abbott's essay on the WNSU in *Comrade*, (Oct., 1902), 3–4.

67. *Appeal to Reason*, Apr. 16, 1904.

68. Abbott and Dunham sent regular reports to the Socialist press. See, for example, *Iowa Socialist*, Mar. 7, 1903; *Appeal to Reason*, June 27, 1903; *Los Angeles Socialist*, Nov. 7, 1903. For Kansas reports, see *Appeal to Reason*, Feb. 27, Apr. 16, 1904; *Los Angeles Socialist*, Apr. 16, 1904.

69. Wenonah Stevens Abbott in *Vanguard*, 2 (Mar., 1904), 20; *Los Angeles Socialist*, Mar. 12, 1904.

70. *Vanguard*, 2 (May, 1904), 18–19; (June, 1904), 17–19; *Los Angeles Socialist*, May 21, 1904. Critical commentary appeared in *Iowa Socialist*, May 7, 1904.

71. "Let's Talk about It," *Vanguard*, 2 (Apr., 1904), 17–19.

4 The Woman's National Committee, 1908–13

Out from the cloister recesses,
    Where moulder heredities' claims:
Out from the passions' excesses
    With the clank of its rust-eaten chains;
Out from base toil with its discord,
    Out from fashion's mad whirl,
Out! O my sisters in bondage—
    Out into the heart of the world!

Out from the wisdom of sages,
    Usurping the spirit's control,
Out from time's obsolete pages
    That enslave the omnipotent soul,
Out from barren assumptions
    That sit with free banners unfurled,
Out! O my sisters in bondage—
    Out into the heart of the world!

Ellen T. Wetherell, "Out! O My Sisters in Bondage"
International Socialist Review (1908)

Around 1907–8, with the appearance of women's branches in urban areas and the rise of a younger generation of leaders, the Socialist women's movement reached a new stage. The movement was still regionally and ethnically complex, no closer to resolving internal differences than in 1904. It showed signs, however, of adapting to shifts in the centers of Socialist activity. The women attached to the municipal party, as in New York and Chicago, or gaining stature within the regional bureaucracies were ideally situated to chart a new course. They acquired a sanction unknown to their predecessors. Not that the party ever wholeheartedly encouraged women to organize or allocated significant resources for that end, but after 1908 it did officially recognize women as a constituent element of the class struggle. This change in policy marked the final eclipse of the independent sector of the Socialist women's movement and the inauguration of a new era.

Changes within the Socialist movement in general influenced the course of women's activities. The party's formative years had been marked by an aura of self-confidence. Traces of dogmatism, considered the legacy of nineteenth-century Socialism, fell to disrepute, even while writers more regularly quoted Marx to justify their interpretations of history or current events. But agitators also recited common-sense explanations of the causes of social injustice, the evils of capitalism, and the promise of Socialism; they rarely haggled over the fine points of theory. At most, various sectors complained of the party's insuf-ficiently "proletarian" character, only to receive the answer that active recruit-ment rather than phraseology would induce the desired changes. In many areas the locals grew into well-oiled machines, gaining votes and support with almost every passing year so that Socialists began to calculate the probability of a million-fold membership and national electoral victory. Membership in this crusade required little more than an avowal of faith in the Cooperative Com-monwealth and commitment to recruit new members. However heterodox, women found a warm welcome.

As the party passed the propaganda stage and became a political contender to the major parties, it lost some of its flexibility. The leadership bent to the needs of a tighter organizational structure and more distinctive political profile. Simply to service a rapidly growing network of locals, leaders demanded greater centralization and more efficient bureaucratic mechanisms for coordinating programs. Local prerogatives gave way somewhat to the directives of the national office in Chicago, despite the party's firm commitment to the principle of local autonomy. The party press was perhaps the best measure of this shift in mood, as the journalistic staple of propaganda paled next to the growing numbers of articles on strategy, tactics, and internal party policy. The agitational giant, the *Appeal to Reason*, declined in prestige as many readers turned to the new dailies more closely attuned to party protocol, such as the *Chicago Daily Socialist*, the *New York Call*, or even the maverick *International Socialist Review*, which pointedly bucked party labor policies. National party politics had hardly mattered in 1901 or 1904; the rank-and-file seemed then to care only about the presidential candidate and campaign, the slate of "immediate demands," and the stock of leaflets supplied by the national office. By 1907 the national office had asked these local members—including women—to hew to a narrower line.

In addition to changes in national policy, European turns also cast their influence over American events. The well-organized and highly respected Socialist women's leadership of Germany had for years been raising the woman question at various meetings and finally in 1907 prepared a salient resolution to be presented at the upcoming Stuttgart conference. German women advocated that all member parties undertake a serious campaign for woman suffrage and, most important, insisted that Socialists conduct their agitation under the sole auspices of the party and apart from the mainstream women's movement. In sum, German women were asking for the highest tribunal of Socialists to recommend a comprehensive program for women that would specify both methods of propaganda and modes of organization. If adopted, their resolution would oblige American Socialists to follow suit.[1]

These developments at the national and international levels necessarily affected the course of the nascent Socialist women's movement, especially as the party began to bolster its appeal to women. The secretary of Local Cook County, for example, sent a memorandum to each city branch demanding that special programs be instituted to attract women to meetings. Various locals debated the issue of women's dues, and resolved that women relinquish their privilege of reduced rates and accept along with the party's pledge of equality a full measure of financial responsibility. A few important newspapers, including *St. Louis Labor* and the *Chicago Daily Socialist*, followed the precedent set by the *New Yorker Volkszeitung* and converted their pages of fashions and recipes to politically sophisticated women's departments. Several key women's clubs responded to such pressure by requesting formal affiliation as branches of the local. The remaining clubs, once merely troublesome, now took on the character of organizational renegades. Left to themselves, the various sectors of the Socialist women's movement might have reached a compromise on the weighty questions of affiliation and style, probably by continuing to abide by local customs. The trend toward centralization within the party at large, however, reduced their options; the resolutions presented by German women and adopted by the Second International in August, 1907, narrowed choices still further.[2]

Party leaders meanwhile sought to foreclose immediately on women's organizational autonomy. Writing in the *International Socialist Review*, John Spargo chided men for their indifference to women's issues and failure to win women's trust. Naturally, he concluded, women had taken matters into their own hands and formed their own, separate organizations now on the verge of blossoming into a national movement. To quell this tendency, Spargo suggested the creation of an official bureau or committee for women's affairs *within* the Socialist party.[3] In January, 1908, the National Executive Committee responded by approving a formal resolution specifying the appointment of a national lecturer to conduct an agitational campaign among sympathetic yet independent women.[4] At its next convention, scheduled for May, 1908, the party would for the first time address the question of women's status in the movement and, most important, outline an official policy on the form of organization.

Not all Socialist women fell passively into line. Josephine Conger, for her part, encouraged women to take advantage of the new mood to accelerate their work but on their own terms. With the help of her husband, the prominent Japanese Socialist Kiichi Kaneko, she created a new magazine, the *Socialist Woman*. With a list of only twenty-six subscribers she brought out the first issue in June, 1907, dedicated to the awakening of women, their training in basic concepts of Socialism, and their recruitment to organized activity. Over the next several years her magazine would serve as the single most important source of propaganda and news of the women's sector. Although Conger-Kaneko fully utilized party resources, she remained heterodox, as indicated by her rapid departure from the seat of the national office, Chicago, and resettlement in comfortable Girard, and by her adoption in 1909 of a new name, *Progressive Woman*, which she hoped would attract a larger readership.[5]

Especially during its first year of publication, the *Socialist Woman* gave the appearance of being a daughter publication to the *Appeal to Reason* and the column Conger previously edited. She published now, as before, a sample of letters from the rural readership cut off from the larger Socialist movement except by mail. A cover photograph lionized a newsworthy woman, and an inside biographical sketch touched upon aspects both personal and political, such as her particular conversion to Socialism, philosophy of women's emancipation, or household skills. Conger's own inspirational poems and short stories accompanied expository essays on women's status or movements for equality both in the United States and abroad. In the pages of the *Socialist Woman*, as nowhere else, the didactic lessons of class struggle faded to the moral imperative of womanhood so common to nineteenth-century woman's literature.

By sentiment and by journalistic attainment, Conger-Kaneko was in a strong position to reaffirm the necessity of women's organizational autonomy and the validity of their own agitational styles. Under ideal conditions, she reflected, it would be preferable to have men and women working side by side in every phase of the Socialist movement. But such ideal conditions included "a group of women who are advanced sufficiently to be willing to work in the mixed locals, and a group of men who are sympathetic and responsive to those needs of women which lie outside their own." Such was not the case in most locals. Rather, "We have known [too many] instances where the local was made a sort of man's club—a place where men met and talked and smoked, and split hairs over unimportant technicalities, transacted a little business, talked and smoked some more, and adjourned until the next meeting's program, which consisted of practically the same line of procedure." Not even the party's public events, like lectures, appealed to the "mere woman" who was "seeking for the first steps" toward knowledge. Conger-Kaneko concluded:

There is a very great deal that women need to learn about themselves, about their history, and the traditions of their sex. These things can best be learned, as a rule, in a separate organization, where the mind can be better centered upon the matter in hand. A woman's organization, with alternate evenings devoted to business meetings and to study, is a very good school for the average woman seeking after the Socialist interpretation of life—feminine life as well as masculine. The members of such an organization *must feel*, however, that their work is as essential to individual and social progress as is the work of any other progressive society. . . .[6]

Conger-Kaneko began to prepare women to defend their independent status at the party convention. She urged her readers to consider the gravity of the situation. "Women are tired of being 'included,' " she warned, "tired of being taken for granted. They demand definite recognition, even as men have it." Although she welcomed the party's new concern, she wished to remind the comrades that most women knew "their interests and men's interests have not been identical since the dawn of human history and it will take something more than a mere statement of the fact to make them believe they will be identical under Socialism." Spargo's proposed bureau or committee might speed the pace of women's organization but at the price of their assimilation into a male-dominated institution. What would be the fate of the Socialist women's movement, Conger-Kaneko asked, under the direct discipline and leadership of the party's mixed local?[7]

To answer this important question, the unaffiliated Socialist Women's League of Chicago invited its sisters to attend a series of meetings just prior to the national convention. Held on May 12, 1908, the first meeting harkened back to the 1904 assembly, the issue of organizational affiliation dominating all discussions. A few women expressed interest in joining the Woman's National Progressive League, chaired by Mary Wilshire, as an alternative to party discipline. Most participants, however, adamantly opposed formal ties to an organization not firmly pledged to the class struggle. As in 1904, Socialist women, clear on their points of disagreement, could not reach a consensus. The following day a more intimate gathering of eighty-five party members chaired by stalwart Corinne Brown continued the discussion; they, too, failed to outline a solution amenable to all sectors and merely appointed a committee to study the matter further.[8]

Their organizational fate now in its hand, women flocked to the national convention. Although wives often coupled their husband's business trip with a family vacation, a shopping spree, or simply a renewal of old friendships, an unusually large number gathered in the convention hall in 1908. The *Chicago Daily Socialist* reported the presence of nearly 200 women, fourteen with babies in arms, observing from the galleries.[9] On the floor twenty women served in delegate capacity, a record number but scarcely proportional to the size of the women's sector of the movement.

At the last session before adjournment a special committee appointed to review the question of women's status presented its report. The committee approved the earlier appointment of the national lecturer to work among women and requested additional provisions for special propaganda beyond the mere arrangement of speaking tours. Its report outlined plans for systematic educational work among women and children, the publication of special propaganda materials, and the sponsorship of an investigation into the conditions of women's labor. Most important, it recommended:

1st. That a special committee of five be elected to care for and manage the work of organization among women.

2nd. That sufficient funds be supplied by the party to that committee to maintain a woman organizer constantly in the field as already voted.

3rd. That this committee co-operate directly with the national headquarters and be under the supervision of the national party.

4th. That this committee be elected by this national convention, its members to consist not necessarily of delegates to this convention.

5th. That all other moneys needed to carry on the work of the woman's committee outside the maintenance of the special organizer be raised by the committee.

6th. That during the campaign of 1908 the woman appointed as organizer be employed in states now possessing the franchise.

Although one member of the committee dissented and issued her own "minority report" condemning all special programs for women including agitation for woman suffrage, the delegates approved the plan as outlined and sanctioned the formation of the Woman's National Committee.[10]

The inauguration of the WNC marked a major turning point in the Socialist women's movement. While the independent women's clubs continued to ponder the pros and cons of affiliation, those newly formed and fully sanctioned women's branches of the party gave the WNC their full support and gained representation for their views. May Wood Simons, Antoinette Konikow, Winnie Branstetter, and Marguerite Prevey, the first members, were all unrelenting party loyalists and strongly opposed to organizational autonomy. Only one member, Meta Stern, favored the continuation of separate women's clubs. The WNC consequently interpreted its collective assignment as a mandate to eradicate the independent clubs and to recruit women directly into the party. The WNC directed each local to elect its own women's committee from its members, drafting men if women's ranks were too thin, and to initiate special agitational programs to attract women to the regular mixed local. Once only a voice of protest, the opponents of organizational independence had finally gained an official status and commensurate leverage.[11]

Success, however, did not come easily or immediately to the WNC. The first national organizer of women, Marguerite Prevey, did not receive the promised assistance from party locals and resigned her post after only a few months in the field. Other women filed similar complaints. Josephine Conger-Kaneko noted that the Kansas Socialist movement, once a flourishing center for women's agitation, had not done "one thing toward interesting women in Socialism." Although self-serving, her point had a basis in reality, for the party had failed to provide sufficient funds to cover the expenses of the national organizer or to print an ample supply of propaganda literature. As Conger-Kaneko had warned, the party's historic inertia on the woman question would not be easily overcome despite the new pledges.[12]

The WNC determined to triumph over these difficulties and to gain more cooperation from the party leadership. By September, 1908, the Kansas state organization had complied with Conger-Kaneko's request for a special organizer and sent the remarkable Caroline Lowe into the field. Lowe organized women's committees in such numbers that by June of the following year she could call a delegate conference of over seventy-five representatives. Kansas women congratulated Lowe, deeming her an organizer "in the front ranks of any . . . in the country."[13] Although few states could match Kansas's record, Socialist women in several areas echoed the claim of their Indiana comrades that a "woman no longer sits alone at a meeting. . . . Now it is a matter of comment if there be no women in the Socialist propaganda meetings; and the men agitators print on their bills: 'Women Especially Invited!' "[14]

These initial achievements of the WNC decisively weakened the position of women favoring organizational autonomy. Meta Stern, who resigned from the WNC after a brief tenure, believed that the plan to recruit women directly into the mixed locals was premature and that separate clubs or leagues were still "eminently satisfactory."[15] Only a few independent organizations, however, survived. The Socialist Women's League of Chicago and the statewide Women's Socialist Union of California continued to thrive, and Wilshire's Woman's National Progressive League held on to clubs mostly in small towns. More frequently the independent clubs followed the example set by the New York Social Democratic Women's Federation, which requested official party status. Especially in urban areas, women's organizations asked for such recognition, and the party local usually complied by designating the existing women's club as the official women's committee required by the new program. The promises of even limited financial assistance, now guaranteed by formal affiliation, proved an extra inducement. Accusations of disloyalty also carried more weight now that the party had pledged itself to agitation among women, and most young organizers, with little reason to distrust the leadership, fell into line with the work of the WNC.[16] The older comrades, who might have led the opposition, could no longer compete with this vivacious younger generation; Wenonah Stevens Abbott, Mary Garbutt, Marion Dunham, and Corinne Brown, all nearing seventy, stepped gracefully aside, witnesses to the disappearance of the independent Socialist women's movement.

If there were any lingering necessity to clarify the situation, the National Executive Committee rendered a final judgment. The corresponding secretary of the WNC, Winnie Branstetter, asked the leadership to specify the party's position on the remaining independent clubs. The NEC replied: "In our opinion the WNC and the National Organizer was created as a committee of the Socialist Party and their efforts should be directed toward increasing the membership of women within the party organization and not to the formation of separate organizations."[17]

WNC AT HIGH TIDE

The Woman's National Committee succeeded in coordinating many aspects of the Socialist women's movement. Although political differences among the various sectors never abated entirely, the WNC mediated the most troublesome disagreements. The WNC displayed neither a romantic faith in womanhood *per se* nor an ambivalence on the principle of sex equality or the desirability of woman suffrage; its members responded sensitively to the special needs of its female constituency yet upheld the class struggle as the sole solution to the woman question. Organizationally, the WNC also provided a practical compromise by allowing the local women's committees to retain customary rituals and by raising at the same time party membership as the key to participation. By its high point in 1912 the WNC had replaced earlier experiments with a smooth-running, relatively sophisticated program.

A large part of this success was due to the talented women who served on the WNC. All prominent figures in the national party, these women were consistently outspoken on the woman question and capable of commanding respect for their work from even the most recalcitrant male comrade. Equally important, their styles differed from their predecessors of either the auxiliary or independent sectors and allowed them to rise above both traditions. Together—as organizers, propagandists, and theorists—they reshaped the political character of the Socialist women's movement.

Two outstanding organizers, Anna A. Maley and Caroline Lowe, chaired the WNC during its prime. A generation younger than the women who had founded the first clubs and auxiliaries, Maley and Lowe had joined the Socialist movement at a time when the exceptional and persevering woman might attain a position within the regular mixed local or regional bureaucracy. This is not to say their roads were smooth; to the contrary, they waged a ceaseless battle against discrimination at all levels. Maley and Lowe nevertheless looked upon male egotism as a fact of life, even among Socialists, and considered it a major problem but no barrier. Similarly, neither Maley nor Lowe organized exclusively among women. Indeed, in joining the Socialist movement they both bypassed the preparatory stage of membership in a women's club or auxiliary; they would have found the social life of either unduly and unnecessarily restraining. As young women they were anxious to strike out for themselves, even if it meant foregoing some of the amenities of female culture. Both were single and free to give their time and energy to the slow task of national organization. Lacking a large feeling of sisterhood, Maley and Lowe were also psychologically distant from their largest constituency, wives and mothers still loyal to old customs and values.

Anna Maley, who succeeded Prevey as chairwoman in 1909, established the WNC on firm ground. A stenographer by profession, educated at the state university in her native Minnesota, Maley had already achieved acclaim as an intellectual and as a highly effective platform speaker.[18] She applied her talents to a rigorous and extensive field work, hoping to lay the basis for a national network of women's committees. During the summer months of 1909 she toured New England, a vanishing sector of the Socialist movement, and focused on the industrial cities like Springfield, Holyoke, Westfield, and the suburbs of Boston. She described a typical tour:

> At Lynn, Mass., a picnic audience listened with interest to a talk on women and the movement on the afternoon of July 10th. With the aid of Mrs. Margaret Goebel, I took thirty-six subscriptions for The Progressive Woman at this meeting. . . .
> Fall River, a town of 100,000 has at least 30,000 textile operatives, largely Portuguese [sic], badly organized and very poorly paid. We held but one street meeting there and elected the following woman's committee. . . . The general movement here is in a very slow condition but the interest in the discussion was lively and the sale of literature considerable. . . .
> The Lowell movement is full of inspiration. This is a textile town of about 100,000, with 70 paid-up members in the Socialist club. I addressed a meeting on the South Common of upward of 1,000 on July 19th, on the subject of Woman's Suffrage From the Socialist Standpoint. The interest was close and a good collection was taken. The following night more than 100 comrades assembled in the party headquarters. . . . The finest spirit was displayed in this meeting and the following [women's] committee was elected. . . . Lowell has a number of interested women but not many members. The men agree that they can and will get them. Watch the woman's work grow in Lowell.[19]

From New England Maley pushed westward, into Pennsylvania and Ohio during September, reaching South Dakota by the following February. At the party congress in May, 1910, she reported having visited some 150 towns and having organized 125 women's committees, twenty-three in Pennsylvania alone.[20]

Refusing to rest upon her laurels, Maley demanded more help from the party.

She knew her brief visits were insufficient. Although she corresponded with as many local women's committees as possible and offered advice, she could not achieve her goal without more assistance. At the 1910 party congress Maley asked the delegates to bolster the WNC. She gained their approval for a larger committee of seven members, a headquarters at the national office in Chicago, a paid secretary to handle the growing correspondence, more independence from party bureaucracy, and direct access to the treasury. Equally important, she gained a new position, as delegates replaced the office of national organizer with a more manageable "general correspondent." As general correspondent, Maley would direct from her station in Chicago a team of regional organizers. She would draw on some of the most capable veterans, such as Nellie Zeh, and arrange tours with the guarantee that each field organizer would stay in the assigned community for at least several days. Meanwhile, Maley could turn her attention to developing a more coherent program for the women's committees, hoping thereby to create a tighter, more homogeneous national network.[21]

After delineating this new task, Maley resigned in 1911 and turned over her office to her successor, Caroline Lowe. A similar dedication had been Lowe's signature. Daughter of a timber worker, Lowe had joined the Kansas City branch around 1903, when she was employed as a school teacher. In 1908 she took to the field and, using contacts established during her previous work for the Kansas City Teachers' Association, began organizing women's committees in southeastern sections of Kansas. Unlike the Kansas towns where a mystical, Christian Socialism had flourished, this region was dotted with coal towns where class-conscious miners filled the party's ranks, although their wives played a more marginal role. Lowe sought to recruit these women through schoolhouse meetings in towns like Pleasanton, Fort Scott, and Englevale. She sold subscriptions to party publications and distributed thousands of membership applications. During the summer of 1909 she toured the encampments of Oklahoma and achieved regional fame as a popular speaker. An experienced and successful organizer, Lowe extricated herself with difficulty from these local involvements, traveled to Chicago, and took office as general correspondent of the WNC.[22]

Under Lowe's direction the WNC excelled as an educational service. It produced a massive supply of propaganda materials designed to attract sympathizers and to convert the ignorant to Socialism. It also encouraged the composition of sophisticated texts directed at the membership. In 1911 Lowe developed a yet more comprehensive program. She designed a series of monthly lessons and directed each local women's committee to use these texts as the basis of their meetings. Through this three-tiered program, Lowe hoped to recruit more women and to provide the converted with a "scientific" and, equally important, uniform education in the principles of Socialism.[23]

Since the early days of the movement Socialists had regarded good propaganda as the open-sesame to successful recruitment. Socialist women similarly upheld the efficacy of persuasional literature, especially those appeals combining rational arguments for Socialism with moralistic preachments. To reach their female audience, however, they believed a special, intimate approach was most effective. "A woman can understand anything if presented from her personal standpoint," Josephine Conger-Kaneko had argued. Another agitator called for "an expression of love and sympathy" in even the most hard-nosed polemics.[24] The WNC fully agreed with these notions and coordinated propaganda along the prescribed lines. Lowe regularly solicited contributions from the best stylists in the movement and reprinted solid essays that had appeared in the party press. The four-page leaflet became her staple, for this short item meshed well with the techniques of distribution at rallies, factory gates, or street corners and demanded little time for busy women to digest. Its message was straightforward and its request simple: whatever the problem, the solution lay in Socialism; for further information, the reader should contact the local branch of the Socialist party, address enclosed. By 1913 the WNC claimed a stock of nearly thirty leaflets directed at special constituencies such as women in the trades, farmers' wives, workingmen's wives, members of women's clubs and suffrage societies, and teachers. After 1910 the WNC produced leaflets aimed at recent immigrants and translated the most popular into German, Polish, and Yiddish.[25] Eugene Debs, beloved for his sentimental reverence for womanhood, contributed a few very popular leaflets. Debs's message easily reached his rural followers, as did Kate Richards O'Hare's sardonic *Wimmin Ain't Got No Kick*, which began, "I spoke one night not long ago in a typical country town of two thousand, a town just like thousands of other towns, and after I had finished a man came up and spoke to me, a typical man, just like millions of other men. He said he liked my speech and thought most of it was true, but that my husband was evidently a poor specimen to allow me to gad about the country, and that I would better be home caring for the babies, and, as a last crushing blow to my presumption, he declared: 'Well, no matter how bad things are, wimmin ain't got no kick.' "[26] O'Hare, of course, supplied a ready answer. Other leaflets merely summarized the Socialist party platform in regard to women's rights or explained its position on woman suffrage, trade unionism, or child labor.

The WNC asked local Socialist women to "band together . . . and carry our literature to the women in bondage everywhere."[27] The distribution of literature was considered the obligation of all party members, and women used many occasions for this purpose. The women of Pasadena, California, had pioneered the idea of "petticoat pockets," a special pouch sewn on undergarments and filled with leaflets, a notebook, and a pencil to jot down names of potential recruits.[28] Through a variety of means, Socialist women distributed propaganda literature in droves, in 1913 alone dispersing over one and a half million leaflets. That same year the WNC also circulated via the party's press service forty-three agitational pieces that reached an estimated audience of three million readers.

The WNC also took up the *Progressive Woman* as a propaganda sheet and as a broader educational mechanism. Maley had utilized the magazine for this purpose from her first days in office. She sent copies of the *Progressive Woman* to secretaries of all local women's committees and advised them to store additional copies at the party headquarters "so that our women may carry them in pocket or handbag and distribute them to store clerks and working women wherever they meet them." Maley also asked Socialists to place copies in their town libraries and to persuade their friends and neighbors to subscribe. In return for this assistance, Conger-Kaneko, who managed to build a monthly subscription list of 15,000, produced special issues on timely subjects like suffrage and temperance with runs up to 100,000 for mass distribution. Through the pages of the *Progressive Woman* the hitherto unacquainted onlooker, the sympathizer, or even the party neophyte might learn what opportunities and responsibilities lay beyond the portals of elementary knowledge of Socialism.[29]

The *Progressive Woman* served as a bridge to the second tier of the WNC's program by supplying along with its agitational appeals a modicum of theoretical analysis. "Leaflets and small booklets have their place," May Wood Simons explained, "but an effort should be made to bring the Socialist women to make a more careful study than is contained in a five-cent leaflet. The movement is getting far beyond the stage where its efficient work can be done without a broad, more comprehensive knowledge than is found in a few printed leaflets."[30] The diffuse membership and sympathetic following of the movement could be welded together in a cohesive unit, the functionaries believed, only by a common theoretical comprehension. Conger-Kaneko's enthusiastic agreement with this postulate made her *Progressive Woman* all the more valuable. "Victory Will Follow Knowledge," she once titled an editorial. To achieve this end, she requested her readers to describe the type of education they believed most effective. Invariably, respondents stressed the importance of a broad field, including the physical and natural sciences, the social sciences, and liberal arts.[31] Conger-Kaneko took their recommendation to heart.

The *Progressive Woman* guided its readers through a morass of literature on many subjects, its editor insisting that such exercise would teach women to think in a systematic and abstract way and prepare them for an understanding of "scientific" Socialism. Conger-Kaneko designed reading lists including Darwin's *Descent of Man*, Spencer's *First Principles*, Buckle's *History of Civilization in England*, Ward's *Pure Sociology* and *Dynamic Sociology*, as well as other weighty texts, and advised local women's committees to study them thoroughly. Whether Socialist women in Coffeyville, Kansas, for instance, followed her advice is impossible to ascertain, but most women's committees did at least attempt to crack the major works of Darwin and Ward. Socialist writers and speakers were unquestionably familiar with these classics and commonly excerpted large sections to illustrate their points. Many women did concede, however, that these texts were too dry and advised their local women's committees to engage only the most experienced lecturers who could interpret and expound in a plain but able way. The *Progressive Woman* itself often filled that role.

The third tier of the WNC's program included a rigorous training in the materialist conception of history as related to women's status. The WNC aimed to educate its constituency to the primacy of economic organization as the focal point of all human history and to provide a uniform interpretation of the woman question from the Socialist standpoint. The *Progressive Woman* regularly included pertinent essays, and various writers contributed a handful of booklets for this purpose. The WNC refused to rely on haphazard methods, however, and recommended formal study classes to provide each woman with basic instruction in the finer points of theory. More than any other innovation, this aspect of the WNC's program heralded a consolidation of the Second International ideological persuasion.[32]

Although each women's committee elected its own president and secretary, the party local appointed the leader of its study class. The class leader, selected because she had demonstrated a knowledge of standard precepts, planned the lessons, selected the readings, and directed the education of her sisters. In preparing for each meeting she drew up a list of questions, which she would preface with a short lecture. Taking her questions one by one, she called on members in turn, so that they could not leave the meeting with the "subject matter confused in their brains." After a round of questions the leader would direct a general discussion. The class leader additionally assigned special readings to individuals and asked them to prepare short papers to be read before the committee. Such training might enable women to become proficient in theoretical analysis as well as confident in discussions, eventually skillful lecturers and writers themselves, capable of filling the demand for more teachers in the Socialist Sunday schools and lyceums.[33]

The WNC also recommended a standard lesson plan, beginning first with a study of the materialist conception of history. The class leader took her students through a set of detailed lessons tracing the evolution of society through savagery, barbarism, and civilization. She explained the basic principles of production at each stage of history and described the parallel developments in the family and in the status of women. Bebel's *Woman under Socialism* usually served as the primary text, and the class leader drilled her students on its contents.[34] The class leader could also draw upon a series of lessons published in various Socialist newspapers and magazines. In 1908, for example, the *Socialist Woman* published an outline designed by the Socialist Women's League of Chicago, which included topics for discussion as well as specific questions, such as "who is supposed to have domesticated the first animals and cultivated the first gardens, and why?" and the answer, "Women, because they were left to attend the fire and look after the children when men hunted, and thus had the time and opportunities for new discoveries." The object of such detailed lessons was to provide women with a close understanding of the shifts in women's status with every new economic development and to show how their subordination had been fixed by the system of private property. Most important, such lessons presumedly made Socialism seem less an act of faith and more a scientific theory of society.[35]

The WNC took its responsibility for the education of its constituency quite seriously. Socialists believed that any woman, if trained carefully, could grasp the fundamentals of Socialist doctrine and thereby become a devoted and useful worker for the cause; if already awakened, she would become proficient in spreading the word. "We Socialists do not simply say we should like to liberate [women]," Luella Krehbiel explained, "but we have a scientific process by which it shall be done." The materialist conception of history was, of course, the base line in all Socialist pedagogy.[36]

The special emphasis on women's plight carried lessons in other directions as well. Class leaders discussed the history of workingwomen in the United States, traced the changes in production and provided statistical verification, explained the necessity for unionization among the ranks of women workers, and documented the progress of women in several trades. They took up special topics—intemperance, white slavery, prostitution, child labor, infidelity, and divorce—from a Socialist perspective. Woman suffrage, of course, earned special attention for its historic importance to all politically concerned women. Sometimes class leaders merely tried to quell women's alleged fears about Socialism. For example, in the monthly lessons designed by Maley, the program entitled "Socialism and the Home" included the class leader's salutory remarks: "You have heard that Socialism will break up the home. We have gathered here this evening to discuss this subject, earnestly and quietly. At the close of this evening's program, we are willing to leave the decision to you. . . . In our program this evening we wish to call your attention to some of the existing evils that are destroying the home. We wish also to show you just a few benefits that will be brought to every home through Socialism."[37] Other programs followed a similar pattern, each demonstrating some aspect of women's oppression under capitalism, its roots in the system of private property, its eradication only with the dawning of the Cooperative Commonwealth.

The WNC did not, however, overlook the need for inspiration and sociability at committee meetings. Besides the rote memorization of particular tenets and aphorisms, each participant was allowed ample opportunity to express her own opinions and to receive the friendly, supportive criticism of her sisters. Together they also joined in song. "Arise, Brave Woman," sung to the tune popularized by the "Battle Hymn of the Republic," opened with the refrain

> Arise! Arise! Brave Woman! There is work for you to do;
> Show the world that love is wisdom and Love promises are true;
> Break the bonds that hold you captive for the world has need of you
> And We'll go marching on.

"My Papa Is a Socialist" and "The Marxian Call" were also common choices. "We're Going to Win," which concluded the program, brought out a high-spirited chorus. Occasionally, children were trained to recite short poems. "A little girl comrade" once provided the favorite:

> I'd like to be a clinging vine
> And twine around some sturdy oak;
> No leaves should be so green as mine
> Nor tendrils cling with softer stroke.
>
> But if no sturdy oak were near
> I'd have to creep and crawl around;
> And then some cruel foot I fear
> Might press my green leaves in the ground.
>
> So I'll just lift my head up high
> And be a pretty tree so straight
> Forever reaching toward the sky
> I'll brave the winds of any fate.
>
> Who knows! Perhaps when I'm grown tall
> And am a lovely, graceful tree,
> The sturdy oak beyond the wall
> May reach his brawny arms to me,
> And we'll shake hands, my comrade tree. [38]

Sentimentalism and didacticism were the twins of the WNC's internal education. But behind these techniques remained the nineteenth-century traditions of women's own institutions and Socialist orthodoxy, now merged into a standardized ritual. At least in a social sense, the inner life and atmosphere of the local women's committee preserved elements from earlier years, its new official form disguising a remarkably tenacious content. By intent or by necessity—because women from various backgrounds formed the membership and contributed many selections—the WNC thus compromised its "scientific" program and continued to provide the requisite "full evening's entertainment."

But the standardization of education was no sham, for the word-for-word recitations supplied a large dose of Second International orthodoxy. Of course, it is impossible to infer what small-town rank-and-filers made of these lessons; the loose structure of the Socialist movement was such that different interpretations of party programs coexisted and were tolerated short of factional outburst. Yet one conclusion is apparent. Although women had been engaged in self-education for decades, in various women's clubs and temperance societies, the WNC succeeded in changing the source of initiative from the grass roots to the leadership and in giving the "scientific" bias a particular Socialist context. What the WNC might do most conclusively was to plot the general direction of women's education.

With regard to its propaganda arm, the WNC reached remarkably far, touched many thousands of women with its leaflets, and brought at least several thousand close to the movement. Ordinary propaganda, however, could no more complete the conversion of neophytes than dry theory could prove palatable to any but the most abstract-minded readers. Clumsy applications of Marxism threatened at all times to push out sophisticated interpretations. But lacking an American Marx or Bebel, Socialist propagandists took their responsibility seriously and tried to reach the widest audience of women. Although accurate figures were unavailable, Caroline Lowe estimated that by 1912 women constituted between 10 and 15 percent of the party membership. Women served as secretaries of six state organizations and 158 locals, and sixteen states had appointed special correspondents to coordinate women's activities. By and large, Lowe judged the propaganda efforts a success and looked upon this achievement as a testimony to the viability of the WNC.

The WNC achieved its greatest triumphs rarely where the roots of the Socialist women's movement were shallow, as in the South, or where they had been severed by demographic or political shifts, as in New England. Rather, the WNC succeeded in making the best of existing strengths, pulling the diverse urban and rural, eastern and western sectors into closer proximity with each other and with the party. The *Socialist Woman/Progressive Woman* represented the premier model of this amiable cooperation. Born independently of the WNC, Conger-Kaneko's little magazine reached a peak through distribution provided by the WNC, while its didactic essays, sentimental stories and poems, and study lessons constituted a vast service to both Maley and Lowe. Moments of tension assuredly remained. Most activists were, however, willing to use the apparatus created only partly by themselves and to enlist the maximum level of support for its operation. The ultimate role of the WNC would depend upon many factors, not least the women at its helm.

THE SOCIALIST "NEW WOMEN"

By its own lights, the Woman's National Committee had brought the Socialist women's movement out of a lingering adolescence into a full maturity, provided a needed coherence, and established the basis for women's integration into the regular party apparatus. This achievement marked an important change in policy, as the majority of independent women's clubs and auxiliaries acquiesced to new leadership and sought formal affiliation with their respective locals. More subtly, outside the range of most contemporary observers, the Socialist women's movement had undergone a more profound cultural shift, symbolized by women's new role and status within the party. The emerging leaders experienced both the joys and sorrows of this transition, lauded for unprecedented accomplishments and haunted by personal insecurities about their significance.

The new generation of leaders, like Maley and Lowe, eclipsed the older traditions. Their predecessors, nearly vanished by 1910, had been hewed from cultural patterns informed by a distinct nineteenth-century political vision. The single greatest element in previous agitation, a legacy from indigenous radicalism running from abolitionism through Populism, had been a romantic faith in womanhood. For them as for no other generation, the task of Socialism was to release the potential power of womanhood against the incursion of capitalism and male debauchery. This sentiment often had a Yankee tinge, a self-assuredness whether flavored by life in Boston, Kansas, or California, and a recurrent strain that set spiritual values and morality above economic determinism. The ethnic counterpart, maintained by German-Americans, showed a faith in womanhood but sought to encourage not its independent expression but its service to the proletarian family and party alike. The gap between these two interpretations had been too wide to be spanned in the Gilded Age, but the two sectors of Socialist women, despite their contrasting rituals and differing beliefs, unwittingly disclosed a common trait: they clung to a culture delineated by separate spheres for men and women and made this culture the fount of their political wisdom.

The next generation of Socialist women, born in the 1870s or afterward, espoused few of the old values or aspirations. The culture they knew was both different and more homogeneous, expanding socially and commercially over the continent and across the world. The booming newspaper and magazine press, the availability of mass-produced goods, as well as the sheer vitality of city life encouraged new interpretations of social life, especially a sense that women had gained at least a foothold in man's world.

These profound developments altered the social dynamics of the Socialist women's movement. New waves of educated women ascended in the urban leadership, while their blue-collar sisters conducted militant strikes. That these women would after a period return to the home as wives and mothers only heightened the significance of the changes. The "new women" located little political vitality in domesticity, or in the regalia of the German ethnic society, or in the mystic passwords of New Thought—all meaningless for women rushing toward their destiny in the "real" world. Few of the outstanding women who exemplified the Socialist "new woman" had any strong family link to the older party traditions or the woman's movement; the particular bough had been snapped, and now a new movement of women refused to add the seemingly dead weight of tradition to the already heavy load they were compelled to bear as pioneers.

No group of women felt these newer impulses more sharply than the emerging stars of the movement, members of the Woman's National Committee. Other women might selflessly serve the cause yet respond to the personal ties pulling them back to family or career as the movement flagged. The WNC functionaries appeared single-minded in their determination and received deserved recognition in the party press and among the anonymous rank-and-file. But they paid a price, both personal and political, and a certain ambiguity ultimately darkened their triumphs.

The most prominent woman in the national Socialist party was Lena Morrow Lewis. An outstanding organizer and platform speaker, she had served as a state representative to the Woman's National Committee and as the first woman appointed to the party's highest governing body, the National Executive Committee. She was an ardent suffragist and staunch defender of women's prerogatives at all levels of the party bureaucracy. Like other members of the WNC, she also opposed the separate organization of women. She believed that any woman could struggle within the male-dominated movement if she willed to do so. She purposefully flaunted her own achievements not to brag but to set an example for others to emulate. She tolerated neither the protective milieu of the women's clubs nor the service mentality of the auxiliaries, and deemed the establishment of the WNC a distinct improvement in women's status in the Socialist movement. As a member of the WNC, Lewis aimed to bring women directly into the Socialist fold and to train them to accept their responsibilities on equal terms with men.

Lewis herself needed no preparation. Born in December, 1868, and raised in the farming district of Warren County, Illinois, daughter of the minister of the local Presbyterian church, Martha Lena Morrow graduated from Monmouth College in 1892 and immediately became a political campaigner. For the next six years she served the WCTU. She became district president of the Freeport union and attended several national conventions. Always on the move, Lena Morrow toured the small towns and villages of northwestern Illinois, organized new WCTU chapters or revitalized old ones, and spoke regularly at local women's clubs and churches. During her last year in office she delivered over 120 addresses during the season.[39] Although she retired from the temperance crusade in 1898, even in later years she described it as revolutionary "within its own field."[40] In a logical progression of interests Lena Morrow turned from temperance to the suffrage campaign. In 1899 she became secretary of the Illinois Equal Suffrage Society and worked primarily among trade unions of Chicago to secure their endorsement of woman suffrage for the state legislative referendum.[41] In 1900 the National American Woman Suffrage Association (NAWSA) dispatched her to Oregon, where she once again worked among trade unions and assisted the local equal suffrage association.[42] Along this path she had met many Socialists and trade unionists and finally joined the Socialist party in 1902.[43]

As soon as she transferred her allegiance to the Socialist movement, Lena Morrow directed all her agitational energy toward its cause. As she later recounted, her dedication to women's emancipation began to fade during these years on the West coast; she had discovered, she wrote, "that a man without a job was about as badly off as a woman without a ballot. In fact, a little worse, for we can live without voting, but we cannot live without eating." By this time she had come to understand that "women are victims of class distinctions more than of sex distinctions," and having perceived that fact, she wrote, she "changed . . . [her] course of action and whatever revolutionary spirit [that was in her] finds expression . . . in the Socialistic movement." Henceforth, she would concentrate solely upon party organizational work and the task of educating the comrades, upholding electoral victory of the party as her ultimate goal.

This shift in political consciousness did not retard her activism. She surveyed the West coast political scene and concluded that the central and northern parts of California were poorly organized but rich in potential. She took it upon herself to conduct a massive canvass, abandoning even the usual itinerary arrangements because the towns were so scattered and communications with the Socialist movement so poor. Unassisted, she entered each community with a bundle of literature under her arm and set herself up on a central street corner. Even bolder were her periodic visits to the lumber camps, many accessible only by riding the engine of a work train. In the camps especially, women were scarce and warmly welcomed, and Morrow's presence and literature were greeted with enthusiasm. Her touring was temporarily restricted when she married the noted Socialist party lecturer, Arthur Lewis, in 1903. For the next two years she limited her agitation to the Bay Area, taking only a dozen or so trips out of state. She dramatized local street-speaking by defying the police crackdown during the city election campaign of 1903, calling upon her new husband to bail her out of jail.[44] In a few years she and Arthur divorced, and she returned to the lecture trail with ferocity. Indeed, in a movement that relied upon soapbox agitation, she took much pride in her extraordinary record, regularly cataloguing her travels for the Socialist press.

Lewis believed she provided a model of what Socialist women could do. In Montana, for example, she reported that her lecture stand was tipped over by a crowd in a panic at a runaway horse, her dress, the main one she used for traveling, "torn into smithereens."[45] Badly bruised, she nevertheless continued her tour. After appearing at the Texas summer encampments, the West Virginia mining fields, and the metropolitan Socialist strongholds, she could report having spoken in every state of the union. In her own mind her dedication was unusual but not peculiar. "The price I personally have paid," she wrote in 1911, "has been to relinquish any and all ideas of a home. Not that it matters. I am used to it now. . . . Seventeen years touring as a lecturer, and in all that time I have never slept for fourteen consecutive nights in the same place. I have rested for ten or twelve days and nights. But that is the longest. I have not yet touched the two weeks mark . . . to be truthful, I have quite forgotten the sensation of having personal belongings about me, other than my clothing."[46]

Lewis was evidently not the sort of Socialist woman to accept any political vision that accentuated the differences between the sexes. She was adamantly opposed to separate organizations for women and had little faith in the efficacy of sex solidarity. "What we need is to develop the idea," she wrote, "that woman is a human being," thoroughly capable of refusing any chivalry or concessions offered by men and strong enough to measure up to whatever standards were required for revolutionary service. "The woman who will be a real and permanent service to the Party," she argued, "is the one who maintains her place in the movement and her right to work solely and only on the grounds of her merit and fitness to do things." Lewis had only one standard: the best interests of the party. It was not that women might need the party, for as she tirelessly reiterated there were already special associations like the WCTU or the woman suffrage movement to cater to women's needs; rather, the Socialist party required the energies of all comrades, male and female alike. "Comrades," she addressed her sisters, "the overthrow of the capitalist system, the deposing of the capitalist class . . . is no prayer-meeting job, and the woman who is afraid of a few men who are trying to secure the same thing she is working for, or who can be driven away by the men who persist in smoking, even at the incovenience of others, had better go back to her sheltered nook and give place to the woman of courage."[47]

Not that Lewis became indifferent to the struggle for woman's rights. She was an active member of the WNC, a frequent contributor to the *Progressive Woman*, and perhaps the most loyal and consistent advocate of woman suffrage within the national leadership. She drew a sharp line, however, between women's historically determined condition and their potential. Trained in the science curriculum at Monmouth College and encouraged by the evolutionary humanism common to late nineteenth-century reform circles, Lewis believed that woman remained "primarily a more social creature than man" because her maternal functions had encouraged a basic altruism of character. "Downtrodden women, just listen to this and take heart!" she pleaded. "You are in reality superior to man, and if you hadn't been you could never have survived all the centuries of servitude and persecution that have been put upon you."[48] In the past woman's resources had been used against her by a male-dominated hierarchy whose ideology of woman's inferiority remained from earlier times. "The men of all ages have as a class," Lewis wrote with Lamarckian logic, "developed brain cells that respond to harmonize with their past economic development." Women could challenge these masculine brain waves not by clinging to their assigned female sphere but, rather, by overthrowing the ideology of male supremacy in the most important institutions of society.[49]

Lewis asked women to reject the notion that public participation was "unladylike."[50] "Because a man labels himself Socialist," she warned, "does not endow him with brains nor make him broad-minded and liberal in his views. Some men think that all a woman is good for in any organization is to raise money for them to spend. It is quite enough for women in the church (where they are taught to be submissive to man) to do this sort of a thing," but inappropriate in an organization dedicated to their emancipation. "The prejudice of small-minded men should not be catered to," she insisted, and women must openly confront all vestiges of male egotism wherever they appeared. Women should not request what Lewis termed special dispensations.[51]

Despite her own self-confidence, Lewis paid a price for audacity. Although most party members respected her for an undeniably selfless devotion to the cause, honored her with praise, and named her to positions of leadership, a few comrades deemed her style improper, especially for a woman of national prominence. Hoping to protect her reputation, a well-meaning comrade introduced Lewis as a dainty woman "with ridiculously small hands and feet," or as "a very little woman to be secretary of a very large association."[52] Following her divorce, Lewis was dragged into a scandal that rocked the national office in 1910–11. She was accused of nothing more than consorting with the chief "free love" advocate, National Secretary J. Mahlon Barnes, going out with him from the office in the afternoons, drinking whiskey, and throwing her feet up on the office desks. For some critics these were sufficient grounds to demand her resignation from the National Executive Committee. After the scandal disappeared from the pages of party bulletins, she declined renomination and returned to the less conspicuous organizational trail.[53] Perhaps choosing a self-imposed exile, she accepted an appointment in 1913 as organizer for the Alaskan territory and spent the next four years living alone in a two-room cabin in Juneau. Seemingly undaunted, she set up study classes for women and children and conducted a course of lectures for the general public on cultural and political topics. She also became editor of the *Alaska Labor News*, vice-president of the Alaska Labor Union, candidate for Congress on the Alaskan Socialist party ticket in 1916, and even a prominent member of the Juneau Woman's Club.[54]

Women in the Socialist movement were justly proud of Lena Morrow Lewis.

She had accomplished the remarkable feat of rising to the top of its male hierarchy and stood as one of the outstanding lecturers and organizers in the party. Her appointment to the NEC was considered a victory all could share, for it seemed to affirm the party's pledge to women's equality. But the ultimate lesson proved as ambiguous as Lewis's own position. Mary Marcy, an editor of the *International Socialist Review* and noted critic of the Socialist women's movement, insisted that Lewis's appointment be interpreted as an honor not to her sex but to "her ability [to work] for Socialism." Lewis did not "need to be pampered with easy tasks that nobody else thinks are worth doing; that nobody finds it necessary to strew roses in her path to remove the difficulties," Marcy concluded. "No, Lena Morrow Lewis needed nobody," Anita Block rejoined; "neither did Susan B. Anthony, nor Mrs. Pankhurst, nor we are convinced does Mary C. Marcy." For every Lena Morrow Lewis, Block added, "there are thousands of women so saturated with tradition, so atrophied by sex-slavery that they actually barricade themselves within their own prison, the Home." These women required a helping hand to find Socialism, special mechanisms within the Socialist movement to secure their position. Despite the honor the leadership paid to Lena Morrow Lewis, Block warned that "most Socialist men are still regrettably male" and incapable of extending fair treatment to ordinary women.[55]

A similar ambiguity marred the accomplishments of May Wood Simons. Chosen as delegate to national conventions and to the international congress of 1910, Simons had narrowly lost election to the National Executive Committee in 1912. She served on the National Woman's Committee and stood as a strong proponent of woman suffrage. May Wood Simons was, however, strongly opposed to separate organizations of women. As Lewis had once shared the platform with her prominent husband, May Wood Simons worked alongside her mate, prominent intellectual A. M. Simons, on his editorial assignments at the *International Socialist Review, Chicago Daily Socialist,* and *Coming Nation.* But, unlike Lewis, Simons envisioned her struggle always in common with her husband's. In representing yet another type of Socialist "new woman," May Wood Simons sought to be both a devoted wife and an intellectual companion.

May Wood first had to reject much of her past life in Baraboo, Wisconsin, where she was born and raised. A devout Presbyterian, May had longed to become a medical missionary and, after two years teaching school in Sauk County, had managed to save enough money to attend Northwestern University. Unlike Lewis, the young May Wood did not adapt easily to the new environment and retreated to the small-town Wisconsin classroom. Finally, in 1897 she married Algie Simons, and together they moved to Chicago, mingled briefly with the residents of the University of Chicago settlement, and joined the Socialist party.

Whereas Lewis excelled as an organizer, Simons found a niche as party intellectual. She decided to develop her writing skills and turned to study women's condition. *Woman and the Social Problem,* one of her earliest contributions, received a wide distribution, and within a few years she emerged as a leading scholar on all aspects of the woman question. She was, however, still dissatisfied with the quality of her work and aspired to produce a distinguished theoretical treatise. She returned to college, earned her Ph.B. from the University of Chicago in 1905 and A.M. from Northwestern University in 1910, her master's essay awarded a locally coveted prize in economics. May also joined Algie on the party's National Educational Committee and found a practical application for her formal training and inclinations. Heavily influenced by the works of John Dewey and Maria Montessori, she, too, became a teacher. She served as lecturer for the Intercollegiate Socialist Society and National Socialist Lyceum Bureau and taught at the experimental Ruskin College and for a brief time in the Milwaukee school system. On behalf of the WNC, Simons conducted several long lecture tours and accepted numerous short engagements.[56]

May Wood Simons became one of the most prestigious women in the national Socialist movement; an admirer claimed that she had "entered into the modern opportunities for women most fully."[57] Despite her achievement, Simons could not shake self-doubts. Nor could she submerge herself into work as Lena Morrow Lewis had done. Rather, she seemed torn between a dedication to the cause and a desire to experience fully the joys of a secure family life. Each public lecture, she recorded in her diary, taxed her sensitive nervous system and brought on a severe bout of anxiety. Following the death of her first child early in her marriage, she suffered a severe emotional collapse and never fully recovered. She barely tolerated absences from her husband. Once when Algie was called away from their Girard home, May wrote in her diary: "Never in all the years of my life have there been days as sad and lonely as these. . . . I cannot sleep, everything seems gone without [Algie]. If ever we can be together again, and we three can be together and be well I shall ask nothing else. I am trying so hard to do the things Algie wants done."[58] Unduly protective of her remaining child and extremely dependent upon her husband, Simons could never escape the phantoms which haunted her daily.

Simons was never able to smooth the contradictions in her personal life or political world view. At times she served as one of the most pronounced defenders of domesticity and the home. She was unquestionably sincere. She recorded in her diary a heartfelt aspiration to be a good wife to Algie, to maintain a pleasant home, and to contribute her share to the household budget. Publicly she emphasized the value of women's contribution to family life. She answered an inquiry from Conger-Kaneko as to why women should be Socialists: "Socialism would restore the home in which women will ever be the center."[59] At other times Simons undercut her own apotheosis of domesticity. She often described housewives as reactionary or conservative. The conditions of household life over the centuries, she wrote, had managed to "make woman physically weak, mentally narrow, politically powerless."[60] Whereas Socialists might hope to recruit women who were politically conditioned by the sociability of wage labor, she predicted, they had only a poor chance of reaching housewives. Simons described rural women who were confined to their homes—"so closely bound by petty social affairs, old tradition, and sometimes so isolated"—as outside the orbit of political agitation altogether.[61] She thus encouraged women to forsake domesticity and to move into more modern, public roles. To be deprived of the opportunity to follow professional or artistic inclinations, to be forced to remain within the "womanly" existence of the household, represented in Simons's estimation the greatest injustice meted to contemporary women.

Eventually the tension became too great. The more Simons doubted the wisdom of her own public position, the more she expressed confidence in the party's ability to solve the woman question. Socialism became a *deus ex machina*, a means to resolve the conflict between the desire for domestic fulfillment and professional aspirations. But even this faith was fleeting. Simons never attained her intellectual goal, for she and Algie broke with the party during World War I and soon abandoned the Socialist ideal altogether. If Lena Morrow Lewis had steeled herself against the personal crises endured by ordinary women, May Wood Simons lifted the contradictions to a nearly intolerable level and fled the scene at an appropriate historic moment.

Whatever their limitations, Lewis and Simons played important parts in fostering the exhilarating advance of women's agitation during the peak years of the Woman's National Committee. They secured for women a greater measure of equality of status than ever before within the Socialist movement. With Simons and Lewis in the forefront, rank-and-file women rose within the party bureaucracy to become branch secretaries, state functionaries, lecturers, and journalists. For neophytes and veterans alike, it was a heady moment, the more so because the influence of the Socialist party and optimism about the political future had reached an all-time high.

Yet hidden in these gains were losses that could scarcely be measured at the time. Protests over the final liquidation of independent women's organizations fell upon deaf ears, although the issue remained. The personal touch Socialists had deemed so necessary in organizing women became almost impossible for the rising leaders to achieve in the larger movement, and the gap between the organizer and the rank-and-file grew into a chasm. Itinerant speakers who had no stake in the home found themselves culturally distant from the blue-collar housewives who accepted, even if they did not particularly glory in, the finality of their own domestic lives. Similarly, women who worked in party offices could not expect to sustain the easy give-and-take that the parlor setting had afforded. And the "new woman," slightly uncomfortable within the women's sector, evinced condescension, however slight, for her "less sophisticated" sisters. In short, the new leaders tended to sever the cultural roots that had blossomed earlier as the Socialist women's movement while they gladly picked the flowers.

Individuals like Lena Morrow Lewis and May Wood Simons suffered dearly for the absence of a sustaining milieu. Lewis in her scorn for the luxury of private life, Simons in her low estimate of domestic women's perceptions, and both in their faith in the party to resolve all key questions, cut themselves off from the collective female network that might have supplied meaningful emotional support for their work. Neither Lewis nor Simons inclined to retreat into a comforting milieu during times of personal trial. Perhaps every leading woman in the movement experienced this problem in one way or another. The acceptance of women by the party leadership had been enough to draw a handful into the spotlight but insufficient to give even those bold few the certainty of status and role. Partly as a consequence of this ambiguity, the political mortality of the younger generation was high. Whereas the Gilded Age leaders not uncommonly spanned decades, their less notable sisters bound to the movement in one way or another through most of their lives, the Socialist "new women" often faded within a decade or so.

At their worst, the Socialist "new women" nurtured a self-deception both personally and politically destructive. While Mila Tupper Maynard described May Wood Simons as "the woman who seems . . . to have reaped the fullest harvest from the new ideals and possibilities of our time both in public and private life,"[62] she painted a picture bearing little resemblance to the self-doubting, confused Simons straining to care simultaneously for the cause and for her family. And Simons herself sought in her dedication to the party an external measure of success that private life seemed destined to deny. That unquestioned loyalty, however, promoted a blanket reasoning unchecked by reality or common sense, while the reductionist element in Second International doctrines reinforced the most wooden elements. If economic determinism held sway and the working class as a whole tended toward uniformity, then sensitivity to women in varying neighborhoods, regions, or stations in life was no great priority. The political line would loom paramount, adapted downward for the time being until women were ready to accept it unilaterally. The limitations of this approach, characteristic of both Simons and Lewis, were obvious to any organizer with strong roots in her locality. The neighborhood resident who carried on the day-to-day agitations learned often quite painfully that hard facts and fancy theories were insufficient, that sentimentality often retained a power amidst the greatest array of intellection, and that didactic lessons could not replace the bonds of female friendship.

The deepest truth in the history of the Socialist women's movement was the constancy of change and the unceasing necessity of adaptation. The pace of change from the late nineteenth century to the eve of world war might best be inferred from a task personally undertaken by the WNC general correspondent in 1912. In order to answer a frequent question, she visited the headquarters of the National WCTU to "ascertain for the benefit of the Party" whether Frances Willard had really made the statements attributed to her in the popular leaflet *Frances Willard on Socialism*. However far physically the Evanston home of the WCTU was from the Socialist party national office in downtown Chicago, the political distance had become so vast that rank-and-file Socialist women had scant knowledge of the history of their own movement. Willard herself had commented on another occasion about the effect of the new realism in literature, that the ascending form robbed women of a sustaining romanticism and, consequently, the heroic vision necessary to a revolutionary movement. Certainly the members of the WNC would never be mistaken for devotees of Frances Willard or romantics of any kind, whatever their personal dedication to the cause. Willard's task had been to rouse the latent political consciousness in women, to direct a campaign against the incursion of capital on woman's sphere; Socialist women after 1910 lived in an age of steady disillusionment, when the determining shifts in political power were being made. Willard might call for the gleam of heaven to light the way toward a truly Christian practice. The later Socialists had to prepare a more mundane but also more inclusive strategy in order to realize the familiar goals of women's emancipation—their right to labor, to enfranchisement, and to the fruits of a new morality.[63]

The mass movements of the twentieth century commanded Socialist women's intervention. They had successfully laid the basis for a network of local women's committees, gained the formal endorsement of the party and the attention of functionaries. Now they were called upon to reach far outside the comfortable party ranks in order to implement their medium-range goals of women's emancipation. Beginning in 1909 with the outbreak of the shirtwaist makers' strike in New York City, continuing until world war and the Russian Revolution combined to overturn the foundation of their movement, Socialist women took leading parts in the path-breaking strikes of workingwomen, the last crusades of the woman suffrage movement, and the renewed campaigns to stamp out prostitution. If these efforts still did not hold out the inherent promise of Socialism, party women carried their ideals as far as circumstances would ever allow.

The Woman's National Committee played no important role in these primarily local events, but supplied the ideological rationale demanded by the party. The women functionaries adapted the general party position to each situation, specifying a class analysis for the problems of women's economic, political, or sexual oppression, establishing the root of women's disability in the system of private property and promising their emancipation with the arrival of the Cooperative Commonwealth. On strategic questions the Second International had already spoken the final word: Socialist women were to cling to the party and resist the temptation to ally with the mainstream women's movement. In firming this perspective, the WNC gained support from the urban rank-and-file, the elder German-American veterans and the young Jewish and native-born women who espoused absolute loyalty to the International. Because the key mobilizations of the 1910s took place for the most part in major metropolitan areas, with New York City the focal point, the affinity between the WNC and the urban activists proved crucial for the entire trajectory of the Socialist women's movement. Women with other predilections, overshadowed and outvoted, took the voice of Cassandra.

The grand mobilizations tested the capacity of Socialist women to act upon their ideas, and so put on trial the principles embodied in the WNC. In a deeper sense the whole theoretical matrix of Socialism came into question around these campaigns for women's emancipation. Relative to their European counterparts, American Socialists female and male were notoriously naive about the details of historical materialism, the economic paradigms outlined in *Kapital*, or the Hegelian underpinnings of Marxism. Yet they felt compelled to rationalize practice, fructify its stated aims, by a comprehensive statement of general social "laws" and a surpassing prediction. For the very sense of this logic, the ultimate value of Second International orthodoxy and the training of women cadres in "scientific" paradigms grew steadily in doubt. Each step in a progression of gender-conscious campaigns—from labor support to suffrage agitation to the hopeful inauguration of a new morality—revealed gaps in the Socialist perspective on the woman question. Contradictions presumably dissolved by ideological fiat returned to haunt the movement.

Thus, while Socialists could rally without hesitation to the cause of workingwomen, suffrage agitation raised old, unanswerable questions about the significance of a sex rather than a class struggle. Issues of sexual morality proved in the end most troubling of all. Although Socialists could easily combat—albeit in a somewhat self-serving manner—prostitution as the spawn of capitalism, they faced a major dilemma when a small group of radical intellectuals challenged the cherished class analysis and dedication to female purity as restraining the development of a truly modern perspective. The standardized education had not even provided a common vocabulary for this discussion, let alone settled the divisive arguments in advance. Moreover, a new sector of the Socialist movement, women recently immigrated from southern and eastern Europe, stood entirely outside the dialogue.

The WNC faced several tests in waging these three great campaigns. Would the policy of integrating women into the party stand up amidst the major mass mobilizations? How could Socialist women participate en bloc in campaigns that by their very nature joined a range of different groups of women? Could the WNC mediate between the different elements of its own constituency, between the rural and urban, foreign- and native-born women, and—most important—between the old and new generations of activists? Could the WNC salvage the best of the nineteenth-century traditions and create institutions solid enough to pass on to its own successors? The WNC faced the familiar challenge, the strategic merging of the class struggle and the advancement of women. But, unlike its predecessors, the WNC stood at the helm of a mature political movement.

NOTES

1. Werner Thönnessen, *The Emancipation of Women* (London, 1973), 65.
2. Dues for party wives became a major issue in 1909, as the WNC urged members to vote against a resolution to offer women not engaged in gainful occupations reduced rates; see the Socialist party's *Official Bulletin* (Chicago), May, 1909. Again in 1912 the Butte, Mont., local proposed instituting family rates so that husbands and wives on tight budgets need not choose between themselves; see *Wheeling (W. Va.) Majority*, Feb. 22, 1912. For reports of activity in Chicago, see C. T. Fraenckel, the secretary of Local Cook County, in the *Chicago Daily Socialist*, July 13, 1907; activities among the women's branches and clubs appeared frequently, especially in the *Daily Socialist*, Apr. 10, 30, Sept. 19, 1907. See also "Socialist Women of Chicago," *Socialist Woman*, 1 (Oct., 1907), 8.
3. John Spargo, "Woman and the Socialist Movement," *International Socialist Review*, 8 (Feb., 1908), 449–55.
4. *Official Bulletin*, Jan., 28, 1908; reprinted in part in *Chicago Daily Socialist*, Feb. 4, 1908.
5. Josephine Conger-Kaneko, "Why the Socialist Woman Comes into Existence," *Socialist Woman*, 1 (June, 1907), 4. For a full description, see my essay in Joseph Conlin, ed., *The Radical Press in the United States, 1880–1960*, 2 vols. (Westport, Conn., 1974), II, 442–49.
6. Josephine Conger-Kaneko, "Separate Organizations," *Socialist Woman*, 1 (Apr., 1908), 5. Conger-Kaneko endorsed separate organizations in the *Appeal to Reason*, Oct. 10, Nov. 14, 1903.
7. Josephine Conger-Kaneko, "Are the Interests of Men and Women Identical?" *Socialist Woman*, 1 (May, 1908), 5. For extensive discussions, see issues of the *Chicago Daily Socialist* and *St. Louis Labor* published around the time of the party convention. Two informative articles are: Jessie E. Molle, "The National Convention and the Woman's Movement," *International Socialist Review*, 8 (May, 1908), 688–90, and "A Word to Our Comrades at the National Convention," the first entry in an exchange between Meta Stern and Sherlie Woodman, *Socialist Woman*, 1 (May, 1803), 3.
8. On preconvention meetings, see "Socialist Women in the Garrick Theater," *Socialist Woman*, 1 (June, 1908), 11; "Socialist Women Hold Meeting during Convention Week," *ibid.*, 9; *Chicago Daily Socialist*, May 9, 12, 1908.

9. *Chicago Daily Socialist*, May 13, 1908.

10. *Proceedings of the National Convention of the Socialist Party, May 10–17, 1908* (Chicago, 1908), 301–6.

11. "Hebe" [Meta Stern], "The Socialist Party and Women," *Socialist Woman*, 2 (July, 1908), 8–9; May Wood Simons in *Chicago Daily Socialist*, June 20, 1908.

12. A biographical sketch of Prevey, born in Nova Scotia in 1869, appeared in the *Chicago Daily Socialist*, May 19, 1910. Her resignation as national organizer appeared in *ibid.*, Jan. 6, 1909.

13. *Appeal to Reason*, Sept. 19, Oct. 10, 31, 1908. Reports of the conference are summarized in "Conference of Socialist Women in Girard, Kansas," *Progressive Women*, 3 (July, 1909), 9.

14. May McDonald Strickland in *New York Call*, Jan. 11, 1909.

15. "Hebe," "Socialist Party and Women," 8–9.

16. "Report of Committee for Furtherance of Women's Organizations," *Socialist Woman*, 2 (Jan., 1909), 7.

17. *Chicago Daily Socialist*, Dec. 28, 1908. See also May Wood Simons, "Aims and Purposes of Women Committee," *Progressive Woman*, 3 (Oct., 1909), 2.

18. Maley was born on Jan. 6, 1873. A brief biography appears in *Woman's Who's Who in America, 1914–1915*, ed. John W. Leonard (New York, 1914), 535. Maley's early activities may be traced in the New York County Local Papers, 1907–1911, Reel 1, Tamiment Library, New York University. For a brief description of her contribution to the Socialist movement, see *Socialist Woman*, 3 (June, 1909), 5.

19. "Report of Anna A. Maley, National Organizer of the Socialist Women," *Progressive Woman*, 3 (Oct., 1909), 15. Maley's Massachusetts stint was reported in "Notes on the National Movement," *ibid.*, 2 (Aug., 1909), 15. See also "Work of Woman Organizer," *ibid.* (Nov., 1909), 13.

20. *Official Bulletin*, Feb., 1910; *Proceedings of the Socialist Party National Congress, May, 1910* (Chicago, 1910), 179.

21. *Proceedings of the Socialist Party National Congress, May, 1910*. Theresa Malkiel describes the gains in the *New York Call*, May 31, 1910. On the routing of Nellie Zeh through Illinois, Alabama, Tennessee, and Florida, see *Official Bulletin*, Nov., 1910.

22. Caroline Lowe was born on Nov. 28, 1874, in Cottom, Essex County, Ontario. Although biographical information is scarce, historian Neil Basen interviewed Lowe's niece and learned that Lowe's father had been an itinerant timber worker from Indiana, her mother a descendant of a Loyalist family which had moved to Canada at the time of the American Revolution. Lowe had attended public school in Oskaloosa, Iowa, before moving to Kansas City when she was sixteen. Lowe's early organizational work for the Socialist party in Kansas and Oklahoma was reported regularly in the *Appeal to Reason* from 1908 through 1910.

23. For an excellent summary of Lowe's intentions, see "Notes from Woman's Department—National Headquarters," *Progressive Woman*, 4 (Jan., 1911), 10, and *New York Call*, Dec. 27, 1910. See also Caroline Lowe, "Work of Women in the Socialist Party, 1912," *Progressive Woman*, 5 (May, 1912), 3, 13.

24. Josephine Conger-Kaneko, "Victory Will Follow Knowledge," *Socialist Woman*, 2 (Jan., 1909), 6. See also Luella R. Krehbiel, "Woman and Socialism," *ibid.*, 2 (July, 1908), 7.

25. Many of these leaflets are located in the pamphlet collections of the State Historical Society of Wisconsin, the Women and Children File of the Socialist

Party of America Papers, Perkins Library, Duke University, and the Tamiment Library, New York University.

26. Kate Richards O'Hare, *Wimmin Ain't Got No Kick*, Socialist Party leaflet (Chicago, n.d.).

27. Luella R. Krehbiel, "Woman, the World Is Waiting for You," *Socialist Woman*, 2 (May, 1909), 4.

28. *Common Sense* (Los Angeles), Jan. 7, 1905.

29. "The National Movement," *Progressive Woman*, 3 (Nov., 1909), 13.

30. May Wood Simons, "The Woman's National Committee—Its Work," *ibid.*, 5 (May, 1912), 5.

31. Anna Rappaport and Agnes Downing, "What Kind of Education Is Most Needed for Women Today?" *Socialist Woman*, 2 (Oct., 1908), 12–13.

32. See, for example, Theresa Malkiel, "The Truth about Socialism," *Progressive Woman*, 3 (Sept., 1909), 10.

33. "How to Form a Study Club," *Socialist Woman*, 2 (Mar., 1909), 15.

34. Luella Twining, "A Word about August Bebel," *Progressive Woman*, 5 (Aug., 1911), 5. Anita Block praised Bebel's contribution in the *New York Call*, Aug. 31, 1913.

35. *Socialist Woman*, 1 (Apr., 1908) through 2 (Oct., 1908). For a similar series see Mary Oppenheim's contribution published in the "Woman's Department" of *Wilshire's Magazine*, Fall, 1910.

36. Luella R. Krehbiel, "How Will Socialism Liberate Women?" *New York Call*, Jan. 30, 1910. See also "Must Woman Emancipate Herself?" *Progressive Woman*, 5 (Feb., 1912), 8.

37. Program for March published in *Progressive Woman*, 4 (Mar., 1911), 10–11.

38. Verses by Nannie Parker, published in *ibid.* (Feb., 1911), 12.

39. *Woman's Who's Who in America*, 1914–1915, 489; *The Past and Present of Warren County, Illinois* (Chicago, 1877), 128; *The Annex* (Monmouth College), 1 (Oct. 25, 1889), 3 (May 20, 1892), 8 (Nov. 11, 1892); *Minutes of the Woman's Christian Temperance Union, 22nd Meeting* (Chicago, 1895), 71; *Minutes of the Woman's Christian Temperance Union, 23rd Meeting* (Chicago, 1896), 11; *Minutes, State Presidents Addresses and Reports of Work of Woman's Christian Temperance Union of the State of Illinois and the Twenty-fifth Annual Convention* (Chicago, 1898), 122–23.

40. Lena Morrow Lewis, "Experiences of a Socialist Propagandist," reprinted in several newspapers including the *Chicago Daily Socialist*, July 3, 1907; *Common Sense*, Apr. 1, 1905.

41. Unmarked clipping from a Chicago newspaper, Feb., 1899, in Lena Morrow Lewis Papers, Tamiment Library, New York University.

42. Abigail Scott Duniway, *Path Breaking* (New York, 1914), 118.

43. Lena Morrow Lewis dated her membership to Apr., 1902, in a letter to Morris Novik, 1936, in Lewis Papers.

44. Lewis, "Experiences of a Socialist Propagandist." The wedding was announced in *California Socialist* (San Francisco), July 25, 1903.

45. Clipping from *Montana News*, n.d. (1906?), in Lewis Papers.

46. Quoted by Ethel Lloyd Patterson, "Lena Morrow Lewis: Agitator," *Masses*, 1 (July, 1911), 13.

47. *Chicago Daily Socialist*, May 10, 1907.

48. Clipping from *Omaha Daily News*, June 27, 1909, in Lewis Papers.

49. Lena Morrow Lewis, "The Sex and Woman Questions," *Masses*, 1 (Dec., 1911), 7.

50. Lena Morrow Lewis, "Women and Social Problems," *Dallas Laborer*, Apr. 25, 1914.

51. *Chicago Daily Socialist*, May 19, 1907.

52. Patterson, "Lena Morrow Lewis: Agitator," reprinted in the *Emporia* (Kan.) *Convincer*, Feb. 24, 1912.

53. The scandal was covered in the *Christian Socialist* (Chicago), 1911, and the party's *Official Bulletin*. Lewis declined renomination in a letter printed in *Progressive Woman*, 5 (Dec., 1911), 16.

54. Letter from Alaska, printed in *New York Call*, Mar. 1, 1914. The *Call* reported Lewis's Alaskan adventures with some regularity, as did the *Alaska Labor News*.

55. Mary Marcy in *New York Call*, May 8, 1910; Anita Block in *ibid.*, May 15, 1910.

56. Kent and Gretchen Kreuter, *An American Dissenter* (Lexington, Ky., 1969), a biography of A. M. Simons, covers May's life in some detail. See also *Woman's Who's Who of America*, 1914–1915, 747; May Wood Simons, "How I Became a Socialist," *Comrade*, 2 (Nov., 1902), 32.

57. Mila Tupper Maynard, "Our Women Delegates to the International," *Progressive Woman*, 4 (Aug., 1910), 10.

58. May Wood Simons Diary, July 17, 1913, May Wood Simons Papers, State Historical Society of Wisconsin.

59. May Wood Simons, "Why Women Should Be Socialists," *Socialist Woman*, 1 (June, 1907), 1.

60. May Wood Simons, *Woman and the Social Problem* (Chicago, 1907), 5.

61. Simons, "Woman's National Committee—Its Work," 5.

62. Maynard, "Our Women Delegates to the International," 10.

63. Frances Willard, *How to Win: A Book for Girls* (1888), quoted by Gail Parker, ed., *The Oven Birds: American Women on Womanhood, 1830–1920* (New York, 1972), 11–12. Parker describes in the introduction to this anthology the general shift in women's political assessment from sentimentalism to realism, and notes that Elizabeth Cady Stanton also shared Willard's estimation of the change. On inquiries as to Willard's Socialism, see *Party Builder* (Chicago), Oct. 23, 1912.

5   Women's Labor

> I walk through the bustling streets, it is already six
> o'clock after noon—in dark rows Jewish daughters drag
> along harassed.
>
> O Jewish daughters of the factories! In your gaze I see
> hidden the charm of the small Jewish town, the glimmer
> of the faraway home.
>
> You stride upon stony streets, where sky and earth are
> concealed from your eyes—but your skirts still retain the
> aroma of your native field.
>
> And when I observe you more closely I behold much
> more: The ancient crowns of millenniums are shining
> through the yoke.
>
> For princesses are you all, nobility rests calmly in your
> gaze. How enslaved have you become now! Who shall
> bring you back to the King?
>
> Anna Margolin, "Daughters of the Old Country"
> In *Modern Yiddish Poetry* (1927)

Theresa Serber Malkiel appeared to her comrades and political
enemies alike a paragon of Socialist womanhood. As a young woman she had
conducted pioneering agitation in the women's sectors of the Jewish labor
movement. Twenty years later Malkiel was directing the New York Socialist
campaigns to aid workingwomen, although she now operated through the
party's women's branches rather than the unions. Through her life history one
could trace Socialist women's commitment to workingwomen, their joys and
frustrations, borne out especially in the great "women's strikes" of 1909–13.

Malkiel had helped create the legend of the Jewish woman *qua* militant
unionist. Born in Bar, Russia, on May Day, 1874, she had immigrated to the
United States with her family in 1891. Like many of her generation and
although little more than a child, she found a job in New York's rapidly expanding garment industry. Malkiel was lucky to enter one of the better-paying sectors
open to women, the "reefer" or cloak-making trade. From her first days in the
shop, Malkiel proved a fighter. She moved to the center of a group of seventy
women who formed the Infant Cloak Makers' Union of New York in October,

1894. Incited by the most severe depression industrial America had yet witnessed and by the growing competition within the sweated trades, Malkiel and her co-workers had decided they would no longer tolerate further wage reductions and worsening conditions. As she later recalled, "with great dignity" the Infant Cloak Makers joined the city's central labor bodies, the United Hebrew Trades and the Central Labor Federation, and demanded the prerogatives of even such as themselves as legitimate trade unionists.

The Infant Cloak Makers' Union made front-page news. Metropolitan newspapers began to run feature articles on women in the trade, and employers likewise heeded the women's activity. Then, as the industry geared up for the busy season, the bosses set lower wage rates and determined to break the union's tenuous hold on the workers' loyalties. In Malkiel's shop a key worker refused to accept the lower standard and was discharged. Malkiel and five other women left in protest, "shaking off the threads of slavery from our garments," Malkiel later recalled, by "declaring war" upon the employers. The newspapers pictured the striking women as "Seven Debses in Skirts," more accurately than they knew in pinpointing Malkiel as a female labor savior.

At its peak Malkiel's union became avowedly radical. Like other sectors of the garment trade, the Infant Cloak Makers' Union expanded into a social organization, with fund-raising functions, theatrical performances, and even special recreational branches. A flagship in the Jewish trades by affiliating with the Knights of Labor's "socialist" center, New York District no. 49, the Infant Cloak Makers' Union eventually broke with the Knights to follow the DeLeon-led faction into the Socialist Trades and Labor Alliance. Unfortunately it could not organizationally survive the bitter factionalism precipitated by the move, or the worsening conditions that followed as the depression hit bottom. The Infant Cloak Makers' Union had nevertheless set a precedent for later efforts. Lacking every resource but will, Jewish women had demonstrated their determination to create a militant and radical labor movement.

Malkiel had meanwhile became the first woman to rise from the factory floor to Socialist leadership. A member of the Russian Workingman's Club as early as 1892, she had achieved the status of a party militant. Malkiel served as a delegate to the Socialist Trades and Labor Alliance's first convention in 1896 and was known as an intimate of the SLP's highest circles. Only in 1899, when the last significant bloc of orthodox Socialists broke with DeLeon, did Malkiel exit to join the Social Democratic party, which merged two years later into the Socialist Party of America. Had Malkiel remained in the shops, she would have likely become a leading political figure in the garment unions formed at the turn of the century; she would have found a natural platform within her own trade reorganized in 1899.

But, true to custom, she left the shop to set up housekeeping. In 1900 Theresa Serber married Leon Malkiel, a longtime comrade and prominent

Socialist functionary. Together they moved from Manhattan to Yonkers. Now
at a distance from the labor community, Theresa Malkiel created a new role
for herself—"soldier in the ranks" of the Socialist party, no less a "model housekeeper." She soon organized other housewives into the Woman's Progressive
Society of Yonkers, which later became Branch One of the Socialist Women's
Society of Greater New York. Although Malkiel emerged as a leader of the
local women's sector of the party, she could not forget her sisters in the garment
trade and gravitated toward the Women's Trade Union League. At the outbreak
of the "women's strikes" in 1909, Theresa Malkiel was a hardened veteran of
the Socialist movement, out of the shops but well prepared by experience and
position to assume a prominent role.[1]

Malkiel's was only a dramatic case study of the many unsung Jewish militants. Fierce devotion to Socialism and work in the sweated trades for at least
a youthful phase marked the lives of many women. Their story is, first, a Jewish
story, for the rise of militant trade unionism had its roots in the key economic
roles women had filled within the old-country *shtetls*. Frequently hand laborers
or petty merchants while their menfolk attended to holy duties, Jewish women
assumed a major financial responsibility. Even if denied formal education, their
political participation sharply limited, such women had a sanction in paid labor
that many other immigrant women, especially German-Americans, lacked. The
close-knit character of the Jewish population in the new land, the Socialist spirit
rife in the 1890s ghetto, made radical trade unionism a natural outlet for idealistic Jewish women. Their distance from American traditions of women's reform,
their proximity to European Socialist ideology, gave their unionism an all-
encompassing character and self-conscious proletarian spirit that English-
language women's associations rarely possessed.

Within the Jewish community the workingwoman was so much a fact of life
that she became a central cultural figure. Poets, prophets, editorialists, and
argumentative correspondents produced a mixture of paternalism and idealism
to assess the proletarian woman. In the blossoming Yiddish Socialist press of
the 1890s, assorted writers discussed woman's purported ignorance and reticence; the temporary nature of woman's stint in the shop they deemed preferable
to man's life-long drudgery. Among the picturesque and beloved sketches,
stories, and poems of the rising literary giants, however, the workingwoman
gained a pathos unprecedented in either German-language or other Socialist
texts. Pioneering feuilletonists, like the cap maker Z. Libin, who first popularized the one-column short story, described the workingwoman's personal
tragedy as evidence of capitalism's evil. Calamities abounded, like the beautiful
daughter dragged into the machinery and killed before her father's disbelieving
eyes, the mother prematurely aged by her family's suffering during the slack
season, sisters driven to starvation or prostitution. If a light glimmered, it
reflected the inherent beauty and instinctive goodness of the working girl. In
the phrases of Leon Kobrin, a painter in words of slum life,

> You stand and marvel: How does she come to be here? How could she have grown up there, behind those gray walls, in this stony world, without a green sprout, without sun-light, and without air? How has the shop not withered her by now?
>
> When the eye-lids lift, a pair of eyes look out, so black and shiny that all the sooty, gray environs are illumined and brightened. . . .
>
> Oh, young Jewish beauty, you bloom and grow by the light within you which tenement house and shop have been unable to extinguish![2]

The heroic deeds of a few revolutionary Jewish women, lionized in the Yiddish-American press, seemed to suggest that despite oppression, despite the age-old obscurantist faith in God and tradition, the workingwoman would rise to a secular, radical perspective and to class-conscious action.

The handful of radical women who spoke for themselves in this early era envisioned Jews as fostering the emergence of a distinct female proletariat. Departing from the German-American Socialist tradition, which clung to the ideal of the class-conscious *Hausfrau*, correspondents to the Yiddish press argued that married women were less fortunate than men precisely because they suffered from isolation in the home, were punished for living upon love of family alone while men entered the exciting world outside. Women's salvation, they insisted, lay in wage labor, women's potential to be realized through the union's advance. Their cry—"Working Women, Organize Yourselves!"—echoed into the twentieth century.[3]

Leading Jewish women like Malkiel combatted lingering opposition to women's wage labor, the old Lassallean desire to restrict women's role to a blessed domesticity. Earlier, Augusta Lilienthal and Johanna Greie had similarly implored Socialists to lend their official sanction to women's right to labor, but they had lacked the resources to be more than a counterbalance to prevailing sentiment. Slowly, reluctantly, and under the pressure of changing economic conditions and a broadened ethnic coalition, Socialists accepted the finality of women's wage labor under capitalism. The party leadership, however, neither altered its political priorities nor directed its energies toward this newly recognized sector. Rather, Malkiel and a few others created a contingent of women organizers under the party's banners, and through their deeds in the union and on the picket line set a new standard of Socialist womanhood.

The new standard also proved imperfect, for it misrepresented the majority inclinations of wage-earning women. Malkiel and her militant co-workers raised unrealistic goals: they demanded a place within the Socialist ranks but as class-conscious fighters rather than as women, and they deemed participation in both union and party the highest form of dedication. The division between the leaders and the ranks, always great in the Socialist movement, made a world of difference here. Workingwomen, even those sympathetic to the Socialist evangel, lacked time and energy for political activities. And, as in the late nineteenth century, the new generation found its most trusted allies outside the

Socialist movement proper, among women activists who dedicated their lives to the advancement of their sex.

During the famed garment strikes of the 1910s, Socialists etched a heroic page in their history. Despite their accomplishments, troubling questions forced them back to basic principles at the very moment that workingwomen advanced to the center of American social and political life.

THEORY OF WOMEN'S LABOR

By the turn of the century Socialists had developed a general theoretical perspective on women's labor. They finally acknowledged the claims of the nineteenth-century woman's movement that women's emancipation was tied to their advancement into wage labor, that women's autonomy rose in proportion to their economic independence. For the most part, however, Socialists drew from contributions closer to their own sensibilities. With Bebel's *Die Frau und der Sozialismus* their major text, party ideologues discussed the entry of women into the labor force as a logical component of capitalism and as the signal for women's direct participation in the class struggle.

Socialists were unable or perhaps unwilling to treat women's labor as a unique entity. On the one hand, they preferred to consider as epiphenomenal the distinctive characteristics of women's situation, such as their segregation into low-paying jobs, the frequently temporary or intermittent nature of their wage earning, or their responsibility for the care of the household and children. On the other hand, they minimized the important contribution women continued to make to the family economy. Defined as outside "real" production, housework measured up short compared to modern factory labor, and women's domestic role—once sentimentally revered by the elder Socialist generation— now reigned as the source of women's backwardness.

Although twentieth-century Socialists acknowledged the permanency of women's wage labor under capitalism and acceded its emancipatory potential, they nevertheless clung to a reductionist logic. They interpreted this significant historical development in a one-dimensional fashion and emphasized the coalescence of women's interests and those of workingmen. In this perspective the special qualities of women's lives became insignificant because they were subsumed by their new proletarian identity.

Women's unique position thus fell prey to the hallowed labor theory of value, the heart of Socialist doctrine, which named the proletariat as the central agent of history. One of the most widely read texts in the United States, Ernest Untermann's *Marxian Economics: A Popular Introduction to the Three Volumes of Marx's Capital*, captured the essence of this perspective. Untermann followed "labor and capital through their long journey from primitive times to the present," tracing in detail the "antagonism between exploiters and exploited" until,

Organized by the requirements of capitalist production itself, the proletariat adapts its economic organizations to the form of modern centralized industries, transforms its craft unions into industrial unions, unites its economic and political organizations in a well-planned division of labor, conquers the political power, and enables its economic organizations to take hold of the great sources of production and distribution in the interest of the working class, which remains the only essential class in society.... Capitalism leaves the field to Socialism.[4]

Whereas earlier political economists had developed theories reflecting the growing predominance of the entrepreneurial and capitalist classes over the broken feudal barons, this new historical outline—"the crowning work of the life of Karl Marx"—incorporated the endeavors of the industrial proletariat to "present its own interests and erect its own milestone" within the existing economic system.[5]

Party theoreticians expounded upon the precise role of the proletariat in the coming of Socialism, especially its paradoxical status as the creator of value and exploited class. Marx, they explained, had answered the profound question of how capitalistic marketplace laws regulated the exchange of products and the estrangement of labor from its human possessors. His resolution, derived through a lifetime of study, specified that value grew from a relationship among people. All societies since the dawn of humankind had been based upon a division of labor, from agriculture and handicraft of the most primitive order to modern machine manufactures in recent times. Every system of divided labor had been a system of distributed labor, from the family or clan through the class system of modern civilization. Under capitalism, however, the forms of production concealed the workers' essential contribution by creating a "commodity," an object estranged from them and seemingly worth whatever price it gained in the marketplace. In reality, as Socialists interpreted Marx, the "real" value had been created by the workers, including not only the cost of their transformation of nature and the price of their own maintenance but the capitalist's profit as well. The capitalist usurped the "surplus value" for his own needs, while the working class, denied its full share, sank into increasing immiseration.

Here was the kernel of Socialist analysis. The same dynamic that degraded labor impelled workers to recognize their central place in civilization, one day to reclaim the fruits of their toil. In Socialist lexicon socialized labor by its very nature provided workers the discipline, unity, and organization to take this step. As party theoretician Louis Boudin cogently noted, the "fight . . . in itself develops the desire for ultimate freedom and educates the workingman to an understanding of the causes and the conditions of the struggle, thus making of him an active and intelligent opponent of the present order."[6] Whereas apathetic workers might see themselves as mere cogs in the productive machine, industrial unionism and political Socialism together developed the instinctive comradely solidarity into an awareness that all industry rested upon the collectivity of labor already a fact of modern production. This wide awareness blossomed into a consciousness inherently revolutionary, as the individual worker experienced a sense of hope and renewal. As class conflict sharpened, good faith would turn to steely will. At last, Socialists quoted Marx, the "knell of capitalist private property sounds. The expropriators are expropriated."

The role granted the wage laborer inherently devalued the importance of any other social sector. While pro-AFL and pro-IWW Socialists might argue about *which* wage laborer, and the agrarian radicals steadily refuse to ignore the small or tenant farmer's place in the struggle, party theoreticians generally reaffirmed the centrality of the industrial proletariat as set out by the European masters and upheld by their nineteenth-century German-American counterparts. Not labor in general but labor organized "in a determined social form" of commodity production created value. Following Marx's distinction between use value produced under any system of labor and exchange value known only to the marketplace, Socialists measured wage labor's contribution through a negotiable "labor power" (sold generally at its value like other commodities), nonwage labor apparently valueless by contrast.[7]

The implications of these abstruse notions for women's role were twofold. Socialists tended to exaggerate the significance of wage labor in women's lives and simultaneously discounted the importance of the work women performed in their homes. In both cases their theoretical analyses lacked precision and, one might add, credibility. Socialists of course recognized that the reproduction and maintenance of the working class took place outside the factory and acknowledged the abstract importance of procuring the necessities of daily life. But the social nature of this process remained a mystery within the economic framework, women's essential contribution obscured.

Socialists did not develop a coherent analysis of household labor and exhibited a strong negative attitude toward women's domestic work. Household drudgery, they maintained, equaled the "final annihilation of the self," for it brought little personal satisfaction and lacked the status of wage labor. The solution lay in the socialization of household maintenance, the reorganization of basic tasks along the industrial lines proposed earlier by Edward Bellamy and Charlotte Perkins Gilman. A few individuals might advocate for the interim cooperative housekeeping arrangements wherein various family members or friends shared the unpleasant burdens. Such schemes, however, held slight promise for the future; they were little better than, in Anita Block's estimation, grafting "the glorious wings of a bird on the crawling body of a reptile." Like so many details of daily life, the precise solution to this aspect of the woman question must be deferred until further technological innovation and the ascension of Socialists to power.[8]

Fortunately, Socialists believed, the transformation had already begun, as industrial capitalism transferred women's work "from fireside to factory." Such tasks as the making of candles and soap, preservation and preparation of food, spinning and weaving of textiles, construction of finished garments—all had already passed into the hands of socialized labor. The manufacture of consumer goods expanding tremendously since the Civil War promised still more improvements. With so many tasks taken over by modern industry, it was "only natural and inevitable that woman should follow her work, that she, too, should accomplish the transition from her age-old work-shop, the family homestead, to the world's new work-shop . . . the factory."[9]

Socialists were not blind to the hardships of women's lives under capitalism, their submerged role at the bottom of the labor market and the "double burden" of domestic responsibilities. Women were allowed only a small portion of men's wages for comparable work and, feared as competitors, they drew men's wrath instead of sympathy. Women not only took the dregs of industrial occupations but also experienced the sting of social ostracism as they invariably violated norms of femininity. Yet working-class women, however stigmatized and exploited, could not afford to quit their jobs. Advancement thus proved a two-edged sword, one side cutting the historic ties that bound them, the other scraping cruelly against their delicate sex.

Yet there was no turning back. Clara Zetkin in *The Question of Women Workers and Women at the Present Time* (1889) had issued the definitive statement. She explained that the advance of capitalism, by dragooning working-class women into the labor force and by reducing the household tasks of the upper class, had eroded the objective basis of women's position in the home. Women's new economic power, Zetkin insisted, now lay in their developing class consciousness as proletarians. American Socialists of the twentieth century refined Zetkin's perspective but maintained its thrust. As Meta Stern stated, "Woman has come into the world of affairs, and she has come to stay. With the tremendous growth of industry and commerce, with the economic and intellectual development of the nation, woman has grown and developed and has stepped forever from those narrow confines in which the economic conditions of the past maintained her." Women would survive this transformation and, with men's aid, they would conquer.[10]

Socialists thus envisioned the realization of womanhood in modern production. For men, the heightening of class consciousness signified a steady but gradual realization of their role as creators of society's wealth. The change for women was more convulsive, their evolution rapidly accelerated from the homebodies of yesteryear to the fully socialized proletarians of today and free worker-citizens of the morrow. Because they faced such a cataclysmic change in their roles, women even better than men could appreciate the underlying significance of the shifts in production which drew them into the labor process. They could feel the golden rays of approaching Socialism with special warmth, for they readily grasped the new society not merely as an improved form of production but as a new civilization, as the reclamation of female dignity lost since the Golden Age.

"The future of the world is in the workingmen's hands," Theresa Malkiel explained, and "the working woman must learn to share the burden of her brothers and together work for the common emancipation of mankind—the Socialist regime—the only true exponent of complete equality and political economic independence."[11] Malkiel's admonition was unquestionably a variant of orthodox Socialist views: woman's unique consciousness must transcend personal and domestic concerns and merge with the class struggle.

Theoretically satisfying, this perspective on women's wage-earning role to a large extent disguised reality. The adaptation of Marxian economics included not so much the entire realm of women's economic contribution as the accepted fact of their new status as wage earners. If the evolution of modern production inevitably brought women into the class struggle, the precise means by which women might actually participate had not been specified, save as men's helpmeets.

STRATEGIC DILEMMAS

During the first decade of the twentieth century social forces seemed to conspire to bring the Socialist dream to life. The percentage of breadwinners in the female population jumped significantly from 20.6 to 25.5 percent, an unprecedented rise in a ten-year period. Women had made inroads into traditional male bastions, such as commerce, transportation, and communication, an advance which many observers interpreted as the beginning of women's integration into all areas of economic life. In selected trades, such as steam laundries, retail sales, food processing, and almost all areas of light manufacturing, so many women found employment that their place in modern industry had been established once and for all.[12]

The expansion of women's work in the garment industry was especially dramatic. New York City's shirtwaist trade had grown from a handful of shops in the mid-1890s to more than 500 by 1900 employing nearly 18,000 women. Philadelphia, Baltimore, and a scattering of smaller cities also had sizable populations of women shirtwaist makers.[13] Concurrently the expansion in the men's clothing sector created spaces for thousands of women. In Chicago, the major center of this line, the industry had become the city's largest employer of women, and women made up over 55 percent of its men's wear work force by 1900. Rochester, St. Louis, and other smaller centers replicated this pattern, spawning a female proletariat where only a few years before there had been virtually none.[14]

Socialists were optimistic about recruiting from these growing ranks of work-ingwomen because so many represented ethnic populations that dominated the urban party. In Chicago over half of the women aged sixteen and over employed in the garment industry were Poles or Bohemians, with Jews, Germans, and Italians constituting the bulk of the remaining work force; sectors of all these ethnic groups participated in the city's radical movements. In New York nearly 60 percent of native-born white women of foreign or mixed parentage, aged sixteen to twenty-four, were gainfully employed by 1910. The rate was similarly high among recent immigrants.[15] Either as self-supporting or (more likely) as important contributors to their families' small incomes, these could easily be viewed as prototypes of future proletarian women. Many demonstrated an integrity and resourcefulness that Socialists hoped would find full expression in the labor and political movements. Especially among young Jewish women of New York's Lower East Side, the sympathetic observer could find a milieu potentially seething with resistance. Journalist Hutchins Hapgood, infatuated with these seemingly exotic women, described in 1902 the "ghetto heroines . . . willing to lay down their lives for an idea, or to live for one."[16] Among New York's waistmakers, nearly 55 percent Jewish, these radical leanings were to have a special salience.

Socialists were also optimistic, although to a lesser degree, about their prospects in other areas where large numbers of women worked. Wherever mass industries had taken over the economic base, the population of workingwomen loomed far in advance of national averages. Paterson and Trenton, New Jersey, Reading, Pennsylvania, Yonkers and Rochester, New York, Milwaukee, St. Louis, and even Muscatine, Iowa, had sizable populations of young working-women, and local Socialists claimed a political organization ready to spring to their aid.[17]

Surveying these promising developments, Socialists prepared to foster class consciousness among workingwomen. The party's women's committees were now in full operation and eager to take on this task. Recalling the difficult battles waged when only handfuls of comrades conducted painstaking agitation, many veterans encouraged their younger sisters to take full advantage of the situation. No longer as an act of faith alone did Socialist women ready themselves to reach out to this vital constituency.

Socialists confronted two compelling strategic alternatives: a formula dictated by the party that obscured women's special interests in the name of class consciousness, and a tradition inherited from the woman's movement that raised sex solidarity as the preferred means. Although most Socialists disdained the latter, they were forced along the course of least resistance. The strategy sponsored by the party could not bridge the distance between themselves and young factory workers, and women's institutions proved stubbornly viable into the first decades of the twentieth century. Without relinquishing their goal of gathering workingwomen under the party's banner, Socialists once again met their match in an organization committed to women's advancement.

Socialist women were bound to the party's so-called "two-arm" labor strategy. With a long and rocky history, the fundamental idea boiled down to the notion that the class struggle comprised two essential components: an economic aspect, the trade union; and a political aspect, the party. The precise relationship between these two "arms" had troubled Socialists for decades and still posed formidable problems. For a period the SLP had tried, with disastrous consequences, to dictate policy to the labor movement. Seemingly having learned a profound lesson, most contemporary Socialists now took a more reserved posture and resolved to maintain the autonomy of each arm. Nevertheless all Socialists recognized their responsibility to build both arms of the movement, to aid the trade union wherever possible and to maintain a party always ready to provide workers with solid political education.[18]

Applied to workingwomen, the two-arm labor strategy was deceptively simple. Socialists aimed first to shake the apathy they perceived among these young workers. Many, they believed, harbored a sense of futility about their positions and saw in marriage the sole answer to their personal unhappiness. Socialists sought to combat this attitude. They argued tirelessly for collective action, claiming that only organized women could refuse low wages and poor conditions. By joining men in the trade union, workingwomen could not only improve their position but afford to postpone marriage until true love presented itself; by joining the party, workingwomen could struggle for their rights as citizens. The union and the party together—as for the male wage earner—spelled salvation.

As their first priority, Socialist women determined to bring more workingwomen into the party. They published dozens of pamphlets and leaflets and regularly grouped themselves into propaganda brigades stationed at the factory gates. They tried, too, to make the party more accessible to hard-pressed workingwomen. They learned quickly that women who worked ten or twelve hours a day could not attend the afternoon meetings arranged to match a housewife's routine and rescheduled some events to early evenings. They called meetings in halls where workingwomen regularly gathered, such as New York's Cooper Union or Clinton Hall, both popular spots on the Lower East Side. They also planned programs to attract workingwomen in particular, such as lectures on economics or debates on workingwomen's need of the ballot.

Were these measures effective? Large numbers of workingwomen did attend various special programs. But even more rarely than their male counterparts did workingwomen turn these occasional bursts of enthusiasm into organizational discipline. At times, amidst union drives or strikes when energies were high and propaganda brigades stormed the community, party membership rolls gained new names. Yet even those workingwomen who paid dues usually declined to participate in day-to-day party affairs. Socialists thus had to be satisfied with subtle signs of success: a sympathy or openness for the Socialist cause among workingwomen, and the prominence of several party members in the union movement.

Never faltering in their faith in mass recruitment, Socialist women fought a Sisyphean battle and received few rewards for their ceaseless efforts. Many members could remember what it had meant to be a "working girl"; others still knew the sting of economic discrimination, although they earned their livelihoods in a school room or office rather than in a factory or store. But however heartfelt their empathy, Socialist women could not bridge the social distance between the two sectors, and the women's branches remained the bastions of housewives and professional women.[19]

The organization of women into labor unions had proved even more difficult. The best hopes for women's organization, the Knights of Labor and Socialist-influenced craft unions of the late 1880s and early 1890s, had fallen since the depression of the mid-1890s. The American Federation of Labor, emerging from economic hard times after the turn of the century, regarded women workers as it did the majority of the unskilled, as competitors who lowered the wage scale and were unsuited for organization. The proportion of female members in the unions had thus declined precipitously during the first years of the new century.

Fortunately, the "new unionism" held high promise. Named for the organization of unskilled dockworkers in England, industrial unionism also had roots in America's coalfields, western mining camps, railroads, and breweries. As the garment industry grew in the 1890s, "new unionism" found an additional pocket of strength among radical workers. The national leadership of the International Ladies' Garment Workers' Union (ILGWU), formed in 1900, condoned the Socialist character of its principal New York locals and permitted the expression of political Socialism in its newspaper and at conventions. Surely the ILGWU, a minority voice within the AFL, and other sectors of the new union movement within the garment industry would prove pioneers of women's organization.[20]

Several women determined to take advantage of this situation. In 1903 Rose Schneiderman, a Russian emigré working as a lining maker in a cap factory, and a friend sought out officials of the United Cloth Hat and Cap Makers' Union, asking if a local could be formed among their co-workers. The union officials assented, and Schneiderman became secretary of the new local. Ignoring her mother's warning that such business would cause her to end up "an old maid," she threw herself into union activities.[21] The only woman on the Cap Makers' executive board, Schneiderman appeared as a sign of women's ascendancy in the new union movement. Pauline Newman, a youthful member of the New York Socialist party's women's committee, also worked in the needle trades. An emigré from eastern Europe, she found a job in 1901 at the Triangle Waist Company. Starting at $1.50 for a seven-day work week, laboring from 7:30 A.M. until 6:30 P.M. in the slack season and longer during the busy months, she rose by 1909 to the "good" wage of $5.50 per week. Enduring the long hours, harsh supervision, customary harassment of "pushing," and unsanitary and oppressive conditions that fostered a sense of degradation, she felt the keen resentment of many garment workers at the worsening conditions, subcontracting, and speed-ups brought by increasing competition between manufacturers. Newman, like Schneiderman, turned to the union. [22]

Despite a promising beginning, militant women faced many obstacles. One was the doldrums weighing down the labor movement in general. Even the best-organized and funded sectors of the AFL suffered from rapid changes in the production process and the overpowering strength of monopolies; the least favored sectors, notably in the women's trades, suffered more. Then, too, male union leaders accounted for another large share. Despite their radical pronouncements, most male unionists continued to harbor reservations about the feasibility of organizing women. Pauline Newman, for example, gained little assistance from the ILGWU leadership in her lengthy struggle against the company union at the Triangle factory. And, as Schneiderman's case suggests, union leaders rarely took the initiative. For a variety of reasons—raw prejudice and insufficient resources—the new unionism failed initially to live up to its promise.

For Socialists, the failure had deeper implications: the two-arm labor strategy had broken down in practice. In theory, the economic and political arms drew upon different although complementary energies and reinforced one another's strengths; in reality, an ill-assorted and outnumbered band of idealists fought unsuccessfully against overwhelming odds. At this point Socialist women had no recourse but to turn to alternative schemes. Not suprisingly they found a mediation in a tradition rooted not in Socialist theory but in the historic woman's movement.

A different strategy, dating to the urban woman's movement of the late nineteenth century, promised a solution. Although the New York Working Women's Society and the Illinois Woman's Alliance had collapsed in the 1890s, old reformers remained in the field. These women had never completely abandoned the dream of a cross-class alliance of women, but they now faced more complex labor, government, and philanthropic mechanisms—some created by themselves—setting up larger barriers between middle-class reformers and workers. Perhaps by cooperating with women with roots in working-class communities, they might offer workingwomen the solidarity, the logistical aid, and the publicity they sorely needed. By default, Socialist women turned to this mobilization inspired by the feared gender consciousness via the Women's Trade Union League.

Formed at the 1903 AFL convention, the Women's Trade Union League was a curiously hybrid institution. Not an official union but rather a quasi-educational organization, the league operated as the industrial wing of the mainstream women's movement. Its founders had direct ties to the late nineteenth-century precursors. Veterans of the Illinois legislative campaigns, Jane Addams and Mary Kenney O'Sullivan were prime initiators; Abby Morton Diaz's successor in the Women's Educational and Industrial Union, Mary Morton Kehew, became the league's first president. The WTUL membership was open to anyone, wage earner or not, who promised to render assistance to the organization of women into trade unions. The league thus joined working-class unionists with middle-class "allies," as they were called, forming an assembly destined to split. For a period, however, especially after 1907 when the league focused on the garment industry, it appeared a promising vehicle for the organization of workingwomen.

Leonora O'Reilly offered personal testimony to the viability of this tradition. At age sixteen she had joined the Knights of Labor and had simultaneously helped organize the New York Working Women's Society. Although she became disillusioned when the society turned to consumer rather than union issues, O'Reilly stayed close to her philanthropic allies. Throughout the 1890s, working ten hours a day at a shirtwaist factory and organizing a women's local of the United Garment Workers' Union, O'Reilly joined her friends at the Henry Street Settlement, the Social Reform Club, and the Society for Ethical Culture. Her middle-class friends reciprocated her loyalty and funded her education at the Pratt Institute of Brooklyn, a vocational school. By the time she graduated in 1900, O'Reilly had emerged as a leading New York personality, defender of the labor movement and friend of the progressive middle class, prime candidate for the Women's Trade Union League.

Although she resigned for a brief period in 1905 in protest over the role of allies in shaping league policy, O'Reilly seemed fairly comfortable within its milieu. She became a member of the WTUL's first executive board and vice-president of the New York league in 1909, when she received a lifetime annuity which would allow her to work full-time for the league. Until 1914, when ill-health curtailed her activities, O'Reilly spoke regularly from its platform.

O'Reilly also recruited many trade unionists and Socialists who might ordinarily have stayed away, like Rose Schneiderman, who became a league vice-president in 1906. Pauline Newman also eventually joined. Newman and Schneiderman, a generation younger than O'Reilly and rooted in the Jewish radical community, often shared lingering reservations but steadily looked for assurance to their older comrade. As a radical bloc within the League, O'Reilly, Newman, and Schneiderman created space for other Socialists.[23]

Socialist women played important roles, especially within the New York WTUL. Party stalwarts Theresa Malkiel, Anna Maley, Bertha Mailly, and Meta Stern served for a time on its local executive board. Nonparty sympathizers Gertrude Barnum, Ida Rauh, Violette Pike, Rheta Childe Dorr, and Harriot Stanton Blatch with fewer restraints participated more fully. Party member Helen Marot worked full-time until 1914, serving as executive secretary of the New York branch, while other lesser-known comrades intermittently contributed their services. [24]

Socialists never fully overcame their suspicions, however, and were especially critical of the league's loyalty to Samuel Gompers and the anti-Socialist bureaucracy of the AFL. Yet they recognized the league's success in drawing public attention to conditions in the shops, its direct aid in securing women doctors and rest rooms for tired workers, its well-attended agitational meetings, and its quieter legislative campaigns. However the WTUL might disavow the class struggle and remain nonpartisan toward political movements, it had proven itself a valuable ally of workingwomen. Moreover, it dispelled the feeling of impotence Socialist women had gained from their experiences within both the party and the union mainstream.

A shared dedication to workingwomen thus formed the basis for a dynamic cooperation. The most sanguine Socialists might prescribe a three-pronged strategy, the "extra arm" to supplement orthodoxy as necessary to address the unique problems raised by this new sector of the working class. How far this path would lead depended upon factors beyond the control of any one element in the coalition. Women's unionism would not run the smooth course Socialists predicted, nor would it unfold as the militant sisterhood the women reformers had planned. Most unsettling, women's unionism did not prove the open-sesame to class consciousness and political activism that party members had hoped. But its explosive character, its combative energies, the spirit and institutions created largely by workingwomen themselves encouraged a sense of fullfillment.

THE WOMEN'S STRIKES

The "women's strikes" of 1909–11 moved the question of women's labor beyond its theoretical phase, and women's unionization from the pioneering effort of a few women to a mass concern. Although all party members instinctively supported the landmark New York shirtwaist strike of 1909 and the Chicago garment strike of 1910, Socialist women recognized they had a special responsibility. Few in number and with slight financial means, they might suffer from too little pre-strike contact with workingwomen and fail to mobilize their own ranks as quickly and completely as they desired. But they could make up for deficiencies through sheer will, by utilizing the resources at hand to spread the message of solidarity among strikers and within the community, by rousing support within organized labor, and sometimes by sustaining the strike momentum after others gave up the cause as lost. Never would Socialist women experience a greater trial or triumph. Their ability to provide aid and leadership to workingwomen would now be put to the test—as would their alliance with the Women's Trade Union League.

New York shirtwaist makers commenced the first round, which lasted from November, 1909, to February, 1910. The "Uprising of 20,000," as their strike came to be called, affected over 500 shops and virtually stopped production in the garment industry. Some 75 percent of the strikers were women, most between the ages of sixteen and twenty-four. Hundreds, sometimes thousands, never before members of labor organizations enrolled in the ILGWU. More than a mere conflict between employers and workers, the shirtwaist strike stood, as contemporaries noted, as the "largest strike of women ever known in the United States."[25]

The strike began in September, 1909, when workers struck the Triangle and Leiserson shops. Witnessing constant police harassment and unlawful arrest of pickets, WTUL leaders who had joined the effort decided to place themselves in jeopardy. New York police finally took WTUL president Mary Dreier to jail, an act which inspired the New York press to give sympathetic coverage to the strike. Meanwhile a committee within the ILGWU considered the possibility of reaping the benefits of favorable publicity by extending the strike to other shops.

As the strike spread quickly throughout the garment district, the ILGWU planned an open meeting to discuss the situation. On November 22 an overflow crowd filled Cooper Union and heard speeches endorsing the moderate tactics set forth by the union leadership. After two hours a young workingwoman, described as a "wisp of a girl, still in her teens," spoke from the back of the hall. Her words in Yiddish fell upon the crowd like an Old Testament miracle: "I have listened to all the speakers and I have no further patience for talk. I am one who feels and suffers for the things pictured. I move we go on general strike!" Responding to the enthusiasm of the crowd, the chairman grabbed the young woman's arm, raised it high, and cried in Yiddish: "Do you mean faith? Will you take the old Hebrew oath?" With right arms raised, the crowd pledged, "If I turn traitor to the cause I now pledge, may this hand wither from the arm I now raise." The general strike had begun.[26]

The young woman catapulted to sudden fame was Clara Lemlich, a striker from Leiserson's and not quite the ingenue publicists like to portray. Lemlich's flair for rebellion was well developed. She had fled Russia with her family during the Kishinev pogrom of 1903, already having cracked the Russian classics and having learned the revolutionary songs of the Ukraine. On her way to the United States she attended anarchist meetings in London. Within her first week on American shores, fifteen-year-old Clara Lemlich found a job in New York's shirtwaist industry and soon thereafter reconvened her political activities. She continued her education at a nearby branch of the public library and joined a trade union discussion group which met during lunch breaks. In 1906, after receiving advice from the editors of the *Jewish Daily Forward*, Lemlich and her co-workers formed Local 25 of the ILGWU. A member of its executive board, Lemlich participated in the undramatic but important strikes leading up to the 1909 conflict. By 1909 she had become well known as a leading trade unionist among waistmakers, not yet a member of the Socialist party but in attendance at so many meetings that the comrades simply assumed she had already enrolled. Lemlich was, in fact, part of a Socialist cadre in the making. [27]

From the onset, Socialist women and the WTUL worked in close alliance and together played a decisive role. The financial weakness of the union and the conservatism of its leadership demanded assistance if order were to reign over chaos. Later, as the press played upon the novelty of a strike led by such young women, other civic organizations and prominent citizens offered their services. By that time women from the WTUL and from the Socialist party had become so deeply enmeshed in the strike machinery that they were vital to its smooth operation.

Socialists aided the strikers first by assisting their union in several key ways. At the strike's onset the ILGWU was only a shadow of what it was to become and lacked organizers to sign up new members and to orchestrate the picket lines. Socialists leaped into the breach by appointing a committee which in turn placed a small army of party members in dozens of halls throughout the Lower East Side. Socialists proceeded to enroll up to 1,500 members in the union per day. Socialists also joined the more exciting and hazardous work of picketing, and provided personal assistance and financial aid to arrested strikers. Prominent women in the party, such as Rose Pastor Stokes, Theresa Malkiel, and Carrie Allen, addressed mass meetings held daily for the strikers and thereby generated enthusiasm for the union drives. Socialists also conducted fund-raising campaigns to build the union's nonexistent treasury. The Italian branch of the party established a special bureau to conduct the difficult work of reaching their ethnic sisters, some 35 percent of New York's garment trade. [28]

Socialists also joined the WTUL's programs designed to garner community support for the strikers. A few days after the general strike broke out, a protest march organized by strikers, with Socialist and WTUL assistance, led several thousand people in a procession to City Hall. Two days later, on December 5, over 7,000 persons filled the Hippodrome in a rally financed by WTUL angel Alva Belmont to hear Rose Pastor Stokes, Leonora O'Reilly, and others deliver what newspapers called a combination of "socialism, unionism, woman suffrage and what seemed to be something like anarchism." The following week

Socialists held their own rally, drawing a large crowd of waistmakers to hear the famous coalfields agitator, Mother Jones.[29] While Socialist newspapers in several languages daily hammered home the importance of the strike, rank-and-filers canvassed union members and neighborhood sympathizers, requesting financial support and help with picket duty. More than at any time perhaps since the late 1880s or early 1890s were Socialist women able to bring to life the radical sentiments in various pockets of Manhattan's communities.

In mid-December, as arbitration began, Socialists moved into yet closer alliance with the WTUL. They hosted a grand reception for women who had just been released from the workhouse and thereby revived the sagging spirits of several thousand strikers who attended the gala event. Together with WTUL organizers they formed shop committees, which assisted those workers who had already settled with their employers in maintaining their unions intact. Socialists and WTUL leaders waged a mass boycott campaign aimed at housewives who might ignore the strike and search for bargains among non-union goods. At the strike's high point Socialist women supported the strikers in their courageous rejection of the proposed contract. They also increased their appeals for funds, fearing public interest was waning just as the strike headed into the winter's hardest months. On December 29, two days after the strikers had refused the first offer at settlement, the *New York Call's* "Strike Special" hit the stands. This strike edition, with sections in Italian, Yiddish, and English, was the production of two Vassar graduates, Elsie Cole and Elizabeth Dutcher, Socialists working for the WTUL, and 45,000 copies were sold on the street by waistmakers affectionately called "strike newsies."[30]

The production of the *Call's* strike edition best characterized Socialists' role in the strike. As one writer put it, the strike newspaper had three essential purposes: to raise money for the union, to tell the full story without concealing any facts, and to keep the public informed of the strike's progress.[31] In other words, Socialists were to serve, not lead, the workers' cause. Socialists thus had added their energies to the monumental and tedious clerical tasks of membership drives, their human warmth to the emotional support strikers required in their times of despair. And they raised thousands of dollars for the union treasury. In short, Socialists and especially the women who threw themselves wholeheartedly into this effort proved themselves loyal friends of workingwomen.

The significance of the contributions of Socialists may be measured by comparing situations in New York and Philadelphia. The New York events had touched off a sympathy strike in nearby Philadelphia. Two-thirds of the local waistmakers left their shops and engaged in combative picketing only to suffer similar political harassment and arrest. Although Socialists threw their resources into the strike campaign led by the WTUL, they were far less organized than in New York and consequently were unable to play an instrumental role. After a few weeks the Philadelphia strike faded, and the strikers gained few of their demands. This relative setback seemed to suggest that enthusiasm alone would not suffice, and that the difference between victory and defeat depended as much on the quality of strike support within the community as on the strength of the union proper.[32]

Not that New York strikers gained their full objectives. By early February union leaders urged strikers to settle although the key demand of a union shop could not be achieved. But as a prominent trade unionist later remarked, the shirtwaist strike had provided an "educational lesson on the grand scale," the full fruits of which would not be picked for years.[33]

Contemporaries observed that the "Uprising of 20,000" had created a new mood in the labor movement inaugurating an era of women's militancy. Indeed, the shirtwaist strike commenced a series of strikes. Although St. Louis workers had conducted the first significant strike in the men's wear sector, the New York waistmakers inspired the workers in Chicago's garment trades, who struck in massive proportions in September, 1910.

The situation in Chicago was unique. A sizable portion of garment workers were men, although heroic young women emerged as strike leaders. As in New York, there were many Jews and Italians, but workers represented many Slavic nationalities as well. Strike literature had to be printed in nine languages to reach all the crucial constituencies. In addition, if the ILGWU leadership in New York had been skeptical of women's capacity for union organizing, the United Garment Workers was not merely reluctant to conduct a strike but archaic by its craft structure and simply incapable of organizing a far-flung, sustained struggle. Socialist women had to weigh these various factors, which offered a different range of choices than New Yorkers possessed. If they seemed less able to maneuver, to parlay alliances into a functioning machine within— and, if need be, outside—the union structure, they were also forced to make more sacrifices and exhibit an even greater dedication to the cause of workingwomen.

Young women initiated the Chicago garment strike. A small group first went to the offices of the UGW to describe the oppressive shop conditions, which were exacerbated by a new rate- and wage-cutting system. The long hours, low wages, and unsanitary conditions were, as in New York, standard fare in this highly competitive industry, but the speed-up had made the workday intolerable. As the union leadership seemed slow to respond to their grievances, sixteen young women took matters into their own hands. Refusing to accept yet another cut in rates, they walked off their jobs. A committee tried to speak with the employer, Hart Schaffner and Marx, but met with no success. The young women then proceeded to visit workers in other shops. At the end of the week they blew their whistles and were joined on the city's streets by 2,000 enthusiastic supporters. The strike had begun.[34]

While the union leadership pondered the situation, Chicago Socialists stepped in. On October 7 they published a special edition of the *Daily Socialist*, featuring detailed stories on shop conditions and the extent of the walk-out. The chief journalist in charge, Robert Dvorak, reportedly threatened to print a call for a general strike if the union leadership continued to stall on the matter. Finally, after 18,000 workers had walked off their jobs and Socialist publicity proliferated, the UGW called a general strike. Fifty thousand copies of the *Daily Socialist* containing the call were distributed throughout the city, and within a week over 41,000 workers had joined the struggle. [35]

Because the garment workers lacked a cadre of experienced leaders, the other groups in the community were even more central than in the New York affair. On October 20 the Chicago WTUL offered its services to the district council of the UGW, which accepted the offer a week later. The WTUL then organized a strike committee and drew upon its extensive network of prominent citizens, especially among the settlement houses and the Chicago Federation of Labor. The Chicago WTUL rendered services to the strikers, as their sisters in New York had done for the waistmakers, and its contribution far outweighed anything the UGW could offer. Publicity, picketing, legal protection, and union organizing thus fell into the hands of the WTUL and its allies. Because the strike involved entire families rather than primarily young women, relief funds were a major concern. When the UGW's treasury ran dry within a few weeks, the WTUL's strike committee took over and rallied neighborhood retailers to contribute goods and services. The strike committee also established a commissary to feed the strikers and organized additional subcommittees to secure rent money, coal, and milk for babies. [36]

Socialist women were well situated to assist these efforts. Like the local garment industry, the Socialist organization had grown up along neighborhood lines, and Socialist women regularly worked within their own communities. Although the garment strike marked their debut, Socialist women had prepared for sustained agitation by regularly leafleting factory gates, sponsoring public forums on issues of women's work, and serving as representatives to various workingwomen's organizations. Their community connections proved decisive in building the support network. Socialist women helped spread the message among sympathetic doctors, druggists, barbers, grocers, butchers, songwriters, and artists, and extracted services from all. They also housed and fed homeless strikers and their children.

Socialist women worked, as in New York, in alliance with the WTUL and likewise found their greatest public role as fund raisers and publicity agents. A special subcommittee formed by the local Women's Agitation Committee took up this task, bringing together women from the party and the WTUL to plan a special strike edition of the *Chicago Daily Socialist*. Socialist women attended strikers' meetings to recruit young women to help edit the paper. Ellen Megow, a local speaker, gave up to seven performances daily to make the public aware of the project. Once the paper was produced, Socialist women planned its distribution, organizing "strike newsies" to cover the entire Chicago Loop district. By the time the strike fizzled in February, 1911, after a second special strike edition of the *Daily Socialist*, Socialist women had secured over $3,000 for the relief fund, the largest sum raised by any save organized labor. [37]

The strikes of 1909–11 prompted Socialists to reaffirm their faith in workingwomen. Women wage earners had proven not only heroic in their own right but capable of stirring the larger unskilled working class into aggressive action. Unionists previously condescending toward workingwomen now praised the strikers. The Socialist cadre within the unions basked in the party's accolades, tightened ranks, and stressed the importance of strengthening the ties between the union and the party. If Socialist women could not foresee the disappointment ahead, they at least enjoyed a temporary gratification.

Unquestionably the New York and Chicago strikes had transformed the garment industry. The waistmakers' strike came to be known as the "spark" that touched off the New York cloakmakers' strike of 1910, which in turn roused the entire Jewish community to new heights of class consciousness and established the model "protocol of peace" in the cloak industry. In 1913 workers in the women's trades would sign similar protocol agreements granting a fifty-hour week, increases in wages and piece rates, various improvements in working conditions, and the long-desired "preferential union shop." Even in its failure, the Chicago garment strike had laid the foundation for the industrial union, the Amalgamated Clothing Workers, which would displace the UGW a few years later during the wartime upswing of labor militancy. Alongside these major strikes, many minor incidents in other cities dramatized women's role in the labor movement. [38]

Socialists drew political conclusions equally unprecedented. The party's oldest daily newspaper, the *New Yorker Volkszeitung*, praised the waistmakers for their heroism. Its leading woman journalist, Meta Stern, hailed the strike as the definite proof of solidarity among the most sorely oppressed sectors of the working class. The *Jewish Daily Forward*, the leading popular Socialist daily, announced that the waistmakers had instituted a "revolution" in the trade on which Jewish-American destiny depended. Tales of heroic deeds were supplemented by the pen-sketches of the movement's most beloved litterateur, "teardrop millionaire" Morris Rosenfeld. Never before had any strike received such extensive coverage in the Yiddish Socialist press. Even outside the metropolis, a craft-labor paper like the *Cleveland Citizen* responded to the events by instituting a column for workingwomen's interests. Across the nation Socialist newspapers increased their coverage of women's news and conveyed an image of women workers at the center of the class struggle. [39]

This reportage also meshed smoothly with more formal theoretical paradigms. Socialist writers thus dramatized the process of "awakening" allegedly experienced by the young women. Prior to the action workingwomen had seemed hapless, almost oblivious to the exploitative circumstances of their labor. Then suddenly these women, "who had gone through life as in a trance," Malkiel wrote, "had with one gigantic effort torn asunder the fetters of ancient custom and tradition determined for this once to wage an earnest battle for the right to live. . . . [T]he very spontaneity of the strike brought about a revolution in their minds." After centuries "bent under the yoke of subjection," women responded to their industrial suffering, their new social consciousness at last penetrating "behind the thick factory wall, the flimsy tenement building."[40]

This process of awakening gained a special quality, in the writers' estimation, from the youth of the workingwomen. Their precious teenhood swallowed up by commodity production, the strikers appeared at once pathetic and heroic. Socialist women reached out because they were loyal to the working class but also because they felt a profound sense of sisterhood with the young working-women who would accomplish what the older generation had longed to see in its lifetime. Meta Stern, writing during the New York strike, appealed in a highly sentimental poem on behalf of this "frail little girl" as the "outcast of today / but the pioneer of tomorrow." Stern was not patronizing the strikers but attempting to describe the unique dignity they inspired in all socially conscious women. As Malkiel explained, the strikers understood their struggle as something grander than merely a fight for a better standard of living: "They have suddenly caught a glimpse of a new fairyland and are stretching hurriedly their long idle wings, raising their bowed heads preparatory in taking flight into it."[41]

Local activist Nellie Zeh similarly emphasized the strikers' nobility of character. A leader of the Chicago strike, Alberta Hnetynka, personally exemplified the ideal: pretty, young, cheerful but no less militant, strong, and assertive—all the best qualities expected in the coming Socialist womanhood. Young workingwomen lacked the emotional frills bourgeois girls flaunted: "There was no posing, no unnecessary 'furs and feathers'; no simpering, giggling or non-sense; nothing but simple strength and power in their every word, action and hand-clasp as they looked one frankly in the face and talked the situation over with intelligence and understanding." To Zeh, women's ability to cooperate with men during the strike disproved the commonplace notion that women were too weak or too "feminine" to undertake the fight. Women's experience in wage labor, as Socialists had predicted, had apparently strengthened their character by giving them access to the economic power men previously monopolized; workingwomen in alliance with politically advanced women would now forward the liberation of their sex.[42]

Despite the evident simplicity of this analysis, writers like Malkiel and Zeh were reaffirming the basic principles of the Socialist theory of women's labor. National leader Caroline Lowe might rephrase their interpretation in more familiar terms: "Solidarity among working women on the industrial field and on the political field is rapidly assuming a strength that will hold the balance of power in the class struggle that is now on. Clear foresight, unfailing and unswerving loyalty are the only attributes necessary to ultimate and speedy victory." Local and national leaders thus agreed on the significance of recent events, the strikers' bold actions serving as both "revelation and prophecy" of things to come.[43]

By drawing such conclusions, Socialist women also reaffirmed their allegiance to the two-arm labor strategy. Both the union and the Socialist party had proved the worthiness of their special mission. Socialist women had performed a range of indispensable tasks, their union support work, rounds of speech-making, fund-raising programs, and the special strike editions the products of careful planning. As Zeh summarized, the "success of the enterprise was entirely due to the fact that there was a machine that was well oiled with harmony and good will and that the workers made use of it for their own profit."[44] Now that workingwomen stood equal to their proletarian brothers, they would take the next step and search for the political education only the party could provide. No doubt their recruitment required a special approach, but the key lay in a creative application of the lessons at hand. "Comrades," Malkiel exhorted, "every movement has its opportunities; this is ours."[45]

The excitement of the moment swept away doubts and reservations that might have proved salutary during the difficult times ahead. Male indifference, even outright hostility, toward workingwomen was deeply rooted in the labor and Socialist movements, and the evident shift in attitude during the women's strikes, while promising, could prove temporary, especially because no new structure within the party or union guaranteed the continuation of good will. In turn, the very success of the strikes had rested upon an unstable and explosive combination—women activists and class-conscious loyalists joined in a single cause. Too many factors outside the two-armed formula impinged on strategic certainty; too easily did Socialists conclude that heroic action alone resolved major theoretical dilemmas. The more Socialist women hoped to consolidate their victory, the more they met a painful frustration.

In the spring of 1911 more than 300 Socialist women crowded New York's Labor Temple to discuss the prospects for the next, great political leap ahead. Having endured a long period of "indifference, contempt and opposition" within the party, they believed a turning point had finally been reached. The strike had justified their demands for special propaganda among women. Now the party must move speedily to meet its historic responsibility to the female proletariat. But how was it to accomplish this goal?

Conference attendees found no simple answer. Should the party create special branches to prepare women for membership or recruit them directly into the mixed local; should agitation committees offer special activities for workingwomen or conduct house-to-house canvasses among housewives; should the women's committee push woman suffrage propaganda or work on behalf of the union—few could speak with authority, let alone decisiveness. Long-standing disagreements remained. Not even the most spectacular uprising of workingwomen in American history offered a panacea to strategically troubled comrades.[46]

In only one important respect had the situation changed significantly. The party recruited successfully among the strike leaders and simultaneously catapulted its own cadre into important positions within the union and WTUL. Trade union women who had rarely expressed their political views prior to the strike now publicly declared their loyalty to the Socialist movement. Rose Schneiderman and Leonora O'Reilly, who achieved a sweeping notoriety during the strike, were only two of the most prominent converts. Long-standing Socialists and sympathizers, similarly hurled into the limelight, capitalized on their fame to the party's benefit. Pauline Newman gained a paid position as organizer for the ILGWU and over the next several years regaled her union audiences with the Socialist message. Clara Lemlich, proclaimed the "Joan of Arc" of the young women's revolution, joined the WTUL executive board shortly after the strike and, blacklisted from most factories, devoted herself to political activities, including the Socialist party's woman suffrage campaign.[47]

But the anticipated rise in party membership failed to materialize. As the strike fever faded into memory, fewer workingwomen applied for membership while recent recruits drifted away. This melancholy outcome returned Socialist women to basic problems of organization: political apathy continued to stalk voteless young workingwomen despite their moment of triumph; the killing pace of wage labor combined with union duties precluded their full participation in the political organization. Socialist women, housewives and professionals removed from the industrial epicenter of class struggle, had navigated vast territories during the strikes but returned at last to their original organizational stasis.

This ambiguous outcome forced women trade unionists deeper into their own institutions while provoking among the political cadre an increasing sense of isolation and loss. Emerging labor functionaries like Schneiderman and Newman did not require a mass Socialist constituency—a faithful membership and dedicated leaders could do their work without carrying party cards—and bent their energies to more immediate tasks. Hardened politicos like Malkiel, lacking any direct link to the unions, took little solace in the new respectability accorded Socialist idealism. Trapped and frustrated by the meager political gains, they turned their rage against the middle-class women who had seemingly denied Socialists their full rewards.

Few could deny the crucial role of the WTUL during the garment strikes. But from the Socialist viewpoint, the league had committed sins of omission and commission. Cautious lest they offend anti-Socialist AFL leaders, WTUL officials acknowledged the party's contributions in reports published for their membership but rarely praised Socialists publicly. They had also allowed certain scions of capitalists, like Anne Morgan, to donate their time and money as well as their anti-radical venom. In Chicago WTUL leaders, along with the local Federation of Labor and (admittedly) a large number of Socialists, had deserted the uncompromising strikers at a crucial moment while Socialist women held tight. Worst of all, the WTUL rather than the Socialist party had emerged the public champions of workingwomen.

Theresa Malkiel had spotted this danger during the early days of the New York strike, but the Carnegie Hall meeting at the apex of events proved the case beyond question. The pageantry of this occasion, highlighted by a tableau performed on stage by strikers themselves, had illuminated the dark corners of Socialist hopes and fears. Malkiel, who had served on the planning committee for this celebration, believed the WTUL financial backers had ruined their prospects by issuing an ultimatum that no Socialist could appear on the dais and by prohibiting all Socialist leafleting. Morris Hillquit, the waistmakers' own attorney, appeared despite the proviso but only to spark unfavorable commentary in the press. Anne Morgan charged Hillquit and the beloved Leonora O'Reilly with misusing the occasion to preach Socialism; AFL executive Eva McDonald Valesh called the Socialist party a disruptive element in the labor movement. Malkiel lost no time in responding. She countered that the real danger to the strike and to trade unionism lay "in the pretended friendship of the Miss Morgans, who came down from the height of their pedestals to preach identity of interests to the little daughters of the people." Socialists, she warned, must guard against such subterfuges by refusing to cooperate with "bourgeois" reformers. [48]

Socialists like Malkiel might find in this decision a reassuring affirmation of their faith in the class struggle, but they missed an important point. Whatever its limitations, a cross-class alliance of women had in fact sustained the garment strikes and helped secure the partial victories. This truth might have suggested a series of corollary questions: why had women been able to rise so suddenly from their apparent lethargy? What special factors, such as their lowly position in the labor market, the cyclical nature of wage and household labor, and the unique attitudes positive and negative that they carried into the workplace, remained theirs alone even after they joined the union? If women activists had barely begun to probe such matters since their ground-breaking work of the late nineteenth century, they had created at least a fund of relevant experience. Socialist women could benefit from this tradition only insofar as they, too, came to grips with the practical problems women faced in the marketplace and adjusted their vision to the reality of the actual situation. Such a task remained incomplete, impossible for the faithful cadre to undertake.

Socialist women had nevertheless proven what so many male comrades previously doubted, the ability of a militant minority to mobilize working-women who were ready for battle. Not only did the women's sector supply indispensable human and financial resources, but they offered strike support creatively adapted to a constituency ignored by both the Socialist and labor movements. Future mobilizations of workingwomen, in the garment trades and elsewhere, did little to improve on these methods.

FROM POLITICS TO UNIONISM

Since the late nineteenth century Socialists had vacillated on their interpretation of the class struggle, stressing as paramount first its economic side, then its political. For women, because they played a comparatively minor role in the labor movement before 1910, the party had served concurrently as organizational home and as subtle reminder of their inability to participate directly in economic struggles. The "women's strikes" seemed at last to abolish this dichotomy. After the celebrations were over, however, the strategic dilemma returned with a new twist. While a cadre of militant trade unionists carried forward the party's labor program for many women in the garment trades, the parent political movement faded away.

The new unions soon had an institutional weight among workingwomen that the party's circle of women had never attained. Progressive leaders female and male made, especially during the war years, admirable efforts to knit together women workers and housewives, Jew and Catholic, immigrant and native-born, and to lay the groundwork for a variant of a mobilization Socialist women had long advocated. But the desired political coherence and alliance among all sympathetic women lay beyond reach. As Socialism in the unions increasingly became more a matter of personal faith than collective discipline, activists could well ponder the ultimate significance of their hard-fought victories.

The Socialist party and its women's sector reached the limits of their influence upon the labor movement during the Lawrence, Massachusetts, and Paterson, New Jersey, textile strikes of 1912–13. The coalition which had successfully served the garment strikers failed on unfamiliar terrain, and Socialists found themselves yet further removed from the dynamic of the class struggle. With the WTUL now sidelined by the AFL leadership, there were no middle-class scapegoats.

Slave to a textile industry already suffering from the competition of southern mills, Lawrence had previously offered few trade union opportunities. Yet its largely female work force showed a fighting spirit as millowners reduced wages and announced a statutory reduction in hours. On January 12 a group of Polish women walked out and ignited a general strike. The IWW hailed the event as the apotheosis of industrial unionism, the promise of a "new society" of foreign-born workers "on trial" against the parasites and their nativist lackeys. The Socialist party, in contrast, lacked ties with the Italians and various eastern European nationalities which constituted Lawrence's blue-collar population. Eager to provide aid, Socialists could play only a minor part in the strike drama.[49]

The leading female role fell to IWW organizer Elizabeth Gurley Flynn, the celebrated "Rebel Girl." Conducting agitation among the unskilled and newly immigrated workers outside the Socialist centers and Jewish networks, Gurley Flynn had come to appreciate the special needs of working-class women. In the eastern textile towns like Little Falls, New Bedford, Lawrence, Fall River, Paterson, and Passaic, where women and children constituted the majority working in the mills, Gurley Flynn had spearheaded the IWW organizing drives of 1910. To aid women in strike situations and after, she advocated programs like sex hygiene classes for women and alternative schools for children along with the usual strike kitchens and other emergency institutions. Despite her sympathy with women's plight, she never strayed from her fundamental goal, to build the union along gender-neutral lines. Although she joined the Socialist party in 1911, shortly after its valiant efforts on behalf of women strikers, she shunned its women's sector and remained unswerving in her basic principles. Helping to create the romantic Wobbly archetype of the agitator who "fanned the flames of discontent," Gurley Flynn bypassed the models offered by her gender-conscious comrades.[50]

Socialist women moved by sisterly feeling for the striking women of Lawrence did, however, assist Gurley Flynn. New York women under Margaret Sanger's leadership arranged the transportation of strikers' children from Lawrence to New York, Philadelphia, and other cities where they were cared for while their parents continued the strike; this newsworthy exodus garnered widespread sympathy for the strike. Socialist women also raised money through lavishly publicized meetings, entertainments, special leafleting, and newspaper coverage. A handful of New York women stationed themselves in Lawrence for the duration, while local sympathizers like Wellesley professors Vida Scudder and Eleanor Hayes delivered speeches under the auspices of the Lawrence Socialist women's club. The partial victory of the Lawrence strike encouraged Socialist women who relished their role as servant to the class struggle. But the distance between the cohesive neighborhood organizations of New York or Chicago, and the party's inability to establish roots in the Lawrence community, foretold a fleeting gratification.[51]

The Paterson, New Jersey, textile strike of early 1913 further dampened their prospects. Here, silk-loom weavers sought to resist accelerating production paces and continuing low wages. Women workers again proved crucial. The

IWW led the strike, while Socialists in nearby New York raised money, conducted publicity campaigns, and helped arrange the vast spectacle staged by the strikers in Madison Square Garden. The strike nevertheless sagged. Facing defeat, Socialists and IWW leaders began to exchange hostilities: Socialists criticized Wobblies for acting irresponsibly in issuing antipolitical propaganda; Wobblies accused Socialists of draining precious energies into the Madison Square Garden event which failed to produce significant funds. The defeat uprooted the entire IWW eastern organizing drive, for the time being restricted industrial union advances to the needle trades, and deepened bitterness on all sides. [52]

The subsequent falling out between Wobblies and the party leadership shook the Socialist women's sector to the core. The recall of IWW leader William D. Haywood from the party's National Executive Committee for the advocacy of industrial sabotage ignited protests and resignations, including those of several prominent women like Gurley Flynn, Sanger, and WTUL leader Helen Marot. A precipitous decline in party membership during 1913 turned pro- and anti-IWW factions at each other's throats, leaving Socialist women and their allies scattered among opposing blocs, sharing mainly discouragement. [53]

For Socialist women the Lawrence and Paterson strikes represented a major turning point. Although they continued to join their allies in the WTUL in response to subsequent strike calls, notably in sectors of the garment trade, their importance receded as the unions took on a greater role. The party's women's committees became a weak appendage to the growing garment unions, while the WTUL fell into disarray at the national level, losing its minimal backing from the AFL leadership and retreating to its former policy of legislative reform. In the meantime the economic downturn of 1913 eclipsed the entire strike momentum, flooding the market with unskilled workers male and female. As the war clouds gathered in Europe, the very subject of women's unionism lost the primacy it once enjoyed. The era begun with the shirtwaist makers' strike was now closed. [54]

The next phase in Socialists' relations with organized labor began with the war years. The demise of the party's influence contrasted sharply to the successful unionism Socialists had so long advocated. Now in key positions of authority within the unions, individual Socialists experienced an understandable measure of satisfaction. At the same time their growing skepticism toward electoral politics and party discipline attenuated the very links Socialists had once considered strategically vital. Radical women in the unions no less than men felt compelled to make the union movement encompass the ideals that the party had failed to realize.

The economic situation was favorable to this transformation. Booming profits promoted rapid industrial growth while international hostilities reduced

immigration, permitting workers to change jobs more readily and to insist upon
better pay. Each year from 1915 to 1919 record-breaking numbers of strikes and
lost hours brought union recognition and shorter hours to new sectors. Garment walk-outs of 1915–16 revived many women's locals that had collapsed
several years earlier and established permanent organizations not only in New
York but also in Philadelphia, Chicago, and Boston. For the first time significant numbers of Italian-American women successfully organized, utilizing
methods the party's women's committee had pioneered. Women textile operatives, department store clerks, telephone operators, and others struck, in some
cases forming the first successful unions in their trades. [55]

These events simultaneously deflated the most grandiose hopes of radical
organizers. New unions sprang up mostly within the AFL, whose leadership
pledged loyalty to government war aims and expressed absolute enmity toward
the "treasonous" Socialists. Some of the most successful and militant unions,
like the Amalgamated Clothing Workers, secured their victories at the bar-
gaining tables with the aid of the Wilson administration's War Labor Board.
The general character of the union drives, wholly set upon bread-and-butter
issues, thrust the Socialist political aims out of sight. It was as if the old craft-
union Socialists had been vindicated in their two-arm labor strategy—but one
of the arms had now practically ceased to exist so the other might grow strong. [56]

In the needle trades, where the organization of women was most successful,
the union tended to displace the party in all but name. Radical women from
New York's ILGWU Local 25 emerged in the ten years after the 1909 strike as
the firebrands of the industry, feverish with expectations especially as the Russian Revolution rekindled their homeland nostalgia and simultaneously gave
them faith in a worldwide revolution. But the Socialist party, politically overextended and closely tied to the moderate leadership, provided no outlet for
such extreme energies. The union's Current Affairs Committee, later to become a center for a Communist-led assault on the ILGWU bureaucracy, thus
demanded that the union itself become "a way of life with vision and a soul."
Wherever this particular idealism might lead, it could not return to the same
political faith endemic among Socialists at the crest of their movement. [57]

In effect, discussions of the woman question also moved from the party to
the unions during these years. In the ACWA and the ILGWU their respective
English-language newspapers *Advance* and *Justice*, along with foreign-language
publications, pressed home the message with special features usually including
a page devoted to women's issues. *Advance* began its regular coverage in 1917
with a statement couched in sentiment clearly drawn from old traditions in the
women's movement:

> Women have not only a special opportunity in the labor movement, but
> they can make to it a contribution of their own. They can bring to it qualities
> which, as a mere man's movement, it often lacks—imagination, devotion,

inspiration. If working girls are once aroused to the wide and deep significance and beauty of the struggle of laboring mankind to free itself from
oppression, they become the devoted and inspired priestesses of that movement. They have much to get and much to give, not only as workers, but
as women. . . .

This Woman's Page thinks too of a woman's sphere, but the sphere of the
woman of the future and not of the past, the sphere of the woman who is
interested in something more than clothes and cooking, a sphere of the
woman who claims the whole world for her province, but seeks an opportunity to see that world in her own light, and to build it according to her
own ideals.[58]

Nor did *Advance* disclaim the source of its inspiration. Reviewing every major
pamphlet on women published by Socialists, the paper urged its women readers
to take their political education seriously. Socialist union leaders, such as the
Amalgamated's August Bellanca, paid special attention to the Italian-American
women believed impossible to reach with a sex-conscious message. Posing "La
Questione delle Donne" in more concrete terms than syndicalists or Socialists
had previously managed, the ACWA's Italian-language journal *Il Lavoro* blessed
women's union activities, encouraged women members to reflect upon their
day-to-day problems and to seek out education as well as organization for their
own sakes as well as their daughters'. If familiar slogans of women's special virtues
and their strategic importance to the cause did not in themselves cut through
the logic of unionism dominated by male workers and their needs, the sincerity
of the editors, authors, and organizers could not be gainsaid. Unionists who had
patiently tilled their fields while accepting the primacy of party politics now
seized the opportunity to create full-blown labor organizations, for women as
well as for men. They were joined by former syndicalists and political Socialists
who saw the handwriting on the wall and put aside old standards for the new
discipline of the union. For a rare period trade unionists tried to address women
in their several roles, as citizens, housewives, and workers.[59]

The final suffrage drive and wartime consumer problems offered important
arenas for experimentation in union policy toward women. Garment unions
produced propaganda literature on suffrage and, especially in New York, urged
members to work in the Socialist party's 1917 suffrage campaign. "Vote for
Revolutionary Socialism and Woman Suffrage," an *Advance* banner headline
characteristically read on election day. Unions responded to housewives' "riots"
and assaults upon meat dealers and others who charged exorbitant prices by
forming union-linked committees distinctly in place of any direct effort conducted by the Socialist party. The Socialist Consumers' League in New York
thus worked primarily through the garment constituencies rather than party
circles proper. Unionists formed a "grand army" of consumers in Chicago,
Cleveland, and other cities similarly appended to the Amalgamated and its
Socialist sympathizers.[60]

In the formation of far-reaching educational and recreational programs, unionists adopted the style of comprehensive social organization common to the nineteenth-century German-American (or contemporary European) Socialist movements. For the first time in the United States workingwomen became the vital center of such efforts, suited to fill their new leisure hours and their aspirations for self-education with a communal enterprise. Juliet Stuart Poyntz, Columbia University lecturer turned education leader of the ILGWU, put together an extensive program to meet the needs of young, politically inexperienced shop women. Along with other union leaders, she emphasized organized recreation. The ILGWU Local 25's Camp Unity typified this effort. After a summer outing at Camp Unity an entranced Pauline Newman wrote: "Here I am, trying hard to convey the beauty, the fellowship, the spirit of the place—in vain. It is beyond words. Only a Galsworthy could do that . . . I tried to sleep but could not. Never was there a night of such beauty and dream tranquility."[61]

This striving toward completeness in women's lives and aspirations harkened unconsciously back to the roots of women's reform traditions, consciously toward the ultimate fate of the woman worker. The formation of women's garment locals, more tactically expedient than principled, nevertheless echoed a sense of autonomy and self-assertion that union leaders like the Amalgamated's Dorothy Jacobs praised and encouraged as necessary to workingwoman's being. Juliet Stuart Poyntz, whose personal identification with workingwomen (including the learning of Yiddish) gave her a larger-than-life status similar to the nineteenth-century reform hero, utilized the columns of *Justice* to elucidate this message more fully. Woman the worker and woman the citizen had outgrown her past limitations, stepped firmly and irrevocably forward, and now bid fair to make her claim upon the whole of society.[62]

But how was this claim to be realized? The best organizing drive and internal education program, vigorous support for women's political advancement and links between consumers and unionists, the most comprehensive union program for communal leisure—none could replace the need for broader ties among various strata of women. The garment unions were mighty by contemporary labor standards. But they were no more than a geographic and ethnic wedge for women's progress, not even a vanguard in those cities and farms, offices and factories distanced from the effort. Socialists male and female had given themselves wholeheartedly to this effort because unions seemed to offer so much to workingmen and women, held a promise of dignity and emancipation from apathy. But they also not infrequently found in unions solace for their political disappointments: a little socialism because the big Socialism had failed.

In their single-minded dedication, union activists returned to a defensive posture that had in the nineteenth century disavowed American political life as too treacherous to navigate. If the key unions had become gender-mixed con-glomerations of the unskilled and semiskilled rather than the preserve of craft workers, the missing dimension of outreach toward nonwage-earning women remained maddeningly elusive. So, too, the absence of anything resembling a cross-class sisterhood, especially following the decline of the Women's Trade Union League, suggested that the legacy of the woman's movement had not been truly transcended but merely bypassed. Socialists had good reason to con-gratulate themselves for their efforts, but the original *telos* of the Socialist women's movement was nowhere to be found.

CONCLUSION

"The problems of the working girl," Juliet Stuart Poyntz wrote in 1919, "become more peculiarly her own and more differentiated from the problems of the working man as we advance from minus to plus, from the struggle for existence to the organization of life."[63] This insight typified the best observation of unionists and threw into relief the difficulty Socialists had experienced in seeking to adapt abstract notions of class consciousness to the concrete problems at hand. By providing comprehensive organizations and educational programs for workingwomen, the garment unions accomplished, at least for a time, what the Socialist party could not. Socialists could claim inspiration for the spirit of the programs, even fill numerous leadership positions, but as political activists they had fallen short.

Obviously, Socialist women could not possibly offer workingwomen the range of services provided by the unions. There were many legitimate reasons why they found workingwomen difficult to reach directly, from the absence of a collective labor heritage to the cyclical nature of women's labor-market ex-perience. That the entire responsibility for propaganda and recruitment rested upon the party's women's committees, none too highly regarded by the lead-ership and comprising women dedicated to but personally removed from the ranks of wage earners, only inflated the inherent difficulty of the task. Short of a breakthrough in membership and influence on the European scale, Socialists could not possibly have built their own women's sector in the labor movement. But that knowledge offered cold comfort to the militants who had expected so much.

Some thirty-odd years after German-American Socialists had abandoned their official opposition to women's wage labor for a more positive (if hardly enthusiastic) acceptance of the fact, the party's strategic formulations advanced very little. Party theoreticians concocted an ideological alchemy: they inter-preted women's new role in the labor market as proof that special considerations were no longer necessary. Unlike Juliet Stuart Poyntz, most Socialists failed to understand that the growing numbers of workingwomen did not herald economic equality, that women were to become more and not less segregated into special occupations, and that the demands of the workplace would continue to vie with traditional responsibility for the home. Socialist women who recognized the problems nevertheless could not formulate an adequate alternative.

The traditions inherited from the late nineteenth-century woman's movement offered a more fruitful approach than Socialists could easily acknowledge. The WTUL affirmed unrelentingly the right of all women to labor and called upon their sex for mutual support across class lines. Socialist women, even while deploring the Manchester economics of the gender-conscious reformers, drew the older traditions of women's solidarity unto themselves as they rallied workingwomen. For brief but crucial interludes, they cooperated with middle-class opponents of Socialism. Where the basis of cooperation crumbled, or where Socialist women themselves lacked ties with the working-class community, they made fewer gains. The garment unions at their peak fused the traditions and inspired a militant sisterhood bound to working-class sentiment. No one, not unions, nor Socialists, nor women reformers, had foreseen this outcome. And by the time the lessons could be drawn, most of the key players had retired from the scene. The continuity remained obscure to the aging veterans of the older movements, no less to those who had renewed the legacy. Such were the pitfalls of a force which hardly knew the strengths it displayed intermittently, which never gained a full sense of its own historic potential.

In serving the cause of workingwomen, Socialist women had triumphed more than they appreciated. They cut through party orthodoxy and union pessimism by dint of perseverance, class loyalty, and undying idealism. They tortured themselves with expectations far beyond the potential of the conditions they faced. But even in self-professed failure, they had done more than anyone to establish the basis of women's unionism in the twentieth century and to impel women—from native- to foreign-born, East to West—to recognize in the struggles of their sisters a hope for a common emancipation. Suffrage and questions of sexual morality would further test the mettle of their movement to confound its own dogmas and to grow beyond its limitations.

NOTES

1. Biographical sketch of Theresa Malkiel may be found in *Progressive Woman*, 2 (May, 1909), 2. For a fuller description, see Sally M. Miller, "From Sweatshop Worker to Labor Leader: Theresa Malkiel, a Case Study," *American Jewish History*, 68 (Dec., 1978), 189–205. Malkiel also recounted "Our First Strike" in the *Chicago Daily Socialist*, Feb. 5, 1910. See also Morris U. Schappes, "The Political Origins of the United Hebrew Trades, 1888," *Journal of Ethnic Studies*, 5 (Spring, 1977), 13–14.
2. Leon Kobrin, "The Tenement House," in Henry Goodman, trans., *The New Country: Stories from the Yiddish about Life in America* (New York, 1961), 32.

3. *Di Arbeter-Tseitung* (Yiddish—New York), Apr. 25, 1890.
4. Ernest Untermann, *Marxian Economics* (Chicago, 1907), 248–49. For a comprehensive discussion of these ideas, see Paul M. Buhle, "Marxism in the United States, 1900–1940" (Ph.D. dissertation, University of Wisconsin, 1975), Ch. I.
5. Untermann, *Marxian Economics*, 165.
6. Louis B. Boudin, *The Theoretical System of Karl Marx* (Chicago, 1907), 226.
7. *Ibid.*, 70–73.
8. Anita Block in *New York Call*, Sept. 28, 1913. The issue of women's economic contribution to the household puzzled many Socialists and periodically aroused a great deal of controversy. Throughout the spring of 1914, for example, readers of the *Call* undertook a major discussion published as letters to the editor of the "Woman's Sphere." See also the special issue on "House Drudgery," *Progressive Woman*, 7 (May, 1913), or such theoretical essays as Lida Parce Robinson, " 'Work' and Housework," *Socialist Woman*, 2 (Aug., 1908), 5.
9. Meta Stern Lilienthal, *From Fireside to Factory* (New York, 1916), 26. See also Lulu Sours, "The Effect of Economic Development upon the American Home," *International Socialist Review*, 11 (Aug., 1910), 112–15; Theresa Malkiel, *Woman and Freedom* (New York, 1915); Mary E. Marcy, *Breaking Up the Home*, Socialist party leaflet (1913).
10. Lilienthal, *From Fireside to Factory*, 42.
11. Theresa Malkiel in *Chicago Daily Socialist*, Jan. 25, 1910.
12. The cyclical and seasonal nature of women's labor patterns makes all statistics suspect. These percentages were derived from the U.S. Census monographs, and were compiled by Joseph A. Hill, *Women in Gainful Occupations, 1870–1920* (Washington, D.C., 1929). For an analysis of women's work at the turn of the century, see Edith Abbott and Sophonisba P. Breckinridge, *Employment of Women in Industries: Twelfth Census Statistics* (Chicago, 1906), a pamphlet reprinted by the Chicago Women's Trade Union League from *Journal of Political Economy*, Jan. and Feb., 1906.
13. Louis Levine, *The Women's Garment Workers* (New York, 1924), Ch. XV and XXI.
14. U.S. Senate, Doc. 645, *Report on the Condition of Women and Child Wage Earners in the United States*, vol. II, *Men's Ready-Made Clothing* (Washington, D.C., 1911).
15. U.S. Senate, *Men's Ready-Made Clothing*, Ch. I, on the labor force details ethnic patterns. For statistics on New York City, see Hill, *Women in Gainful Occupations*, Table 158, "Percentage of Native White Women of Foreign or Mixed Parentage Engaged in Gainful Occupations, for Cities of 100,000 Inhabitants or More: 1920, 1910, and 1900, with Marital Conditions for 1920," and Table 159, "Percentage of Foreign-Born White Women Engaged in Gainful Occupations, for Cities of 100,000 or More: 1920, 1910, 1900, with Marital Condition for 1920."
16. Hutchins Hapgood, *Spirit of the Ghetto* (New York, 1902), 78.
17. Hill, *Women in Gainful Occupations*, Tables 158 and 159.
18. Sometimes called the "Milwaukee Idea," this position was defined clearly by Victor Berger. See, for example, Berger's "A Labor Movement with Two Arms," *Social Democratic Herald* (Milwaukee), Mar. 23, 1907.
19. The women's columns in the *New York Call* and the *Chicago Daily Socialist* are the best sources for documenting Socialist women's aspirations along these lines.

20. Andre Tridon, *The New Unionism* (New York, 1914); John Laslett, *Labor and the Left: A Study of Socialist and Labor Influence in the American Labor Movement, 1881–1924* (New York, 1970).

21. Rose Schneiderman with Lucy Goldthwaite, *All for One* (New York, 1967), Ch. 1–6. Rose Schneiderman Papers, Tamiment Library, New York University, also contain biographical information.

22. Barbara Wertheimer, *We Were There* (New York, 1977), 293–95; Alice Kessler-Harris, "Organizing the Unorganizable: Three Jewish Women and Their Unions," *Labor History*, 17 (Winter, 1976), 4–23.

23. Biographical data on Leonora O'Reilly (1870–1927) supplied by Charles Shively in *Notable American Women*, ed. Edward T. James, Janet Wilson James, and Paul S. Boyer, 3 vols. (Cambridge, Mass., 1971), II, 651–53. Leonora O'Reilly Papers, Schlesinger Library, Radcliffe College, contain ample biographical materials.

24. Nancy Schrom Dye, *As Equals and as Sisters: Feminism, the Labor Movement, and the Women's Trade Union League of New York* (Columbia, Mo., 1980), offers a full and fascinating history of the New York league. See also Dye, "Feminism or Unionism? The New York Women's Trade Union League and the Labor Movement," *Feminist Studies*, 3 (Fall, 1975), 111–25; Robin Miller Jacoby, "The Women's Trade Union League and American Feminism," *ibid.*, 126–40.

25. Quoted by Levine in *Women's Garment Workers*, 144. Levine's Ch. XXI, "The 'Uprising of the Twenty Thousand,' " provides a detailed narrative of the strike, as does Philip S. Foner, *Women and the American Labor Movement* (New York, 1979), Ch. 18. See also Agnes Nestor, *Woman's Labor Leader* (Rockford, Ill., 1954), Ch. 9. The *New York Call*, Sept., 1909, through Feb., 1910, contained excellent daily coverage of the strike.

26. This famous incident has been described many times. The *New York Call* gave front-page coverage to the Cooper Union meeting and quoted Lemlich in its Nov. 23, 1909, issue. See also "Two Little Heroines," *Progressive Woman*, 3 (May, 1910), 2–3.

27. See the biographical sketch of Lemlich's long history in radical organizing by Paula Scheier, "Clara Lemlich Shavelson: 50 Years in Labor's Front Line," *Jewish Life*, 8 (Nov., 1954), 4–11. Morris U. Schappes, editor of *Jewish Life*, kindly supplied a copy of this article.

28. Described by Levine, *Women's Garment Workers*, 155–56. On the selection of the Socialist party's committee to aid strikes, see *New York Call*, Nov. 26, 1909. Socialist women's speaking engagements were covered in the *Call*, especially Nov. 27, 29, and Dec. 1, 1909.

29. March to City Hall reported in the *New York Call*, Dec. 4, 1909. Hippodrome meeting described in *ibid.*, Dec. 6, 1909. Quotation from the *New York Times* as cited by Levine in *Women's Garment Workers*, 160. Mother Jones's appearances before strikers reported in the *Call*, Dec. 9, 1909.

30. *New York Call*, daily reports in Dec., 1909. For report on the production of the "special edition," see *ibid.*, Dec. 31, 1909.

31. *Ibid.*, Dec. 29, 1909.

32. Beginning on Dec. 1, 1909, the *New York Call* offered detailed daily reports on the Philadelphia shirtwaist makers' strike, especially the role of Socialists and the support offered by the Jewish community.

33. Alice Henry, *Trade Union Woman* (New York, 1973 ed.), 101. Henry concluded: "Everywhere on the continent the results of these strikes have been felt, women's

strikes as they have been for the most part. The trade unionists of this generation have been encouraged in realizing how much fight there was in these young girls. All labor has been inspired. In trade after trade unorganized workers have learned the meaning of the words 'the solidarity of labor,' and it has become to them an article of faith" (113).

34. For histories of the strike, see "Chicago at the Front, a Condensed History of the Garment Workers' Strike," *Life and Labor*, 1 (Jan., 1911), 4–13; Amalgamated Clothing Workers of America, *The Clothing Workers of Chicago, 1910–1922* (Chicago, 1922), 15–47; State of Illinois, 47th General Assembly, "Report of Special Committee on Garment Workers Strike in Chicago," *Senate Journal*, 1911, 423–28.

35. Robert Dvorak's articles in the *International Socialist Review* also contain detailed reports, including the role of Socialists in encouraging the strikers: "The Fighting Garment Workers," 11 (Jan., 1911), 385–93; "The Chicago Garment Workers," 11 (Dec., 1910), 353–59. The *Chicago Daily Socialist*, Oct.-Dec., 1910, provided detailed coverage of the strike.

36. "Chicago at the Front."

37. Anna Epstein, Ellen Megow, and Emma Pischel served on the committee working with the WTUL; see *Chicago Daily Socialist*, Oct. 15, 1910. The announcement of plans for the special strike edition were made to workers' meetings on Nov. 14 and reported in *ibid.*, Nov. 15, 1910. For reports on distribution, see *ibid.*, Nov. 21, 1910. The contributions collected by Socialists were recorded in the Chicago Women's Trade Union League's *Official Report of the Strike Committee* (Chicago, 1911), 46.

38. Levine, *Women's Garment Workers*, Ch. XXV, details events leading to the "protocol of peace" adopted in 1913. Mary Snowden Nichols, "General Strike in the Needle Industry," *Progressive Woman*, 6 (Feb., 1913), 10, supplies a contemporary analysis.

39. *New Yorker Volkszeitung*, Dec. 5, 23, 25, 1909; *Jewish Daily Forward*, Nov. 24, 1909, and generally from Nov. 17 through Dec. 9, 1909. Rosenfeld's comments appeared in the *Jewish Daily Forward*, Dec. 11, 1909. The first column on women workers appeared in the *Cleveland Citizen*, Feb. 25, 1911. For a brief assessment and documentation of Socialists' activities, see Mari Jo Buhle, "Socialist Women and the 'Girl Strikers,' Chicago, 1910," *Signs*, 1 (Summer, 1976), 1039–59.

40. *New York Call*, Dec. 4, 1909; *Chicago Daily Socialist*, Feb. 26, 1910.

41. Meta Stern's poem "The Striker," which she published under her pen-name "Hebe," appeared in the *New York Call*, Jan. 9, 1910, and was reprinted in Buhle, "Socialist Women and the 'Girl Strikers.' " Malkiel's comments appeared in the *New York Call*, Dec. 4, 1909.

42. Zeh's "The Girl Striker—A Prophecy" appeared in *Chicago Daily Socialist*, Nov. 21, 1910, and was reprinted in Buhle, "Socialist Women and the 'Girl Strikers.' " For similar statements in praise of the New York strikers, see Elizabeth H. Thomas, "Heroines of the Needle," *Chicago Daily Socialist*, Dec. 31, 1909, and William Mailly, "How Girls Can Strike," *Progressive Woman*, 3 (Feb., 1910), 6.

43. Caroline Lowe, "Solidarity among Women as Shown by the Garment Workers' Strike in Chicago," *Progressive Woman*, 4 (Aug., 1911), 4. Zeh's assessment of the strikers' action is quoted from "The Girl Striker—A Prophecy."

44. "Why the 'Special Strike Extra' Succeeded," *Chicago Daily Socialist*, Nov. 29, 1910, and reprinted in full in Buhle, "Socialist Women and the 'Girl Strikers.' "

For an assessment of Socialists' role in the New York strike, see the editorial in the *New York Call*, Feb. 16, 1910.

45. *New York Call*, Dec. 4, 1909.

46. *Ibid.*, May 28, 1911.

47. Wertheimer, *We Were There*, 278–79, 308.

48. Carnegie Hall meeting reported in *New York Call*, Jan. 3, 1910. Socialists quoted Anne Morgan as deploring "fanatical statements of Morris Hillquit, Leonora O'Reilly and others," in *ibid.*, Jan. 4, 1910. Malkiel's description of the Carnegie Hall affair appeared in the *Chicago Daily Socialist*, Feb. 21, 1910; her statement on Morgan appeared in *ibid.*, Jan. 12, 1910. Valesh was quoted in a New York paper, Jan. 22, 1910, as saying, "There's nothing constructive about Socialism. It just makes those ignorant foreign discontent, sets them against the government, makes them want to tear it down"; see unmarked clipping in Leonora O'Reilly Papers, Box 15, Folder 335. Theresa Malkiel's *Diary of a Shirtwaist Striker*, a fictional account published serially in the *Call* and released as a book in 1910, issues a strong polemic against middle-class women and bourgeois suffragists and stands as her clearest political interpretation of the significance of the strike. A French edition, *Journal d'une Gréuiste par Theresa Serber Malkiel* (Paris, 1980), is introduced by Françoise Basch and translated by Marianne Sirgent.

49. See Justus Ebert, *The New Society on Trial* (n.p., n.d. [Cleveland, 1913?]); Melvyn Dubofsky, *We Shall Be All* (Chicago, 1969), Ch. 10.

50. A biographical sketch appeared in *Chicago Daily Socialist*, Sept. 17, 1907. See also Rosalyn Baxandall, "Elizabeth Gurley Flynn: The Early Years," *Radical America*, 8 (Jan.-Feb., 1975), 90–102; Elizabeth Gurley Flynn, *Rebel Girl* (New York, 1973). On party membership, see *International Socialist Review*, 12 (July, 1911), 56.

51. See, for example, "The Women of Lawrence," *Progressive Woman*, 6 (Aug., 1912), 6, and *New York Call*, Aug. 11, 1912, on New York women's mobilization. For women's role in general, see Foner, *Women and the American Labor Movement*, Ch. 23. Robert E. Snyder, "Women, Wobblies, and Workers' Rights: The 1912 Textile Strike in Little Falls, New York," *New York History*, 60 (Jan., 1979), 29–57, makes an interesting comparison with Lawrence; this essay documents the role of Socialist women in community relief organizations.

52. William D. Haywood, "On the Paterson Picket Line," *International Socialist Review*, 13 (June, 1913), 847–51; Patrick L. Quinlan, "The Paterson Strike and After," *New Review*, 2 (Jan., 1914), 26–33; Dubofsky, *We Shall Be All*, Ch. 11.

53. James Weinstein, *The Decline of Socialism in America, 1912–1925* (New York, 1969 ed.), 28–29, describes Haywood's expulsion.

54. See, for example, *Buffalo Socialist*, Mar. 1, May 3, 10, 17, 1913; Elsa Untermann, "When Girls Go on Strike," *Western Comrade*, 1 (Nov., 1913), 258; *California Social Democrat* (Los Angeles), Sept. 6, 1913; Martha Bensly Bruere, "The White Goods Strike," *Life and Labor*, 3 (Mar., 1913), 73–75; Dye, "Feminism or Unionism?"

55. Maurine Weiner Greenwald, *Women, War, and Work: The Impact of World War I on Women Workers in the United States* (Westport, Conn., 1980); David Montgomery, "The 'New Unionism' and the Transformation of Workers' Consciousness in America, 1909–1922," *Journal of Social History*, 7 (Summer, 1974), 513–16; Edwin Fenton, "Immigrants and Unions: A Case Study of Italians and American Labor, 1870–1920" (Ph.D. dissertation, Harvard University,

1957), 524–27; Ellen Gates Starr, "The Chicago Clothing Strike," *New Review,* 4 (Mar., 1916), 62–64; Levine, *Women's Garment Workers,* 292–304; *Justice* (New York), Mar. 29, 1919.
56. Buhle, "Marxism in the United States," 127–32.
57. Benjamin Stolberg, *Tailor's Progress* (New York, 1944), 109.
58. *Advance* (New York), June 22, 1917.
59. *Advance,* Oct. 12, Nov. 9, 16, 23, 30, Dec. 7, 14, 21, 1917, Mar. 1, 1918; *Il Lavoro* (New York), Feb. 17, Dec. 15, 1917, Sept. 7, 1918, Feb. 1, 8, 11, 1919.
60. *Advance,* June 15, Oct. 19, 26, Nov. 2, 1917, Apr. 5, 1918.
61. *Justice,* Aug. 31, 1917, Feb. 22, 1919. On Poyntz's biography, see Theodore Draper, *Roots of American Communism* (New York, 1957), 193, and *American Labor Who's Who,* ed. Solon DeLeon (New York, 1925), 188, which states that Poyntz was born in 1886 in Omaha, Nebr., received a bachelor's degree from Barnard and a master's degree from Columbia, and studied at Oxford and the London School of Economics.
62. *Advance,* May 3, July 27, Sept. 28, Oct. 26, 1918; *Justice,* Jan. 25, Mar. 1, Apr. 12, 1919.
63. *Justice,* Jan. 25, 1919.

6 Woman Suffrage

Said the Socialist to the Suffragist:
  "My cause is greater than yours!
    You only work for a Special Class,
    We for the gain of the General Mass,
  Which every good ensures!"

Said the Suffragist to the Socialist:
  "You underrate my Cause!
    While women remain a Subject Class,
    You never can move the General Mass,
  With your Economic Laws!"

Said the Socialist to the Suffragist:
  "You misinterpret facts!
    There is no room for doubt or schism
    In Economic Determinism—
  It governs all our acts!"

Said the Suffragist to the Socialist:
  "You men will always find
    That this old world will never move
    More swiftly in its ancient groove
  While women stay behind!"

"A lifted world lifts women up,"
  The Socialist explained.
    "You cannot lift the world at all
    While half of it is kept so small,"
  The Suffragist maintained.

The world awoke, and tartly spoke:
  "Your work is all the same;
    Work together or work apart,
    Work, each of you, with all your heart—
  Just get into the game!"

Charlotte Perkins Gilman,
"The Socialist and the Suffragist"
In *The Forerunner* (1912)

Native-born Socialist women had for decades professed woman suffrage as a basic political principle. Ida Crouch Hazlett, for example, rarely failed to remind her younger comrades that the struggle for women's enfranchisement was their natural inheritance. Crouch Hazlett herself was a living testimony to this tradition. She had, according to family legend, supported woman's rights from early childhood, throwing a tantrum at age five when she first learned her mother could not vote. As a youth she won a reputation for being a disciple of Susan B. Anthony, although she had not yet heard the name. A few years later this daughter of Illinois farmers followed a familiar path. After graduating from a state normal school, she exercised her political prerogative in one of the few ways possible, as a candidate for a county school board on the Prohibition ticket. Shortly thereafter the promise of work lured Crouch Hazlett to the first suffrage territory, Wyoming, where the ballot carriage made a special stop at the schoolhouse to transport teachers to the polls. She recalled casting her first ballot as easily as naming her favorite candidate in the local Emerson club.

Crouch Hazlett also acted directly on her inclinations. After a stint as a newspaper reporter in Colorado during the state's exciting Populist heyday, she joined the national organizing staff of NAWSA and toured with Susan B. Anthony, Anna Howard Shaw, and Carrie Chapman Catt during the pivotal California campaign of 1896.[1] The campaign failed, and the suffrage movement fell into a prolonged period of doldrums. During the difficult years that followed, Crouch Hazlett gained fortitude. As she later reminisced: "I am sometimes amused at hearing a group of Socialist speakers talking about the hardships of their tours. I have never found the hardships of Socialist work anything to compare with the early suffrage work. . . . [I]n those days, if women did believe in voting, they were afraid to say so; the few women who were outspoken were considered cranks of the community, and there was but scant welcome to the workers." She might find nowhere to stay one night on the road in Illinois, and the next day be treated to a grand reception in Iowa by the renowned widower of Amelia Bloomer.[2] In any event, Crouch Hazlett learned to care for herself, locate allies, convert the uncommitted, and energize the apathetic.

The skills she learned as a suffrage agitator allowed Crouch Hazlett to rise quickly within the Socialist movement. She became a state organizer for the Colorado party and frequent participant in the arduous national lyceum tours. Success came easily but not, she insisted, because she was unusually talented. Rather, she simply knew how to use the ever-crucial network of women sympathizers she had created during her suffrage years.

Crouch Hazlett was one of many Socialist women who would not forsake the suffrage movement. She might regret what she perceived as a rightward turn in NAWSA, above all the new leadership's appeal to the conservative religious vote "against the oncoming proletarian tide."[3] On the other hand, the Socialist party's notable complacency on the suffrage issue forced women to find allies wherever they could. National party luminaries Lena Morrow Lewis, Winnie Branstetter, Meta Stern, and Caroline Lowe among others personally granted an unofficial sanction to this practice, for each had likewise retained membership in NAWSA despite a greater allegiance to the Socialist movement. In many localities, particularly in the Plains states and California where ties to the woman's movement were still strong, Socialist women collaborated freely with their suffrage sisters.

Nor was such fealty restricted to women in the party. No Socialist showed himself more the old-fashioned idealist than Eugene Debs, whose support of woman suffrage was unquestioned. Like the women veterans, Debs had advocated women's enfranchisement long before converting to Socialism. As a local labor dignitary in the 1880s, he had personally invited Susan B. Anthony to address the citizens of Terre Haute. A hometown newspaper might say in 1917, with only slight exaggeration, that this paragon of American Socialism was also "a man who had devoted more time and interest than any other man in the United States to bringing about political freedom for women." Debs rarely missed an opportunity to speak on behalf of woman suffrage or to push its support in intraparty councils. Wherever possible, he lent his charismatic presence and immense personal prestige directly to local suffrage campaigns.[4]

Debs and Crouch Hazlett represented, however, a distinct sector of the Socialist movement rooted in older traditions and geographical regions of former strength—the Plains and Rocky Mountain states and the Far West. They could take satisfaction in the fact that this region delivered the first suffrage referenda victories of the twentieth century. To the east, especially in the major industrial centers, the situation was less promising and more complex. The party platform might demand at least a tacit endorsement, but many urban Socialists could not accept a casual relationship between the party and a woman suffrage movement so patently at odds with the immigrant masses. Urban Socialist women themselves broke ranks with their small-town and western sisters, and with each other, over the ambiguous aspects of local suffrage campaigns. Woman suffrage, an article of faith for the likes of Debs or Crouch Hazlett, became in the East a matter of extreme controversy.

Not only policy but the very integrity of the party was at stake, according to urban comrades. A period of calm discussion had ended in 1907–8, they noted, when mainstream suffrage organizations moved suddenly forward in urban areas, and the proximity of state victories opened a new era. "The fact that the demand of votes for women has ceased to furnish topics for parlor talks, but has become an immediate vital issue for the vast majority of women," Anita Block reflected, "brings to the attention of Socialists the most practical problems connected with women assuming their rights of citizenship."[5] Socialists must, she argued, begin to consider their responsibilities and especially their bearing upon a burgeoning middle-class suffrage movement. Should Socialist women continue to work as individuals within a middle-class suffrage movement? Had they the power, and the rightful prerogative, to organize their own distinctly Socialist suffrage organizations? And what would they do if prominent trade unionists chose to work instead within the "bourgeois" suffrage movement? These problems and others vexed party loyalists most of all because their very existence seemed to pose the question of whether Socialists as *Socialists* had anything decisive to contribute to the struggle for women's political emancipation.

The converse of this last question, whether women's emancipation had any direct bearing upon the final triumph of the proletarian revolution, stood not far behind. Support of the strikes of "working girls" had proved comparatively easy—at least in principle—because the demands of class conflict overrode misgivings some Socialists had about women's destiny as wage earners. Socialists knew that their action on behalf of workingwomen had demonstrated their willingness to work as able comrades. Support of woman suffrage implied, no matter how cautiously formulated, a struggle for political emancipation across class lines. Could the Socialist movement safely broaden its tactics to become an all-encompassing democratic force? Would involvement in woman suffrage campaigns represent no more than a necessary deviation from the principles of industrial and parliamentary class struggle to complete the bourgeois revolution? How well would Socialists fare in a mass movement not of their own making, indeed carried on for decades against the indifference and outright hostility of their own forebears?

These questions prompted some of the most heated debates on the woman question in the history of the Socialist movement. They also inspired imaginative political formulations, as Socialists specified the precise grounds upon which their comrades should take up the struggle. In many instances the proposed rationales functioned transparently as rationalizations. And yet, at the best of times, Socialists overcame nagging doubts and participated forcefully in local suffrage campaigns, so much so that the continuing dialogue over tactics stood in stark contrast to the actual crusades. Although they demanded an unambiguous and public role, Socialist women could not stay upon the sidelines.

THEORIES OF WOMAN SUFFRAGE

If Socialists had long slumbered in blissful complacency about the theoretical ramifications of woman suffrage, the enthusiastic campaigns of the twentieth century rudely awakened them. Many at first hoped to lighten the task by classifying woman suffrage with other democratic reforms like the referendum or direct election of senators. In this view, woman suffrage deserved its place in the party platform because it promised to extend political democracy, but it did not merit any special consideration. Most Socialist women, in contrast, demanded a more precise examination of the issue and invited a handful of sympathetic men to join them in filling the theoretical void. Hard-pressed for time to develop their ideas beyond the level of propaganda, Socialist women sought to explain the historic importance of the woman suffrage campaign, the party's unique responsibility, and the overall implications for the advancement of the class struggle.

Socialists aimed foremost to differentiate their perspective from that of the mainstream suffrage movement. They therefore compared the idealist natural rights component of "bourgeois" suffrage thought with their own materialist analysis and described women's struggle for political rights as a corollary to the intensification of the class struggle under developing capitalism. Socialists traced the demand for universal suffrage to the bourgeois revolutions of the late eighteenth century, when the rising entrepreneurial class demanded male suffrage as a means to uproot the last vestiges of feudalism by securing its own political hegemony. By the early decades of the nineteenth century, Socialists added, the wives of this class had made analogous claims for themselves. Socialists paid generous homage to the founders of the woman's rights movement for having given "voice to and crystalizing the demand" for the vote, but warned that within the modern context bourgeois suffragists lacked legitimacy and even turned against their own liberal heritage. In the twentieth century, Socialists explained, the struggle for woman suffrage coincided with the ascendancy of the industrial proletariat, and women's destiny rested therefore not with the bourgeoisie but with the ultimate force of political reconstruction, the working class. The new generation of suffragists, still clinging to an outdated natural rights philosophy, was consequently not as "brilliant, courageous and sacrificing" as its predecessors and desperately needed guidance. Socialists were ready to step forward and throw off the old natural rights theories, strip the suffrage movement of its middle-class biases, and fulfill the democratic promise of the historic movement for women's emancipation.[6]

Despite their bold claims, Socialists overestimated their own role and disguised similarities between themselves and mainstream suffragists. Whereas suffragists might quote John Stuart Mill, Socialists flavored their arguments with phrases cribbed from the writings of Frederick Engels and August Bebel. But as manhood suffrage had enjoyed far less than universal consent among a nascent bourgeoisie, so too the tacit endorsement many Socialists gave to woman suffrage in the twentieth century created complications that no simple reductionist analysis could resolve. Equally important, the insistence upon a theoretically "correct" and distinctive argument for woman's vote led Socialists down a tortuous, often circuitous ideological path.

Socialists erred most obviously in naming natural rights as the principal component of the rival mainstream suffrage ideology. On the one hand, suffragists did not enjoy a monopoly on this archaic philosophy. Socialists also drew upon the republican traditions and frequently argued in the name of Jefferson, Lincoln, and Elizabeth Cady Stanton: "Freedom has always been measured by the right to vote. Tyranny is measured by the absence of that right."[7] Especially in the Midwest, such appeals were popular well into the twentieth century, and Socialists and suffragists regularly argued for women's enfranchisement on the ground of absolute justice. On the other hand, both mainstream suffragists and Socialists tended to downplay the natural rights basis of women's political rights in favor of more pragmatic, expedient arguments for the vote.

Socialists and suffragists were, in fact, twin heirs to the world view of the late nineteenth-century woman's movement, especially its sociological emphasis. Thus what Socialists termed "capitalism" and suffragists preferred to label "industrialism" became homologous concepts in a common theoretical framework that treated all questions of morality, rights, and duties not as static notions but as changing by-products of social evolution. The advent of machine production in the nineteenth century, Socialists and suffragists agreed, had fundamentally altered women's role by drawing large numbers of women into the work force and by simultaneously transforming the nature of the household itself. The major conclusion stood prominently: the political subordination of women was not merely unjust, as earlier woman's rights advocates had argued, but no longer served the needs of modern society. Socialists and suffragists thus argued that since many American women had emerged as individuals in their own right, they required all the political and legal privileges commensurate with their new status in the public sphere.[8]

The sociological basis of such arguments is apparent in one of the most frequently employed forms, the "government as housekeeping" analogy shared by Socialists and suffragists alike. The significance of women's changing role frames this argument. Socialists described the many ways that industry took over the functions of the home, thereby freeing women from traditional responsibilities and simultaneously raising what were once merely domestic problems to important affairs of government. A contemporary woman, Socialists explained, would "find that clothes made for her children may have been made in a tenement sweatshop and contain germs of disease. The milk, the food she gives them, concerns her vitally. She must investigate, as a body, the manner in which the streets are cleaned, sewers drained, manufactures carried on. She has a social responsibility toward her children and her sister's children." Social evolution had thus forced a dramatic transformation of the "oldest, most time-honored profession," motherhood. And if the "whole vast knowledge and experience of mothers" were to be "socialized for the good of the entire race," women must be able to exert their wills. Only through the intelligent use of the ballot could modern woman regulate conditions she had previously controlled in her home.[9]

This type of argument, pioneered by the WCTU, had widespread appeal in the twentieth century and served Socialists on many occasions. In an Italian-American community that upheld women's family-centered activities, Socialists argued that landlords and shopkeepers were eager to keep women out of politics because wives who possessed the ballot could protect their families while preparing the next generation to struggle on. Croatian-American Socialists took a similar tack and admonished mothers to take "control over government in [their] own hands."[10] Other Socialists stated more lyrically the opportunity before the modern woman: "You are destined to be the greatest force for social justice this country ever had. Yours is the work to help banish industrial robbery and political corruption, and this task when performed will result in the elevation and emancipation of the race. Hence your sphere is not confined to the thing misnamed 'home' but to the larger sphere of world services—social services—human service."[11] However sentimental the rhetoric, such arguments gave twentieth-century Socialists and suffragists alike a way to grapple intelligently with the historic shifts in women's roles and employ at the same time traditional approbations of domesticity.

Although Socialists readily employed an assortment of commonplace arguments for woman suffrage, they nevertheless insisted that their propaganda bear the distinctive imprint of their movement. Many Socialists with roots in the woman's movement were less insistent on this matter, but a large sector, hoping to cut the Gordian knot with the woman's rights tradition, believed that any slight to the class analysis invited disaster. If the main purpose of the suffrage struggle from the Socialist perspective was, as one writer contended, to help the proletarian woman "fight her way from the veritable beast of burden she is to-day to the free and glorious human being it is her right to be," then energy spent appealing to all classes of women was wasted.[12] Many Socialists thus demanded that propaganda for woman suffrage be framed not principally as a plea for women's rights *per se* but as an argument for the advancement of the proletariat.

Socialists emphasized the difference between the goals of the woman suffrage and Socialist movements. They described the intentions of the suffrage leadership as reformist rather than revolutionary. Suffragists, Socialists contended, merely hoped to secure women's place within the great plurality of interest groups—farmers, laborers, business representatives, consumers, and others—so that women might exert their influence within the existing political system. To those aiming to overthrow that political system, such a goal was anathema. Socialists had no desire to affirm a theory of government based on a false notion of political democracy. As one comrade wrote: "With millions of women spending their energies on social service, child labor, prostitution, long working hours for women, the liquor traffic, degrading poverty, ugly towns, [and] political boodling, the vast accumulations of unearned wealth flourish upon every land anyway." Woman suffrage in itself could not eradicate these horrible conditions or end the vast and increasing disparities between rich and poor; only class-conscious voters of both sexes could wrest the means of production "out of the hands of the few who control into the hands of the many who must use them."[13] Only class-conscious voters would use the ballot to protect their families, to improve their working and living conditions, and to advance the class struggle. Although Socialists did not deny the natural right of all women to the ballot, they addressed their arguments primarily to working-class women who might see their cause as tied to that of the proletariat. Even a devoted suffragist like Lena Morrow Lewis contended that Socialists advocated woman suffrage "not because women need the ballot on account of their sex rights but because of their class rights."[14]

Although woman suffrage was by its nature a sex and not a class demand, Socialists tried valiantly to incorporate it within a class analysis. To arrive at a satisfactory formulation, they conducted interminable discussions covering the same ground and battled phantoms words alone could not conquer. The more strongly Socialists advanced "class" reasons for women's enfranchisement, the more their overall logic suffered.

Logically stymied, Socialists faced a *cul de sac*. To fail to support woman suffrage in some way was, as one writer put it, to stand in the shadow of the party platform as "hypocrites drunkenly jealous of our unfair artificial advantages over the sex of our mothers and wives, cravenly terrorized by fear of one-half the human race whom [we Socialist men] profess to love and protect."[15] Yet those who appealed on behalf of all women ran the risk of "class collaboration." For Socialists striving to determine a strategic approach, especially as the mainstream suffrage movement moved forward at great speed, this problem provoked many disagreements and exposed the fragility of the entire Socialist stand on the woman question.

THE QUESTION OF STRATEGY

By 1908, as Ida Crouch Hazlett noted, the Socialist party seemed to be "waking up on the woman question," moving beyond mere words to deeds and formulating strategy for an all-out woman suffrage campaign.[16] This was a new road for Socialists. In the nineteenth century the SLP had curtly dismissed all agitations associated with the "bourgeois" woman's movement; as late as 1907 movement veteran Josephine Cole had confessed that she had never heard a party speaker give more than passing reference to the issue of women's political rights.[17] Throughout 1908, in contrast, Socialist papers carried reports of local suffrage activities and short essays on political theory. Position statements filled a greater portion of various women's departments and spilled over—as the woman question rarely did—into the regular editorial columns of many newspapers. Suddenly, it seemed to longtime observers, the Socialist party shook itself from slumber and took on a new role.

Two developments awakened Socialists to their responsibility. The mainstream suffrage movement itself experienced a revival during the first decade of the twentieth century and tacitly challenged Socialists to fall into step. Concurrently, the Second International issued a directive which called upon its member parties to inaugurate a distinct campaign for women's political rights.

In different ways both the Second International and the woman suffrage movement forced Socialists to clarify their theoretical position on the issue, especially with regard to the bearing of women's enfranchisement on the class struggle. Consequently, over the next decade Socialists discussed, heatedly at times, their proper role in the last grand campaign of the historic woman's rights movement. They asked: should Socialists cooperate with the well-organized but middle-class woman suffrage movement? Or should they wage an independent campaign inbued with class consciousness and sponsored by their own organization? There were no easy answers to these questions, and the heightening of the political climate in 1912, with challenges left and right, exposed long-standing differences within the women's sector of the party.

The Second International took the lead in reaffirming the class nature of woman suffrage and called upon Socialists to conduct a campaign along proper lines. Responding to the rise of woman suffrage movements across Europe and the United States, the Second International at its 1907 meeting in Stuttgart adopted a resolution encouraging Socialists to agitate "strenuously" for woman suffrage. As to the appropriate form, the directive was unequivocal: "The Socialist women shall not carry on this struggle for complete equality of right of vote in alliance with the middle class women suffragists, but in common with the Socialist parties, which insist upon woman suffrage as one of the fundamental and most important reforms for the full democratization of political franchise in general."[18]

This directive posed special problems for American comrades. The German women who had sponsored the resolution had sound reasons for proscribing cooperation with "bourgeois" suffragists; they faced the German Union for Woman Suffrage, an elite, conservative group organized in 1902, and they were determined to combat its growing influence.[19] Although American Socialists understood the situation abroad and appreciated their sisters' efforts to secure a formal endorsement of woman suffrage agitation, they harbored ambivalent feelings about the stipulation demanding abstention from all campaigns waged by middle-class suffragists. Many Socialist women had spent their formative years within the suffrage camp and could not look upon their suffrage sisters as class enemies. Despite its clarity, the International's directive became an item of controversy in the United States.

American Socialists responded first by increasing their suffrage agitation. Several state organizations instructed party speakers and local organizers to include special suffrage appeals in their repertoires. Anticipating the next national convention scheduled for May, 1908, several locals requested the formulation of official policy in line with the International's declaration; they asked specifically for a strong suffrage plank in the party platform and the inauguration of an active campaign.[20] The party assigned this task to the Woman's National Committee, created at the 1908 convention, and within a year plans were laid for the publication of leaflets, the routing of suffrage lecturers, and the discussion of uniform strategy.

The creation of Woman's Day was the most tangible sign of this new commitment. The National Executive Committee directed locals to arrange mass meetings on the last Sunday of February, 1909, to celebrate woman's rights. Socialist newspapers carried special supplements, usually a page or section edited by the newly designated women's committee in their area. Party leaders joined women in these efforts. Although some comrades complained that this once-a-year affair might serve as an excuse to ignore the woman question the other 364 days, most Socialists participated enthusiastically and established Woman's Day as a permanent institution. By 1915 the metropolitan gatherings achieved the scale of mass spectacles. A New York meeting in Harlem's Pabst Coliseum drew an overflowing crowd for a program featuring speakers ranging from party functionaries Theresa Malkiel and Meta Stern to trade unionists Pauline Newman and Juliet Stuart Poyntz, and Congressman Meyer London.[21] Had there been any doubts about suffrage agitation as a drawing card, they were surely dispelled.

Despite the party's new commitment, many Socialist women continued at first to work with local and national suffrage societies. Even the WNC maintained ties to the mainstream suffrage movement. In the spring of 1909, just after the first Woman's Day celebration, the WNC decided to participate in NAWSA's "monster petition" campaign and asked Socialists everywhere to cooperate. The WNC nevertheless justified its tactics, claiming that time was too short to circulate the petition under the sole auspices of the Socialist party. The WNC also affixed the party seal to each list of signatures collected before relinquishing petitions to NAWSA officials. The committee reminded the comrades that the United States was not Germany and a few deviations from the International's directive were thus allowable. The committee had therefore decided to further "our common cause" even if it meant going "part of the way with women of the other classes."[22] Other Socialists supported the petition without reservation, some calling it a "splendid field for Socialist propaganda."[23]

It was, in fact, Socialists who pushed the petition drive over the top. NAWSA officials admitted that the Socialist party had given "generally the heartiest support to the petition."[24]

The 1909 petition drive was one of the last cooperative ventures sponsored by the WNC and endorsed by the party. Even in this case the alliance was uneasy. At its conclusion a sector within the party protested and asked leaders to take a firm stand against cooperation with the mainstream suffrage movement.

New York Socialists emerged as the primary opponents of cooperation and pushed the issue to the center of party business. Many leaders of this faction had strong roots in the Germanic sector, such as the Social Democratic Women's Federation, which had finally gained a semiofficial party status and inclined to support the Second International on most issues. As party loyalists, German-American women heaped scorn upon compromisers with the mainstream suffrage movement, passed resolutions against Socialist participation in NAWSA parades, and in general condemned the whole mode of women's agitation that seemingly turned attention away from organizing factory workers.[25] They found support throughout the city organization. Antoinette Konikow affirmed their position, warning that Socialist women must be wary of anything that "obscures the issues of class struggle," including mainstream suffrage agitations.[26]

Social relations in New York City gave this position a certain measure of authenticity. The distance between the parlors of genteel reform and the sweat-shops of industrial agitation seemed unbridgeable to former shopworkers like Theresa Malkiel. Midwesterners and westerners, small-town and rural folk were for better or worse more likely to adapt to local customs; New Yorkers, on the other hand, often believed that the rest of the nation should be catching up with the European style of uncompromising class-conscious radicalism. Tradition, ethnicity, and loyalty to the International bolstered the logic of "straight" Socialism.

While Socialists might see New York as "little Europe," the rising suffrage leaders viewed the city as both the working model for a new level of agitation and the nerve center of the national movement. Once the cradle of the woman's rights movement, New York state had fallen into the shadow as the momentum for suffrage moved to the West during the last decades of the nineteenth century. Yet by the turn of the century New York City was obviously rich in material resources and personnel required to create a new type of organization. "Fashionable ladies," once reluctant to take up the cause, had swelled the movement; indeed, wealthy New Yorkers lent so much prestige that NAWSA had recently moved its headquarters from a small Ohio town to this potentially lucrative center. Then, too, institutions like the Women's Trade Union League were also headquartered here; suffragists hoped to broaden their constituency by establishing links between the upper- and working-class women. The Equality League of Self-Supporting Women, formed by Harriot Stanton Blatch in 1907, gathered 19,000 supporters and introduced "militant" tactics such as the mass parades that broke the polite atmosphere of Victorian suffragism and restored the crusading spirit lost since the nineteenth century. New York City also hosted the premier suffrage organization in the United States, Carrie Chapman Catt's Woman Suffrage party, formed in 1907; its 20,000 members would grow to a half-million by the time the suffrage amendment met victory. It was Catt who later attested that New York "proved in the end the political lever with which the final moves" for the vote "were successfully made."[27]

New York Socialists revealed a deep apprehension about these new, bouyant movements. They rightly feared that "respectable" leaders would seek to limit their participation. Even a grass-roots suffragist like Ida Crouch Hazlett dolefully corroborated the existence of a "snobbish truckling to the women of influence and social position" among the new suffrage forces. Then, too, the introduction of "militant" tactics added a new wrinkle. Although most Socialists welcomed the new techniques, the major result, as Crouch Hazlett noted, was to make suffrage agitation yet more fashionable, virtually chic. Younger women especially, as well as some Socialists of standing like Florence Kelley, drew close to the mainstream "militants" instead of the laboriously theoretical Socialist party. The principal benefactor was indeed the mainstream.[28]

Socialists, now outnumbered and "outclassed," lost their standing among local suffrage forces. Once the vanguard, representatives of the only major party besides the Prohibitionists to carry the suffrage banner, Socialists found themselves on the sidelines. The Woman Suffrage party had effectively usurped their position; worse, it made its stand within the two-party system and wooed individual Democrats and Republicans. Socialist women therefore feared that their efforts rallying workingwomen and blue-collar voters would be manipulated by mainstream suffragists, overshadowed in the press by society women's role, and outmaneuvered and outfinanced by women least likely to use their vote to advance the class struggle.[29]

Socialists waged a series of polemical forays against their adversaries until they found the proper occasion to call for open warfare. The shirtwaist strike of 1909–10, which had uneasily joined suffragists and Socialists, proved fortuitous. Attacked by conservative "allies" in the WTUL, Socialists responded in kind and charged that middle-class women, especially Alva Belmont, had not only tried to discredit the contributions of Socialists but had misused the strike to advance the cause of woman suffrage. New York Socialist women came to distrust all cross-class alliances and demanded formal obeisance to the letter of the Second International's directive.

To discuss the issue of cooperation with "bourgeois" suffragists, New York Socialists called a major conference. On December 19, 1909, over 200 participants gathered at the Labor Temple on East 84th Street. Tempers ran high. Theresa Malkiel charged Alva Belmont with a list of political crimes against the working class and expressed her outrage at being asked to organize work-ingwomen into "Belmont's organization." "The Suffragists ask us to go to a mass meeting and sit in a box we pay $10 for and put our banner outside it, but they don't want us to speak," Anna Ingerman confirmed. After more than five hours' debate the conference declared against cooperation with mainstream suffragists.

Party loyalists undoubtedly derived a large measure of satisfaction from their victory, but they also tested the limits of their influence, even among their own ranks. Trade unionists tended to judge the issue of cooperation in practical terms rather than for its toll on Socialist dignity. Rose Schneiderman warned that advising workingwomen to stay away from bourgeois suffrage meetings merely limited their education. Leonora O'Reilly, the leading Socialist in the WTUL, agreed. "If this is an educational work and these other women say 'Come on our platform,' why not go and use it as a school for educating other people?" Socialists could not always choose their arenas, she added, and some-times "you have to close your ears to the name of a school you don't like." Hard-line party members had their priorities, trade unionists like O'Reilly had others. In a few years O'Reilly would be heading the industrial division of the Woman Suffrage party with Socialists (in their own minds) on the other side of the barricades. The December conference had perhaps drawn the lines too sharply.[30]

Many Socialists were fully aware of the danger and sensed a turning point ahead. No true Socialist could fail to recognize the legitimacy of the complaints against the mainstream suffrage organizers, but how to address those complaints was not an easy matter. Meta Stern, who had presented the unsuccessful mi-nority resolution at the December meeting, admonished her colleagues that the Socialist movement was still weak; to break with the suffrage mainstream would isolate Socialists "as a group of relentless and uncompromising theorists." She warned,

> Whether or not the suffragists as a body recognize the class struggle is of no consequence, for the suffrage movement is not a class question, but a sex question. We iterate and reiterate that class is more important than sex, but in this particular problem all our assertions about class struggle and class-consciousness are meaningless. For it is not a class, but a sex—the entire female sex—that is disfranchised in the United States. . . . Therefore, the struggle for enfranchisement is a distinct and common cause of all women. . . . Therefore we should welcome every woman who works honestly for the liberation of her sex.[31]

Stern hit the proverbial nail on the head. The debates over cooperation had disguised a more weighty matter, the relationship between Socialism and women's emancipation in general.

Across the country, Socialists discussed the implications of the New York conference. In proletarian Seattle the women's committee filed its enthusiastic support. Elsewhere one might hear the affirming voices of German-American Socialists and elderly comrades who had never reconciled themselves to the suffrage agitation. Old opponents of autonomous women's organizations, like May Wood Simons, seized the opportunity to lash out against all who would "wipe out class lines and build up sex lines."[32] Still, others were shocked by the New Yorkers' action, the more so when ill-advised male comrades renewed their attack on any form of suffrage agitation. In Chicago the Socialist women's movement almost split over the issue of cooperation with local suffragists. Socialists in several localities finally called upon the party to settle the matter at its next convention scheduled for May, 1910.

The discussions at the national convention set a new standard. Before 1910 the leadership had never treated the woman question as an important item on their political agenda. The creation of the Woman's National Committee at the 1908 meeting had stirred little controversy. But as Chicago women joined their New York sisters, forces aligned for a showdown over the meaning of the Stuttgart resolution, not merely an endorsement of suffrage agitation but a stipulation as to the "correct" context. Both sides dug in for a major battle.

Despite the intensity of discussions, delegates failed to resolve the matter. The Woman's National Committee, making its first report to a national convention, chose a compromise formula; it asked the party to renew its *pro forma* pledge to the suffrage cause and to enlarge the plank in the platform dealing with equal political rights. Opponents of bourgeois suffragists might infer that a stronger party platform militated against cooperation; others might read the resolution as a mandate for the status quo. Perhaps, as Josephine Conger-Kaneko reflected, such was the best that could be expected from political activists of such strikingly different backgrounds and predilections. Indecision promised, if not a unified position, at least a reasonably permissive atmosphere for the differences to play themselves out.[33]

Unfortunately, events inside and outside the party conspired against an easy resolution. The upsurge of suffrage agitation coincided with dramatic changes in the party's demographic make-up and a fierce, unprecedented series of internal struggles over its control. Over the long run, the hard-won process of "Americanization" would be reversed, new immigrants mostly from eastern Europe displacing the older German and indigenous cadre. In the meantime, heightened labor struggles and the prospect of political victories raised the question of strategic priorities to an almost unendurable degree. Woman suffrage, along with other issues, became not merely a controversial matter but a football tossed between Left and Right.

Self-defined "revolutionary" Socialists had for years associated suffrage agitation with "pink tea" or "parlor" Socialism. In 1908, for example, a group of IWW women issued a declaration against the suffrage number of the *Socialist Woman* and the magazine's "natural rights hobbies."[34] Only a minority shared this assessment, however, so long as Socialists had confidence in political education and assurance that "direct action" had failed to create a mass movement.

The great strikes of 1909–13 had the unwonted effect of placing political education and woman suffrage in the worst light. The newly immigrated workers evidently demonstrated their class consciousness in action rather than in discussion of political doctrine, and solidified their communities primarily against factory owners and police rather than against local political officials. The young women who emerged as labor militants seemed unlikely to develop their class consciousness as voters. In the prose and poetry of Italian revolutionary writers in particular, "Syndicalist Woman" became an almost unearthly ideal—shamed, degraded, bound by the Church, and illiterate the day before, she rose in direct action to claim her dignity. Compared to her, the "fine ladies" of the woman suffrage movement took on a sinister mien. The treacherous NAWSA leaders and perhaps even their Socialist allies seemed to condescend to immigrant women only to divert them from active class consciousness to a more abstract transclass loyalty, from the vision of the general strike to an endless electoral tug of war. The extreme character of the contemporary struggles at Lawrence, Paterson, and elsewhere, the laurels that the IWW and Italian syndicalists drew upon themselves, and the growing tension within the Socialist movement gave such views a following they lacked in calmer times.[35]

The Right faced its own crisis in the appearance of the Progressive party headed by Theodore Roosevelt. The colonel, known for his promise to "crush" Socialism, outraged the party faithful by drawing off many left-leaning municipal reformers and other erstwhile sympathizers with his platform, which strangely resembled the party's own "immediate demands," including woman suffrage. Among the most prominent recruits to the Progressive party were women reformers Jane Addams, Margaret Dreier Robins, and Mary Dreier, and even a few outright defectors like Florence Kelley. As party membership wavered after the 1912 election, many Socialists became convinced that women's vote would go, at least initially, to the bourgeois reform parties.[36]

The question of woman suffrage thus assumed a peculiar place in what might be described as the Socialist crisis of faith. Neither Left nor Right had any monopoly on misogyny or good will toward women. If the Right declined to take seriously the militancy of young workingwomen, the Left vented its spleen on the woman's movement. Although Socialist women did not align themselves with either faction, they did become ensnared within the larger conflict.

But after all the grand pronouncements of the Second International, the internecine quarrels among the various sectors, and the attacks left and right,

Socialist women could not risk an ultimatum on "correct" strategy. It therefore remained for local groups of Socialists to carry the woman suffrage agitation through the difficult years ahead. In the midst of raging debates Socialist women learned to live with a range of strategies dictated by geopolitical variations in the mainstream suffrage movement and by the weight of traditional loyalties. They demanded a platform broad enough to allow some women to place sex unembarrassedly on a plateau with class and to join hands with broad masses of women when circumstances allowed.

STATE AND LOCAL CAMPAIGNS

Socialist women followed the International's directive only in New York. In other areas orthodoxy never weighed heavily, and Socialists cooperated freely with mainstream suffragists. Especially as state campaigns entered the final round, Socialists in at least a half-dozen key states moved ahead, one might say, on political instinct. They campaigned vigorously not because they hoped to recruit new party members or to spread the Socialist gospel but because they, like other progressive Americans, believed woman suffrage was in itself a compelling issue. Neither pressure to abstain from joint ventures, nor lack of financial resources or substantial party assistance, could prevent Socialist women from joining a crusade now three-quarters of a century old and on the eve of victory.

In most regions Socialists intervened rather straightforwardly. The party used its political offices wherever possible to introduce suffrage resolutions in state legislatures, urge voter support, and carry through an active campaign to secure passage of the bills. In Massachusetts, for example, where a weak Socialist movement experienced a brief revival in the early 1910s, Boston-area Socialists became the first in the United States to draw up a bill for the state legislature. The sole Socialist representative duly introduced the bill, while Socialist women testified at hearings and organized demonstrations and parades. In this case NAWSA followed the Socialist lead, almost sheepishly, as its own prerogative had been usurped.[37] Socialist municipal officials likewise played key roles, Mayor J. Stitt Wilson of Berkeley in the front ranks of supporters.

Socialists also acted as democratic leaveners in some NAWSA-led campaigns by actually opposing restrictive bills carrying literacy, property, or nativity requirements—"class suffrage" in Socialist lexicon—or limiting women's vote to municipal elections. Where Socialists worked within NAWSA, as in Wisconsin, they pushed their suffrage sisters to demand full political rights; where NAWSA committed itself to restricted suffrage, as during the Oregon referendum campaign of 1911, Socialists agitated against the bill because of its literacy proviso and prided themselves in its failure.[38] Socialists consistently demanded the broadest measure of suffrage possible.

Socialists also campaigned alongside suffragists, especially in the West where the "doldrums" of seventeen years finally ended in the 1910 Washington victory. The Socialist national office had sponsored a special state tour of Anna Maley and Eugene Debs, who gathered huge, wildly enthusiastic crowds and secured the official endorsement of local progressive labor unions.[39] More instrumental than the work of individual luminaries was the intensive agitation conducted by hundreds of rank-and-file Socialists who cooperated freely with mainstream suffragists. Only New Yorkers found reason to criticize; they claimed that NAWSA failed to acknowledge the Socialist contribution. Western Socialists and suffragists, paying no heed, embraced in celebration.[40]

The California referendum campaign of 1911 served as a viable model of judicious cooperation between suffragists and Socialists. California Socialist women had maintained their own statewide organization, the Women's Socialist Union, and could easily mobilize their troops. Always independent-minded, they were above all firmly rooted in women's own political traditions and eager to cooperate with their longtime suffrage allies. For the final effort, practically all women's organizations in the state—WCTU, women's clubs, suffrage societies, and the Women's Socialist Union—formed a loose federation to coordinate tactics. Their campaigns were the first in the country to demonstrate the new, flamboyant agitational techniques which would mark the suffrage movement's last phase. Suffragists staged spectacular parades, door-to-door pollings, special mass events from fund-raising dances to the ubiquitous card parties by the hundreds, strategically emphasizing the "swing" districts and garnering support of leading politicians. Socialist women participated freely in most activities but preserved their own identity at all times. Although a few individuals joined suffrage mobilizations directly, the mass of Socialist workers adhered to their own organizations and paraded under the party banner. Sometimes they added a special class-conscious note to the local campaigns. In Los Angeles, for example, Socialists cooperated with the Union Labor League and helped organize the Wage Earners' Votes for Women Club and sponsored a series of meetings held in the local labor temple. When the amendment passed, Socialists claimed special credit, reporting that while suffrage ran poorly in the city's wealthy districts, the vote carried two to one in Los Angeles working-class neighborhoods. They took pride in their contribution and claimed that their work had been conducted "most scrupulous[ly] along class lines." NAWSA acknowledged Socialists' generous support, and the campaign ended joyously for all concerned.[41]

Socialist women in western states lacking a comparable independent organization could not easily create the apparatus for participating *en bloc* in NAWSA campaigns. But, like their Californian sisters, they were determined to join. Especially after 1912, when the party bureaucracy and many state organizations grew too weak to offer any but moral encouragement, local activists ignored the International's admonitions. As one longtime Socialist suffragist commented wryly, there were no Mrs. Belmonts on the plains of Oklahoma.[42] Instead many mainstream suffragists welcomed Socialists to their ranks. In the Kansas campaign of 1912, when even the nominally pro-suffrage *Appeal to Reason* failed to cover the event in any detail, Socialist women agitated in the community with zeal, energy, and a selfless political anonymity. Socialists also played central roles in Nevada and Montana in 1914. Mining areas with practically no middle class, these states lacked the chief components of metropolitan NAWSA leadership. Small-town Socialist women—teachers, miners' wives, and a scattering of other professionals—acted in place of the suffrage mainstream, worked with the party in polling the labor movement, pushed the bill in the state legislature, and campaigned vigorously. Socialists claimed the Montana victory, while the party's decisive contribution to the Nevada effort won praise in newspapers across the country.[43]

Farther to the east cooperation with NAWSA was more problematic. Socialist women who joined NAWSA or worked on its fringe had to defend themselves from attacks by party orthodoxists on the one hand and NAWSA conservatives on the other hand. Yet many Socialist women chose the pragmatic solution.

Although unique for its large German population and strong Socialist movement, Wisconsin represented a typical situation. The state NAWSA affiliate not only spurned Socialists' assistance but conducted in 1912 an elitist temperance-ridden agitation, certain to alienate German-American workingmen however progressive their inclinations and forcing Socialists to conduct a separate canvass. When the referendum lost by a heavy margin, Socialist leaders thus pointed to their influence in the Milwaukee neighborhoods where the pro-suffrage ballot ran neck-and-neck with the party vote. Leading Milwaukee functionary Elizabeth Thomas concluded that suffrage was most definitely a "class issue," and advised her comrades to support suffrage outside and against the reactionary NAWSA organization.[44] Meta Berger, however, could not be pursuaded and aimed to bolster NAWSA's weak progressive leanings. She set out to change its public image, arguing successfully at her first convention for the union label on all NAWSA-printed materials and for the elimination of prohibition literature from the agitational lists. When NAWSA leaders advanced a campaign for limited suffrage, Berger insisted that they hold out for a full suffrage bill and won the day. These shrewd moves paid off. In 1915 in the aftermath of yet another referendum defeat, NAWSA invited Berger to accept the presidency of the state organization. She refused, she later recalled, because she feared her Socialist identity would become a public issue and splinter the organization. She did, however, accept a position as first vice-president. She had not sought to control NAWSA or to give it an openly socialistic bent. She worked loyally within its ranks because, as she put it, "as Socialists we believe in equal rights."[45]

Over the years hundreds of other Socialist women played lesser, more anonymous roles in state suffrage organizations and in local societies. Like Winnie Branstetter of Oklahoma, they occasionally served as delegates to state and national suffrage conventions.[46] Blessed with delegate status or not, Socialists attending NAWSA meetings, from the early years of the century through 1916, could look out into the gallery and spot sister comrades in the audience. Most of these women chose to work within NAWSA, not because they refused to listen to those who warned against cooperation, nor because NAWSA provided a comfortable arena for agitation. Meta Berger recalled, for instance, that her Wisconsin suffrage cohorts had once rumored that she must be in the pay of the brewers to own such a fancy dress, the one fine gown reclaimed, she remembered, from her husband's first term in Congress.[47] Yet personal slights could not inhibit her; the political conservatism of NAWSA merely toughened her spirit. Despite obstacles, many Socialist women like Berger stayed in the suffrage camp as long as they could, insisting upon universal franchise, special agitation among immigrant and workingwomen, and alliances with the local labor movements. In short, they pushed the maintream suffrage movement against its own historic tendencies, preserving and extending the nineteenth-century democratic spirit as much as possible. Lacking significant support from their own party leaders, Socialist suffragists did battle with the best means at hand.

The heavily industrial, densely populated eastern states presented special problems for Socialist suffragists. With the West falling into line and as Illinois gained presidential suffrage, the spotlight was thrown upon the region where the dichotomy of suffrage and temperance on the one hand, and the boss system and the immigrant and often organized labor on the other, made Socialist cooperation with NAWSA virtually untenable. Ohio, Massachusetts, and New Jersey suffrage campaigns were defeated in 1915–16 by humiliating margins; Pennsylvanian suffragists rather expectant of an important victory were likewise disappointed. Veteran suffragists who had lived to see a quarter- and even half-century of consecutive defeats in the East as much as threw up their hands in desperation, naming liquor dealers, the indigent, and the foreign-born as scapegoats. The single bright spot on the horizon was New York, where progressive sympathies of a wide popular stratum promised a counterbalance. Generations of labor and Socialist agitation, along with unique demographic factors, had a leavening influence in particular on the blue-collar community, whose new congressman, Meyer London, prominently advocated woman suffrage. That the Empire State presented a special case could not be denied. But the very specialness of New York City, its newsworthiness around the nation, guaranteed that results in any form would have a significant impact on all future developments.

For suffragists, New York was the "swing" state, and a victory there might change the course of political history. For Socialists, the New York City agitation conveyed equally grand implications. The Second International policy of "class-conscious" campaigning under the direct auspices of the party would be vindicated here or nowhere. In a deeper sense the entire orthodox interpretation of the woman question was on trial. Socialists claimed to be the true emancipators of women, but, as the western suffrage campaigns seemed to indicate, perhaps they served better as aids and allies. From a purely practical standpoint, however, Socialists had to design a unique campaign, probe the party's political conscience, demand financial aid and ideological sanction sufficient to call out comrades who never considered suffrage agitation crucial, and finally appeal to a younger generation of women drawn to the competing, more dramatic campaigns.

Theresa Malkiel hoped she was equal to the test. As soon as she left the 1910 party congress, Malkiel began to set the machinery into motion. By the early winter months she had founded several Socialist suffrage clubs designed to reach those women presumably ignored by the mainstream movement. Malkiel encouraged her co-workers to create an atmosphere both politically attractive and socially amenable to workingwomen. The clubs tried a variety of programs; they sponsored musical performances, engaged popular speakers, held dances, teas, and ice cream festivals, conducted rallies, and organized bazaars for woman suffrage. Club members also convened every two weeks to discuss the class aspects of the ballot and to instill a Socialist message into all propaganda for women's enfranchisement.[48] Malkiel thus followed the International's directive to the letter.

Malkiel was relatively successful in creating a network of Socialist suffrage clubs reaching from the Lower East Side to Harlem, into Brooklyn, the Bronx, and Queens. The numbers of affiliates continued to grow through the spring of 1911. But in surveying her accomplishment she realized that the majority in attendance at club meetings were not workingwomen but party stalwarts merely adding one more meeting to their political calendar. Few women outside the ranks were being recruited. Because she followed party policy so scrupulously, Malkiel also expected Local New York to offer considerable support. Consequently, when results proved disappointing, she blamed the party for its indifference and infidelity to the Second International program. Malkiel's assistant, Sarah Volovich, agreed that their efforts to establish Socialist suffrage clubs had been merely "tolerated" by the local and deprived of sufficient financial backing.[49] They nevertheless had no choice but to plod ahead.

The impetus came at last from outside the movement Malkiel had created. By 1912 the state suffrage campaign verged upon a breakthrough as mainstream organizations swelled with enthusiastic new members. Socialists imbibed this spirit. Their Woman's Day celebrations grew into massive meetings; over 5,000 comrades joined the citywide suffrage parade, creating "a brilliant mass of red

sashes, banners, and red torches."[50] In 1913 the state legislature finally passed
a referendum bill that would place the issue directly before the voters in 1915.
Socialist luminaries joined mainstream suffragists in an assault on Albany,
while local Socialists turned to lay the groundwork for intensive agitation
among the voters.[51] If Malkiel's program were indeed viable, the 1915 campaign
would be the test.

Socialists began slowly in the early months of 1914. The party's women's
committee, badly disorganized in the wake of the Progressive splash, responded
feebly. Pauline Newman complained that there were only 700 dues-paying
women members in greater New York and of that number only a dozen participated regularly in committee work. Was the party, she asked bluntly, going to
"leave this thing to the Suffrage Association?" Newman refused to be down-
hearted, and she planned an automobile tour of the state. Meanwhile Theresa
Malkiel covered New York City. In late March, 1914, a meeting of 300 Socialist
women under Malkiel's leadership pledged themselves to the boldest campaign
hitherto. They collected names of hundreds of volunteers and began the initial
work of agitation.[52] For its first task the committee scheduled open-air meetings
and distributed literature, some 125,000 leaflets in the first four months of its
work. Socialist women singled out foreign-born women as a special, crucial
constituency and prepared leaflets and recruited volunteers to assist immigrant
women in obtaining their naturalization papers. After a six-month delay the
central committee of Local New York funded a salaried woman organizer to
work full-time in the suffrage agitation. By the end of the year Meta Stern, who
had inaugurated a "Votes for Women" column in the *New York Call*, proclaimed the Socialist suffrage campaign "in full swing."[53]

During early winter, 1915, Socialists throughout New York state prepared
for the big campaign. They elected a state committee to coordinate activities,
circulated a suffrage petition which would be presented to the state legislature,
and appointed a special woman's correspondent to circulate the necessary information among the various locals. Theresa Malkiel directed the New York
City campaign and simultaneously conducted a women's column in the *Jewish
Daily Forward*.[54] Within three months her campaign committee, which began
with only ten members, spawned subcommittees in each borough; by the end
of March it had sponsored approximately sixty suffrage meetings and had distributed over 5,000 leaflets. The language federations also joined, the Finnish
and even the German branches having initiated their own agitational committees for this campaign.[55] John Sloan, popular artist for the *Masses*, designed
a Socialist suffrage stamp symbolizing the "ideal comradeship and perfect cooperation of men and women in the Socialist movement" and selling for a
penny apiece.[56] In Manhattan and Brooklyn Socialist suffrage brigades canvassed the various neighborhoods and distributed literature. Within each district the campaign committee arranged special meetings, held either in private

homes or in public schools. This local agitation, although difficult to orchestrate smoothly, was important, for it reached many women who could not
escape domestic responsibilities to travel to downtown rallies. [57]

By mid-March the campaign committee began to plan for the second stage
of agitation. A conference of over 200 delegates and visitors discussed the
program for warmer months, when open-air meetings and intensified work
could begin. Socialists ambitiously adopted a slogan, "One street meeting for
every square block in the city before November 2,"[58] and almost reached this
goal. During the summer months they held from twenty-five to thirty open-air
meetings weekly, which by the close of the season in September totaled over
500. At the summer's end they increased their efforts and scheduled forty
meetings weekly for September and October. The amount of literature distributed reportedly topped all previous totals for any agitational effort sponsored by
the party.[59] Feeling confident, Socialists agreed to ban all party banners or
inscriptions in the gigantic parade which ended the campaign. Eugene Debs
led 2,000 men, followed by a Socialist fife, drum, and bugle corps from Queens
and thousands of Socialist suffragists.[60] During the final weeks of the campaign
Socialists claimed to have increased their agitation "six-fold."[61] No one could
say that Socialists fell short during this round.

Socialists were bitterly disappointed when voters defeated the suffrage referendum. But more heartbreaks were ahead. The party's central committee responded to the defeat by recalling its delegates from the suffrage campaign
committee and by withdrawing all financial backing. The resilient Theresa
Malkiel protested this action. She pointed out that despite the party's minimal
support it had gained a 25 percent increase in city membership during the year
of suffrage agitation. Moreover, the suffrage referendum had actually passed in
those districts where Socialists had been most active. The hard-won agitational
machinery, she warned, could not be dismantled now except at great cost.
Malkiel tried to maintain an informational network with only scarce funds and
personally oversaw the few remaining volunteer workers. But the spirit was
irretrievably gone.[62]

In more ways than one the 1915 campaign marked a turning point. The
victorious 1917 referendum would not spark such enthusiasm. Malkiel did try
to revitalize the Socialist suffrage campaign committee but met with only
marginal success. But such was the fare of the mainstream movement. NAWSA
leaders similarly reported that the campaign of 1915 had been one of "highways, and of spectacular display," that of 1917 of "byways, of quiet intensive
work."[63] There was good reason: world war.

The logic of political Socialism, the slow task of mass education failed during
the conflict. Some Socialists turned to the peace movement; some joined
consumers' leagues to fight inflation and high food prices; some concentrated
on the trade union drive booming during this period; some disbanded after

party newspapers were virtually banned from the mail; others, including a few of the party's most prominent intellectuals, renounced their Socialist convictions in a burst of unanticipated patriotism. Even where the party mounted vigorous electoral campaigns, it could no longer unite these disparate activities into a simple logic.

The New York Socialist suffrage campaign committee barely survived this crisis. By early spring, 1917, the committee had renewed public agitation and began to plan additional meetings for the summer months ahead. Meta Stern resumed her "Votes for Women" column in the *Call*. Despite the similarity with the 1915 agitation, world war demanded a different, more guarded course. New York Socialists of course had always preserved their political identity, but they had on occasion, like the mass suffrage parades, shared the arena with mainstream suffragists. In 1917 few Socialists would be so casual in their behavior. On June 1 the Socialist suffrage campaign committee thus pledged to work only "under the auspices of and in closest cooperation with the Socialist party," while several subcommittees adopted similar resolutions condemning any cooperative efforts with middle-class suffrage societies.[64] With fewer workers, scant finances, and no problematic alliances, Socialist suffragists continued the struggle.

Meanwhile NAWSA leaders succumbed to wartime patriotism. In 1914 the *Woman's Journal* had publicized the call of suffragists from twenty-six nations for peace and attacked editorially the "unbridled ambitions" of "war-crazed men."[65] By 1916 many NAWSA activists had joined the preparedness campaigns and soon praised the American entry into the conflict. The *Woman's Journal* now became the *Woman Citizen* and proclaimed the government "an intimate part of ourselves . . . [standing] for our own effort to hold ourselves coherently to group action, group control, group process. . . ."[66] NAWSA president Carrie Chapman Catt attacked industrial radicalism then under the gun from unprecedented government harassment, and defended her organization by contrast as a "bourgeois movement with nothing radical about it," rather "representative of the most coherent, tightest-welded, farthest reaching section of society—the middle."[67] As they joined the Wilsonian crusade for "world democracy," NAWSA leaders were as never before one with the existing state of American social and political life.

With so many NAWSA activists involved in bandage-rolling and other patriotic activities, New York Socialists and their labor allies did the bulk of campaigning and bore the fruits of wartime events. In an election where a nominally anti-war candidate defeated the mayoral incumbent, and Socialist Morris Hillquit received the largest radical vote for that office since the Henry George campaign of 1886, suffrage swept in. The symbol was patent. Once upstate New York, the "burned over district," had given the suffrage movement life, and Manhattan stood as the site of ignorance and reaction. Now the New York City vote defeated an adverse upstate majority. It was left to the foreign-born community, aided by radical agitators, to raise the issue to completion.[68] Although prohibition among other factors obscured this tendency nationally, in New York City the voting patterns were clear enough to elicit florid commentary.

As champions of woman suffrage, Socialists did not necessarily win new friends. Political conservatives attacked Socialists for inaugurating a reign of anarchy. The *New York Times* agreed, suggesting editorially that Socialists were indeed responsible for the lamentable suffrage victory. The president of the State Association Opposed to Woman Suffrage noted that her group "had always maintained, that when radicalism and socialism prevail, woman suffrage will carry."[69] The president of the National Association Opposed to Woman Suffrage circulated a pamphlet among congressmen, charging that all suffragists were at heart pacifists and Socialists.[70] NAWSA leaders, drawing up in horror at these insinuations, now devised charts purporting to illustrate the lack of Socialist influence on voting patterns, and at the mass meetings celebrating the victory excluded Socialist speakers on principle.

Many Socialists did not know how to respond to this situation. The editor of the *New York Call*, in answering the *Times* editorial which called woman suffrage a "gift from Socialism," replied whimsically: "Really, fellow citizenesses, we blush at this praise. Modesty forbids us from even hinting that we Socialists presented the franchise to you as a gift. But the *Times* has no shame, and seems not to care what it says. And then, after telling you this, it reverts to its usual stupidity, and suggests that you use the gift to club the givers. . . ."[71] With less humor Morris Hillquit, addressing a Socialist rally in Madison Square Garden, claimed the issue "ceased to be one of speculation and has become one of mathematical demonstration." He pointed to the 150,000 increase in the Socialist vote, which correlated (presumably) with the rise in votes for woman suffrage. Socialist candidates, Hillquit insisted, came out for women's enfranchisement if only to save their own political necks. He added that Socialists did not really expect recognition "from the conservative women of the rich, and their frantic disclaimers . . . only amuse us."[72]

More serious was the disappointment experienced by individual Socialist women. They had only to look back less than ten years to recall NAWSA's praise for their contribution to the 1909 petition campaign. Although times had changed, especially with the onset of war, many Socialists felt stung by NAWSA's disclaimers.

This perplexing situation cast its shadow over the final stage of the national campaign. Socialists had retained friends among the National Woman's party (NWP) dedicated to securing a federal amendment. Socialist women admired the young, militant suffragists similarly repelled by NAWSA's patriotism and overlooked their mainstream partisan involvements; in turn, NWP activists looked favorably upon Socialists enmeshed in both suffrage and anti-war agitation. They shared a martyr in Inez Milholland, who died during the 1917 New York campaign and who had prominently represented Socialists among the NWP leadership. Outside New York, Socialists occasionally dropped their membership in NAWSA to join the militants. Berger, who credited the NWP cadre with "guts and courage," organized a state affiliate in her Milwaukee home after failing to gain NAWSA support for a local peace initiative.[73] Thus it came as no surprise when a meeting called to celebrate the 1917 New York victory, to demand the release of the jailed White House pickets, and to call upon Wilson to endorse suffrage brought Socialists and NWP members together with joined hands. Nearly a thousand women cheered Socialists to the rafters for their "magnificent support" in California and New York and listened with shared enthusiasm to anti-war diatribes.[74] Unfortunately, no mass movement could be generated from this zeal. NWP remained a mere cadre unable or unwilling to generate any larger socialistic current.

This last dilemma was symptomatic of the Socialist suffrage agitation at large. Footsoldiers in the battle for the vote, they had been repeatedly out-maneuvered at the national level by NAWSA leaders. Although the western state victories and the New York triumph in which Socialists had played a significant role had set the stage for the final act, they received slight credit. The drama of National Woman's party picketing, the symbolic importance of Wilson's belated endorsement, the fact of prohibition's success along with woman suffrage—all blurred the meaning of Socialists' grass-roots contribution. Carrie Chapman Catt added to their disappointment. In her address to the last NAWSA convention (and first meeting of the League of Women Voters), Catt gave definite shape to her political philosophy. The danger of American life, she averred, stemmed equally from the "mass illiteracy" at one end of the social scale and from the "extreme hurried men, busy with big risks . . . knowing commercial America only," at the other. She advocated a "prompt redress of legitimate grievance" as the "safeguard against revolution and violence."[75] She had at last explained clearly what the suffrage mainstream had believed for close to a decade: the twin enemies of the republic were reaction and radicalism. Now this philosophy achieved a finality it had previously lacked. As the greatest political campaign ever waged by women concluded, Socialists saw their role eclipsed, their contribution swallowed up, forgotten.

Not that Socialists had given up. Throughout the ratification campaign they urged special programs and promoted the duty of new voters toward their sisters. They hoped enfranchised women would use their hard-won political rights to advance humanitarian causes. "Unlimited are the vistas of public usefulness that have opened up before us. Boundless is the field of social service upon which we enter as full and equal human beings at last," one Socialist cheered.[76] Meta Stern thus retitled her column first the "New Citizens" and finally "To the Woman Voter," and aimed to accelerate an educational campaign, especially among the foreign-born workingwomen who required naturalization before they could vote and express their presumed radical interests. Socialists in the communities simultaneously organized registration campaigns, along with a broadened appeal for party membership.[77]

There were, however, no great victories ahead. Even the enfranchisement of women scarcely affected the Socialist vote. As early as 1915 Socialists in Butte, Montana, blamed women voters for turning their administration out of office, and a few similar stories appeared subsequently. But a survey conducted in 1917 by the national office uncovered no discernible patterns in women's vote.[78] To the extent that Socialists tried to seize upon the new voting potential by offering oustanding women candidates, they reaped encouraging returns. In 1914 the first Socialist woman was elected to the California legislature. Later a number of other women, especially in the West, won a variety of offices or ran ahead of the national ticket in local elections.[79] But many of these victories were based upon a constituency fast slipping away from the Socialist movement. It was likewise gratifying that a few suffrage veterans finally proclaimed their radical sympathies. Alice Stone Blackwell, Lucy Stone's daughter, and Harriot Stanton Blatch were doubtless the most prominent recruits to the Socialist party.[80] Politically, however, their affiliation was unimportant. For every new member drawn from the suffrage movement, tens and hundreds moved further away, with a fear induced by government repression on the one hand and the Russian Revolution on the other and, above all, with the sense that the great day for Socialism had passed.

CONCLUSION

In 1912, when prospects for a Socialist America seemed bright, propagandist Morris William opined that Socialism and the struggle for women's enfranchisement were inherently related:

> The Socialist Party when it first flung its banner to the breeze, declared for woman suffrage. Not only declared for woman suffrage but practices woman suffrage every single day of its existence. Women have been elected delegates to the Socialist party conventions of all kinds at a time when a woman that thought about politics was laughed at, scorned, and considered little better than a woman of the streets. The Socialist Party in those days knew what was right, and it continued in its way of equality between its women members and men members. . . . If a member of the Socialist Party were to declare himself as opposed to woman suffrage, the party constitution would expel such a person from its membership.[81]

The numerous factual errors in this peroration suggest not so much hypocrisy as self-deception. Contrary to this myth, it was not the Socialist party as such but a militant minority who seriously dedicated itself to suffrage; it was not through the supposed broad highways of full party backing but by the backroads of underfunded agitation, involving politically fragmented committees and overextended organizers, that Socialist suffrage campaigns progressed. Neither had woman suffrage been the class question Socialists claimed; it was, rather, an issue which compelled party activists to live up to the egalitarian ideals they professed or to expose themselves as shams. Attempts to seek out theoretical formulae distinct from mainstream suffrage ideology were likewise spurious; efforts to create independent, "class-conscious" campaigns proved heroic but indecisive.

Socialists nevertheless made a decisive contribution to the suffrage campaign, especially in forcing suffragists to seek a full measure of political emancipation. Socialists had no simple answer to NAWSA's xenophobic or racist leanings but managed to insist that foreign-born groups were a proper constituency of any democratic movement. They endeavored to validate this faith by spearheading agitation in working-class neighborhoods. If their contributions were belittled by mainstream suffragists, or exaggerated by political enemies seeking to link woman's vote with disorder, Socialists did not take to heart the disappointment, for they faced greater problems in the postwar political world.

The Socialist-led suffrage campaign also had an impact on the Socialist movement itself. Orthodox Socialists had heretofore treated the woman question as a sentimental fillip upon the main message of class struggle. By forcing the issue of woman suffrage, Socialist women smoked out sources of hidden opposition and raised the woman question to its true dimensions. In so doing, they went far in creating new standards, toward which all but the most recalcitrantly misogynist comrades felt bound to pay lip service. Socialist women learned to convert the latent sympathy of a minority into an active campaign, although within the larger Socialist movement they could only tip the balance slightly from passive acquiescence to significant support.

Socialist women did not succeed, any more than Marxist theoreticians, in formulating the full implications of their endeavor, for their party or for the women's movement at large. In the context of the suffrage campaign they raised perhaps the most significant questions possible—about the strategic relationship of the Left to reform movements in general and the relationship between the class struggle and women's emancipation. Here were problems worthy of the finest minds in America, if only the terms of discussion could be recognized. Despite the endless rounds of cogitation and feverish attempts at clarification, Socialists generated little universal wisdom on this issue. Their contributions to posterity were not to be found in treatise or tome.

True to the inclinations of American Socialists in general, suffrage activists devoted their energies rather to a practical application of their commitment and proved the viability of local initiative. No blanket policy could cover the full range of variation within both the mainstream suffrage movement and the national Socialist organization. Region by region, Socialists adapted strategy to fit the specific situation. In New York, where political Socialists, especially Jews, could create a discernible and decisive voice for woman suffrage, Socialist women wisely chose an independent course; in the West, where Socialists lacked an organic community and maintained friendly relations with the woman's movement, Socialist women demonstrated their catholicity by co-operating freely with various suffrage societies. This varied adaptation, at once pragmatic and idealistic, contained the elements of a larger theoretic-strategic formulation just beyond the grasp of Socialists. Time ran out on the quest.

Ida Crouch Hazlett, who had made the advancement of woman's cause through Socialism her life's task, served as well as any figure to illustrate the political stasis at the end of her campaign. Among prominent Socialist women she was rare in her fidelity to the party after 1920. Unrelenting agitator, she continued making tours of the West. But now she met reaction and vigilante "justice" rather than the open arms of suffrage-minded school teachers. She was kidnapped at least once by American Legionnaires, driven hundreds of miles, and dumped in a desert.[82] She was not broken by this experience, but she was weary and perhaps somewhat disillusioned. What was the final meaning of the struggle for woman suffrage in this new age of economic prosperity and rebellious resistance to prohibition? Nothing in her background suggested an answer.

The historic woman suffrage movement had formally ended. The problems beyond the vote were not so much legal as social and seemed to require agencies and activities outside the usual political institutions. Perhaps, many activists and radical sympathizers concluded, individual initiative would act more effectively than any collective venture.

NOTES

1. *New York Call*, Mar. 4, 1917. Biographical sketches of Hazlett were published in *Common Sense* (Los Angeles), July 29, 1905, and *Toledo Socialist*, June 3, 1905. See also *American Labor Who's Who*, ed. Solon DeLeon (New York, 1925), 51–52. Ida Crouch was born Aug. 7, 1862, and married Val Hazlett in 1892. Her early suffrage activity is recorded contemporaneously in *Burchard (Colo.) Times*; see especially issues for Oct. 15 and 29, 1897.
2. *New York Call*, Mar. 11, 1917.
3. *Ibid.*
4. *Terre Haute Tribune*, Feb. 28, 1917. For Debs's association with Anthony, see "Debs on Susan B. Anthony," *Socialist Woman*, 4 (Jan., 1909), 3, and Ray Ginger, *Eugene V. Debs* (New York, 1970 ed.), 240–41. The magazine which Debs edited in the 1890s, the *Locomotive Firemen's Magazine*, boasted a very progressive "Woman's Department," edited by Ida Husted Harper, who was to become Susan B. Anthony's biographer and editor of the later volumes of the *History of Woman*

Suffrage. Debs wrote on the woman question in the mid–1890s; see, for example, his comments on the "new woman" and on bloomers in *Railway Times* (Chicago), Oct. 1, 1895.

5. Anita Block in *New York Call*, Dec. 19, 1909.
6. Theresa Malkiel in *ibid.*, Mar. 9, 1915. See also Lena Morrow Lewis, "The Woman Suffrage Movement," *Progressive Woman*, 4 (Mar., 1911), 4, 7; Anna Ingerman, "Suffrage and the Historical Mission of Woman," *ibid.*, 3 (Mar., 1910), 6.
7. May Walden, quoted in a clipping from an Elgin, Ill., newspaper, dated Mar. 1, 1909, in May Walden Kerr Papers, Newberry Library, Chicago.
8. On twentieth-century suffrage ideology, see Aileen S. Kraditor, *The Ideas of the Woman Suffrage Movement* (New York, 1965).
9. Meta Stern in *New York Call*, Mar. 1, 1915. See also Stern's leaflet *To the Woman of the House* (n.d.), Women and Children File, Socialist Party of America Papers, Perkins Library, Duke University. Josephine Conger-Kaneko made a similar argument in "Women and Socialism," *Progressive Woman*, 5 (Aug., 1911), 8.
10. "Mammina," *La Fiaccola* (Buffalo), Nov. 5, 1910, and "Virtus," *ibid.*, June 22, 1912; *Radnicka Straza* (Chicago), Oct. 31, 1919, translated by the *Chicago Foreign Language Press Survey* (Chicago, 1937).
11. Barnett Braverman, "Home Is Woman's Sphere, a Fantastic Claim," *Progressive Woman*, 7 (Aug., 1913), 2.
12. Anita Block in *New York Socialist*, July 18, 1908.
13. Anna A. Maley, "The Suffrage and Freedom," *Socialist Woman*, 1 (Feb., 1908), 10.
14. Lena Morrow Lewis, "Woman Suffragists and Woman Suffragists," *ibid.*, 3.
15. Murray Schloss, "Men! Let's Turn in and Help," *Progressive Woman*, 6 (Dec., 1912), 4.
16. Ida Crouch Hazlett, "The Socialist Movement and Woman Suffrage," *Socialist Woman*, 1 (June, 1908), 5.
17. Josephine Cole, "The International and Woman Suffrage," *ibid.* (Nov., 1907), 3.
18. Quoted in *ibid.*
19. Richard J. Evans, *The Feminist Movement in Germany, 1894–1933* (London, 1976), 71–114; Werner Thönnessen, *The Emancipation of Women* (London, 1973), 65.
20. Report by Winnie Branstetter, in *Chicago Daily Socialist*, Feb. 7, 1908.
21. *New York Call*, Feb. 15, 1909, Feb. 23, 1914, Mar. 1, 1915.
22. Socialist party's *Official Bulletin* (Chicago), Mar., 1909.
23. Anita Block reporting for New York locals, *Progressive Woman*, 2 (Mar., 1909), 15; *Chicago Daily Socialist*, Apr. 17, 1909.
24. Harriet Taylor Upton, ed., *Forty-first Annual Report of NAWSA* (Warren, Ohio, 1909), 35–36.
25. See, for example, *New Yorker Volkszeitung*, Oct. 10, 23, Nov. 13, Dec. 25, 1910, Jan. 15, 1911.
26. *New York Call*, Dec. 12, 1909.
27. Carrie Chapman Catt and Nettie Shuler, *Woman Suffrage and Politics* (New York, 1923), 282–83.
28. See Crouch Hazlett's remarks in "The Socialist Movement and Woman Suffrage," 5; *New York Call*, Mar. 11, 1917. For a similar assessment, see Mary S. Oppenheimer's essay in the *New York Call*, July 25, 1914.

29. A retrospective analysis by Anita Block appeared in the *Chicago Daily Socialist*, Feb. 23, 1910.
30. *New York Times*, Dec. 20, 1909; *New York Call*, Dec. 20, 1909.
31. *New York Call*, Dec. 19, 1909.
32. *Chicago Daily Socialist*, Feb. 26, 1910.
33. *Progressive Woman*, 4 (June, 1910), 4. For reports on discussions at the convention, see Socialist Party of America, *Proceedings of National Congress, 1910* (Chicago, 1910), 181–211.
34. Anna B. Bouroff in *Industrial Union Bulletin* (Chicago), Apr. 4, 1908.
35. *Il Proletario* (New York City), Oct. 30, 1908, Feb. 25, June 30, 1910, June 8, 1911, Apr. 5, 1912; *Lavoratore Italiano* (Pittsburg, Kans.), Dec. 10, 1909.
36. Lena Morrow Lewis in *The World* (Oakland, Calif.), Oct. 19, 1912; Anita Block in *New York Call*, Aug. 18, 1912; Josephine Conger-Kaneko in *Chicago Evening World*, Oct. 8, 1912. See also William English Walling, *Progressivism—and After* (New York, 1914).
37. May Wood Simons in *Coming Nation* (Girard, Kans.), Mar. 4, 1911.
38. For an excellent description of state Socialist efforts, see James Weinstein, *The Decline of Socialism in America, 1912–1925* (New York, 1967 ed.), 60.
39. Editorial, *Woman's Journal*, Nov. 19, 1910; "A Woman in the Race," *Western Comrade*, 1 (June, 1913), 86–87.
40. *New York Call*, Nov. 17, 1910.
41. Agnes Downing, "The Work in Los Angeles," *Progressive Woman*, 5 (Dec., 1911), 4, and "Woman Suffrage in California," *ibid.* (Sept., 1911), 3; Mary Garbutt in *Chicago Daily Socialist*, Sept. 9, 1911; Dorothy Johns in *Revolt* (San Francisco), Oct. 21, 1911; Kate Gordon, on behalf of NAWSA, *Woman's Journal*, Dec. 3, 1910.
42. J.C.K. [Josephine Conger-Kaneko], "Notes on the Congress," *Progressive Woman*, 4 (June, 1910), 4.
43. May Wood Simons, who campaigned in Kansas, credits Socialists in *Cleveland Socialist*, Jan. 18, 1913. For Montana, see the *American Socialist* (Chicago), Oct. 17, 1914, and *New York Call*, Nov. 7, 1914; for Nevada, *New York Call*, Nov. 6, 1914.
44. *National Socialist* (Washington, D.C.), Mar. 5, 1913; "Wisconsin and Woman Suffrage," typed news release, Socialist Party of America Papers.
45. Unpublished autobiography, Meta Berger Papers, State Historical Society of Wisconsin.
46. NAWSA, *Proceedings, 1911* (New York, n.d.), 179; NAWSA, *Proceedings, 1912* (New York, n.d.), 86, 103; Socialist party's *Monthly Bulletin*, 9 (Nov., 1912). On Socialists and NAWSA in Oklahoma, see Ida Porter-Boyer to Carrie Chapman Catt, Apr. 4, 1910, Socialist Party of America Papers.
47. Unpublished autobiography, Meta Berger Papers.
48. *New York Call*, Dec. 23, 1910, Jan. 4, 21, Feb. 1, 8, 1911.
49. "Report of the Organizer of the Women's Committee, Local New York, for the period March 11–May 25, 1912," Socialist Party, Local New York Minutes, Microfilm Reel 4, Tamiment Library, New York University; Malkiel's protest, *New York Call*, Feb. 14, 1911.
50. Anita Block in *New York Call*, Nov. 17, 1912.
51. Ida Husted Harper, ed., *History of Woman Suffrage*, VI (New York, 1921), 455, 456.
52. Newman's challenge, *New York Call*, Mar. 29, 1914, followed by almost daily reports through July. Report of conference, *ibid.*, Mar. 30, 1914.

53. Detailed reports may be found in *ibid.*, particularly May 2, 6, 17, 24, June 13, Dec. 15, 1914. Stern's "Votes for Women" column appeared for the first time on Dec. 5, 1914, and provided excellent coverage of the 1915 campaign.
54. Meta Stern in *ibid.*, Jan. 10, 12, 22, Feb. 2, 19, 1915.
55. *New York Call*, Feb. 19, 1915.
56. *Ibid.*, Feb. 21, 1915.
57. *Ibid.*, Mar. 6, 8, 1915.
58. *Ibid.*, Mar. 22, 1915.
59. *Ibid.*, July 18, Sept. 5, 1915.
60. *Ibid.*, Oct. 16, 1915; *New York Times*, Aug. 17, 1915.
61. *New York Call*, Oct. 25, 1915.
62. Mary S. Oppenheimer, "The Suffrage Movement and the Socialist Party," *New Review*, 3 (Dec. 15, 1915), 359–60. The May Day anniversary and international labor issue of the *New York Call*, May 1, 1916, contains a brief history of the 1915 Socialist suffrage campaign.
63. Mrs. Ellen Hawley Crosset in Harper, ed., *History of Woman Suffrage*, VI, 435.
64. Stern's column reappeared in the *New York Call* on Feb. 19, 1917. For spring plans of the Socialist suffrage campaign committee, see *ibid.*, Mar. 30, May 28, and June 6, 1917.
65. *Woman's Journal* (Boston), Aug. 15, 1914.
66. *Woman Citizen* (Boston), Sept. 28, 1918.
67. *Ibid.*, July 7, 1917.
68. For post-election analyses of the 1917 campaign in the German and Yiddish Socialist dailies, see *New Yorker Volkszeitung*, Nov. 11, 28, 1917; *Jewish Daily Forward*, Oct. 20, Nov. 3, 6, 10, 1917. From the Slavic group with its head-quarters in Chicago, similar statements appeared in *Radnicka Straza*, Oct. 31, 1917, translated in the *Chicago Foreign Language Press Survey* (Chicago, 1937), Reel 9. For the role of immigrants in the New York state suffrage victory, see Doris Daniels, "Building a Winning Coalition: The Suffrage Fight in New York State," *New York History*, 60 (Jan., 1979), 58–80.
69. *New York Times*, Nov. 8, 1917.
70. Mary Garret Hay, "Report" to the 1917 NAWSA convention, in Ida Husted Harper, ed., *History of Woman Suffrage*, V (New York, 1922), 537.
71. *New York Call*, Nov. 9, 1917.
72. *New York Times*, Nov. 23, 1917.
73. Unpublished autobiography, Meta Berger Papers.
74. *New York Times*, Nov. 12, 23, 1917.
75. *Handbook of the N.A.W.S.A. and Proceedings of the Jubilee Convention* (New York, 1919), 250.
76. *New York Call*, Nov. 14, 1917. See also Anita Block's "Women at the Cross Roads" in *New Age* (Buffalo), Feb. 28, 1918.
77. These activities were covered in the *New York Call* in Meta Stern's column in late 1917 and early 1918.
78. *Montana Socialist* (Butte), Apr. 24, 1915. Typscript of the survey conducted by the national office may be found in Women and Children File, Socialist Party of American Papers.
79. The first Socialist woman legislator elected in California was Mrs. Estelle Law-ton Lindsey, a Los Angeles journalist, reported in the *New York Call*, Nov. 6, 1914. Lena Morrow Lewis ran well in Alaska; her campaign was covered by the *Alaska Labor News* (Anchorage) in 1916; see especially the report published in the Nov. 4, 1916, issue.

80. *Oklahoma Leader* (Oklahoma City), July 10, 1920, reprinted a letter by Anita Block entitled "Harriot Stanton Blatch Joins the Socialist Party." Block quoted Blatch: "After the big suffrage fight was over, I must admit that I did not feel like getting right into another big fight. And very likely under different conditions, I would have gone quietly on, just voting the Socialist ticket. But all the events since the war have made such a course impossible. . . . This I felt laid a duty upon me, as pure American, with strong anti-slavery traditions. . . . The fight is on and the time has come for alignments. Long ago I made the choice inside and now I must make it openly." See also Blatch's *Why I Joined the Socialist Party*, undated leaflet (1922?), Women and Children File, Socialist Party of America Papers. Harriot Stanton Blatch and Alma Lutz, *Challenging Years: The Memoirs of Harriot Stanton Blatch* (New York, 1940), 316–20, describes her ultimate departure from the party.

81. *National Socialist*, Oct. 26, 1912.

82. *New Day* (Chicago), Aug. 20, 1921.

7 Sexual Emancipation

Sex attraction and joy in reproduction are primal; they
come down to us from the far-gone past before society
existed. They were a part of life before civilization
dawned and became the complicated thing it now is. Of
late, however, we are beginning to question whether this
primal impulse will survive our complex civilization. In
the contest of learned minds, the artifices of busy brains,
and the roar of machinery, in the ever increasing intensity of the struggle for existence, the little god Cupid
seems hustled aside. We are discussing very gravely what
shall be Cupid's ultimate fate when civilization shall
have dethroned him and reduced life to a mere mechanical process.

Kate Richards O'Hare
The Sorrows of Cupid (1912)

"Is the elimination of Love the price of Progress," Kate Richards
O'Hare asked, "or can we have Love and Progress too?" This was an important
question because, O'Hare explained, her generation was witnessing a tumul-
tuous change in sexual relations. She documented her case by culling evidence
from the federal census which suggested that men and women were resisting
the natural attraction of marriage, that the number of celibates in the population
was increasing, that permanent marriage seemed incompatible with modern
civilization, and that Americans were losing their "fruitfulness . . . becoming
sterile." Among these ominous tendencies was yet another peril, a "pestilential
miasma creeping up from the underworld to invade our homes"—prostitution,
or the Social Evil. "The toilers who feed and clothe and shelter the race,"
O'Hare warned, were demanding answers. They had already called upon the
clergy, the fine theoreticians, honored scholars, and the rulers of capital but
had received no satisfactory response. Now the humble toilers would take
matters into their own hands. Socialists, O'Hare concluded, bore a unique
responsibility at this stage in historical development: they must step forward
and act upon these monumental shifts in manners and morals.[1]

Kathleen Richards was born in 1877 in Ottawa County, Kansas, where her
parents, homesteaders from Kentucky, had built a prosperous ranch and pro-

duced five children. Kate's rural childhood was short-lived. During the severe drought and recession of 1887 her father lost the ranch and, seeking salvation, brought his wife and brood to Kansas City.

The "sin city" of the Plains states was the site of the young Kate's political awakening. Her father did well enough as a machinist to finance a daughter's customary education. Kate attended normal school in Nebraska, but one winter in a rural schoolhouse dampened her enthusiasm for this feminine occupation. She soon found her way back to Kansas City. Kate then became an apprentice in her father's establishment and flouted tradition further by joining the International Association of Machinists, a union not especially receptive to women members. However heterodox her vocational calling, Kate's political inclinations were not in the least unusual. Like so many other socially concerned women in this center of Populist agitation, much like Donnelly's heroic Sophie, Kate enlisted in the campaign to assist young women new to the city, especially those thrown upon their own resources.[2]

Kate joined the staff of the newly opened Florence Crittenton Mission and Home. Named for the deceased daughter of a wealthy New York businessman, Florence Crittenton missions could be found by the mid-1890s in most major cities. Charles Crittenton himself had conducted a cross-country evangelistic tour, often working in conjunction with local chapters of the WCTU, and founded dozens of rescue missions to provide prostitutes with shelter and moral uplift and to encourage drunkards to mend their ways. Crittenton visited Kansas City in 1895, and a year later the mission and home opened to receive guests. It stood prominently in the city's red-light district as a beacon to women desiring "to lead a better life." The first floor served as a meeting room and contained some chairs, an organ or piano. A open Bible shared the center stage with a fresh lily, symbol of purity and subtle inspiration to the patrons. Florence workers often patrolled the city's streets, entering taverns and dance halls and inviting the presumably outcast men and women to accompany them to the mission. Beginning usually around 9:00 P.M. each evening, Florence workers would lead the audience in prayer, scripture readings, and songs, aiming to fill the hours of temptation until early morning when the assembly could safely disband. Within a year of its opening, over 60,000 men and women had attended these services. Others took advantage of the mission's other services. The second floor served as a temporary living quarter sheltering ten to twelve young women at one time. During its first year the home received over 200 young women, offered maternity care to some, referred others to parents or hospitals, or placed them in "respectable" employments.[3]

Kate's involvement in rescue work left an indelible mark on her political consciousness. Like other volunteers, Kate came to this cause a devout Christian, and she considered entering the ministry of the Disciples of Christ until overcome by a painful crisis of faith. She began to question the means she had chosen to tackle such pressing problems as prostitution. The writings of Henry George, Henry Demarest Lloyd, and Ignatius Donnelly served to broaden her intellectual horizons, while the political ferment in Kansas City provided a substitute for her religious activism. Yet Kate lost none of her dedication to the lowly, and little of her evangelical spirit. She maintained ties with the local woman suffrage movement and the WCTU and continued to focus on women's issues. The hardships women endured in earning their livelihoods, especially their subjection to sexual violence, remained at the center of her concerns.

At the turn of the century Kate Richards O'Hare brought the social purity crusade to the doorstep of the local Socialist movement. When Mother Jones's oratory inspired Kate to join the new Socialist party, the acolyte lifted her understanding to a yet higher level but did not abandon her earlier commitments. She soon became the most popular woman orator in the Socialist encampments and continued to direct her polemical outbursts at the liquor traffic, "race suicide" and divorce, white slavery and prostitution, all now consistently interpreted as the spawn of the capitalist system. Speaking to the hearts of thousands of mid- and southwestern women who had made a similar transition to the Socialist movement, O'Hare proved the political viability of the social purity heritage.

After 1910 other political demands lured O'Hare from her original calling and ultimately altered her perspective on woman's plight. As a Socialist of international repute, O'Hare weathered the factionalism, labor upsurge, antiwar mobilization, spectre of repression, and the day-to-day rigor of collaborating on one of the Socialist movement's most popular newspapers, the *National Rip-Saw*. Rubbing shoulders with a variety of progressive politicians and intellectuals, she gained over the years a cosmopolitan outlook unattainable to her rank-and-file sister comrades. Of the midwestern leadership O'Hare most easily acclimated herself to a new campaign for sexual emancipation—family limitation. Although she supported its mobilization and assisted its key activists, she did not become a leading figure in the birth control agitation as she was in social purity causes. Yet even this limited involvement was notable, for the majority of her peers played no role whatsoever.

Unlike women's wage-labor and political rights, the issue of sexual emancipation divided the Socialist ranks along generational lines. Virtually all Socialist women regardless of age wished to aid workingwomen in their struggle for bread and, when circumstances allowed, rallied to assist their efforts at unionization. Although the woman suffrage campaign raised many questions about correct strategy, it nevertheless gathered the energies of most party women. Women's sexual oppression under capitalism stirred no such uniform response. Rather, sections of the Socialist movement created two relatively autonomous campaigns, each addressing the problems of sexual oppression in a distinct and, at least on one level, contradictory manner.

Like the youthful O'Hare, most Socialists responded readily to the image of female sexual degradation. Reared upon the sensationalist tales of seduction, they envisioned capital's great crime against woman as her moral ruination. Prostitution, the most heinous example, thus drew many party activists to attention, so that by 1912 they spearheaded several major agitations against white slavery and organized crime.

The birth control agitation was the child, so to speak, of a constituency new to party environs. Younger and more formally educated than the party regulars of 1912, this sector broke many traditions and sought to create a wholly different framework for considering the weighty questions of sexual morality. Whereas the social purity–oriented majority hoped to stave off the invasion of capitalism into personal life and attempted to preserve the ideals of a presumably pre-existing sexual morality, the young radicals who instigated the birth control agitation accepted instead the tendency of capitalism to foster new social relations among women and men as the basis of a moral system adequate to modern life. Rather than envisioning woman as the victim of capitalist degradation, they located in her a potency for sexual expression unimaginable to their predecessors.

The issue of sexual emancipation brought Socialists to a crossroads on the woman question. They could no longer conserve their sentimental regard for woman, for she had begun to become a subject in her own right. Woman's self-realization, moreover, ultimately lay beyond the economic sphere where Socialists could comfortably and confidently supply the answers. An updated view of Socialism thus demanded a new perspective on the recreation of human purpose, a new view of culture.

SOCIALISTS AND SOCIAL PURITY, 1901–12

Socialists transmitted the ideal of social purity from the late nineteenth-century reform movements to their own modern campaigns. They continued to describe the defense of the family against ruination, of womanly virtue against despoliation, as necessary concomitants to electoral victory. Veteran women agitators spearheaded the campaigns, and an unusual number of men responded sympathetically. German-American Socialists, wedded to the romantic tradition, interpreted women's sexual oppression especially in prostitution as the most profound example of capitalism's evil. Shrewd strategists found other reasons to join the campaign. In part to clear Socialism's good name from slanderous charges of immorality, in part to outmaneuver municipal reformers in their campaigns for good government, many party activists became vocal defenders of pure womanhood. Heartfelt or expedient, the avowal that only Socialism would herald the end of woman's sexual exploitation added a unique touch to the somewhat timeworn pursuit of social purity. From another standpoint, the emphasis upon this aspect of woman's plight underlined Socialists' own difficulty in grappling with the changing patterns of manners and morals.

"Official" Socialist theory, elaborate if not particularly neoteric, situated woman's sexual oppression within the standard materialist framework championed by the Second International. The classic work in this genre, Frederick Engels's *The Origin of the Family, Private Property and the State* (1884), adapted the modish anthropological scholarship on marriage and kinship to a political analysis of the family at various stages of historical development. Following the evolutionary paradigm popularized earlier by J. J. Bachofen and Lewis Henry Morgan, Engels traced the history of sexual relations through early stages of social organization. Savagery, Engels wrote, had been marked by a communistic sharing of persons and things, as men and women mated promiscuously in group marriage. When economic development had created more wealth and consequently fostered more complex forms of social organization, mankind entered upon barbarism, an ominous step for women. So long as paternity had been unknown, the collective property of the kinship group passed through the female line, and women enjoyed the status and power commensurate with their relatively secure place in the social order. Under barbarism, a system of pairing marriage guaranteed the accumulation of property within a single family unit now ruled by the male. The emergence of the patriarchal family thus represented, in Engels's view, "the *world historical defeat of the female sex*" and illustrated effectively how the subordination of women paralleled the rise of private property.[4]

Engels's analysis significantly avoided the problem of modern sexual relations save to decry woman's oppression under capitalism. With the onset of private property, Engels argued, man became absolute ruler and "woman was degraded and reduced to servitude, she became the slave of his lust and a mere instrument for the production of children," that is, sexual chattel. Engels blasted the prevailing double standard of morality which dictated chastity for women but allowed men free sexual reign; adultery and prostitution, the most blatant injustices of patriarchy, maintained the inequitable system. Engels predicted sexual harmony only with the dawn of Socialism, as men and women joined freely on the basis of "real" love alone, and "monogamy, instead of collapsing, at last becomes a reality—also for men."[5] Whether Socialism might allow for other possibilities—women in the future like men in the past choosing a diversity of love objects, erotic impulses playing a more prominent place in the society of universal cooperation—Engels did not specify.

Although an English-language version of *The Origin of the Family* appeared in the United States only in 1902, Socialists had already mastered the book's central thesis. Bebel had summarized Engels's contribution in the wide-circulating 1891 edition of *Die Frau und der Sozialismus*. German-American

Socialists had simultaneously produced dozens of tracts simplifying Engels's complex documentation of the history of the family. Native-born theorists like Ward, Bellamy, and Gilman had taken a complementary tack, linking female sexual oppression to an economic system that denied women the right to independent livelihoods. Socialists of various stripes could thus agree with the turn-of-the-century propagandist who wrote: "the institution which the beneficiaries of capitalism are so afraid the socialists will destroy, is too often not marriage at all, but a hateful slave-compact. . . . It is only private property expressed in human lives."[6] Scarcely any would draw openly the corollary conclusion, that the abolition of private property might end the artificial legal restraints of marriage bonds.

Whereas Bebel quoted Bachofen to hint that the "end of social development resembles the beginning of human existence," the Golden Age of equality returning at last, American Socialists distinctly chose to confute all implications of promiscuity however egalitarian. Most could agree with the first American translator of *Die Frau*, Daniel DeLeon, that the German visionary had erred and the "moral, as well as the material, accretions of the race's intellect, since it uncoiled out of early Communism, bar . . . all prospect—I would say danger, moral and hygienic,—of promiscuity, or of anything even remotely approaching that." The monogamic family, "enobled" by "conjugal, paternal and filial affection," DeLeon insisted, would "bloom under Socialism into a lever of mighty power for the moral and physical elevation of the race."[7] DeLeon spoke for a large sector of Socialists who believed Bebel had surpassed the boundary of "scientific" observation of society.

All the more curious, then, was the pride taken by American Socialists in fulfilling the rigorous materialism of the Second International in regard to the woman question. By imposing upon their historical schema the social purity ideology which sought to turn back capitalism's intrusion into the home, Socialists planted a permanent feature amidst an otherwise dynamic system and thereby raised doubts about the credibility of the entire edifice.

There were a number of sources for such self-deception. Modern production in the great factories had seemingly created a tangible basis for Socialism while the home rendered up no such literal images. Socialists also endured, often in a life-and-death struggle for the sympathy of working-class groups, the charges by clerics and political opponents that Socialism meant free-love debauchery. For union organizers and political agitators in such neighborhoods, dangerous slanders had to be dispelled quickly and more pressing matters attended. And finally, predisposed by their own leanings, Socialists observed that most women believed men already had too much sexual freedom. Practical considerations for better and worse overruled any prospect of theoretical consistency.

The most frequent public attack upon Socialism centered on the issue of free love. In its literal meaning, the concept had perfect consonance with the notion of sexual equality and relations unscathed by the cash nexus. In the public mind, however, free love meant promiscuity and Socialists were its chief advocates. Although Marx had defended the European movement against this charge since the 1840s, the popular imagination continued to see in Socialism not only the impending violence of class warfare but the destruction of the family and the ruination of women. As a wave of panic about the future of the family swept over many middle-class Americans at the turn of the century, Socialists again became prime targets of hostility. Their opponents pointed to the decline in the birth rate, the increase in the population of unmarried persons, the rise in the divorce rate, and the numerous scandals about adultery and illegitimacy cropping up in recent years. Religious leaders, politicians, and educators had joined these discussions and offered a variety of reasons to explain this apparently dangerous shift in moral standards. Many concluded that the middle-class family, the proverbial foundation of the state, had been imperiled by women's recent advances. They denounced women for seeking careers instead of motherhood, as sociologists followed the first graduates from the new women's colleges into unusually late marriages and atypically small families. The cry of "race suicide" echoed from the chambers of the White House and Harvard College to the small corners of middle America. Even those women who did marry appeared "restless" as indicated by their perceptible apathy toward domestic responsibilities or retreat into neurasthenia. To ward off such phantoms, a notable sector of the populace struck out at the women's movement and its Socialist allies and accused them of conspiring to destroy the family.[8]

Rather than developing deeper analyses of marriage and family life, Socialists expended their polemical energies fending off such false and damaging charges. Especially in the Midwest and Plains states, where Socialists campaigned within a socially conservative milieu, the taint of free love could prove an extreme liability at the polls. Party leaders regularly cautioned local standard bearers to keep questions of marriage and religion off the platform, although eager polemicists often ignored this directive to turn free-love accusations back upon their attackers. In a few cases local Socialists quoted passages from the Bible and listed publicly the "immoral" sexual habits of leading home-town Democrats and Republicans. The national leadership might disapprove this tactic, but especially around election time expedience won out.[9]

Although the political climate mitigated against even a reasonable argument on behalf of the ideal of free love, Socialists were never ready advocates. Capitalist society, most believed, did not provide a supportive milieu for sexual innovation by those lacking the basic political and economic resources to enter nonbinding arrangements on equal terms. As propagandist Allen W. Ricker warned: "Man will debauch woman, so long as he has the power, just as he always has since he gained dominance over her. Woman's virtue is seldom safe in the keeping of man. You know it. Woman knows it, and the whole world knows it, so don't make a fool of yourself by denying it."[10] To ask the average working-class woman to put aside moral and legal sanctions and to trust her companion in his declaration of love was, in the popular Socialist view, extremely naive.

The chivalrous underpinnings of such arguments nevertheless protruded through the reassuring rhetoric. If the mainstream woman's movement of the nineteenth century had named man the potential debaucher, Socialists had substituted capitalism and its masters as the curse of maidenly virtue. Their depiction of pure womanhood, victim of lust, had a ring of unquestionable sincerity, likewise their promise that under Socialism woman would gain control over erotic relations, finally "settle the sex question, and settle it right."[11] Who would heartlessly deny Kate Richards O'Hare's appeal to "Love, home and babies" as the "three graces that make the trials, struggle and suffering of life worth while"?[12] Maternal sensibility, national ideology, and Socialist aspiration seemingly coincided at this point, regardless of other complications.

If a toll were to be exacted for such indifference to the changes sweeping over modern womanhood, Socialists were for the moment blissfully ignorant or, rather, righteously looking in another direction. Notoriously weak on theoretical matters generally, they excelled as creative propagandists and skilled agitators. They reacted with instinctive vigor, therefore, when the one definite issue of contemporary sexual politics allowed them to define their roles as defenders of womanhood. Commercialized vice and "white slavery" found the Socialists in their stride as warriors: at the leftward edge of the mainstream, they could press a radical perspective and hold out a Socialist solution without endangering their public support of the family, legitimately assail "bourgeois" morality and hypocrisy while leaving unresolved the revolutionary alternatives.

During the first decade of the twentieth century the war against prostitution gained new life as municipal reformers took up the cudgel. Previously, women had shaped the campaign. As moral reformers during the early years of the nineteenth century, women had directly named men as the aggressors and had hoped to "redeem" the so-called fallen woman by providing her with spiritual guidance, moral uplift, and the means to sustain herself. Toward the end of the century women reformers had adopted a broader social approach; they designed large-scale educational programs to impart to young adults sufficient knowledge for self-protection, and worked to improve women's chance for economic survival in the city. Progressives took a different tack. In the twentieth century prostitution still conjured up the image of distressed womanhood but suggested other dangers as well.

Progressives treated the Social Evil as but one of many blights upon urban society. They came to agree with women reformers that it was not weak character but low wages that drove many women to desperate acts. But as prostitution had grown tremendously in recent years, Progressives believed that other factors as well were at work. White slavery was the clearest illustration. Rather than slipping into the wily snares of a seducing "bestial" male, the modern Clarissa would be captured, drugged, sexually violated, sold to a cunning madame, and then imprisoned in a brothel. In league with the procurers, the madame would destroy the young woman's clothing and force her to become addicted to alcohol and drugs. "Return" to society was thus no longer a moral or even an economic choice for the modern prostitute; a captive imprisoned by walls or by drugs, she had little recourse but to serve her masters. In rendering this analysis, Progressives continued to appeal to the public's sense of outrage at the vile destruction of womanhood. They tended to emphasize, however, the wide-scale, even international organization behind the white slave trade. The polit-ical corruption, the collusion of the police, ward politicians, and city hall in graft, bribery, and payoffs—these were the key issues. Thus prostitution became an issue in the Progressive campaign for good government.[13]

It was no small issue either. During the first decade of the twentieth century the attention given to prostitution was unsurpassed. Many municipal govern-ments instituted commissions of citizens' committees to study the problem in order to formulate legislation that might eliminate the heinous system. Major city newspapers veered toward yellow journalism as the white slavery exposé naturally lent itself to lurid descriptions and to melodrama. And the statistical reports proliferated. If one investigator could find only 10,000 prostitutes in Chicago, another easily located at least 100,000 in New York City. The National Purity Congress estimated the total number in the United States at more than 230,000. No city, no small town was safe.[14]

Socialists joined this war against prostitution and played roles not unlike the Progressives. The publication of statistics on the extent of prostitution, descrip-tions of the crippling effects of venereal disease, reports of the demise of young women captured off the streets and locked in brothels, such was standard fare in the Socialist as well as the muckraking press. The headline "Girls Fed to Ghouls," penned by a Socialist editor, captured the mood.[15]

Socialists always emphasized, however, that it was the capitalist system, not merely organized crime, that made women prey for white slavers and pimps. At least 90 percent of all prostitutes, they wrote, were working-class women who looked upon prostitution as merely the lowest rung of the economic ladder. Financially and spiritually dragged down by frequent unemployment, sickness, poverty, and despair, these women simply succumbed to the temptations around them. Socialists frequently quoted the official reports produced by the various vice commissions and highlighted the causal relationship between low wages and woman's fall. They also drew the analogy suggested by Engels, that mar-riage and prostitution mirrored the system of private property.[16]

Claiming a unique and correct perspective on the problem, Socialists took up their pens for woman's cause and produced a sizable body of literature on the subjects of prostitution and white slavery. Most productions appeared as short sketches, newspaper or magazine essays, or pamphlets. Some of the most moving treatments of white slavery were penned by midwesterners, like Kate Richards O'Hare, who wrote with the poignancy and flare that her Populist background inspired. Joseph Greer, M.D., lent his medical authority to *The Social Evil and the Remedy* (n.d.), which described the plodding life of women wage earners. Charles H. Kerr published *What Did Gracia Do?* and its sequel *Was It Gracia's Fault?* (1899), the former a lyric poem on the subject of seduction, the later a strict materialist analysis in prose form. Toward 1910, as the Progressive campaigns began to set the tone, Socialist journalists joined the muckraking foray. Newspapers overran with articles on prostitution. Josephine Conger-Kaneko responded by producing a special issue of the *Progressive Woman* and almost lost her mailing privileges for her candid treatment of sexual abuse. [17]

Although historical analysis and exposé were propaganda staples, the most effective literature drew upon case studies of real life. Cast into fictional form, the story of woman's fall drew upon a popular genre of seduction literature and touched many hearts. The two most widely read works were, if more sentimental than realistic in tone, comprehensive in their political treatments and gripping as dramatic stories. Estelle Baker's *The Rose Door* (1911) followed three women of differing social classes and ethnic backgrounds to their respective falls and featured a Socialist propagandist who seemed to know several of Bebel's chapters by heart. *The Rose Door* was very popular among Socialists, but Reginald Kauffman's *House of Bondage* (1910) became a national best-seller. Within one and one-half years of its publication, the book went through sixteen printings. It was well timed with the era's major investigations of white slavery and prompted a wave of fiction concerning the Social Evil.

In *House of Bondage* Kauffman presents a class analysis of white slavery. The story details the various evils associated with organized prostitution but focuses on the victimization of an innocent woman. Mary appears first as a young, overworked, and mistreated daughter of a working-class family in Pittsburgh. In the midst of this unhappiness she meets a handsome and dashing suiter, Max, who promises romance and escape. Offering his hand in marriage, Max persuades Mary to run away with him to New York City. Max, of course, turns out to be a procurer for the white slave trade and sells Mary to Rose Legere, the unscrupulous madame of a brothel. Mary, now called Violet, cannot escape but is caught within an elaborate political web of organized vice. Kauffman stabs at the naivete of settlement workers who try to offer protection to prostitutes like Violet. He illustrates the extent of corruption in the city government. Finally, a minor character delivers the insightful analysis. Hermann Hoffmann, a Socialist, supplements his Marx with statistics to show "dot big system as makes us all vork for less as ve earn, und makes us all pay more as ve can" is the single cause for prostitution. The solution: "Von vay—und only von. . . . Do avay vith poverty. Reorganize de whole of de industrial system; gif effery man und voman a chance to vork; gif effery man und voman effery penny dey earns."[18] In the meantime, Hoffman explains, more and more people should be made to understand the pervasive nature of organized vice so that they can see the necessity of this comprehensive solution. Thus Kauffman's novel stood as the outstanding work of the contemporary genre, and Socialists rightfully considered it the finest fictional representation of white slavery, the crowning glory of their own impressive array of short stories and propaganda pieces.

As writers but also as local politicians, Socialists participated in the key campaigns in New York, Los Angeles, Milwaukee, and Chicago. The *Chicago Daily Socialist*, for example, led a controversial and risky attack on the Mayor Harrison administration. For several months during the summer of 1911 banner headlines attracted readers to stories documenting the extent of corruption in the administration and city hall's links to organized crime. Concurrently, the Chicago Vice Commission had issued its own report, but it tactfully held back in naming the individuals indirectly involved in prostitution rings. The *Daily Socialist* determined to crack the "key" to the vice commission's report so that the identity of criminals could be made known to the public. Their reporters succeeded and, using the index to Chicago real estate, were able to name the owners of much of the property used for houses of prostitution. The *Daily Socialist* not only published large sections of the vice commission's report but filled in the names of prominent citizens covertly backing prostitution, including city aldermen, judges, attorneys, bank presidents, and officials prominent in the Harrison administration. During the summer months the *Daily Socialist* reported unusually high sales, so high the paper exhausted its white stock and had to reduce the size of its editions. In other cities Socialists played similar although less dramatic roles.[19]

The agitational and propaganda campaigns against organized vice and prostitution marked the high point of the Socialist party's involvement with issues of sexual morality. In the urban movement large numbers of women and men rallied to the cause, for they, like the Progressives, used the fact of women's sexual victimization to call attention to other political issues. They designed their arguments to meet the Progressive challenge, to expose not mere flaws in the political order, such as dishonest city officials, but the fragility of the entire capitalist system. Unlike trade unionism among workingwomen or even woman suffrage, the white slave hysteria gave Socialists a weapon to fight Progressives on their own ground and, they hoped, to steal much of their political thunder. Party leaders thus managed to take up a popular cause, address it from a Socialist perspective, and draw a Socialist moral.

The campaign against prostitution drew together one final time the diverse strains of the older Socialist movement. European- or native-born, urban or rural, veteran Socialist propagandists harkened back to the nineteenth-century critique of prostitution as capitalism's ultimate degradation. Their crusade against white slavery seemingly refuted the familiar charge against Socialists as free lovers, and demonstrated to all sincere observers that the new regime would bring a purified monogamy.

This attempt by Socialists to rectify American public morals suggests in retrospect a fading photograph of the Socialist past, and faces still vivid with ideological zeal but marred by an archaic pose, a sentimental ambience already out of date. Their fervor to abolish prostitution disguised an inability to grasp the larger changes in sexual morality and the emergence of new behaviors. Save for vague promises of connubial bliss under Socialism—and usually presented in the opaque forms of poetry, songs, or aphorisms—no analysis of woman's oppression did more than reiterate how capitalism degraded woman.

Socialists could hardly be expected to predict with any degree of accuracy the titanic changes in moral standards. Few intellectual observers surpassed the contemporary press, which reacted with great interest but with no profound insights into the nature of the process. All the same, their unwillingness to pursue the subject offered a stark contrast to the depiction of workers' control under the Cooperative Commonwealth, a staple of Socialist literature from the earliest days of the movement. The future sexual morality, or what may be designated "private life" generally, Socialists set aside as a detail. Thus the claim for Socialism as a stage of civilization rather than a mere economic arrangement increasingly lacked conviction.

Before they could fully grasp the significance of events, Socialists paid a dear price for their historic myopia. The demand for sexual liberation framed the context of a different radical ideal, economic institutions as mere backdrop for the changes that inspired the greatest expectation among the young. The campaigns against prostitution, carrying the old moralist standard to the limit, pointed toward the necessity of a positive effort to protect womanhood. But strategy they had none, even ideals they could barely envision. A new generation, ill trained in Socialist theory and little connected with the labor movement or ethnic and grass-roots communities, had to stake out the claims of sexual emancipation by themselves and against the prejudices of the party elders. Rarely had the accomplishments of the Socialist movement so damaged the prospect for its required renovation.

THE NEW MORALITY

By 1910, when the Socialist party seemed to reach its stride in power and influence, an influential group of intellectuals moved close to its ranks. Many had already joined its antiprostitution campaigns or had been impressed by its political showing and its growing strength among the garment unions. In large cities, particularly New York, sufficient numbers gathered to place a new and distinct stamp upon the local movement.

The recruits stood apart from party veterans. On the one hand, they seemed surprisingly and pleasingly young. For years the stalwart of the women's branch had been the German or Jewish matron who, try as she might, could not entice even her own daughter. Now, women in their twenties and thirties appeared at various meetings.[20] Comrades also noted a larger showing of young men and women at special public programs and entertainments sponsored by the party. Although veterans eagerly welcomed these younger activists, they nevertheless were somewhat dismayed by their irregular political stands. The IWW, the anarchist Ferrer School in New York City, the ideas of revolutionary syndicalism, these better excited the fancies of the young than did old-fashioned political Socialism. The new recruits even ignored the standard Socialist texts, turning instead to the works of European social theorists like Nietzsche, Ibsen, Bergson, Sorel, and Stirner, and discussed among themselves all kinds of literary and philosophical notions. Pulled into the Socialist movement—as charmed by its unique character as by the working-class neighborhoods they discovered in Greenwich Village—these young radicals nevertheless found the organizational apparatus much too confining.

The branches occupied by the young recruits became known for their avant-garde mien. Rheta Childe Dorr recalled that intellectuals as well as some individuals of "rougher character" formed the "high brow" branch of the party in Greenwich Village.[21] Its leading lights were Sinclair Lewis, Robert and Martha Bruere, Arthur Bullard, and Ernest Poole. Club A, a nearby cooperative boarding house on Fifth Avenue, frequently hosted writers Mary Heaton Vorse, Upton Sinclair, Jack London, and on one occasion the Russian Maxim Gorki. On the Upper West Side was Local no. 5, which attracted luminaries William D. Haywood, Mabel Dodge, John Reed, and Margaret and William Sanger. During the summer months many fled the city and regrouped on Cape Cod, where they vacationed and sometimes worked together in a theatrical troupe, the Provincetown Players. Crystal Eastman and her brother Max, Ida Rauh, Henrietta Rodman, Floyd Dell, Hutchins Hapgood, Neith Boyce, Jessie Ashley, George Cram Cook, and Susan Glaspell frequently joined the various gatherings.[22]

Despite their somewhat diffident manner, these intellectuals made a decisive impact upon the Socialist movement and enjoyed an influence extending far beyond their centers of activity. Because they touched the pulse of a new national culture in gestation, poet Genevieve Taggard could later write with pardonable exaggeration that they constituted "the most significant group that ever managed to dominate, for a time, an entire generation." Where previously the ranks of the Left included a handful of intellectuals among its autodidact masses, now the Socialist movement attracted scores of college-educated men and women seeking rebellion. They epitomized "the unity of life, the dance of it," and rejected commercial values for the child-like discovery of new wonders. To be sure, as Taggard emphasized, most were summer soldiers; fascinated rather than dedicated, they turned soon enough to other matters. But for a time in the 1910s artist and audience gave a Socialist magazine like the *Masses* an unprecedented vogue. Never before had the upper reaches of American culture—its painting, fiction, poetry, criticism—felt so keenly the influence of individuals spiritually socialistic.[23]

Although the precocious intellectuals themselves barely understood the critique they laid down against the old ways, they sensed that "motion," dynamic activity, was, as Arturo Giovannitti said, "the sole reason for life." And the motion they experienced swept past the usual economic or political criteria into private life. They thus brought to Socialist ideology the notion that psychology had become as relevant as history, the collectivity of the social order no more compelling than the internal growth of the individual.

Known in party circles as "the new intellectuals,"[24] this politically active minority issued the direct challenge that sex be made a major issue of revolutionary politics and women's liberation its substance. They chided their elders for adhering to many Victorian prejudices common in middle America. But even more, they ridiculed Socialists for being too timid to discuss the matter publicly and boldly. In contrast, the new intellectuals sought to comprehend the social function of sex, not to destroy its mystic symbolism but to break the taboos that separated the symbol from interpretation. Lillian Symes, an aspiring journalist, later recalled the young women across the country "pouring over tomes by Ellis, Steckle, Long and Robie, and candlelit tea-rooms [echoing] with discussions of erogenous zones and other similar matters." Admirably defiant of existing conventions, this generation was serious in its revolt, Symes recalled, "wholesome" rather than merely flippant as were the young in the Roaring Twenties to follow.[25] Carriers of the rebellious spirit, the new intellectuals sought to transform the staid world of political Socialism.

For theoretical inspiration they looked abroad. There the growing field of sex research provided the bulk of new empirical data on the nature of sexuality and its prevailing forms in human behavior. The new intellectuals devoured much of this new literature. Especially after Freud's visit to the United States in 1909, they furiously debated his psychoanalytic theory and adopted its vocabulary. As Susan Glaspell later recalled, among her crowd in Greenwich Village one "could not go out to buy a bun without hearing of some one's complex."[26] The new intellectuals likewise found merit in even the German Krafft-Ebing, whose *Psychopathia Sexualis* (1892) broke ground as a catalogue of "deviant" sexual behavior. But whereas Freud's theories were unique to themselves and Krafft-Ebing's informative but uninspiring, other writers had absorbed much of the new empirical information on human sexuality into a political analysis of contemporary social norms. In this area the philosophers of the New Morality provided the new intellectuals with the most coherent and satisfactory examination of sexual relations.

The new intellectuals found kindred spirits among British New Moralists, especially those who had formed the Fellowship of New Life in 1883. They studied the landmark, multivolume study of human sexuality written by the leading British sexologist Havelock Ellis. They produced the plays of the brilliant satirizer of "bourgeois" romance, George Bernard Shaw. Above all, they revered William Morris, whose utopian novel *News from Nowhere* (1890) had established the truth that genuine love could exist only between moral equals, that affection and friendship must loom above romance. Like Morris, the new intellectuals argued against asceticism and demanded greater sexual freedom predicated upon the emergence of an independent woman who could meet man on equal terms, who could be his partner as well as lover.[27]

As proponents of the New Morality, the new intellectuals embraced an enlightened, modern view of sexuality. They emphasized the importance of the sex drive, for they considered it, like other physical needs, natural and healthy. They startled many genteel folk by announcing that women experienced strong sexual desires and nurtured a passion deeper and more pervasive than men's. They issued a harsh critique of all aspects of what they termed "bourgeois" or "puritanical" morality. Sexual love in many forms, inside or outside marriage, between men and women or between individuals of the same sex, must, they insisted, be allowed to flourish without restriction. As sex enthusiasts, the new intellectuals thus found wisdom in Edward Carpenter's statement: "Sex is the allegory of love in the physical world. It is from this fact that it derives its immense power."[28]

The new intellectuals sought in sexual liberation the key to future social revolution, the destruction of "bourgeois" values in general. They therefore linked sexual repression to the spiritual barrenness of middle-class society, its conventions and artificialities. They hoped to destroy "polite society" and thereby recapture a sensuality purportedly lost in a materialistic age. They thus agreed with Nietzsche that contemporary man was suspended in a void, but they equated the entering of the life force with the re-establishment of a natural harmony between men and women. Love, the soul union of two individuals, thus represented the ultimate escape from the existential loneliness of life under capitalism.

While older Socialists turned to Marx, the new intellectuals found their revolutionary prophet in Edward Carpenter. A major defender of the "Intermediate Sex," Carpenter had named the principles of the New Morality as the true basis of Socialism. His *Love's Coming of Age*, published privately in England in 1894 and issued by a major American house in 1911, was the definitive work of the genre. In it Carpenter reviewed the long history of women's oppression, but rather than stressing the civil or economic aspects of women's lowly status, he discussed a greater tragedy: sexual repression and the consequent barriers placed between the sexes. By her relegation to an isolated domestic life, her transformation into an inhumanely chaste symbol, woman had "lost touch with the actual world, and grew, one might say, into a separate species from man—so that in the later civilisations the males and females, except when the sex-attraction has compelled them as it were to come together, have been wont to congregate in separate herds, and talk languages each unintelligible to the other." Because of this distance, social relations had become "perverse" above all in married life. Happiness was soon replaced by "mere vacuity of affection, then by boredom, and even nausea," as husband and wife each came to feel cold, bitterly alone. This tragic condition, Carpenter believed, could end only when women achieved emancipation. Social equality would herald a rapprochement of the sexes as man and woman stood on common ground—lovers, companions, and friends.[29]

As a theory of Socialism, Carpenter's contribution was unprecedented, for it altered both the vision of the future Cooperative Commonwealth and the analytical matrix. "No doubt the Freedom of Society . . . and the possibility of a human life which shall be the fluid and ever-responsive embodiment of true Love in all its variety of manifestations," he remarked, "goes with the Freedom of Society in the economic sense."[30] Socialists had always believed the Cooperative Commonwealth would enshrine love, but, fearful of erotic intensity, they envisioned the promised state as platonic and spiritual, as the realization of old aspirations rather than the efflorescence of new practices. In concentrating upon the germinative manners and morals already forming within capitalist society, Carpenter also shifted the focus from the prehistoric, anthropological past which Engels had described to the future within the present and its prime locus in personal life. Not since the early writings (and in this era still unpublished) of Marx had Socialism represented the economic prerequisite for the constraints of society to fall away, when humanity as children awakening from the nightmare of history realized its *species being*.

Intellectuals in the United States had been especially slow to articulate this existential side of Socialism. A minority voice for sexual freedom had been vivid within the ethnic free-thought circles of the 1880–90s. Robert Reitzel's literary weekly *Der Arme Teufel* described free love and even homosexuality with sympathy, pronouncing marriage the "death bed" of romance. Jewish revolutionaries, strongly influenced by Russian Nihilism, placed free love among the founding principles of the Yiddish labor and political movements. Their poets warned brides that the wedding march was a funeral dirge in disguise, presentiment of the repeated childbearing and financial woes that would drive them down. Journalists translated and popularized the works of Ibsen, Strindberg, and Wedekind long before their English-language counterparts

could identify the names. Much of the hyper-revolutionary rhetoric passed
early, as Yiddish anarchism faded to the background. But a mood remained in
the ghetto, free-love unions a persistent ideal which actual disappointment
could diminish but never eradicate.[31] Native-born Socialists rarely went so far.
The genteel *Comrade*, edited by sentimentalist John Spargo, epitomized the
inclination to shrink back from the actual discussion of sexual questions, to
idealize woman abstractly and to suggest free love only in the distant future
(as in Morris's *News from Nowhere*, which the *Comrade* serialized). American
intellectuals still nodded in innocence when the shifting social patterns after
1910 allowed a new generation to retrieve the European *fin de siècle* legacy, to
discuss openly and to act upon the political ramifications of sexual freedom.

Although they left few permanent monuments in other realms, the new
intellectuals broke through the social purity barriers and established a political
voice for the New Morality within the mainstream American Socialist movement. They openly fought the historic bogey, free love. And as artists and writers
they did much to discredit the self-satisfied materialist interpretations handed
down from Engels and Bebel; they promoted in their place the will to break
away from the existing moral system. No longer the hapless victims of male
debauchery, no longer plagued by phantoms of immorality, women became
true subjects in a revolutionary process; sex as mirror of social conflict necessitated the ideological arming of emancipated women to slay their own foes.
Woman, timeless symbol of romanticism, emerged anew as dynamic symbol
for modernism within the Socialist movement.

The new intellectuals placed the ideal of a sexually emancipated woman at
the center of their cultural aesthetic. They argued their views in the *New York
Call's* Sunday literary supplement and in Anita Block's "Woman's Sphere" sec-
tion, in their own theoretical journal, the *New Review*, and most of all in the
Masses and its successor, the *Liberator*. The *Masses* could claim the best young
realist painters in the nation, John Sloan, Stuart Davis, George Bellows, and
Boardman Robinson, along with several of the sharpest cartoonists of the day,
Art Young and Robert Minor, and lyric symbolist Hugo Gellert. It could count
among its literary contributors the coming giants Sherwood Anderson, Amy
Lowell, Carl Sandburg, Louis Untermeyer, Mike Gold, and Joel Spingarn. In
its prose and visual representations the *Masses* made woman and her liberation
a major subject. Never before had Socialist journalists so avidly depicted the
slum woman as oppressed but nevertheless capable of a profound resistance,
offered so much subjective evidence of an awakening female sensuality, and
devoted itself to the fondest expectation of woman's triumph, politically, economically, and sexually. Woman's situation became for these writers and artists
a way of knowing and believing, a touchstone for revolution.

Although the "liberation of American literature,"[32] as critic V. F. Calverton
had later described the awakening realism, had doubtless begun deep within

the mainstream, the new intellectuals established a positive image for the new woman and her struggle for freedom. The prevailing hostility toward the independent woman exhibited by genteel litterateurs like William Dean Howells had found its opposite number in the naturalism of Stephen Crane, whose *Maggie, a Girl of the Streets* (1893) embodied the depravity of the slums. The publication of Theodore Dreiser's *Sister Carrie* (1900) and a series of novels by Robert Herrick had begun to move toward a more dynamic, vaguely sympathetic portrayal. But artists of the *Masses* and *Liberator* quickened the pace, adjusted the perspective, and moved women's rejection of bourgeois morality into the literary light of day. Sinclair Lewis, Edna Ferber, Ring Lardner, and Fanny Hurst, among other best-selling authors of the 1920s, bore this imprint. Short story artists for the *Masses*, like Mary Heaton Vorse and Susan Glaspell, had earlier and more vividly created female characters as working-class women with capacities to feel intensely, to understand injustice rather than internalizing oppression, and when conditions allowed to strike back at their oppressors.

The women poets of the *Masses* and *Liberator* routinely broke protocol and articulated best an unprecedented frank and erotic female sexuality. Contrary to their genteel ancestors, writers of the nineteenth-century woman's movement, they could look at a man and whisper aloud, "God, what a lover you would be!"[33] or talk of their amours as did Gladys Oaks in "Climax":

> I had thought that I could sleep
> After I had kissed his mouth
> With its sharply haunting corners
> And its red.
>
> But now that he has kissed me
> A stir is in my blood,
> And I want to be awake
> Instead.[34]

By standards of a later generation, these were mild; once said, the erotic statement began to lose its shock value. But the awakening experience of woman as sufficient to herself, no mere object of man's feckless passion but subject of her own, conveyed to contemporaries a major cultural breakthrough:

> Her veins are lit with strange desire,
>   A force of earth, but more than earth;
> The burst of spring, the summer's fire,
>   Is in her mirth.
>
> A mad, wild essence is her blood,
>   She hears the storm when winds are still,
> And all the rushing torrent flood
>   Is in her will.

Quenched fires, stopped flood, defeated spring,
Desire stone-dead within the mould,
And Love that brought you everything—
Has left her cold.[35]

Unlike the nineteenth-century radical authors like Ignatius Donnelly, more determinedly than contemporary mainstream writers like Dreiser and Herrick, the outstanding new intellectual novelists made the sexually emancipated woman the subject of moral revolution. Arthur Bullard, an editor of the *New York Call*, was the outstanding example. Under the pen-name Albert Edwards, Bullard contributed two successful novels, *A Man's World* (1912) and *Comrade Yetta* (1913). As his admirers pointed out, Bullard managed to break from the thematic stereotype of the fat boss or mustacioed villain versus the fair damsel, the stylistic artificiality of thundering emotions, and the alternating moods of outraged moralism so much a part of late nineteenth-century popular melodrama and the Shavian cynicism common to high-brow treatments. Bullard's novels, wrote Andre Tridon, "let life tell us of the forces which are making continuously for radicalism. . . . They do not reduce life to formulas; they make the high lights of life more visible above the dust and haze of numberless phenomena."[36] If *Comrade Yetta* expressed the hopefulness of the archetypal young woman toiling for the Cause while striving to realize herself, *A Man's World* offered a fundamentally psychological portraiture of the "young woman" and her naive suitor. *A Man's World* captured the male perspective on female sexual emancipation.

At a crucial moment in his development, Bullard's protagonist is forced to sort out his uneasy feelings about love and learns the difference between love and sex and the place for each in a total life. He has become friends with a woman "as far removed from cheap sentimentality as any woman" he had known, yet also "strangely romantic." He does not love her but decides nevertheless that he must marry her. To his surprise, the young woman has no intention of marrying him or anyone. Reared by a mother influenced by woman's rights and anarchism, she is committed to her career yet does not believe celibacy the only alternative to a restraining marriage. As she explains her position, Bullard's protagonist ponders the implications:

> My knowledge was so much less than hers. But although it was a relief to find that she would not marry me, there was still a feeling of deep injustice. There seemed a despicable cheat in taking from her so much more than I could give. It seemed ultimately unfair to accept a love I could not wholly return. But she brushed aside any effort to explain. She ran to her room, and bringing a copy of the Rubyat, preached me quite a sermon on the quatrain about Omar's astronomy, how he revised the calendar, struck off dead yesterday and unborn tomorrow. Love, she said, was subjective, its joy came from loving, rather than from being loved.[37]

Other writers pursued this theme. As Louise Bogan wrote:

> Mix prudence with my ashes;
> Write caution on my urn;
> While life foams and flashes
> Burn, bridges, burn![38]

None identified more clearly than Bullard the decisive elements: a woman coolly in control of her own emotions yet possessed of a passionate nature; a dynamic relation between the sexes altered decisively by woman's initiative. How different from Reginald Kauffman's *House of Bondage!* Empowered by her new sense of self, woman sought the very sexuality that had been her sister's downfall and made of it the spiritual regeneration of man.

The implications of this change were diverse, emphatically more significant than the creation of a new literary mode. That man would gain from woman's unchaining had long been upheld abstractly as an article of faith or affirmed in political rather than personal terms. The genteel chivalry of the *Comrade* crowd, the big-heartedness and sentimentality of Debs's small-town following, the generosity of individual comrades of virtually every ethnic and regional description had indicated a warm spot for womanhood. The new intellectuals offered the startling alternative that men might achieve personal emancipation by escaping their own narrowly defined sex roles and by welcoming the liberation of female sexuality. For the first time since the generation of the abolitionists, men avidly joined, not merely supported, woman's cause. The changing social relations between men and women, prime subject of the literary revolution, thus gave self-aware Socialists the means to improve the quality of their own lives while joyfully engaging in struggle.

The new intellectuals boldly took their novel ideas into practice. Although common among Europeans for decades, "lifestyle radicalism" had been rare among American Socialists. The circles of Yiddish and German free lovers of the 1890s had little influence outside the ethnic enclaves, while the mainstream Socialist movement prudently guarded itself from association with irregular behaviors. What had once been a minor, unpopular tendency now headed for supremacy, not in the numbers of men and women who demanded the right to live according to the precepts of their convictions but because the few who did so appeared the avant-garde rather than the eccentric.

Most striking were the women who rejected the prevailing standards for feminine fulfillment. They were usually native-born and well educated, although a number of Jewish intellectuals bearing traces of their radical Russian origins gravitated toward this practice as well. The mirror opposite of the victimized woman so popular in Socialist sentimentalism, this new breed sought love and happiness only in forms that did not vitiate personal independence. Married, they refused to subordinate their desires to the wills of their husbands or to immerse themselves in domestic responsibilities. A few experimented with cooperative household arrangements. Others decided to forego domestic duties entirely, preferring a barren and sometimes lonely apartment to the drudgery accompanying full-scale home care. Upon marrying they often struck up specific agreements with their partners to ensure privacy and autonomy. They kept their professions, their maiden names, sometimes their separate residences, and hoped to maintain themselves financially throughout their lives. Within marriage and without, they were sometimes willing to defy sexual norms, or were at least game to consider the consequences; they refused to be bound to "bourgeois" customs. A few women issued apologies for legalizing their sexual affairs, claiming that had the weight of public opinion been lighter they would have preferred to follow their natural inclination toward unions freely formed and freely dissolved. Openly rebellious yet eminently respectable, these women were unafraid of the free-love stigma and flaunted their newly discovered prerogatives with bravado and style. They adopted a new and often dramatic style of dress, cropped their hair, smoked and drank at the "Working Girls Club"—not a charity home but a saloon in Greenwich Village—and dared any man to dampen their spirit. Few of their male allies had any such intentions. As Floyd Dell later recalled, radical men were drawn to this defiant woman precisely because she "was comparatively freed from the home and its influence; because she took the shock and jostle of life's incident more bravely, more candidly and more lightly."[39] The emancipated woman thus encouraged men to join in the creation of a new lifestyle.

This uniquely close association between men and women set the new intellectuals apart from most elder Socialists, not merely because their private lives were so intense but because even their political organizations bore the impact of heterosociality. For decades most women activists had preferred their own societies, be they auxiliaries, separate clubs, or committees. Although more women now participated in business meetings and held leadership positions, the bulk of party affairs still tended to divide along gender lines. In breaking this tradition, the new intellectuals created in their branches an atmosphere conducive to the participation of both men and women. Men professed, perhaps faint-heartedly, to eschew misogynic posturing or domineering behavior. Hutchins Hapgood attested that because men formally discarded their usual prerogatives, they actually lost ground as women secured ample opportunities to express themselves. Whatever the truth, the new intellectuals had introduced new forms of camaraderie to the Socialist movement. After party meetings, for example, young men and women often adjourned together and continued the discussion. Downtown Socialists flocked to tea rooms and coffee houses; uptown Socialists and their friends customarily reconvened at the apartments of various members and sipped beer or wine until the early morning hours. William and Margaret Sanger often hosted their comrades, but undoubtedly the most well-known setting was the all-white quarters of Mabel Dodge. Dodge regularly threw open her doors and conducted salons for radical men and women. No one could call Dodge's infamous parlor a feminine sanctuary, for it served as an arena for both sexes to take up weighty issues and to revel together in fun. Even that embodiment of unabashed and unreformed masculinity, William D. Haywood, frequently graced this dwelling.

Although older party members tended to disagree with the philosophy and practice of life of the new intellectuals, they sometimes recognized that these young men and women were in the mainstream of the historical current. Relations between the sexes had clearly been changing. The birth rate among native-born Americans had, for example, been dropping for nearly a century, and the smaller family which contemporaries noted with a mixture of curiosity and apprehension seemed to indicate a significant trend. Likewise, the nineteenth-century culture which romanticized separate spheres for men and women continued to fade, as women's presence in the work force and civil society, men's involvement in the new leisure and family-oriented activities, seemed to indicate. The entire era, in short, heralded great changes in social relations, bringing the sexes closer together in all aspects of life from the mundane level of ballroom dancing to the ascendancy of coeducation. The new intellectuals rejoiced in this changing and charged atmosphere, shaped their personal lives around great expectations and created therewith unique forms of cultural expression. The sprightly *Masses*, the emerging art and literature, promised to Socialists of a new generation an enlightened, up-to-date response to America in evolution.

Probably the bulk of new intellectuals scarcely understood the full implications of their aspirations. They tended to push aside the old economic and political priorities and thereby gained for themselves a reputation for superficiality. No more deserved than for the turgid, economistic, and culturally underdeveloped doctrines of their elders, neither was this impression wholly inaccurate. As the campaigns against white slavery resolved in Socialist electoral competitions concerned with woman's plight primarily as a timely issue, so the calls for an emancipated sexuality often became the rationale for retreat from political involvement and submergence in private life. Like the Socialist pioneers, the new intellectuals were publicists and activists rather than deep thinkers. They could not discover just which key unlocked the immense potential before them. How the revolution in mass culture, especially in heterosexual relations, might produce the right constituency and setting for the final assault upon capitalism—no one would hazard a guess so literal and direct as the Socialist congressional majority or a workers' factory council. This was the glory and the fate of the Socialist movement's last generation of creative intellectuals: they could perceive the outlines of the new society but neither reconcile them to their parent forms nor fill in the details of the system to come.

The new intellectuals did, however, impart a vital message. The New Morality specified the cultural absolute that if Socialism could be made from modern society, it would adjust moral customs as much as economic standards; if Socialists were to break the barriers of the old social order in preparing for the great day, they would of necessity confront questions previously deemed too delicate or personal for public agitation. Here the new intellectuals made a lasting contribution.

BIRTH CONTROL AGITATION

The new intellectuals believed a successful campaign for family limitation would encompass populations seemingly immune to the avant-garde spirit but hungry for practical information. Once enticed, these men and women would become participants in a mass movement to challenge the precepts of bourgeois morality and inaugurate an era of sexual enlightenment and freedom. In the process they would transform the Socialist movement, broadening it strategically to embrace the web of social relations remote from the factory realm of production. Although the subject remained taboo in polite society, its public advocacy risky, family limitation thus assumed a place of unique importance and the ensuing campaign took on a portentous meaning for the entire radical movement.

The campaign for family limitation spoke to the political contradictions Socialists faced in the new age. The party loyalists who vigorously and courageously warred against white slavery were apathetic at best, often hostile toward the concurrent birth control agitation. Enraged by capitalistic degradation of women, mainstream Socialists seemed unprepared to fight for their sexual liberation. Neither did the party's style of campaigning condone the conscious violation of laws or address strategically the goal of transforming private life. The straightforward electoral campaigns, the struggle for trade union solidarity, these had always sufficed and continued to do so. What was the purpose of this drastically different agitation, many wondered, if it served to dislocate or place in jeopardy the more certain, time-tested methods?

Faced with this question, the new intellectuals had few certain answers. The working-class constituency of the Socialist movement, especially its growing new immigrant component, stood to benefit most from the birth control agitation; influenced by free thought, the radicalized sector presumably lacked the superstitions and religious qualms that doomed so many proletarian couples to more children than they could afford. Yet while the immigrants might hold out through the most bitter strikes or boldly confront a line of armed police, they remained for the most part shy toward the public campaigns for family limitation. Even if they held no prejudices against contraception, nothing in their political history had prepared them to take up such a different and "personal" cause. The most fervent constituency for birth control, rebellious youth across class lines, were no prophets to take the message to the immigrant masses: better flappers and sheiks than Jennie and Jimmie Higgins, they had fled their backgrounds to seek a different mode of existence. Thus while the new intellectuals and new immigrants might share contempt for Socialist parliamentarianism, they remained on different historic timetables for liberation. Access to contraceptive information might aid the open-minded working-class woman, but whether she could carry her personal decision into a public campaign remained in doubt.

The transcendent significance of the campaign for family limitation rested upon its capacity to redirect the idealistic strain in Socialist theory and practice to modern purposes. Socialists, native- and foreign-born, had long since demonstrated their faith in Socialism as heralding something grander than mere economic adjustment, but they had been unable to put the elusive aspects of life's deeper meaning into a political program. The campaign against prostitution represented an older sensibility, where the sex question had an essentially negative function reinforcing the historic Socialist world view. The New Morality drove a wedge into party orthodoxy by placing culture on a parity with economics. Birth control agitation offered the means to bring this perspective to the masses, to finalize the powers of woman acting on her own behalf in the class struggle and in the Socialist movement—if only, the new intellectuals intuited, time did not run out on their quest.

The concept of family limitation was not unknown even to old-time Socialists. The *Comrade* had published advertisements for Dr. Alice B. Stockham's popular marriage manuals *Tokology* (1883) and *Karezza, Ethics of Marriage* (1898), which included descriptions of nonorgasmic intercourse. Similarly Dr. Joseph G. Greer, who wrote so eloquently on the Social Evil, contributed *The Wholesome Woman* (1902), which contained an explicit chapter on the art of continence during sexual intercourse. Although Socialists left scant record of their own love-making techniques, a few at least were familiar with these and other texts and reaped the benefits of voluntary motherhood. Kate Richards O'Hare, for example, bore four children between 1904 and 1908 and curtailed her childbearing completely at the age of thirty-one. Families among the leadership were small, usually below the contemporary average of 3.56 per white American couple. If unwilling to make a political statement, many Socialists privately accepted family limitation as necessary to their own personal well-being.[40]

Mainstream Socialists began to discuss the theoretical ramifications of family limitation around 1910, primarily in conjunction with the rebirth of European Neo-Malthusianism. Lying quiescent since its origins in the early nineteenth century, Neo-Malthusian doctrine had gained a slight following after 1870.

Most simply, Neo-Malthusians believed that population control abetted the revolution: by reducing the size of its families, the working class could survive the supposed ever-declining standard of living, save itself from succumbing to the moral depravity brought on by extreme poverty, and actually gain stamina and will to fight as fewer children lightened financial burdens. Neo-Malthusian Socialists, especially plentiful in France and Germany, easily adapted the principle of family limitation to the accepted strategic priority, the class struggle.[41]

The strongest proponent of Neo-Malthusianism within the American movement was Antoinette Bucholz Konikow, physician and revolutionary Socialist. Born in central Russia in 1869 and educated in Germany, Konikow had trained as a physician in Switzerland in the late 1880s. Like so many educated Russian women, Konikow moved in radical circles and before her twentieth birthday had joined the Social Democratic party of Russia. In 1893 she immigrated to the United States and worked, along with her new husband, for the Massachusetts Socialist Labor party and for the Boston Workman's Circle. After graduating from Tufts University in 1902, Konikow established a medical practice in an immigrant working-class neighborhood. Now a member of the Socialist party, Konikow clung to European orthodoxy, characteristically speaking out with Second International authority against separate organizations for women and ridiculing those Socialist women who flirted with "bourgeois" suffrage societies. Neo-Malthusianism apparently satisfied her medical as well as doctrinal inclinations.[42]

Konikow was one of the first American Socialists to raise "Die Sexuelfrage" which was common in Germany. In response to those Socialists "who can only think in a straight line," she garnered evidence from the writings of Marx and Engels to illustrate the "wonderful interdependence of the manifold factors of human life, especially the factor of sex relations with the basic ones of economics." Using such arguments, Konikow hoped to combat the party's complacency, the unhealthy attitude that Socialism would automatically bring the necessary changes in sexual behavior. She demanded instead an active campaign, even if Socialists, she admitted, would be merely "trotting in the tracks left by more daring investigators."[43]

Konikow pointed to the exemplary activities of Socialists abroad. Comrades in Sweden and Denmark headed a propaganda campaign and disseminated practical advice on family limitation. In Germany many Socialists cooperated, albeit without party sanction, in the *Bund für Mutterschutz und Sexuel Reform* organized in 1904. Its founders, followers of the Swedish New Moralist Ellen Key, insisted that sexual activity was normal and its free expression a natural right regardless of gender; they rejected the principle of legal marriage and named sexual liberation as an immediate political demand. The Muttershutz League organized programs to introduce contraceptive methods to working-class women and conducted large-scale propaganda campaigns to rally the masses, called for the legalization of abortion, and demanded a system of state welfare to support all women with children. These advanced programs earned the league an international reputation. Among its many prominent promoters were Ernest Haeckel, Carl Hauptman, Otto Adler, Havelock Ellis, George Bernard Shaw, H. G. Wells, and Frank Wedekind. An American writer likened the founding of the Mutterschutz League to the historic, precedent-setting woman's rights convention held in Seneca Falls in 1848. To Konikow it was proof of what a fearless organization could do "to register the truth and work for it," a model for American Socialists.[44]

Urging her comrades to follow the example set by the Mutterschutz League, Konikow found allies in New York City. Anita Block regularly opened her columns to Konikow, Dr. Anna Ingerman, and William J. Robinson, a prolific writer and prominent physician. Describing family limitation as an "effective revolutionary weapon," Robinson also advocated a specifically class-conscious campaign for sexual enlightenment. Konikow meanwhile conducted a course of weekly illustrated lectures on the "physiology of sex" for women of the Lower East Side and discussed with them various methods of contraception.[45] Despite a favorable response from several sectors, Konikow's plans for an organized campaign remained dormant.

The inability of Konikow to rally her comrades indicated the size of the gulf between her aspirations and the real possibilities for an American birth control movement. To conduct an agitation along the lines of the distinctly European Mutterschutz League required a coherent working-class movement and culture. Although the Socialist party in the United States possessed sufficient authority, it could not readily pull together the fragments of its diverse movement. With limited resources spread thin on electoral politics and trade unionism, Socialists were moreover enmeshed in a nineteenth-century sentimentalism seemingly impervious to the free-thought currents that had provided space for discussions of sexual matters in Europe. In an odd way, American Socialists had to pay the price for adapting so successfully to the moral standards of the woman's movement of the Gilded Age. Because it expressed a righteous indignation toward matters Europeans treated more casually, the social purity tradition made the next step more difficult, made even the acceptance of a class-conscious Neo-Malthusianism impossible for the Socialist majority in the United States.

The new intellectuals recognized the odds against a successful birth control campaign. Although they shared the Neo-Malthusian politics of Konikow and her allies, they had little in common with the party's social purity majority. They also had few contacts in the working-class community they needed most to reach; they only abstractly understood its customs and institutions that might impede their cause or increase their chances for success. But they had their own talents: journalistic skill, a flair for publicity, and a keen awareness of generational moods. They possessed a sense, simultaneously wise and foolish, of women's desire for sexual liberation. And they had the perspicacity to direct their attentions both outward toward working-class families and inward toward the latent sympathizers within the Socialist movement. With energy and luck, they could go far.

Margaret Sanger quickly became the bellwether for the campaign. Her early success rested precisely upon her ability to unite various tendencies around a common agitation. A trained nurse, she worked comfortably with radical health professionals. A participant in the heterodox fringe, she became identified with the New Morality avant-garde; Mabel Dodge claimed it was Sanger who taught—indeed, was an ardent propagandist for—"the joys of the flesh."[46] Sanger proclaimed woman's first freedom as the right to control her own body and handled with ease the preferred rhetoric of Neo-Malthusianism with its emphasis upon working-class uplift. Unlike any other figure in the New York environs, Sanger contributed the practical experience and political catholicity necessary at this stage.

Only inadvertently, however, did Sanger play a critical role in shaping the campaign for family limitation. Anita Block had asked Sanger to replace an ailing speaker scheduled to appear at one of the women's branch meetings. Lacking experience in public speaking, Sanger at first demurred and finally accepted on the condition that the topic be her own choice. She decided to speak on hygiene and sex education, especially as related to working-class women. Sanger struck a responsive chord, as her enthusiastic audience clamored for "more health talks." At her next presentation attendance skyrocketed from a typical turn-out of twenty or thirty women to over seventy-five. These meetings generated so many questions that Block invited Sanger to write her lectures for publication in the *Call*. Sanger agreed and composed her first set of essays, "What Every Mother Should Know," which, like her lectures, merely whetted women's appetite for more information. By the end of 1911 Sanger had established herself as the party's chief propagandist for sexual enlightenment, less theoretical in tone than either Konikow or Robinson yet capable of delivering the desired practical lessons.[47]

Precisely because her essays were so explicit, Sanger drew attention to the cause. On November 17, 1912, she began a weekly series addressed to all mothers. Hoping to "revolutionize women's attitude toward sex," Sanger called upon each mother "to clear her mind of prudishness and to understand that the procreative act is natural, clean and healthful." Prejudice, she wrote, must be pushed aside, and mother must come to view the sexual impulse as inspiration of "the highest and noblest thought . . ., the creative instinct which dominates all living things." Sanger thus adapted basic concepts of the New Morality to popular exegesis. She concentrated on female sexuality, describing in great detail the anatomy and physiology of the reproductive system. Too

Caroline Lowe

Anna Maley

Lena and Arthur Morrow Lewis

May Wood Simons

Theresa Malkiel

Rose Schneiderman

Striking Shirtwaist Makers Selling Copies of the *Call*

from *Munsey's Magazine*, Apr. 1910

Ida Crouch Hazlett

Kate Richards O'Hare and Children

Anita Block

Rose Pastor Stokes

bold for Anthony Comstock, the self-appointed protector of morality, the column scheduled for February 8, 1913, was replaced by a wide box bordered in black, containing in bold type after the heading "What Every Young Girl Should Know" the notation "Nothing." For the first time Sanger met the hand of the censor.

The propaganda campaigns for sexual enlightenment, conducted primarily in the pages of the *New York Call* and supplemented by several lecture series, now took on a more poignant meaning than heretofore. Anita Block took pride in her role as editor. She noted that the purpose of Sanger's column had been to "turn the searchlight on all the rotten spots which those in power today find it in their interest to keep dark . . . and keep turning on the light, in one way or another, ever stronger and more penetrating until there is no part of our social structure that will not be clean and healthy and beautiful."[48] She continued to publish articles dealing as explicitly as possible with the principle of family limitation and sex hygiene and invited her readers to forward their opinions. The response to her request was overwhelming. Within a few months the discussion of sexual enlightenment moved observably from the rare circles of the new intellectuals and professionals to the rank-and-file.

Ordinary comrades made their voices heard. Readers favoring the discussion often expressed their appreciation. One woman, sixty-six years old and mother of eight, contended that she learned more from Sanger's essays than from any books or even from her own life! Another woman claimed Sanger's columns had saved her marriage by explaining to her suspicious husband how a woman might lose her virginity "naturally." Above all, such readers emphasized that the knowledge made available in the series was not readily accessible elsewhere and therefore an important service. Readers hostile to this viewpoint took a different tack entirely. Most merely argued that such discussions detracted from the party's main course, the class struggle. One angry man, however, offered to "look Mrs. Sanger in the eye" and inform her that he would "prefer to pass venereal disease on to [his] offspring than wage-slavery." He objected to the publication of health warnings, reasoning that they placed "FEAR and DISTRUST in the minds of hundreds of prospective wives and mothers" and discouraged impressionable female readers from marrying. He predicted that Sanger's column might "produce a panic which would cause women to lose all confidence in men and cause them to withdraw their capital (themselves) from the marriage market." Other male readers shared his opinion and believed Sanger censured "the men too much and the women too little." Other critics simply judged it inopportune to discuss "the lowest, or animal" aspect of marriage. A few argued simply for an "eternal" inferior status for women.[49]

Anita Block assessed the significance of these comments for the projected campaign for family limitation. Clearly the discussion had challenged the prevailing complacency and placed the biological realities of woman's condition at the center of the revolutionary struggle. Yet it was equally clear that unanimous support was lacking. Although she had expected some discord, Block admitted that she had overestimated the degree of open-mindedness among her readership. Socialist men, she concluded, were incapable of responding sympathetically: they were "stirred by the Socialist call for the workers to revolt from wage-slavery but they are unmoved by the Socialist call to women to revolt from sex-slavery." These men, she added, were "too tainted with the sins of their fathers . . . their class-consciousness . . . not yet perfect enough to have wiped out their inherited sex-consciousness."[50]

Block was correct. The party leadership did not endorse the campaign. As a group Socialists more than other sectors of the populace might affirm the principle of women's equality and rail sincerely against their exploitation under capitalism. Most rank-and-file Socialists could discuss intelligently the theories drawn by Engels and Bebel on the origins of the family and women's sexual oppression. But only a small minority judged the campaign for family limitation appropriate for the party to undertake. Some considered it "plain heresy." Especially as Sanger's publications became more newsworthy, many Socialists backstepped further; they disclaimed even Bebel's *Woman under Socialism* as personal opinion rather than official statement.[51] Compared to the antiprostitution campaigns, which the leadership supported wholeheartedly, the question of sexual enlightenment fell upon deaf ears.

Extenuating circumstances, moreover, prompted many sincere proponents of women's emancipation to remain silent. Just as the campaign for family limitation became viable, the party suffered the most open and extreme internecine warfare in its history. For years the industrially oriented Left and electorally inclined Right had disagreed on a wide range of issues. In 1912–13 the drama of the IWW-led strikes and the concurrent cresting of Socialist municipal victories raised the stakes in party strategic decisions. Consequently the defeat of the mass strikes and a subsequent feeling of electoral inertia fell hard. Socialists associated with the Right used Haywood's careless phrases in favor of industrial sabotage to engineer his removal from the National Executive Committee. In scattered locals a relatively minor purge of revolutionary "disloyalists" ensued. Enraged comrades by the thousands withdrew from the party. Those leftist Socialists who did remain were frustrated by the party's old-line leadership and eager to test new methods outside as well as within the organization. Amidst this disarray, Socialists were unlikely to rush into yet another problematical agitation.[52]

Finding few dedicated supporters, Sanger became more extreme in her actions and pushed the campaign further into the camp of notoriety. Although she continued to write for Socialist publications, she turned toward other sectors for assistance, the IWW and Italian-American syndicalists. For a period Sanger veered to the left of even this ultra-radical constituency. Like so many of the new intellectuals who attached their fondest hopes to the working-class uprising of 1909–13, Sanger was haunted by the specter of time running out on the great opportunity of a generation. The failure of Socialists to throw full support behind the Paterson strike exasperated her almost beyond words, as she wrote in the anarchist *Revolutionary Almanac* of the possibilities she had seen in a general strike and concurrent antireligious uprising. The defeat and withdrawal of the IWW from the East, and its subsequent caution on such volatile issues as sabotage, left her, like other ardent sympathizers, to her own devices. At the edge of desperation, with world war evidently nearing, Sanger grew increasingly impatient. "Wherever I turned, from every one I approached I met with the same answer," she recalled, " 'Wait!' 'Wait until women get the vote.' 'Wait until the Socialists are in power.' 'Wait for the Social Revolution.' 'Wait for the Industrial Revolution.' " Nothing less than all-out resistance, she seemed to suggest, could save the day. [53]

During the spring of 1914 Sanger distanced herself from the Socialist movement. She began to publish her own revolutionary newspaper, the *Woman Rebel*, its masthead emblazoned with the anarchist slogan "No Gods, No Masters." Along with rudimentary birth control propaganda, Sanger preached self-reliance to workingwomen. "Build up within yourself a conscious fighting character against all things that enslave you," she wrote, at times even warning women against joining a Socialist movement inadequate to their needs. Sanger called simultaneously for propaganda of the deed, a violent direct-action tactic which only the extremist *Cronoca Sovversiva* advocated openly in the United States. Taunting Socialist women to send rifles instead of letters of sympathy to striking miners in Colorado, Sanger revealed her own confusion between tactics and bravado; she displayed what Max Eastman described accurately as "rebellion for its own sake."[54]

Such defiance earned its advocates neither vindication nor even martyrdom but persecution and isolation. *Cronoca Sovversiva* accelerated an agitation that led to its suppression, the jailing of followers, and the deportation of its editors. Sanger experienced a similar fate. The *Woman Rebel* was suppressed initially not for its illegal publication of birth control information but rather for a defense of political assassination. Fleeing the United States to avoid arrest, Sanger closed this episode flamboyantly and disguised a certain lack of political acumen by playing the victim. [55]

Had the campaign for family limitation rested on Sanger's leadership alone, it would likely have dwindled into an ignominious silence at her departure. Sanger had served most effectively as a catalyst; she pushed agitation from the realm of discussion to practical application. Yet she had seemingly proved incapable of providing the sensitive leadership required for mass mobilization. Her timely exodus thus served as a tonic for an agitation less mired in extraneous slogans and more attuned to a working-class constituency.

Sanger's impatience with the Socialist organization also proved costly. Not that she would have won over the national office or any other center of power. But she might have tested the weak spots in the old social purity edifice and garnered support from the new immigrant leaders who were themselves steeped in free thought. She might have formed a coalition by using the party's resources to their utmost. As it was, her successors had allies in a number of major cities and a fair tactical sensibility, but they lacked the numbers to conduct a sweeping agitation. They fell back upon the tactics of confrontation and publicity, the news splash that might counteract their other weaknesses.

The publication of Sanger's pamphlet *Family Limitation* signaled the next phase and pushed the new intellectuals to the front of the agitation. IWW locals, anarchists, Socialists, and other sympathizers reportedly circulated 100,000 copies during the first months of 1915. The campaign stepped up considerably when Sanger's estranged husband was arrested for distributing the pamphlet, and a common-front legal defense committee formed. Within an astonishingly short time after Sanger's departure, advocates of family limitation created a network of agitators that included some of the most talented and energetic radicals in the country.

Writers and propagandists stepped to the fore. The new intellectuals around the *Masses* and the *New Review* formed a political core for a two-pronged legal defense of Margaret and William Sanger and an acceleration of the birth control agitation. Skilled litterateurs like Max Eastman and Floyd Dell issued a veritable barrage of propaganda. Leading writers in other well-circulated Socialist publications—Anita Block in the *Call*, Kate Richards O'Hare and Eugene Debs in the *National Rip-Saw*, Georgia Kotsch and Antoinette Konikow in the *International Socialist Review*—played an important role. Emma Goldman stepped up her activities and invited Sanger to join her on a national tour. IWW activists Caroline Nelson and Elizabeth Gurley Flynn pressed the campaign in their quarters, including Italian-American communities and enlisting the aid of IWW hero Carlo Tresca. New York activists Rose Pastor Stokes, Ida Rauh, and Jessie Ashley rallied sympathizers within the local labor and suffrage movements.

During 1915–16 this agitation assumed a definite shape in several locations. Goldman, Gurley Flynn, Nelson, Stokes, and others crossed the continent and spoke at IWW and Socialist locals and before various women's groups. Particularly in New York City, Portland, San Francisco, and Los Angeles, local birth control leagues gathered sympathizers under the guidance of Socialist and IWW organizers. Cities like Cleveland and St. Paul, far indeed from the centers of cultural sophistication, likewise became alive through the concentrated work of well-placed radicals. By August, 1915, "Two Comrades" wrote

Sanger and reported that "thousands of people had been immeasurably helped" through this agitation. They might additionally have noted the refinement of the agitation at the hands of veteran activists and enthusiastic militants.[56]

No one saw more clearly the problems of birth control agitation then did Caroline Nelson, a longtime Socialist and west coast IWW organizer. In a letter to Sanger in 1915 Nelson explained her position. Experience had demonstrated ordinary people's fears of association with immorality as well as their eagerness to receive the actual information. Workaday housewives, like erudite Marxists, drew back at the prospect of widespread publicity and could not discuss their needs in public "without giggling and blushing." To carry this agitation beyond the initial stages of publicity, Nelson thus advocated the organization of trained nurses or salaried women, women who knew the mores of the neighborhood and could work comfortably and quietly among the people. Nelson outlined such a campaign. She advised Sanger to return to Canada and to reissue the *Woman Rebel* under a less provocative title, something incorporating "New Moral" on the masthead to "catch the worker's wife and daughter." Nelson explained that "workers are so afraid of being suspected of immorality and they love the word—Moral with an effection [*sic*] worthy of something better than it stands today." Not a radical break with the past and the immediate acquisition of a new set of values, as Sanger seemed to want, but a heightening or shift in the meaning of values working people already possessed—this principle would more effectively guide birth control agitators.[57]

Political Socialists likewise advocated a tempered campaign, particularly a campaign directed at legislators. Kate Richards O'Hare reported that the *National Rip-Saw* had been "flooded" with letters from readers begging for information. Although sympathetic with their request, she explained that Socialists were not "in a position to wage this battle at present," and apologized that she could not furnish Sanger's pamphlet or other explicit literature. "We have too big a job on hand fighting capitalism," she wrote, "to take time to go to jail for swatting one phase of the system." She advised her readers to write to their representatives in Congress and demand the repeal of the repressive laws. Both Dell and Eastman supported this tactic, and several Socialist assemblymen promised to introduce measures in their state legislatures. The National Birth Control League, which had been recently organized by mainly non-Socialist reformers, additionally advocated a legislative campaign.[58]

Socialists advised Sanger to drop the defense of the *Woman Rebel*, to return to the United States, and to rejoin the agitation. Elizabeth Gurley Flynn wrote Sanger and described the tremendous interest birth control meetings elicited wherever she toured; if Sanger were to conduct a canvass of American cities, Gurley Flynn predicted, she would draw huge crowds, raise the much-need finances, and encourage organizers to work with "defense committees" composed of local women who could sustain the agitation after she departed. Debs promised Sanger "a pretty good-sized bunch of revolutionaries" to arm the defense."[59]

It would be difficult to overestimate the value of this comradely advice and proffered aid. A few key Socialists had offered Sanger the opportunity to recoup her earlier losses. With their assistance she might win back a degree of sympathy within the party and learn to act more judiciously in her working-class agitation. More than any other Socialist, Debs epitomized the old-fashioned sentimentalist; if he could envision a transformation of pure womanhood via the birth control agitation, more could be made of residual social purity standards than might otherwise be imagined. Likewise Nelson and Gurley Flynn, who knew the potential constituents, could bolster the agitation; whatever their differences with a political Socialist like Kate Richards O'Hare, they appreciated the worth of steady organization.

By early 1916, shortly after Sanger's return, the campaign to test the legality of restrictive laws was in full swing. Ida Rauh, Emma Goldman, and Rose Pastor Stokes had been arrested on several well-publicized occasions for attempting to distribute literature at huge rallies in Carnegie Hall. Sanger had visited several cities and faced arrest for speaking on birth control; she soon settled in Brownsville, a Brooklyn working-class neighborhood, where she opened a clinic to distribute information and devices, a move precipitating yet another round of arrests and Socialist-led rallies in her defense.

A decisive point had been reached. To provide a forum for discussion of these events, Sanger with the help of radical allies began a second publication, the *Birth Control Review*. Staid in contrast to the *Woman Rebel*, the new journal served primarily as a bulletin for supporters, an exchange of news of local birth control leagues and legislative activity. Jessie Ashley served on the editorial board, Caroline Nelson and Georgia Kotsch reported regularly from California, Eugene Debs submitted heartfelt endorsements, and Anita Block urged her readers to subscribe. Socialists also cooperated with the National Birth Control League in formulating legislation and claimed as a matter of pride that the first bill for the legalization of birth control information had been introduced by New York Socialist assemblymen.[60]

From here, Sanger might have advanced to the ironic status of Socialist champion. Despite her lingering suspicion of Socialist leadership, she could find no other vehicle than the party to supply the working-class contacts her strategy required. And whatever their doubts of her mercurial character, sympathetic Socialists recognized that no one else would seize the initiative to make birth control a major political issue.

The promise died aborning. Sanger precipitously broke with the Left when the Socialist managing editor of the *Birth Control Review* absconded with the mailing list. She soon thereafter abandoned her early allies, bolted from the

National Birth Control League, and moved close to a professional community capable of providing respectability and finances to cover her costly legal defenses. Concurrently, the Left pulled back. Opposition within sectors of the Socialist movement had continued unabated, and despite the enthusiasm expressed by a minority, the party as a whole could never be won over to a wide-scale sponsorship. Nor was failure only a matter of bad faith. Amidst wartime confusion, a number of prominent party intellectuals, including some of Sanger's crucial New York supporters, repudiated Socialism in a burst of patriotism. The *New Review* meanwhile folded under the financial pressure of political defection, the *Masses, International Socialist Review,* and *National Rip-Saw* lost their mailing permits, Wobbly leaders were arrested by the scores, Debs, O'Hare, and Goldman all imprisoned. Government reprisal overnight became the common lot of anti-war radicals and "dangerous subversives." A mass mobilization of the working class in a campaign for family limitation, the inauguration of a New Morality—these dreams faded soon enough.

Short-lived yet dramatic, the campaign for family limitation had depended upon a politically fragile coalition. Whereas the social purity crusade had historic grounding decades old and the benefit of public approbation, the birth control agitation remained jerry-built, politically haphazard, subject to the strain of notoriety forced upon the thin stratum of leaders and local collaborators. Suddenly pushed into the spotlight, virtually deified only a few months removed from obscurity, Sanger herself demonstrated the instability of many overnight celebrities. She and her allies lacked the time, the community contacts, and the camaraderie that allowed the labor and suffrage movements to nurture their strengths, guard precious resources, and carefully plan their moves. The wartime pressures essentially exacerbated the difficulties in maintaining the coalition and thrust the disparate elements back in the direction of their distinct origins.

At another level, the birth control campaign lacked substance because it never gained the basic requirements of a social movement: a constituency motivated toward collective action and able to claim a measure of public legitimacy for its efforts. Unlike strike support, where Socialists and Wobblies essentially aided the mobilization of the community, birth control agitation remained a service; workingwomen gladly received the information but played a slight political role. Unlike suffrage agitation, which built upon a self-confident middle-class base with labor and Socialist support, birth control agitation reached out precisely to those who were least able to take the risks. The status and manner of the agitators, utterly distant from the foreign-born women they sought to help, further inclined the campaign toward drama for the very reason that it lacked the capacity for solid organization. Birth control agitation served the needy and, like the settlement house, placed its advocates in the role of benefactors rather than guides to class-conscious or gender-conscious participation.

Had there been any other possibility? Veteran militants like Caroline Nelson understood what the new intellectuals in their youthful enthusiasm had not stopped to consider. Neither the emancipated sexuality Greenwich Village radicals apotheosized, nor the heroic class violence Sanger briefly linked to women's emancipation, nor for that matter the heterosociality which the new intellectuals raised as their ultimate goal, rang true to new immigrant women. These women had a different set of priorities; the collective struggle for existence buried contradictions so burning for intellectuals beneath the survival of the family and the retention of ethnic values into the next generation.[61] The cultural rebels had something important to contribute but not in the form or with the immediate implications that they had anticipated. A true political movement arising from these circumstances would have to utilize the sentiments infusing the antiprostitution campaigns and make claim upon the protection of the family through the assertion of a sexual freedom that the state and church denied.

To native-born activists, the birth control agitation represented the last outpost of the historic woman question. Only superficially did it contradict or violate the nineteenth-century concept of womanhood. If native-born women had indeed limited sexual activity to achieve smaller families, proclaimed social purity to enforce that decision, the accessibility of contraceptives might allow them to pass onto another stage. At the cutting edge of this possibility, the new intellectuals could not devise a strategy to push the revolution beyond their own private lives.

Despite these limitations, the campaign for birth control had lifted the freeing of woman for her own sake, the strengthening of the working-class family for the revolution, to the limits that one issue could go. And the activists had sought to address those groups upon whose brawny shoulders the future of the Left rested. If they failed, they had confronted odds a millennium in the making.

CONCLUSION

One of the most beloved Socialists of the era, William Morris, had as early as the 1890s touched upon the urgent desires men and women shared for new social relations. Not in "scientific" theory but in utopian fantasy, the "great soul" had proposed a resolution to the alienation of industrial society. Men and women would find peace, Morris predicted, in a sexual love based on equality and friendship.

So simple, Morris's vision of Socialism proved immensely difficult to assimilate into the orthodox canon and practice. Veteran Socialists did not shrink back from failure of nerve but for reasons both expedient and historical. Because they could not fully escape a world view shaped by separate traditions for men and women, the prospect of "true comradeship" remained an abstract principle to most party regulars, a hot-house creature of the small circles of intellectuals. Neither the fading values of sex solidarity perpetuated by the woman's movement, nor the faith in class consciousness renewed by recurrent waves of immigrants, had prepared Socialists for the modern social relations of the twentieth century.

And they were sincere in their loyalty. The late nineteenth-century woman's movement had insisted that moral questions as a matter of course be woman's prerogative and rallied a gender-conscious fervor and brotherly sympathy on a wide scale. Home-grown radicals could not have been true to their inheritance had they failed to grasp the reins when prostitution and white slavery scandals struck once more. The immigrant sectors, old and new, could accept much of this political logic. If German-Americans had romanticized woman's helpmeet role, long hoped Socialism would return her from factory to home, they felt no less strongly the sting of her sexual exploitation. In capitalism they found a culprit whose wantonness seemed sufficient to perpetuate the most vile forms of human degradation.

The Socialist party held fast to this position. The aggressive attack upon capitalism's misuse of human frailty merged smoothly with the defense of woman's moral prerogatives, so smoothly that none might discern the fading relevance of both to twentieth-century social relations. Some concepts could be updated with difficulty to include women workers (as proletarians) and women voters (as citizens). But Socialists could not forsake the archaic notion of woman as sexual victim, her bill of rights a kind of institutionalized chivalry, without plunging into the miasma of modern relations utterly alien to their experience. Neither indigenous nor European radical traditions offered more than clues.

If Socialists clung to their old ways, it was due not only to their misunderstanding of—or indifference to—women's contemporary revolt but to the uncertainty of the road ahead. How could they substitute eros for the sweet sentimentality of yesteryear? How could they abandon the essentially juridical vision of woman's advancement through civil and political rights to full citizenship under Socialism for some concept of woman's emancipation more sudden, potentially explosive, and unpredictable? Veteran women would not sacrifice the sex solidarity which had been a pillar of strength in Kansas parlors and New York ethnic halls for a heterosociality whose implications could not yet be assessed. Socialists male and female hedging their bets for the future hesitated to forsake old ideals.

Furthermore, the Socialist party was not a creature of easy adaptation. In good times its various segments tended naturally to follow their own particular interests, modified only partially by directives from the leadership. During the war years the centripetal forces accelerated dramatically, as trade unionists took solace in their unions, suffragists turned to complete their historic task, many activists concentrated solely upon anti-war or political defense work, and the guiding hand of leadership seemed at times scarcely present at all. The party's women's sector, divided geographically, ethnically, and ideologically among the various segments, suffered under the weight of these conditions. The new intellectuals, small in number and with few ties to the party center, could find only marginal means to work within these elusive milieux.

The revolutionary movement takes up questions as society makes them possible to understand, a mature Marx had suggested. But he might have added that the need for a movement does not always ensure its existence. The Socialist and women's movements alike had outreached their historic moorings in this as in so many other regards, and the new intellectuals merely grazed the surface of modern life. What would fill the yawning gulf ahead?

For a flickering moment the prospects seemed bright, not because the new intellectuals had successfully grappled with the problem but because life itself seemed to suggest a serendipitous understanding. If only for a minority, a new perspective took shape. They found justification and promise in the thousands of shifts in manners and morals then underway, more obvious in the proletarian ballrooms and dance halls of major cities than in the parlors of the rich, most obvious among the self-avowed liberated women and their male companions. From the factory to the dance hall to the domicile, millions of young men and women had felt in themselves some volcanic shift from the lives their parents had led. Youth showed signs of rebellion, more on cultural and moral grounds than on any other. At the same time the mass strikes of immigrant workers, the tottering of the capitalist empires in Europe, seemed to promise a political transformation that would undoubtedly shatter the old system of bourgeois morality. Socialists had no more to replace old standards than to reconstruct the factories singlehandedly; the masses themselves would strip off the constraining fetters and, with Socialist guidance, bring a new society from the ashes of the old.

At their most optimistic, the new intellectuals had moved with the times, and began to support woman as social being because they found the old categories of "worker" and "citizen" obsolete. Men like Max Eastman and Floyd Dell acted not from sympathy but rather from their own desires to realize the revolutionary prospects before them by adjusting personal life to the new standards of women's advancement. They awaited the impending cataclysm: the eclipse of the bourgeois order (including Socialist obeisance to the parliamentary politics of the state) and the free expression of desires purportedly latent in men and women since the dawn of class society. While the mainstream Socialists vouchsafed a modest improvement in morality on the road to the Cooperative Commonwealth, the younger radicals viewed the changes as the *process* by which the political transformation would come. This bold conception, bursting the barriers of staidness on the woman question as on art, music, and other realms, sought to remake Socialism anew and women anew within it at every phase. Contemporary writings about the creativity of jazz dancing, futurist attempts to grasp the motion in a "Nude Descending a Staircase," these and others were playful attempts to make the larger point about revolution. Socialism could not reign victorious, could not save itself without a renewal precisely at this moment in history.

The moment passed as surely as the prospects for political transformation. Less visible than the counterattack against labor militancy, the suppression of Socialist newspapers, or the "Red Scare," the waning of the birth control agitation marked the end of this era of collective experimentation with social relations. On the one side, political Socialism became narrow and economistic in a way it had never heretofore been; on the other side, the youthful rebellion lost its plasticity, its sense of collectivity transferred to the prerogatives of individuals. The Socialist movement suffered greatly from this melancholy exchange. The women's movement suffered more, because it lacked a basis to renew its struggle beyond political rights. And it must be added that perhaps the young radicals were too flippant in casting aside the entire legacy of the nineteenth-century movements. In so doing they broke new ground but also drifted inevitably away from the historic constituencies and their fixed world views toward an uncertain milieu and vague perspective.

And yet the aspirations expressed so vividly for a time in the thoughts and lives of a radical minority had been far from illusory. The New Moralists had made a contribution potentially crucial to the further prospects of Socialism, not because they had discussed physical sex but because sexual questions held a key to subjectivity. Not for bread alone would citizens of industrially advanced nations raise revolutionary banners. By 1910 the equation of the good life with harmonious relations between the sexes had become empty rhetoric in party programs, as the stock details of cultural life in the Cooperative Commonwealth had little bearing upon day-to-day experiences. The march toward a new civilization demanded that Socialists fill in the cracks of the older vision, move from the archaic mixture of economic guarantees and sentimentalism to support the advanced tendencies in modern life. The self-identity increasingly gained by ordinary men and women through work, education, and leisure carried the dual possibilities of ennui and alienation or a more fully realized, emancipated individual than society had ever produced. In phraseology that would have done justice to Whitman, a writer thus foretold the day when "our time-honored masculine standard will be relegated to the limbo of outworn ideals, and whereas we have known the blessed relations of mother and son, father and daughter, brother and sister, lover and sweetheart, husband and wife, with clear vision will come mutual respect and we shall achieve this also—to be friends."[62] Revolutionaries might help tip the balance by offering guidance to men and women who hoped to live and love as equals. Socialists who failed to address this timely question undercut their own trade union and political agitation, deprived it of one side of reality, and doomed themselves to the backwash of history.

NOTES

1. Quotations from *The Sorrows of Cupid* (St. Louis, 1912), 9–14. O'Hare's small book was distributed earlier, in 1904, as *Whatever Happened to Dan?*

2. Kate Richards O'Hare, "How I Became a Socialist Agitator," *Socialist Woman*, 2 (Oct., 1908), 4–5. David Shannon supplied additional information in *Notable American Women*, ed. Edward T. James, Janet Wilson James, and Paul S. Boyer, 3 vols. (Cambridge, Mass., 1971), I, 417–19.

3. O'Hare often discussed her experiences as a Florence worker; see, for example, her pamphlet *Church and the Social Problem*, published by the *National Rip-Saw* in 1911. On the Florence Crittenton Missions and Homes, see Charlton Edholm, *The Traffic in Girls* (Chicago, 1893), and Otto Wilson, *Fifty Years' Work with Girls, 1883–1933* (Alexandria, Va., 1933), especially the brief history of the Kansas City home. The Kansas City magazine *Kings and Queens of the Range* published contemporary reports of the local mission and home. L. Hereward, "A Famous Night Mission in New York," *Westminster Review*, 140 (Sept., 1893), 272–80, details the activities of the mission.

4. Frederick Engels, *The Origin of the Family, Private Property and the State in the Light of the Researches of Lewis H. Morgan* (New York, 1942 ed.), 50; emphasis in the original. J. J. Bachofen, *Das Mutterrecht, Eine Untersuchung über die Gynaekokratic der Alten Welt nach ihrer religiosen und rechtlichen Nature* (Stuttgart, 1861), first described in popular form this epochal transition and the establishment of monogamy. Lewis Henry Morgan, *Ancient Society, or Researches in the Lines of Human Progress from Savagery, through Barbarism to Civilization* (London, 1877), contained a similar analysis based on historical and ethnographical data rather than classical literature and myths. For a brief overview of this intellectual tradition and its importance to American Socialist writers, see Sidney Ditzion, *Marriage, Morals, and Sex in America* (New York, 1953), 289–93, and Ann J. Lane, "Woman in Society: A Critique of Frederick Engels," in Berenice A. Carroll, ed., *Liberating Women's History: Theoretical and Critical Essays* (Urbana, Ill., 1976), 4–25.

5. Engels, *Origin of the Family*, 50, 67.

6. Franklin H. Wentworth, *The Woman's Portion* (New York, 1910), 21. See also Phillip Rappaport, *Looking Forward* (Chicago, 1906).

7. August Bebel, *Woman under Socialism* (New York, 1904 ed.), 348, xvii, xviii.

8. Correa Moylan Walsh, *The Climax of Civilization, Socialism, and Feminism* (New York, 1917), although published late in this campaign, represents the tenor of the genre.

9. Garin Burbank, *When Farmers Voted Red* (Westport, Conn., 1976), 14–43. See also a letter from the former state secretary, J. E. Snyder of Oklahoma, which employed such moral accusations against capitalists, in *Appeal to Reason* (Girard, Kans.), May 18, 1907.

10. Allen W. Ricker, *Free Love and Socialism: The Truth as to What Socialists Believe about Marriage*, Rip-Saw Series no. 7 (St. Louis, n.d.), 17.

11. *Ibid.*, 16.

12. O'Hare, *Sorrows of Cupid*, 9.
13. Robert Riegel, "Changing American Attitudes toward Prostitution, 1800–1920," *Journal of the History of Ideas*, 39 (July-Sept., 1969), 437–52; Egal Feldman, "Prostitution, the Alien Woman, and the Progressive Imagination, 1910–1915," *American Quarterly*, 19 (Summer, 1967), 192–206.
14. Figures quoted by Gustavus Meyers, "The White Slave Traffic," *International Socialist Review*, 11 (Nov., 1910), 278.
15. *National Rip-Saw* (St. Louis), Mar., 1914.
16. See, for example, "The Social Evil," a report prepared by a committee of the New York Socialist party in 1913, in New York Socialist Party Local Papers, Reel 2, Tamiment Library, New York University. See also Victor Berger, "The Social Evil," *Vanguard*, 6 (Nov., 1907), 17–22; Phillips Russell, "Women for Sale," *International Socialist Review*, 12 (May, 1912), 727–29.
17. Kate Richards O'Hare, *Church and the Social Problem*, Rip-Saw Series no. 2 (St. Louis, 1911); *Law and the White Slaver*, (St. Louis, 1911). The white slavery number of the *Progressive Woman*, 4 (Apr., 1910), followed Conger-Kaneko's earlier investigative report published as *Little Sisters of the Poor* (1905) and later serialized in the last issues of the *Progressive Woman* and *Coming Nation*.
18. Reginald Wright Kauffman, *House of Bondage* (New York, 1910), 258–59, 260. Hutchins Hapgood criticized Kauffman's literary style and imagination in *Bookman*, 32 (Oct., 1910), 178. A more favorable review appeared in the New York *Times*, Sept. 17, 1910.
19. *Chicago Daily Socialist*, June-Aug., 1911, ran banner headlines on white slavery. During the summer of 1911 the *California Social Democrat* (Los Angeles) conducted a similar journalistic campaign, although on a smaller scale. For reports of Milwaukee Socialists' endeavors, see *Appeal to Reason*, Nov. 4, 1911, and Berger's statements in the New York *Call*, Aug. 3, 1911.
20. *New York Call*, Apr. 5, 1914.
21. Rheta Childe Dorr, *A Woman of Fifty* (New York, 1924), 215–19.
22. Albert Parry, *Garrets and Pretenders* (New York, 1960 ed.), 267; Mary Heaton Vorse, *A Footnote to Folly* (New York, 1935), 32–35; Margaret Sanger, *Autobiography* (New York, 1938), 74–75.
23. Genevieve Taggard, ed., *May Days: An Anthology of Verse from Masses-Liberator* (New York, 1925), 7.
24. Robert Rives Lamont, "The New Intellectuals," *New Review*, 2 (Jan., 1914), 45–53.
25. Lillian Symes and Travers Clement, *Rebel America* (New York, 1972 ed.), 283.
26. Susan Glaspell, *Road to the Temple* (New York, 1927), 250.
27. Sheila Rowbotham and Jeffrey Weeks, *Socialism and the New Life* (London, 1978); Norman and Jane Mackenzie, *The Fabians* (New York, 1977).
28. Edward Carpenter, *Love's Coming of Age* (New York, 1911), 26.
29. *Ibid.*, 54–55, 48, 79, 80–81.
30. *Ibid.*, 148.
31. See the literary treatment of Yiddish free-love tendencies in David Ignatov's monumental trilogy, *Euf Veite Vegn*, I (Yiddish—New York, 1932), 54–55.
32. V. F. Calverton, *The Liberation of American Literature* (New York, 1932). For a contemporary commentary on this shift in literary modes, see Floyd Dell, "Changes in American Life and Fiction," *New Review*, 3 (May, 1915), 13–15.
33. Anne Herendeen, "The Stranger," in Taggard, ed., *May Days*, 167.

34. Taggard, ed., *May Days*, 170.
35. Annette Wynne, "Her Veins Are Lit with Strange Desire," in *ibid.*, 87.
36. Andre Tridon, "The Novels of Albert Edwards," *New Review*, 1 (May, 1913), 536.
37. Albert Edwards, *A Man's World* (New York, 1912), 80, 86–87. Floyd Dell contributed an incoherent review to the *Progressive Woman*, 6 (Dec., 1912), 11, salvaged by a footnote by Lucian Cary which pinpointed the importance of this novel as an endorsement of women's new freedom, especially in sexual matters. The *Nation*, 95 (Oct. 23, 1912), 384, disdained Bullard's treatment of sex outside marriage. In contrast, Anita Block advised her readers to take up this novel because she judged its depiction of women "so very big yet so very tender"; see *New York Call*, Nov. 17, 1912.
38. Louise Bogan, "Pyrotechnics," in Taggard, ed., *May Days*, 202.
39. Floyd Dell, *Intellectual Vagabondage: An Apology for the Intelligentsia* (New York, 1926), 161. For a close study of these women, see June Sochen, *The New Woman: Feminism in Greenwich Village* (New York, 1972), and Judith Sue Schwartz, "Heterodoxy: A Club for Unorthodox Women" (Master's thesis, San Jose State University, 1977).
40. On the origins of these practices, see Linda Gordon, "Voluntary Motherhood: The Beginnings of Feminist Birth Control Ideas in the United States," in Mary Harman and Lois W. Banners, eds., *Clio's Consciousness Raised* (New York, 1974), 54–71.
41. Rosanna Leadbetter, *A History of the Malthusian League, 1877–1927* (Columbus, Ohio, 1976). For discussions of the impact on Socialists in the United States, see Caroline Nelson, "Neo-Malthusianism in America," *International Socialist Review*, 14 (Oct., 1913), 228–30, and "The Control of Child Bearing," *ibid.* (Mar., 1914), 547–58; William J. Robinson, "The Birth Strike," *ibid.* (Jan., 1914), 404–6; "Shall Child-Bearing Be Made Compulsory?" *New Review*, 2 (July, 1914), 430–32; Robinson's report on Germany and the "Birth Strike" in *New York Call*, July 27, 1913; and various articles in the *Masses*, Oct. and Nov., 1913.
42. *Woman's Who's Who of America, 1914–1915*, ed. John W. Leonard (New York, 1914), 466; Dianne Feeley, "Antoinette Konikow: Marxist and Feminist," *International Socialist Review*, 33 (Jan., 1972), 42–46. Antoinette Konikow recalled historic moments in her lifetime of activism in the *Socialist Appeal* (New York), Nov. 5, 1938.
43. *New York Call*, June 1, 1913. For Konikow's remarks on "Die Sexuelfrage," see the *New Yorker Volkszeitung*, Feb. 11, 1912.
44. Konikow endorsed the Mutterschutz League in the *New York Call*, Aug. 16, 1914. For a contemporary American response, see Katharine Anthony, *Feminism in Germany and Scandinavia* (New York, 1915), 88. Richard J. Evans, *The Feminist Movement in Germany, 1894–1933* (London, 1976), 115–43, details the history of the league.
45. Robinson's statement appeared in the *New York Call*, Dec. 21, 1913. For a report of Konikow's lectures held on Crystie near Houston streets, see *ibid.*, Nov. 17, 1909.
46. Mabel Dodge Luhan, *Intimate Memories*, 3 vols. (New York, 1936), III, 69–71.
47. Sanger, *Autobiography*, 76–77. For contemporary reports, see *New York Call*, Mar. 2, May 31, June 7, 1911.
48. *New York Call*, Feb. 16, 1913.
49. *Ibid.*, Jan.-Sept., 1913, "Woman's Sphere" column.

50. *Ibid.*, Mar. 2, June 1, 1913.
51. Manager of Information Department, National Correspondent, to Alphonse Olbrich, Philadelphia, July 2, 1913, Socialist Party of America Papers, Perkins Library, Duke University.
52. Ira Kipnis, *The American Socialist Movement, 1897–1912* (New York, 1972 ed.), 289–430, covers these events in detail.
53. Margaret Sanger, *My Fight for Birth Control* (New York, 1931), 61. See also Sanger's essay, "The Paterson Strike," *Revolutionary Almanac*, 1914, ed. H. Havel (New York, 1914), 47–49.
54. Sanger describes her publication in her *Autobiography*, 108–9. The attack on Socialist women appeared in an editorial, "Watchful Waiting," *Woman Rebel*, 1 (May, 1914), 24. Eastman's comments appeared in "Knowledge and Revolution," *Masses*, 5 (Mar., 1914), 8.
55. Herbert Thorpe, "A Defense of Assassination," *Woman Rebel*, 1 (July, 1914), was the offending essay. Sanger describes her flight in her *Autobiography*, 110–11.
56. Letter signed "Two Comrades" dated Aug. 23, 1915, in Margaret Sanger Papers, Box 2, Library of Congress. Linda Gordon, *Woman's Body / Woman's Right* (New York, 1976), provides a detailed narrative of radical birth control activities. On Goldman's activities, see Richard Drinnon, *Rebel in Paradise* (Chicago, 1961), 166–71. Elizabeth Gurley Flynn describes her tour in a letter to Sanger in the Margaret Sanger Papers, Box 2, Library of Congress. The Rose Pastor Stokes Papers, Box 2, Tamiment Library, contain numerous clippings of her birth control activities; the Stokes Papers at Yale Library include scrapbooks of newspaper clippings on these activities. For a report on the birth control movement in Los Angeles, see Georgia Kotsch's essays in the *Oakland World*, Feb. 23, 1917.
57. Letter dated June 12, 1915, in Margaret Sanger Papers, Box 2.
58. O'Hare's statement appeared in the *National Rip-Saw*, Dec., 1915. Floyd Dell, *Homecoming* (New York, 1933), 252, recalled turning letters requesting information over to "private individuals" who mailed the information directly to the women. Caroline Nelson also reported having received "dozens of letters" begging for information; she asked correspondents to identify themselves by enclosing their red cards along with their requests for information; see "Neo-Malthusianism in America," 300.
59. Elizabeth Gurley Flynn to Margaret Sanger, n.d., and Eugene Debs to Margaret Sanger, Dec. 16, 1914, both in Margaret Sanger Papers, Box 2.
60. The Carnegie Hall meetings were covered extensively in *Mother Earth*, 11 (Mar.–June, 1916). Block's endorsement of the *Birth Control Review* appeared in the *New York Call*, Feb. 19, 1917. Block also assured the president of the National Birth Control League that she would publicize the journal in a letter dated Apr. 24, 1917, in Margaret Sanger Papers, Box 3. News of Socialist assemblymen's support of the legislation appeared in *New York Call*, Feb. 4, 1917. For Debs's continuing support of birth control, see his "Freedom Is the Goal," *Birth Control Review*, 2 (May, 1918), 7, and the magazine's response to his arrest, Leonine Napiere's "Debs and the Woman's Movement," *ibid.* (Dec., 1918), 11–12.
61. For an excellent discussion of the stability of ethnic culture, see Judith E. Smith, "Our Own Kind: Family and Community Networks in Providence," *Radical History Review*, 17 (Spring, 1978), 88–120.
62. Frances G. Richards, "Some Anti-Feminist Vagaries," *New Review*, 2 (Aug., 1914), 450.

8   Autumn Song

A little song I tried to sing upon a summer's day;
  A song that turned a traitor, an air that used me wrong—
It reminded me of springtime and the happy, happy way
  When I was a young thing I sang the selfsame song.

I looked at my old hands, I harked to my old voice—
  (Oh, voice that was, the song was different then!)
I minded how the yellow sunlight made my heart rejoice
  When I was a young thing and unbeknown to men.

Lydia Gibson, "Autumn Song"
In *May Days* (1925)

In 1962, near the end of a long life dedicated to the Left, Elizabeth Gurley Flynn recalled her decision more than a half-century earlier to cast her lot with the Industrial Workers of the World rather than the Socialist party. Not unfamiliarity but the contempt familiarity breeds motivated her choice. Her parents had been members of the Socialist party, a fact that signaled to the young rebel the old-fashioned, stodgy character of the institution. Influenced by Kropotkin's *An Appeal to the Young* (1880) and drawn to the romantic IWW, Gurley Flynn set upon a path that was to include Syndicalism, Feminism, Communism—everything but the once-fervent dream of Socialist electoral triumph. In her mind, the fate of the Socialist movement had already been determined.[1]

Other young women drawn to the Left came to similar conclusions. The great mobilizations of the 1910s—the "women's strikes," suffrage campaigns, and birth control agitations—had impressed many sympathizers but failed ultimately to contain new energies in old forms. Young women breathed new life into the urban party locals and women's committees, forced the old guard to reassess its position, updated the very vision of Socialism itself—and then they moved on. As young radical women became prime activists in the new unions, the militant wing of the suffrage movement, and various birth control leagues, the Socialist party and its women's committees experienced a net loss.

Young women seemed to care little about the history of the Socialist women's movement, the struggles of native- and foreign-born women that had finally culminated in a genuine movement during the glory years of the Socialist party. Nor did they appreciate the painfully wrought institutions that women had secured for themselves within the party. They looked upon the elder women who had served so faithfully, who personally guaranteed the continuity with past struggles, and noted a deadening air of complacency. But if the veterans threw up their hands in despair at these young iconoclasts, the newcomers could justly complain that they had inherited little in terms of machinery or ideas suitable for the problems at hand.

The Woman's National Committee was a case in point. Since 1908 the WNC had maintained the Socialist women's movement. It oversaw the operation of local women's committees, offering encouragement as well as subsidies in the form of propaganda materials and publicity. The decision of the 1910 party congress to place the WNC on a par with the ruling National Executive Committee had been a proud day, not least because the WNC gained access to the party treasury and space in the party's nerve-center, the national office in Chicago. The definitive "Plan of Work" adopted the following year further coordinated activities and promised to fulfill the dreams of a half-century of activists. All too soon, however, the promise proved illusory, not because it had been false but because the WNC could no longer moderate among various wayward elements.

After 1910 the WNC faced a Socialist movement in the process of transformation. While its determined leaders had managed a compromise between the major sectors which represented the nineteenth-century traditions, they could respond only feebly to the revival of the Socialist movement on a different basis altogether. Accordingly, the ideological underpinnings of the WNC, the fragile *modus vivendi* between gender- and class-conscious leanings, showed signs of wear during this crucial decade and ultimately collapsed. The young, highly educated, native-born women represented one challenge. Concurrently, the last major wave of immigration brought new groups of Socialist women, mostly from southern and eastern Europe, who carried equally striking notions about women's place and responsibility. In dramatically different ways these two groups—the rising generation of Socialist women—allowed no further mediation, and the historic compromise embedded in the WNC ceased to bind. Never more than a rope ladder across two traditions, the WNC now swayed in the winds and strained under the weight of those who grasped at it as their only recourse.

The decade of the 1910s thus took on a character only the eldest veterans could recognize. Native-born women seeking liberation became disillusioned with the Socialist party and searched for alternative identities. Foreign-born women cleaved to the Socialist movement but reinstituted forms now deemed archaic, such as the women's auxiliary. The Socialist women's movement trailed off on exotic courses.

VAGARIES OF FEMINISM

The signpost on one road away from the Socialist movement read "Feminism." The territory resembled the New Morality; it took on many of the same philosophical characteristics, often identical protagonists. But whereas the New Morality concerned changes in the social relations between the sexes, Feminism spoke specifically for the liberation of women. The former connoted a transformed vision of Socialism, forced by its bohemian following upon a skeptical old guard. The latter judged Socialism a complementary but in itself insufficient goal. Feminism also represented an ultimate challenge to the ideological underpinnings of the woman question. For decades radical women had espoused a historicist interpretation of women's destiny, had set their sights upon women's advancement into civil society, and had looked upon the concurrent shifts in class relations as a necessary complement to mass political transformation. Feminists had a different perspective on social change. They downplayed the collective advancement of women into civil society for the practice of personal development and the goal of self-realization. Feminists judged the Socialist party not only inadequate to respond to their needs but archaic in certain key respects. Albeit inadvertently, Feminism represented a secessionist impulse of the young.

Feminism was a vague concept that came belatedly to the United States. Although Europeans had used the term for decades, Americans adopted it only around 1910. Immediately upon its introduction, debates raged over its precise meaning. Writers from the high-brow *Forum* to the popular women's magazine *Delineator* grappled with the new idiom. One journalist observed that novelty as much as substance marked its importance: "We have grown accustomed in these years to something or other known as the Woman Movement. That has an old sound—it *is* old. Therefore, no need to cry it down. But Feminism!" It was difficult to derive an accurate definition, this writer added, because Feminism did not represent a "concrete thing." It was not synonymous with the struggle for the ballot or with the demand for equal wages. Indeed, it seemed to supersede most specific issues associated with the historic movement for women's advancement. Was it possible, contemporaries asked, that a campaign for women's emancipation now almost a century old could take on new and startling dimensions?[2]

Although "Feminism" crept gradually into popular parlance, few users could manage an exact application. There was no doubt, however, that Feminism would become the watchword of the unconventional and daring. For instance, a well-attended meeting at New York City's prestigious Sunrise Club became the setting for just such an explication. The evening's program featured a panel discussion blandly entitled "How Shall We Deal with the Problem of Prostitution?" and included two "large minded and able" male speakers who espoused the customary economic interpretations of woman's ensnarement and disgrace. Not the content but something about the tone of their delivery provoked the two female participants to lash out and criticize the men's condescending manner. Scarcely an important incident in itself, the confrontation seemed to suggest just how eager women were to challenge normative behavior within even the most congenial circles. The journalist who described this exchange believed it aptly illustrated the new mood among women. "Feminism is a fighting weapon for the cause of women," she wrote, "a reaction from the long rule of man and the consequent repression of womankind. . . . It is the surging tide of women in revolt against generations of repression and tragic endurance."[3]

In making such declarations, Feminists did not reject the goals of the woman's movement. They surveyed women's accomplishments since the days of Seneca Falls, noting that in the last half-century women had made truly great strides. Large numbers of women now worked for wages, graduated from college, and maintained important positions in public life. In light of the historic campaigns for women's advancement, these were no mean signs of impending victory. The remaining battles for political and economic parity with men would bring women fully into public life and thereby complete the historic task of the nineteenth-century woman's movement. As public figures themselves, Feminists necessarily embraced these campaigns; economic self-sufficiency and legitimized political expression were minimum prerequisites for women making their way in civil society.

Yet, as the incident at the Sunrise Club suggested, Feminists pronounced their struggle uniquely militant because it emphasized not the legalistic or formal aspects of women's emancipation so much as the behavioral side. Thus Marie Jenney Howe, founder of New York City's premier Feminist circle, Heterodoxy, elucidated the three major components of Feminism as the will to vote, the desire for economic self-support, and the social revaluation of outgrown customs and standards. Although all elements were essential, the last clearly was the most significant. Howe defined Feminism simply as an "appropriate word which will register . . . woman's effort toward development." True liberation demanded more than a changed world, she insisted; it demanded foremost a "changed psychology, the creation of a new consciousness in women."[4]

The spiritual or psychological struggle to develop the self, the "conscious attempt to realize Personality," gave Feminism its singly modern connotation.[5] Women had suffered under the weight of male domination, Feminists believed, since the fall of the matriarchy, had responded selflessly to the demands of their fathers, their husbands, their children, and more recently their society, while reserving little time to reflect upon their own personal needs as women. In the modern age at last women were preparing to reject all forms of subservience, were advancing beyond the rituals of time-worn civilizations to realize their innermost natures. "The new, wonderful, final step which women must take," one writer affirmed, was "to enter upon the free unfolding of her personality as an end in itself."[6]

Feminists thus joined other new intellectuals in rejecting the formalism of prevailing social theory. They praised, for example, the modernist notions explicated by Henri Bergson, the most important philosopher to conduct a frontal assault upon western rationalist thought. "*To know* is to *live*, to feel within a duration, a pure intensity, which no human language can express except by symbols," wrote an interpreter. As the young Walter Lippmann located the "living force" of Socialism not at all in the mode of production but in the "will—a will to beauty, order, neighborliness, not infrequently a will to health," Feminists similarly concluded that the "true" subjects of inquiry should be human beings themselves rather than their institutions.[7]

Although Feminism never gained a precise definition and quickly became (as it is today) an all-encompassing term, it managed nevertheless to convey for a few years and within special circles a meaning distinct from the goals of the established women's movement. Feminists endorsed formal equality but did not consider it synonymous with the greater goal of women's liberation. They criticized, for example, the very standards of prestige and self-worth which were defined for the most part by men's achievements. The women's movement had fought for gains in society because its leaders believed women's entry into the public sphere would transform that sphere and simultaneously secure the means for women's independence; increasingly doubtful that women could alter public life sufficiently to meet their own inner needs, Feminists chose to wage their battles elsewhere—within the interstices of private life. In redefining the ultimate goal as self-realization rather than advancement, Feminists drastically altered the teleology of woman's mission.

Just as Feminism implied a shift in the locus of struggle from civil society to private life, its goal of self-realization suggested a departure from former standards of emancipation. As Havelock Ellis summed, it was "not enough to claim woman's place as a human being—especially in an age when man was regarded as the human being *par excellence*—but . . . necessary to claim woman's place in the world as woman." Feminism thus aimed to establish the "emancipation of woman both as a human-being and as a sex-being"—as woman.[8]

The prophet of Feminism was the Swedish writer Ellen Key. Although Key had begun her literary career in the 1880s and had achieved prominence as a leading educator in Stockholm, she became popular in the United States only well after 1910. She based her theoretical system upon a single premise, the conviction that fundamental physiological and psychological differences between man and woman could never be eradicated. She believed a female principle governed woman's development. To prove her point, she utilized contemporary studies in natural science that had established the sex-linkage of every body cell as the basis of distinct temperaments in men and women. Male aggression, for example, supposedly arose from the tendency to dissipate energy, while female passivity stemmed from the cellular propensity to conserve resources. Human biology therefore established the basis of distinct physiologies of the male and female. Key expanded this "discovery" into a social philosophy.[9]

Key named the great injustice not the denial of equal rights but the suppression of feminine nature, for there was no question that woman's destiny lay in her indisputably unmatched function, motherhood. Key saw in the female sex "an energy of motherliness which had shown itself so mighty and boundless a power" that it remained unchanged through all history, impervious to man's attempt to render it powerless. Motherhood thus stood as woman's most fundamental right. "In a very strong maternal feeling," Key wrote, "there is also a strong sensuous pleasure . . . —a pleasure which thrills the mother with blissful emotion when she puts the child to breast. . . . This harmony makes motherhood the most perfect stage. Self-sacrifice and self-realization, the universal conflicting elements of human life," their "one-ness in mother love; the soul and the senses, altruism and egoism blended."[10]

To liberate female nature, Key proposed a very radical political program. She issued a scathing attack on contemporary sexual relations and strongly criticized Christianity for its role in forcing monogamy upon its female subjects. Calling for the release of female passion, she recommended the abolition of both legal marriage and the patriarchal family. Men and women might love freely, she hoped, but women should not sacrifice their independence or their maternal prerogatives. She thus advocated a system of state protection of motherhood wherein women lived unto themselves and their offspring and had no other duty than to provide nurturant care.

Key's precise notion of motherhood had few proponents in the United States. The leaders of the late nineteenth-century woman's movement had, of course, respected woman's maternal role and believed that woman's station in life had uniquely prepared her for a higher morality. But they never implied a literal application of the concept. Frances Willard, the greatest proselytizer for a distinctly feminine morality, had thus named as the century's premier mother-figure Susan B. Anthony, and thereby demonstrated that the instinct to preserve need not be expressed literally in childbearing. Ambitious career women, contemporary Feminists in the United States were similarly at odds with Key's program of a state-protected maternity to the exclusion of other occupations. They might agree with her that they had nothing in common with the "short-sighted woman's rights woman, who takes pride in being a restless working-machine or a specialist rewarded by diplomas but otherwise half-educated,"[11] but they had scant desire to withdraw from society or from male company.

Despite this important reservation, American Feminists did locate in Key's philosophy a novel emphasis upon what one writer called the "psychic side" of liberation, a revolutionary promise the slow advance into man's world had never fulfilled. [12] Key encouraged women to envision liberation not merely as the accession of formal equality but as a fulfillment attuned to their feminine natures. Dubbed by Floyd Dell "the talmud of sexual morality," Key's leading text, *Love and Marriage,* received a warm welcome when an American edition appeared in 1911. [13] *The Woman Movement* by Key, which appeared the following year, enlarged the grounds for discussion enough that by 1913 American Feminists had initiated a major review of the woman question. Old-time reformers like Charlotte Perkins Gilman might balk at such notions as tantamount to heresy, but young women embraced Key as a kindred spirit. Not since 1869, when the woman's rights movement split into rival camps, had discussions of basic principles waxed so fierce. And so the battle raged, from the Left to the mainstream press, program to definition, a "human" and "female" emancipation locked into a struggle scarcely conceivable a few years earlier. [14]

Socialists necessarily partook of these discussions. Most Feminists were professed Socialists and many gravitated toward the party. But as they would prefer the Greenwich Village branch to other established locals, Feminists maintained their own standards. They retained something of themselves apart, such as their special language with its distinctive symbols, their own rituals and forms of association. And they eventually drifted from heterodoxy to dissaffection.

The reaction within the Socialist party contained mixed elements of sincere welcome, deep suspicion, and outright contempt. Feminists at first seemed to be a preliminary regiment in a new army of young, militant women. If repellent to many old-style Socialists, their peculiar notions had the virtue of linking the party with ascending intellectual currents. By 1913 the sagging movement unquestionably needed the spark Feminists might supply. Once the smoke cleared, however, dissension and confusion accompanied the Feminist challenge.

Discussions moved along two lines. The first involved large numbers of rank-and-file women and resembled that conducted by mainstream women activists; it concerned the nature of femininity and its political ramifications. The second mainly occupied the intellectual leadership and focused on the strategic relationship between Feminism and Socialism. Both lines of discussion inadvertently opened the door to an undisguised backlash against women's participation in the Socialist movement.

Deprived of its specific political context, the emphasis upon motherhood and feminine nature raised unwonted possibilities. On the one hand, new intellectuals like Floyd Dell and Hutchins Hapgood celebrated the wild essence of female passion as a revolutionary potential as yet untapped. "Woe to the more artificial male," Village bohemian Hapgood wrote," dependent on the unconsciously remembered past and on willful desire to maintain the impossible structure of civilization."[15] In Hapgood's mind, the more man exposed the futility of his material striving, the more woman revealed herself the true agent of cultural revolution. On the other hand, the discussions of Ellen Key in the mainstream press brought such a notable misogynist as Theodore Roosevelt to defend "feminism" as an antidote to the woman movement's propensity for "race suicide."[16]

Socialists were not inured to misreadings of Feminism. By 1913 a debate raged in the columns of the *New York Call*. A rank-and-filer had written to the "Woman's Sphere" that Socialists had made a big mistake emphasizing the "idea of economic independence" over motherhood and should now reassess their principles. The subsequent flood of letters concerning "woman's greatest work"—that is, motherhood—exposed the fragility of the hard-won defense of woman's right to labor. Although many Socialists defended their allegiance to women's civil equality, a large number spoke out against women's striving for economic independence as a mark of "bourgeois individualism." One of the party's most popular authors, John Spargo, argued similarly in *Socialism and Motherhood* (1914) that the Cooperative Commonwealth would emancipate womanhood from the "thralldom of the centuries, glorify motherhood, protect the home and insure childhood of its precious heritage and opportunity." Outside the metropolitan environs, readers of the popular *National Rip-Saw* could in 1913 send 25¢ for a hand-set essay, suitable for framing, entitled "Mothers of Men."[17] Feminists did not so much encourage these sentiments as offer unintended ammunition for the champions of traditionalism.

At the same time that Feminists inadvertently invited a resurgence of long-standing grievances against woman's advancement, they also issued a distinctly modern challenge to the old faith and distanced themselves from the Socialist organization. "We will not wait for the Social Revolution to bring us the freedom we should have won in the 19th century," Crystal Eastman announced to the first Feminist congress in 1919.[18] She spoke for the majority who straightforwardly refused to adopt Socialism as the ultimate goal and instead viewed Socialism and Feminism as complementary philosophies and schools of praxis. They expected Socialists to be in the forefront of the battle for women's liberation, their Socialist faith giving them the necessary fortitude to battle restrictive conventions. But Feminists called their own shots, for they were conducting their own struggle "for the destruction of a masculine despotism and for the right of womankind." Although allies like Floyd Dell might advise their comrades to pay heed to Feminism and to appreciate what Socialism might gain from its victory, few party regulars could abide by such a blatant dismissal of the Socialist faith.[19] If Feminists stirred latent reservations about the woman question, they also rallied those who considered all such discussions heretical to the Socialist canon.

Yet even those sincere comrades who believed the revolutionary prospect might well prove illusory unless Socialists came to terms with Feminism could do little in charting a clear map. The basis of such a connection evaded the grasp of the best-intended intellectuals and activists. Feminists themselves knew better what they rejected than what they desired as an alternative strategy. The most optimistic might envision a great two-pronged alliance, Feminists and Socialists negotiating as equals the terms of revolution. Few Socialists, however, could agree to such an arrangement; for even the most sympathetic toward woman's cause, the woman question was, by its very nature, but one aspect of the great social question. Many stalwarts in the Socialist women's movement proper spoke openly against Feminism on these grounds alone.

Rather than winning over the party to a new and revolutionary viewpoint on women, the Feminist insurgency actually diminished the standing of the existing women's sector. The adulation of motherhood, seized upon by those conservative men and women who had never accepted the trajectory of woman's civil emancipation, was turned against the veterans of suffrage, women's journalism, and all the battles for women's prerogatives in party ranks. Feminists themselves responded only weakly to this ominous counteroffensive, for, on the fringes of the party and pessimistic about its efficacy, they could not readily offer their sister comrades the intellectual and organizational support they now badly needed.

In truth, the Feminist emphasis upon an individual rather than collective, private more than public destiny ultimately militated against the strategic impulse of the Socialist women's movement. The New York circle Heterodoxy thus epitomized the demi-organization that many Feminists embraced. Unlike the nineteenth-century associations which aimed to reach outward through agitation and education, unlike the women's network within the Socialist party born of this tradition, the Feminist gatherings tended to reach inward toward the private experience of the individual member. Although women read political papers to each other in a familiar fashion, they also gave formal shape to the discussion of intimate details of daily life and sought to share their existential trials and victories.[20] The sacred concept of self-improvement as but aid to a greater collective service was reversed: the collectivity of the political mechanism could at best erect the basis for a realized self. As one writer explained lucidly: "[S]ince feminism in its essence—if it is anything— is a great personal, joyous adventure with one's untried self, it does not have to be 'organized.' It does not depend on organization nor on outside sympathy. . . . It does depend on the spiritual attitude of the individual woman to herself and to life, to the sense of freedom born within her that no one can give her and no one can take from her. . . ."[21] Feminists thus did not take their mission to the women's sector of the Socialist party. They maintained their own discussion circles and joined several political organizations, such as the National Woman's party, the

Women's Trade Union League, and the Socialist party itself. But their emphasis upon self-development and personal life objectively led them away from formal organizations designed to assist women in the public sphere. Feminism, for all its innovation and flair, for its philosophic wisdom about the trajectory of modern life, failed to salvage the organizational forms of its predecessors.

Seen from a long-range perspective, the outcome has a cast of inevitability. The historic limits of the older patterns in women' collective exertions left a vacuum before the Feminists made their appearance on the American scene. Young women responded to different urges than had their veteran sisters; they were drawn to the promise of womanhood more sexually complete, more emotionally intense than the nineteenth-century vision of proud and productive citizens which still informed the consciousness of elder Socialist women. The difficulty of deriving an alternative strategy made the Feminist yearnings uniquely modern as well as problematical political mechanisms; future generations would continue to struggle over how the personality might become a factor in revolutionary transformation. The direct confrontation of old and new ways, at the turning point in American Socialist history in the mid-1910s, generated much premonitory light but also anxiety among comrades overwrought by the dour implications for a heritage so dearly won. Revolutionary in its purport, Feminism signaled, despite the intentions of its foremost proponents, the final division between the old and the young.

NEW IMMIGRANT TRANSFORMATION

Hardened Socialist veterans might treat the emergence of Feminism as a passing fad, its proponents the ever-vacillating intellectuals important mainly as popularizers. Deeper shifts in the party's class, ethnic, and geographical make-up offered by contrast an absolute challenge to familiar practices. New immigrants, most from eastern and southern Europe, reaffirmed the principle of collective class struggle but interpreted the methods of organization and strategic questions according to their own perspectives. Unlike the handful of intellectuals, new immigrant Socialists could back up their demands with a near-majority of party members by the end of World War I. Once again the woman question faced re-evaluation—by this new constituency full of potential, alien in many ways from the traditions of both the elder German-American and indigenous woman's movements.

The new immigrants gradually changed the structure of the Socialist movement. In addition to the Jews, who by the mid-1890s had succeeded Germans in sections of New York and Chicago, Slavs and southern European groups had by the turn of the century formed small Socialist organizations. Party leaders, at first confused by this "foreign" constituency, postponed the establishment of an official liaison until 1908 and strengthened ties during the mass strikes of 1909–13. By 1912 the party had chartered nearly a dozen distinct "federations," groups which managed their own press, collected dues, and even exerted discipline largely autonomous of the party proper. A small fraction of the party membership, they still seemed to officials more a nuisance than a political asset. During World War I, as the strike wave seized labor's mainstream and grew ever greater, the new immigrants came into their own as a major force within the Socialist movement. By 1915 the foreign-language federations represented one-third of party membership, by 1919 over one-half.[22]

For the future of Socialist women, the new immigrants constituted a crucial sector. Old World customs, however, weighed heavily upon their prospects for organization. The nature of ethnic community life in the United States and, unquestionably, the quality of political leadership offered by the Left also influenced their course. As a result, new immigrant women created organizations as varied as the ethnic sector itself.

At one end of the spectrum were Italian-American women. Although a Socialist movement had grown between waves of repression in the industrializing northern regions of Italy, the majority of immigrants came from desperately poor communities of the rural south, where men and women had staged sporadic hunger riots, created *fasci*, and produced other manifestations of "primitive rebellion." Village provincialism, illiteracy particularly marked among women, religious and civil traditions of female subservience, and the sheer difficulty of life offered scant margin for the standard organizational forms of political Socialism.[23] Still, as newcomers to the United States, Italian-American women showed a remarkable volatility in the face of new hardships and prejudices. Exploited by American business through the *padrone* system, overcrowded into slums, and subjected to severe discrimination, a number of Italian-American communities consolidated rapidly in support of labor actions. Here the increasing stream of young women into industrial occupations and the loyalty of homemakers toward their families offered important sources for mobilization.[24]

The labor movement served as a focus for women's radical sympathies. Not only theoretical considerations but the very nature of the concrete problems at hand induced *Lotta de Classe*, mainstay Socialist journal for the New York cloakmakers, to introduce the first women's column in an Italian-American radical newspaper. Appearing as early as 1911, Socialist women's own appeals to their sister workers took the form of a plea to cast off patriarchal ties to the homeland and "become Americans" by joining the union movement. If relatively few women responded by enlisting in the Socialist party, thousands loyally followed Socialist union leaders, learned from their advance guard and Jewish sisters the meaning of class solidarity, and heard the promise of a better world. Outside the garment trade, Socialist-influenced unions like the United Mine Workers organized extensive women's auxiliaries with a distinctive cultural flavor, like the Dante Alligheri Clubs of the Kansas "Little Balkans" coal-mining district. In the pages of *Lotta de Classe*, the UMW's *Lavoratore Italiano*, the ILGWU's *Giustizia*, and the Amalgamated's *Il Lavoro*, Italian-American women emerged as an important force, their awareness the hope of the future.[25]

"La furia delle donne"—the activity of Italian-American women during the mass strikes and the ripple effect throughout their communities—presented the first significant opportunities for extended agitation and organization. In a scattering of cities, study groups, fashioned on the Ferrer School in New York, helped women organizers to expose their uneducated sisters to modern theories of childrearing, pedagogy, and even birth control, to establish lending libraries, and to urge secular enlightenment especially for children. The defense of Lawrence, Massachusetts, labor martyrs Joseph Ettor and Arturo Giovannitti involved many women; the agitational theatrical groups and above all the *casa proletaire* (clubhouses for radical workers) served as local fraternal associations wherein women could proudly lend their time and energies.[26]

Labor and community organizations aside, Italian-American Socialists did not noticeably succeed in inducing women to join the regular party local. A steady stream of propaganda aimed at recent immigrants never completely lost its abstract quality. Most commonly, writers attacked the historic traditions of women's role, the Church's ideal of virginity and indifference to earthly sufferings, its "false religion" directed against the true religion of humanity. This European-style anticlericalism, shared by virtually all new immigrant Socialist proselytizers, had here an almost fanatic quality. The alternative to Church institutions, like the "free love" (actually, civil) marriages unmarred by the "dirty water" of the priests, however, attracted relatively few outside the already committed radicals. Propagandists touched down to earth with their arguments in favor of family solidarity, such as imaginary dialogues with "mama" about her children's welfare, with sisters and daughters about their glum prospects for marital happiness under capitalism. But the distance between the revolutionary ideal and daily practice remained too great, and Italian-American women were drawn to the Left only insofar as Socialists could provide practical leadership and real services.[27] Not surprisingly, then, the effort to forge a distinct women's sector within the political movement met with little success. The short-lived *Circolo Femminile Socialisme* (women's Socialist circle) and occasional conferences organized expressly for women marked the outward limits. Relatively few Italian immigrant women joined either the Socialist party or the Italian Socialist Federation.[28]

Despite a wealth of human resources, Jewish women likewise did not commonly organize as gender-conscious militants within the ethnic sector. Most young women chose not the Jewish Socialist Federation, which committed itself to resist cultural assimilation, but rather the English-language branches of the party. In Chicago and New York especially, Jewish women had joined the daughters of the old German-American movement to become the prime leaders of the women's committees. The garment unions offered hundreds of other militants the same taste of leadership in their own right, relatively free from the Old World strictures against woman's prerogatives. But in the neighborhoods and among Socialist families where the old ways prevailed, the party did not encourage women to be politically assertive. The all-powerful propaganda institution, the *Daily Forward*, thus reintroduced the woman question gingerly, popularizing Bebel's *Die Frau und der Sozialismus* under such sensationalistic titles as "Why Were Women in the Past More Beautiful than Now?" and "Solomon Had a Thousand Wives and That Was No Sin," until Bebel himself objected. No distinct women's column could be found in the paper until 1915, when an essentially household-and-family page finally appeared. At the historic moment when thousands of Jewish women were mobilizing for the 1915 suffrage referendum in New York, Jewish Socialist luminaries warned in the *Forward*'s columns against placing too much emphasis upon political emancipation.[29]

Jewish fraternalism offered a middle road, melding family-community obligations with a modicum of personal expression. The *Arbeter Ring* swelled from its 1906 membership of 8,800 to more than 80,000 by 1920. Women participated as teachers and administrators in the "Socialist Sunday School" and Yiddish-language school system, served on a variety of internal subcommittees which oversaw the payment of sick-and-death benefits, and naturally graced the many social occasions with their presence. Yet few women achieved individual prominence. Here the secretary of the cemeteries department, there a noted Yiddish author on childrearing—the most notable personalities were, as in the nineteenth-century German-American movement, wives of party or fraternal leaders. Despite these familiar limitations, the wartime upsurge in ethnic self-consciousness and the steady development of fraternal organizations provided a net advance in women's position. Out of the last major waves of immigration, many retained a vivid sense of linguistic identity, from which sprang a revitalized Yiddish culture. The influence of Jewish Socialists in their communities, redoubled by successful union agitation and by the impact of the Russian Revolution, drew thousands of women and whole families into an enriched fraternal system, which supplemented the garment union's programs for organized leisure and adult education. As this fraternal network expanded to become the most extensive in the Left, former and future workingwomen found special places in the children's camps, *shules*, consumer organizations and tenement committees, foreign relief societies, labor defense, and a hundred other agencies spawned by the Left. This level of activity was, to be sure, a far cry from political participation, but it offered ordinary women an opportunity well within their reach.[30]

Eastern European nationalities, save for the Poles, stood in far smaller numbers than Italian-Americans or Jews, but through their very cohesiveness tended to create comparable roles for women. Influenced by the German Socialist movement in the homeland, southern Slavs (Slovenes, Croats, and Serbians) generated a cadre of workers and intellectuals active around the steel mills, packinghouses, and coalfields where their fellow immigrants settled. The fraternal movement more than the political unit served as a rallying point and again proved a natural outlet for women's energies. Few Slavic women possessed the cosmopolitan self-confidence for political assimilation into the English-language sector, although they might well become completely devoted to the labor movement. In Chicago, for instance, Slovakian and Slovenian Socialist women's circles, "Proletarka" and "Nada," organized as early as 1908. After a round of mass strikes in which Slavs played a role secondary only to Italians and Jews, the Slovak Socialist paper *Rovnost Ludu* could boast of the "fair success" of the woman's branch and urged comrades to attend the special lectures on women's issues. Much like Italians, Slav Socialists rained fire upon the clergy in favor of an enlightened womanhood. But the ardent support of woman suffrage and the expressed faith that (in the words of the Croat Socialist *Radnicka Straza*) "woman is just a human being after all, and after that she is a wife and mother" suggested a marked adaptation to American Socialist ideals on questions of women's political emancipation.[31]

As the language federations prospered during wartime, so too women's organizations blossomed. International developments, especially the prospective national liberation of their homelands, frequently permitted Socialists to assume important positions within their ethnic communities. Prominent European Socialist figures, like the Ukrainian Irene Sichyns'ky, toured the United States and encouraged the formation of women's groups. At the same time the fraternal networks began to coalesce fully. Musical societies, children's groups, leisure and educational programs for adults offered new immigrant women, like their German-American antecedents, a rich milieu for service and self-development. If women rarely attained leadership positions within the language federation itself, as workingwomen they supported the rising Socialist labor organizers, as homemakers they filled the fraternal halls, marshaled the children, and supplied the essential services.[32] All these activities were familiar to any veteran of the German-American Socialist movement. But they enjoyed (or suffered from) a leeway created by the discontinuity in ethnic and political traditions, the necessity to begin again the radical contribution to the process of community building.

The Lithuanian Women's Progressive Alliance, centered in Chicago, was a case in point. Both loyalty to the Socialist movement and a deep resentment that women's work had been "considered of less value," its participants "shunted to the rear" of existing organizations, prompted women to form their own society. Although the appearance of the alliance had been greeted with "joy and celebration," its initiates did not yet know how to build upon the momen-

tum, and the "sisters again closed themselves up in their steaming kitchens."
Gradually a small minority developed a more hard-minded political sensibility.
These women seized the responsibility for leadership, cast off their own constraints, and as one veteran related, "in the newspapers, at meetings, and in
private circumstances . . . urged their sisters to enlighten themselves to organize
and fight for their rights." The mobilization of women suited the needs of the
Lithuanian-American Socialist movement, not large in absolute numbers but
nevertheless a vital force in a number of cities and industries. Women also
gained an important measure of self-determination. [33]

Despite the organizational advances of many new immigrant women, the
majority did not develop the gender consciousness characteristic of the English-
language Socialist movement, nor did they create their own press or propaganda
mechanisms. The tenacity of Old World customs and the overwhelming struggle to guard their families against the pressures of "Americanization" and economic distress tended to blunt the sharpness of women's own demands for
recognition. Immigrant Socialists sincerely preached the gospel of women's
enlightenment and equal political participation, but they lacked the milieu
which had produced English-language women leaders and secured for them
an autonomous base for activity. Sometimes, however, they simply lacked the
will. Only in rare circumstances did immigrant women successfully combine
a community- and class-conscious sentiment with an avowed desire for women's
emancipation.

Finnish-American women, relatively few in number, nevertheless possessed
a signal importance. Upwards of 35 percent of the Finnish membership of the
Socialist movement, they enjoyed the kind of influence that Socialists in the
United States regarded as a European feat. Full participants in the fraternal
societies, they also spoke in the name of an emancipation few men could fully
comprehend.

Old-country conditions and the patterns of immigration had a number of
unique qualities favoring radical activism and women's participation. Many
Finns had traveled from farm to city en route to the new land and had thus
experienced both industry and the burgeoning radical movements. The national domination of Finns by the Swedes and later by the Russians placed the
survival of the culture and even the language as a patriotic priority. The spiritual
alternative to temporal power, the Lutheran church, was both authoritarian in
its claims upon citizens' lives and identified with the foreign rulers, so that
widespread free-thought opposition had deep roots in the populace, male and
female. Most important for women's status, the prerogatives they possessed in
the countryside blended well with the rising democratic currents and gained
legal recognition when the Russian duma granted universal suffrage to all
Finnish citizens in 1906. A playwright, novelist, and political theorist, Minna
Cath, took her place among the pioneers of Finnish Socialist thought and

counted among her disciples future editors of Finnish-American Socialist publications. Even as the trek to America began, the precursive path for Finnish-American Socialist women's activities had been cut.[34]

The difficulties of Finnish-American life tempered the immigrants' aspirations and pushed them toward self-improvement activities. Extractive and heavy industries, often isolated geographically like the Minnesota-Michigan copper country, encouraged the dissolute habits of a hard-drinking working class. Now free to develop their own secular traditions in literature, theatrical and recreational programs, Finns fought back and swiftly developed an intense and inclusive practice. Temperance played an important part in these activities, as societies disproportionately composed of women (but supported by men) sprung up. Through the temperance leagues but also many fraternal societies and even the Lutheran synods, Socialist doctrines spread to a wider population. Finnish-American women, many working as domestics or factory operatives, grew politically within this progressive context and moved in significant numbers through church and temperance activities toward a vision of liberation.[35]

Alone of the new immigrant groups, Finnish-American Socialist women established their own press along the lines of indigenous women's publications. *Tyomïes*, the first Finnish-American Socialist newspaper, urged women's emancipation in a heartfelt manner, bringing the seeds of Minna Cath's inspirational doctrine to the new land. A proposal for an autonomous women's sector and press immediately enjoined debate in the Finnish Socialist Federation. Women's letters to the newspaper bristled with the sentiment that "women should have their own paper where they can freely have their say," an argument expressed even more frequently among their own discussion groups. The proliferation of the Finnish-American radical press, the growing prominence of women in the fraternal and political sectors of the movement, and no doubt the influence of the Stuttgart resolution condoning agitation on behalf of women comrades gradually won over the federation. In 1911 the *Toveritar* (woman comrade) was established in Astoria, Oregon, by a group of women who gathered pledges for 3,000 subscriptions; a former woman member of Finland's Diet was installed as its first editor. After several years of experimentation *Toveritar* gained an equivalent to Josephine Conger-Kaneko, editor and intellectual leader par excellence.[36]

Selma Jokela McCone had attended the Workpeople's College in Smithville, Minnesota, and had as a young woman joined the women's committee of the Finnish-Socialist Federation. In this position she sponsored the publication of the first pamphlets specifically directed at Finnish-American women. Several years later, in 1915, she took over a *Toveritar* weighed down with theoretical abstractions and losing ground despite a growing potential constituency. Inspired by the example of the *Progressive Woman*, as her forerunners had undoubtedly been by *Die Gleichheit*, she changed the paper's tone to what she called a "woman's own paper, which would become a close friend, one who is needed every week." Calling herself "Selma-Täti" (Aunt Selma), McCone mixed political essays with fiction and poetry (including her own), household hints, and the instruction of children. She installed an extremely popular children's department and helped to sponsor the burgeoning summer camp activities of Finnish-American youth. Within months she had raised the subscription list to a respectable 5,000 and truly rendered the publication not merely one for women but women's own paper. [37]

The *Toveritar* under McCone and her successors served as the political voice of the Finnish-American women's sector. These Socialist women were unique because they, like their male comrades, played an important role in their immigrant community for considerable periods of time but also because their unrelenting support of woman's cause did not diminish their militant advocacy of revolutionary Socialism. Almost exclusively among the new immigrants, Finnish-American women conducted their own suffrage campaign and avowedly joined in sentiment, if not in organization, the mainstream woman's movement. And they were unique in their cultural creativity, to an extent that few non-Finns could appreciate. Not only the creation of producers' and consumers' cooperatives, along with the usual fraternal components, but a high level of literary attainment marked the leadership of Socialist women. *Toveritar*, and the constituency it represented, could claim achievements other Socialist women frankly considered utopian. [38]

Although Finnish-American Socialist women were *sui generis*, their accomplishment accentuated a pattern shared by other new immigrant women. Working in a new country, severely strained by the ambiguities of assimilation, Slav, Finnish, Jewish, and to a lesser extent Italian women helped erect social movements with strong roots in their communities. At times and places—during the peak of class conflict or within the inner warmth of the ethnic ghettoes—they demonstrated a potential for more, had the call gone out clearly and unequivocally. Their capacity for self-organization within and without the Socialist party suggested that new immigrant women had only begun to coordinate their political work by the early 1910s. But that work had as little in common with the Woman's National Committee and its political prescriptions as did the activities of the Feminists. Like their sister rebels, whose existence they scarcely recognized, the immigrant women set out in new directions.

DEMISE OF THE WNC

Challenged by Feminists and new immigrants, the WNC lacked both staying power and flexibility. For years the leaders had insisted that the local women's committee was not mere form but vital to the solidarity of the Socialist women's movement. In one sense they were correct, for the women's committees had combined the desire for separate institutions with fealty to the party. This synthesis, however, could not survive the 1910s; younger women chose alternative forms to express their socialistic sympathies. The leaders of the WNC responded only half-heartedly to this situation. They once again questioned the validity of any special institutions for women and called upon their sisters to take their place within the regular party local. To those Socialist women who had witnessed the creation of the WNC and had listened to the debates surrounding the event in 1908, the renewed effort to abandon even the semblance of separate institutions had a familiar, disquieting ring.

Widespread complaints against the mixed local should have forewarned Socialists that the WNC plan to integrate women into the party structure might never be fulfilled. A mild furor began in 1911 when a letter in the *New York Call* flatly listed major grievances against the male-dominated branches. "A Mere Woman" described the reception Socialists extended when she brought several friends to demonstrate the famous hospitality. To her dismay party chieftains ignored them to greet young men. During the meeting the few women who took the platform saw the meeting reconvene as if they had never spoken. The atmosphere, politically chilling, was physically "one cloud of smoke." Undaunted, this adventurer and her three friends visited various locals in greater New York and each time reaffirmed their initial impression. With but few exceptions, the locals resembled "a cheap class Bowery dancing hall," male culture *in extremis*. While longtime advocate of separate women's organizations, Meta Stern, noted that the writer had raised serious questions, most respondents simply denied the charges as untrue or irrelevant.[39]

Despite the attempt to downplay such complaints, more were forthcoming. In Seattle, long a bastion of class consciousness, the women's committee passed into open revolt. Women had asked their local to reserve 10¢ per month from each woman's dues as a special fund for propaganda and educational work. The local agreed, and the women's committee opened a room in the party headquarters where each afternoon a woman attended to sell literature and to talk to any strangers who happened by. The program proved successful until, one woman reported, "the local woke up to the fact that women were really handling some money, a part of their own dues, and spending it as they thought best!" The local cut off the fund, and the women resolved to take a "vacation" and re-established their pre-1908 separate organization.[40] Such incidents only reinforced male prejudices. A comrade in 1913 noted with disgust that his peers remained "not one whit enthusiastic" about women's issues, and that the typical "dyed-red-in-the-wool r-r-revolutionary" did not care whether "women fail or succeed. . . ."[41] As the party drifted leftward over labor and wartime issues, the future of women's prospects dimmed.

The WNC for its part simply declined to recognize the dimensions of the problem. Early in its existence the WNC had decried as "foreign to the ideal of equality" a well-intended suggestion that wives be permitted full membership privileges at one-third dues. Refusing special privileges, the WNC never grappled effectively with the difficulties of recruiting and sustaining women in the party. Leading figures such as Theresa Malkiel had appealed repeatedly for national conferences to conduct the necessary far-ranging strategic discussions. The WNC refused on the grounds that it lacked the authority to issue such a call. Lena Morrow Lewis characteristically argued that the very idea of a special women's conference defied the purpose of integrating them into the "domain of the regular party work."[42]

By 1914 reports of diminished ranks trickled in to the women's columns of the Socialist press. New York state correspondent Mary Schonberg supplied sample letters from various local committees requesting information on how to revive their women's organizations. "We used to have a good-sized Woman's Committee, but a year and a half ago a good many of the women would only come out when there were fairs and suppers at which they thought themselves especially useful," read a typical communication.[43] Such was the experience of many locals where women out of the auxiliary tradition had never become comfortable with the more vocal and domineering men. The self-assertive, native-born women in the countryside and metropolis departed for other reasons. The old, gender-conscious activists fell under the lash of political reaction, accelerated by the specter of war and the aroused anti-Socialist nationalism. The rise of local Progressivism after 1912 meanwhile chewed away at the Socialist leadership of urban reform movements, as the image of Woodrow Wilson rose like a beacon to the believers in government regulation. The limits of Socialist influence, some observers perspicaciously predicted, had been reached. And the young, college-educated women, never close to the women's sector, drifted out with the tide.

The Socialist women's movement had come to a turning point where the directives of the Second International and admonitions to party loyalty no longer sufficed. The women's sector, like the hard-hit party as a whole, would adapt or perish. The press and political institutions had to be maintained at all costs. And the new, potential constituencies—cultural rebels not wholly wedded to Feminism, immigrants willing to mediate the differences of logic and form—had to be sought on their own terms.

The party accommodated itself willy-nilly and put up a brave front in electoral campaigns. It conducted vigorous anti-war propaganda that drew immigrant radicals closer and supported wherever possible the labor militance that seemed the most dynamic and promising activity of the Left. The WNC, on the contrary, torn by the party's demands and shy of innovation, seized the moment of crisis to attack the gender-conscious institutions they had ever regarded with suspicion.

The *Progressive Woman* offered a particularly dramatic case in point. For years Josephine Conger-Kaneko had maintained a unique independence for her venture by relying only upon the subscriptions and sales her readers themselves provided. She suffered her first telling blow in 1912 when the *Appeal to Reason* managers retrenched their operation and stopped publishing other periodicals. Determinedly Conger-Kaneko set out for Chicago and the only remedies available: the paid advertising she had heretofore avoided on political grounds and the subsidization only the WNC could confer. Battered by her husband's death, Conger-Kaneko fell back upon the advice and aid of Caroline Lowe, WNC correspondent, who helped negotiate a joint-stock company guarantee by the national office. To this point, the odds against the *Progressive Woman* had grown, but Conger-Kaneko and her circle of supporters held out.

Suddenly the blows fell upon her, one after another. Winnie Branstetter succeeded Lowe the same year and pronounced the joint-stock venture a failure; she urged the dismantling of the company. When the WNC vetoed this proposal, Branstetter took her case to higher circles and assaulted the *Progressive Woman* in the factional hate terms of the day as a "red" sympathizer to the IWW. The controversy raged and stock sales fell. Conger-Kaneko and the WNC parted ways by mutual consent. And still the editor struggled on. She hired a subscription agency, added 12,000 new readers in 1913, and introduced a wide range of subject matter. Seeking to recall the popularity of the remarkable journal of the 1890s, she changed the name to the *Coming Nation*. Now Branstetter sought to remove the magazine from the WNC's literature list on the basis that it was no longer a publication for women! Against the pressure of financial obligations and political isolation, Conger-Kaneko gave up. Once the voice of the independent Socialist women's clubs, faithful to the WNC in its prime, Conger-Kaneko's magazine folded.[44]

Subsequent events are difficult to disentangle. Perhaps its leaders had already determined that a WNC had no place in a weakened party; perhaps they had become so exasperated at the failure to integrate women into the party that they concluded the WNC was counterproductive. Whatever the truth, the winding down of the WNC had a ring of self-fulfilling prophecy: the less it accomplished, the stronger the argument for its dismantling.

The absence of the *Progressive Woman* deprived Socialist women of a voice of protest and even news about scattered activities. Doubtless by 1913 women's committees had declined, but how severely could not yet be known. Josephine Conger-Kaneko, in spite of her wounds, hurried to support a new WNC with Branstetter at the helm, but she warned that the "lack of cooperation at the fountainhead" must be circumvented.[45] Meanwhile, Branstetter herself pressed for abolition.

Significantly, Branstetter's supporter, the first major Socialist woman to promote this course, was May Wood Simons. Prominent author on the woman question, Simons had long been adamant against separate organizations and regarded the WNC's primary function as encouraging women to take their

places within the regular movement. The WNC had failed to accomplish this
goal, Simons pronounced in 1914. Citing scarcity of funds as the chief cause
for dereliction, she hinted that grass-roots resistance to the program of integration had doomed the WNC from the beginning.[46]

Against Branstetter and Simons stood a scattered faithful, unable to rally a
sufficient counteracting force. In January, 1915, the WNC announced that
"great changes will be made in the party machinery affecting special work for
women by the National Committee at the May Sessions." New York and New
Jersey Socialists held an emergency meeting and proposed measures to strengthen
the WNC. In light of Branstetter's divisive role, they urged the WNC to elect
its own national correspondent. To meet Simon's charges, they argued that a full
10 percent of the party's income be regularly set aside for women's purposes, that
the WNC maintain full control of its own budget, and that it be empowered to
raise additional income through solicitation.[47]

These proposals came at a particularly inopportune time. The Socialist party
nearly struck bottom on its membership slide from 1912, facing electoral reverses
and endemic factionalism with a mixture of shock and old-fashioned resolve.
The party leadership streamlined its functions, eliminated many offices, and
placed others under tighter control. Under these conditions the floundering
and divided WNC appeared to many well-meaning members a liability. One
captured the mood with the clumsy analogy, "We have more cars hitched to
the Socialist engine than it can pull, and we are going to have to put some of
the cars on the sidetrack or stall the train." When the National Executive
Committee polled the membership in June, 1915, to amend the constitution
and abolish the WNC, the women's car was definitely shunted aside. It remained to be seen whether the engine could now pull the train better or not.[48]

Most Socialist women resigned themselves to the *fait accompli* as the logical
outcome of protracted decline. Kate Richards O'Hare, in good position "to study
the antics of the male who feels his domain has been treacherously invaded by
a female," used the opportunity to reflect upon her own experiences as a woman
at the top. "Scratch a scientific male Socialist," she concluded, "and you will
find an ordinary he-man. And that he-man will resent as bitterly and fight as
unscrupulously the invasion of women into his domain as possible."[49]

But O'Hare's lesson had broad application. Why did the unreconstructed
male Socialist, willing to sponsor and even finance the WNC at one time, later
turn against this effort? Josephine Conger-Kaneko pinpointed the cause in the
sectarian spirit which leading Socialist women themselves displayed. Looking
back to the early days of women's organization, she recalled the independent-
mindedness of women "active in study clubs . . . from New York to Los Angeles."
She reminded her sisters that it had been the "party convention which gave to
the Socialist women the 'committee' form of organization, officially discrediting
other forms, and thus destroying to a large degree the work already accomplished

by the women." The party had of course offered—and for a time delivered—benefits ranging from funds and literature to official status and publicity. But as Conger-Kaneko recalled, a cynical woman had suggested such perquisites hid the real reason behind the party's welcoming gesture, "to kill the [independent] women's activities in the Socialist party." Indeed, the original advocates of the committee form did later become the primary agents in "triumphantly" voting the WNC out of existence. [50]

This interpretation smacked of a devil theory and disregarded the ardent labors of many women who by reasons of background and temperament could not work comfortably outside the party. At its prime, the WNC had been an irreplaceable mechanism for mediating the differences between groups of Socialist women and thereby provided a sense of national coherence to the intense local and regional activities. It had, moreover, endowed women's agitation with an official status within the Socialist movement, rallied otherwise doubtful men, and raised the woman question considerably higher than it would have otherwise reached. But Conger-Kaneko's theory had a grain of truth: all this had been accomplished at a price.

To orthodox Socialists of the nineteenth century, in most times and places, loyalty had meant a disavowal of the bourgeois woman's movement in favor of class-conscious politics. That Socialists were unable to become a mass proletarian movement reinforced their embattled sensibility of revolutionary prophets in the American wilderness. Twentieth-century Socialists had adapted to indigenous currents and in part owed their greater success to the dilution or abandonment of former principles. For the literalism of class consciousness they substituted a fealty to the party that the middle class, farmers, and assorted *declassé* moralists could more easily accept. Socialists no longer scorned agitation focused on gender rather than class issues, but they drew the line at subordinating their identity within reform movements—thus the spectacle of militant Theresa Malkiel bitterly assaulting the principle of cooperation with mainstream suffragists, thus the sensation of veteran WCTU activist Lena Morrow Lewis undermining the autonomous women's organizations within the Socialist movement. Any other behavior would have raised doubts about their primary dedication to the party.

As long as the party continued to grow, large numbers of Socialist women could tolerate this compromise. Within the ranks, party fealty coexisted with gender-conscious motivations, the independent-minded *Progressive Woman* in service to the WNC the symbol of harmonious relations. In form—and by their own lights, sincerely—most Socialists supported the campaign for woman suffrage, abhorred the evils of prostitution, and most certainly promoted the unionization of workingwomen. As individuals, many doubtless favored the legalization of birth control information and devices. But only a small minority had ever considered the mainstream woman's movement a constitutive, creative force in its own right. When sacrifices had to be made for party survival, when women lacked their historic sources of strength, Socialists could mark off the WNC a tertiary apparatus, expendable.

Fatefully, the leaders of the WNC failed to appreciate the contributions of the independent women's sector of the Socialist movement. Without large numbers of organized and assertive women, no woman would likely have been elected to the National Executive Committee, no WNC would have been formed even with the encouragement of the International. Not the good will of Socialist men, however generous, but the presence of women guaranteed the party's commitment to women's equality. Yet to May Wood Simons, Lena Morrow Lewis, or Winnie Branstetter, to request a special status or undue favors seemed to diminish their accomplishments as individuals. They unknowingly fell back upon the formula first articulated by German-American Socialists in 1876, that within the party the "equality of rights is a principle and is strictly observed." When most Socialist women declined to integrate themselves into regular party locals, the leaders felt they had no recourse but to abandon all compensatory institutions.

"Are we to have this sort of thing forever?" asked Conger-Kaneko in desperation at the close of the WNC, "is there absolutely NO WAY OUT?"[51] The possible solutions had by this time already been foreclosed. Probably the diverse, geographically scattered Socialist women's organizations could not have coordinated affairs, answered the changes in constituency any better than the WNC had done. But they were victims nevertheless of an enduring dynamic— stronger even than the best-willed Socialists—that had rendered Socialism a literal function of class, class a function of wage labor, and the woman question a function of both. During the political crises of the 1910s, the familiar dichotomy between gender- and class-conscious forms, temporarily buried by common consent, had returned with a vengeance.

A FEW CONSEQUENCES

Although Socialist women did not disappear *en masse* following the abolition of the WNC, after 1915 they lacked a means to broadcast their sentiments. They no longer could call upon representatives who might carry their demands to the party leadership, and they found it increasingly difficult to acquire information about women's activities across the country. Lines of communication, once strong across vast stretches, snapped under the dead weight of disorganization. Although many individual women remained active at the local level, the movement that had once sustained their spirits faded into obscurity. For the crucial decade ahead—especially the anti-war campaigns and the defense of Socialists against repression—the absence of a collective voice had dire consequences.

Perhaps the greatest failure was the inability of the WNC to ease the ethnic transformation of the women's sector. A few local women's committees, such as one in Cook County, Illinois, had responded enthusiastically to the prospects of recruitment among new immigrants and reported increases in membership among Finnish, Scandinavian, Bohemian, Slovakian, Latvian, Lithuanian, and even German women.[52] The WNC, however, responded feebly. Its leaders instituted a subcommittee on "foreign relationship" with representatives from various language federations, but managed only to translate a few leaflets. For the most part the WNC played a negative role. Whereas the majority of women in the foreign-language federations maintained their own societies, the WNC badgered them to dissolve their separate organizations and to join the mixed local.[53] Similarly, Branstetter's disparaging remarks about the IWW and revolutionary Socialism could not but offend the left-inclined federationist women. Had the WNC been more sensitive toward the traditions of immigrant women, had it been able to coordinate activities among the various groups, it might have played an important role in reconstituting the Socialist women's movement on a new basis. Instead, its steadfast leaders merely multiplied the difficulties new immigrant women encountered in taking a united stand within the Left.

The WNC did no better in its duty to women directly under its purview, native-born young and old. Its collapse just at the onset of world war robbed Socialist women of a great crusade rich in tradition. Here was a women's campaign with deep roots, dating to the Civil War and the thousands of women's peace societies that had formed in its wake. "Can we . . . as mothers and teachers instill into the minds of our growing generations the horror and cruelty of war?" asked a Driftwood, Oklahoma, woman in 1912. She answered with an affirmation that had resounded through the last five decades: "We as mothers of the race should stand with helmet and shield, at the head of the procession, marching and educating toward the Grand Union for a World of Peace."[54]

As the shades of conflict began to fall over Europe, Socialist women in the United States had begun a vigorous agitation. In May, 1911, the WNC urged women to form an anti-war campaign in their home towns. Although the actual outbreak of the European war threw American Socialists into bitter despair over the failure of the International to take drastic action, they nevertheless sharpened their attack against war patriotism and preparedness in the United States. By 1914 Socialist women had filed the first of many petitions with President Wilson; they asked him to guard the neutrality of the United States and to act forcefully upon the food shortage and inflation by seizing resources from capitalist profiteers. In September, 1914, the WNC produced a special anti-war edition of the *American Socialist*, unofficial organ of the national office. By 1914 the WNC had established a subcommittee on disarmament and militarism, and urged Socialist women to cooperate with all local "peace forces." Women in the party from California to Kansas to New York

rallied their sisters.[55] Much like the mainstream suffragists at this point, Socialist women interpreted the conflict as the apotheosis of male domination at
its last historic moment prior to women's political coming-of-age. A "thoroughly masculine quantity," Josephine Conger-Kaneko called the war. Meta
Stern suggested in 1914, "Soon will women, the peaceful producers, the homemakers, the mothers of men, help to conduct the affairs of the world. . . . They
will compel governments to settle their disputes. . . ."[56]

As dread turned into horror at the potential involvement of the United States,
as the WNC dissolved, the anti-war agitation lost its overall political coherence.
On the one hand, the New York Socialist suffrage campaign committee became
a dynamic center for mobilizing women. New York Socialist women conducted
a huge anti-war demonstration in January, 1916, joined with non-Socialists in
the Woman's Peace party, publicized Meta Stern's antipreparedness pamphlet
Motherhood and the "Bloody Five Laws," and sent Theresa Malkiel on a nationwide speaking tour. Socialists in other cities similarly broke protocol to join
prominent women reformers, suffragists, and settlement house leaders in a last-
ditch effort to force international arbitration. But while a peace campaign raged
among some sectors, others leaned in an opposite direction. Much of middle
America took up national preparedness with zeal, and large numbers of native-
born Socialists grew nearly hysterical in fear and predicted an apocalyptic end
to American democracy.[57] Without the WNC to provide coordination and to
issue policy, these strongly divergent reactions moved Socialist women onto
several different paths.

The entry of the United States into the war nearly completed the division
between various sectors of the movement. Kate Richards O'Hare chaired the
key committee at the 1917 Socialist Party Emergency Convention, which put
the party on record against American participation. But numbers of her comrades drew silent in fear, while a prominent minority turned patriot. May Wood
Simons, for example, became starkly pro-war, as did many others who had
supported woman's cause. By 1918 dozens of Socialist periodicals had been
destroyed by government repression, and party branches had disbanded. The
Appeal to Reason supported Wilson in the name of an early peace, while the
once-vibrant Oklahoma movement, a symbolic center of home-grown Socialism, disintegrated after some of its activists staged a small-scale armed "rebellion." Even New York Socialists experienced defections among seasoned
activists whose hatred of the Kaiser threw them into sympathy with Wilson's
war aims. Such defectors stood in sharp contrast to the Jewish, German, and
other ethnic sectors, which by and large viewed the American entry as an
Anglo-Saxon crusade toward world commercial domination.[58]

Always endangered by the threat of prosecution for anti-war activities, Socialist women could act only under considerable handicaps. Opportunities
nevertheless existed for a revival. The party actually gained a considerable

increase in votes on anti-war and inflation issues in local elections in 1917 and held on the following year where the organization managed to stave off legal repression. In 1918, after women had gained the ballot, the Socialist party in New York City reached a high point in the proportion of women members, nearly 20,000 of the 67,000 registered for primary elections. New bursts of energy could be seen, as around the garment districts, or where industry had given women new prominence, as in Schenectady, New York, center of a growing electrical trade employing large numbers of women, or in southern districts where the Socialist movement had been slow to sink in. However promising these stirrings, they could not grow without leadership and coordination.[59]

The last opportunity for Socialist women to reach across their ethnic and generational boundaries had slipped by, and veterans looked on sadly, sometimes bitterly, as their movement faded away. They could see the party backsliding on its former commitments. Greybeard theorist Ernest Untermann, observing the climax of the suffrage crusade, could thus freely warn his comrades against a "desire of women's rule over men." Chicago Socialists went on record opposing the formation of a new women's branch in that city. The editors of the remaining Socialist newspapers sought to soften the tone of journalism addressed to women. The revived women's column in the *New York Call*, for example, lacked its former punch and now focused on home and fashion at the expense of political agitation. In 1919, for the first time since 1909, the *Call* and other papers significantly failed to give Woman's Day serious attention. Few women openly protested this situation. One wrote to the *Call* in September, 1918: "There is more of a feeling of resentment over the situation regarding women . . . than appears on the surface." Complaints, however, had lost their purpose when women themselves "are feeling that the party is in an inextricable rut. . . ." Ida Crouch Hazlett could only refer to the new women's column in the *Call* as "stupid" and devoid of all the essentials that she and other women demanded in their political work. Not that capable women were missing, another added, but "the lack of cooperation and self-monopolistic egotism of the men" made the few efforts fruitless.[60] In truth, the women's sector was so disorganized it could not wage a counteroffensive. And no one could identify the strategic priorities ahead. The older loyalist thus accepted her misgivings in hopes of a better future; the younger woman followed her instincts out of the movement.

NOTES

1. Elizabeth Gurley Flynn, *Memories of the Industrial Workers of the World (IWW)* (New York, 1977).
2. Edna Kenton, "Edna Kenton Says Feminists Will Give—," *Delineator*, 85 (July, 1914), 17. The prominent author Gertrude Atherton also wrote on "What Is Fem-

inism" in a monthly series in the *Delineator*, 89 (Oct.-Dec., 1916). W. L. George, "Feminist Intentions," *Atlantic Monthly*, 112 (Dec., 1913), 721–32; Evelyn King Gilmore, "Feminism," *Harper's Weekly*, 62 (Mar. 11, 1916), 310; "Same Old Thing," *Harper's Weekly*, 59 (Aug. 29, 1914), 208; and Elisabeth Woodbridge, "The Unknown Quantity in the Woman Problem," *Atlantic Monthly*, 113 (Apr., 1914), 510–20, are examples of the discussion in the popular press.

3. Mary S. Oppenheimer, "The Cry of a Feminist," *New Review*, 1 (Mar., 1913), 412–14.

4. Marie Jenney Howe, "Feminism," *New Review*, 2 (Aug., 1914), 441–43.

5. Kenton, "Edna Kenton Says . . .," 17.

6. George Burman Foster, "The Philosophy of Feminism," *Forum*, 52 (July, 1914), 17.

7. Charles Rappaport, "The Intuitive Philosophy of M. Bergson," *New Review*, 2 (Mar., 1914), 133; Marian Cox, "Bergson's Message to Feminism," *Forum*, 48 (May, 1913), 548–59; Walter Lippmann, *A Preface to Politics* (New York, 1913).

8. Havelock Ellis, "Introduction," to Ellen Key, *Love and Marriage*, trans. Arthur G. Chater (New York, 1911), xiv. See also Katharine Anthony, *Feminism in Germany and Scandinavia* (New York, 1915), 6.

9. Jill Conway discusses the influence of scientific investigation in "Stereotypes of Femininity in a Theory of Sexual Evolution," in Martha Vincinus, ed., *Suffer and Be Still: Women in the Victorian Age* (Bloomington, Ind., 1972), 140–54.

10. Ellen Key, *The Renaissance of Motherhood*, trans. Anna E. B. Fries (New York, 1914), 21; "Motherliness," *Atlantic Monthly*, 110 (Dec. 1912), 565–67.

11. Key, *Love and Marriage*, 284.

12. Florence Geurtin Tuttle, *The Awakening of Woman* (New York, 1915); reviewed in the *New York Call*, May 23, 1915. June Sochen, *The New Woman: Feminism in Greenwich Village* (New York, 1972), demonstrates that most avant-garde Feminists pursued their careers while at the same time hoping to find fulfillment in their private lives. Christina Simmons has ably followed this theme into the 1920s and the popularity of "companionate marriage" among that generation in "Purity Rejected: The New Sex Freedom of the Twenties," an unpublished paper delivered at the Berkshire Conference of Women's History, June, 1976.

13. Floyd Dell, *Women and World Builders: Studies in Modern Feminism* (New York, 1913), 83. See also Helen Zimmern, "Ellen Key," *Putnam's*, 3 (Jan., 1908), 432–39.

14. A great believer in motherhood as a race-preserving force, Gilman had carefully separated biological traits from social ascriptions. Where Key demanded state protection of individual motherhood, Gilman looked forward to a system of child care handled collectively by the state. Professionalization of child care, in her opinion, would benefit women by freeing them to follow their talents into the world of work. See her essays: "On Ellen Key and the Woman Movement," *Forerunner*, 4 (Feb., 1913), 35–38; "The New Mothers of a New World," *ibid.* (June, 1913), 145–49; "Education for Motherhood," *ibid.* (Oct., 1913), 259–62.

In the popular press the dramatic differences in perspective between Gilman and Key served to sharpen the discussion of Feminism: see "Ellen Key's Attack on 'Amaternal' Feminism," *Current Opinion*, 54 (Feb., 1913), 138–40; "A New Conception of Maternity," *ibid.* (Mar., 1913), 220–21; "The Conflict between 'Human' and 'Female' Feminism," *ibid.*, 56 (Apr., 1914), 291–92. For a full treatment, see Emmet Densmore, *Sex Equality: A Solution to the Woman Problem* (New York, 1907), wherein he defends Gilman against the new currents.

15. Hutchins Hapgood, *A Victorian in the Modern World* (New York, 1939), 320.
16. "The Feminism That Roosevelt Admires," *Current Literature*, 53 (Sept. 1912), 310.
17. John Spargo, *Socialism and Motherhood* (New York, 1914), 124. Advertisement, "Mothers of Men," appeared in the *National Rip-Saw* (St. Louis), Dec., 1913.
18. Crystal Eastman, "Feminism," *Liberator*, 2 (May, 1919), 37; reprinted in *Crystal Eastman on Women and Revolution*, ed. Blanch Wiesen Cook (New York, 1978), 49–51.
19. Floyd Dell, "A Reply to Belfort Bax," *New Review*, 2 (June, 1914), 353. See also Mary White Ovington, "Socialism and the Feminist Movement," *ibid.* (Mar., 1914), 147.
20. Judith Sue Schwartz, "Heterodoxy: A Club for Unorthodox Women" (Master's thesis, San Jose State University, 1977). Rheta Childe Dorr, *A Woman of Fifty* (New York, 1924), 270–80, recalls both the intimate discussions and the social facets of Heterodoxy. Inez Haynes Irwin Papers, Schlesinger Library, Radcliffe College, contain materials on Heterodoxy, including a memorable photo album.
21. Kenton, "Edna Kenton Says . . .," 17.
22. See Paul M. Buhle, "Debsian Socialism and the 'New Immigrants,' " in William L. O'Neill, ed., *Insights and Parallels: Problems and Issues in American Social History* (Minneapolis, 1973), 266–76.
23. See Richard Hotstetter, *The Italian Socialist Movement*, I (Princeton, N.J., 1958), and Rudolph J. Vecoli, "*Contadini* in Chicago," in Herbert Gutman and Gregory Kealey, eds., *Many Pasts*, II (Englewood Cliffs, N.J., 1973).
24. Rudolph J. Vecoli, "Italian-American Workers, 1880–1920: *Padrone* Slaves or Primitive Rebels," unpublished essay, kindly lent to me by Professor Vecoli.
25. *Lavoratore Italiano* (Pittsburg, Kans.), Mar. 22, May 3, 10, June 12, 1912; the Italian-language section of the Socialist newspaper *Pittsburg* (Kans.) *Chronicle*, June, Oct., 1915; *Lotta de Classe* (New York), Feb. 3, 10, May 18, Nov. 16, 1912; Edwin Fenton, "Immigrants and Unions: A Case Study of Italians and American Labor, 1870–1920" (Ph.D. dissertation, Harvard University, 1957), 448–90, 527. See also *Il Lavoro* (New York), Dec. 15, 1917, May 25, Sept. 7, 1918, Feb. 1, 1919, Apr. 14, 1920.
26. See, for instance, the formation of theatrical circles, study groups, and *casa proletaire* in Pawtucket, Providence, and Westerly, R.I. as reported in *Cronoca Sovversiva* (Barre, Vt.), July 13, 1912, May 29, 1915, January 20, 1917; *Il Proletario* (New York), Mar. 1, Dec. 7, 1912; *La Question Social* (Paterson, N.J.), Dec. 20, 1914. Commented on in Paul M. Buhle, "Italian-American Radicals and the Labor Movement, 1905–1930," *Radical History Review*, 17 (Spring, 1978), 121–52.
27. *Lavoratore Italiano*, Mar. 1, 1907; *Il Proletario*, May 1, 1907; *Ragione Nuova* (Providence, R.I.), May 31, 1909; *La Fiaccola* (Buffalo), Aug. 20, 1910.
28. *La Fiaccola*, July 30, Dec. 25, 1909; *Il Proletario*, May 1, 1907, June 5, 1908, Apr. 25, 1909, Apr. 19, 1913; *Parola dei Socialisti* (Chicago), July 11, 1909, May 1, 1911; *Lavoratore Italiano*, Mar. 1, 1907; *Cronoca Sovversiva*, Nov. 20, 1909; *L'Avanti* (Chicago), Mar. 1, 1919, *Chicago Foreign Language Press Survey*. On the family, see *La Fiaccola*, Sept. 4, 1909, Apr. 9, June 11, Aug. 20, Oct. 29, Nov. 12, 1910, Jan. 14, 1911; also *La Commune* (Philadelphia), Sept., 1913; commented on extensively in Virginia Yans-McLaughlin, "Like the Fingers of the Hand: The Family and Community Life of First-Generation Italian-Americans in Buffalo, New York" (Ph.D. dissertation, State University of New

York–Buffalo, 1977), 391–404. See also Judith E. Smith, "Our Own Kind: Family and Community Networks in Providence," *Radical History Review*, 17 (Spring, 1978), 99–120, and Buhle, "Italian-American Radicals."

29. Irving Howe, *World of Our Fathers* (New York, 1976), Chs. VI, VIII; Louis Harap, *The Image of Jews in American Literature* (Philadelphia, 1974), 488; *Jewish Daily Forward* (New York), Sept. 11, 14, 1915.

30. A. S. Sachs, *Di Geshikhte fun Arbeiter Ring, 1892–1925*, II (Yiddish—New York, 1925), 505–7, 607, 809–10.

31. Joseph Stipanovich, "Immigrant Workers and Immigrant Intellectuals in Progressive America: A History of the Yugoslav Socialist Federation, 1900–1918" (Ph.D. dissertation, University of Minnesota, 1978), Preface; *Proletarec*, Mar. 10, 31, 1908; *Radnicka Straza*, Mar. 10, 1915, Apr. 19, 1916, Oct. 31, 1917, *Chicago Foreign Language Press Survey*.

32. The best case study is Maria Woroby, "Ukrainian Radicals and Women," *Cultural Correspondence*, 6–7 (Spring, 1978), 50–56.

33. *Naujienos*, March 29, 1916, *Chicago Foreign Language Press Survey*.

34. See A. William Hoglund, "Breaking with Religious Tradition: Finnish Immigrant Workers and the Church, 1890–1915," in *For the Common Good* (Superior, Wis., 1977), 23–64; Hilja J. Karvonen, "Three Proponents of Woman's Rights in the American Labor Movement from 1910 to 1930: Selma Jokela McCone, Naiji Nurmi and Helmi Mattson," in *For the Common Good*, 196–97.

35. Carl Ross, *The Finn Factor in American Labor, Culture and Society* (New York Mills, Minn., 1977), 26–35.

36. Karvonen, "Three Proponents," 198–200. See also the essays in the special sixty-fifth anniversary issue of *Naisten Viiri* (Superior, Wis.), successor to *Toveritar*, July 9, 1976, and quotations from "Feminism versus Socialist Work for Women," describing the commentary hostile toward feminism by *Toveritar's* third editor, Lydia Gritchef.

37. *Naisten Viiri*, July 9, 1976; Karvonen, "Three Proponents," 200–206.

38. Karvonen, "Three Proponents," 208–14; *Naisten Virri*, July 9, 1976. See also Paul George Hummasti, *Finnish Radicals in Astoria, Oregon, 1904–1940: A Study in Immigrant Socialism* (New York, 1979), 49–55.

39. *New York Call*, Jan. 20, 24, 1911.

40. Reported by Anna Burgess in *ibid.*, July 16, 1911. A similar disagreement developed within the New York local, when Louise Kneeland donated a large sum to be held in reserve for women's propaganda, as reported in *ibid.*, Jan. 21, 1912. The dispute over the money, between the women's committee and the local, may be traced in correspondence dated Feb. through Apr., 1914, in the New York Socialist Party Local Papers, Tamiment Library, New York University.

41. Barnett Braverman in *New York Call*, May 9, 1913.

42. Lewis was quoted in the Socialist party's *Official Bulletin* (Chicago), Nov., Sept.-Oct., 1911. For discussion of women's dues, see the Socialist party's *Weekly Bulletin*, May 8, 1909, and *Official Bulletin*, May, 1909.

43. *New York Call*, May 24, July 5, 1914. Schonberg reported that she estimated a membership of 1,618 women in seventy-eight locals, compared to 12,338 men in the state of New York.

44. Mari Jo Buhle, "*Socialist Woman/Progressive Woman/Coming Nation*," in *The Radical Press in the United States, 1880–1960*, 2 vols. (Westport, Conn., 1974), II, 442–49.

45. "National Committee Convention," *Coming Nation*, n.s., 1 (May-June, 1914), 10.
46. *American Socialist* (Chicago), Jan. 9, 1915.
47. WNC's plans for renovation were announced in the *American Socialist*, Jan. 30, 1915. Local Socialists' suggestions were published in the *New York Call*, Apr. 5, May 9, 12, 1915.
48. Allen W. Ricker, quoted in the *New York Call*, May 31, 1915. On the official polling of the membership, see "Report of the Woman's National Committee," Majority Report and Minority Report, Socialist Party National Committee Session of May, 1915, Socialist Party of America Papers, Perkins Library, Duke University. For contemporary reactions, see *New York Call*, May 15–31, 1915.
49. O'Hare's comments appeared in *New York Call*, June 7, 1915. Anita Block published a profusion of letters in the "Woman's Sphere" column, all issuing important statements on women's status in the Socialist movement; see *ibid.*, May and June, 1915.
50. *American Socialist*, July 10, 1915.
51. *Ibid.*
52. See Cook County Socialist Party Executive Committee Minutes, 1914–16, University of Illinois–Chicago Circle; *Labor Action* (Providence, R.I.), May 18, 1913; *Party Builder* (Chicago), Aug. 9, 1913; *American Socialist*, Aug. 15, 1914.
53. *Official Bulletin*, Sept.-Oct., 1911; *Party Builder*, July 5, Aug. 30, Oct. 18, 1913.
54. *Constructive Socialist* (Alva, Okla.), Apr. 17, 1912; *Montana Socialist* (Butte), May 4, 1913.
55. *Official Bulletin*, May, 1911; Winnie Branstetter to National Executive Committee, Sept. 3, 1914, Socialist Party Papers, Milwaukee County Historical Society; *New York Call*, Sept. 26, 1914; *American Socialist*, Oct. 17, 1914, Jan. 2, 1915; *New York Call*, Jan. 6, 1915; *Workers' Chronicle* (Pittsburg, Kans.), Mar. 10, 1916; *Appeal to Reason*, Nov. 27, 1915; *New York Call*, Oct. 18, 1914.
56. *Oakland* (Calif.) *World*, Oct. 30, 1915; *New York Call*, Aug. 30, 1914.
57. For a striking Socialist literary depiction of civilization's demise, see George Allen England's *Darkness and Dawn* (Westport, Conn., 1976 ed.), originally serialized in *Munsey's Magazine*. *New York Call*, Jan. 17, 20, May 1, June 17, July 2, 1916, Feb. 23, 25, Apr. 2, 6, May 7, 1917. See also documents on the Woman's Peace party of New York, in the R. P. Phelps Stokes Papers, Yale University Library.
58. On the character of the defections, see James Weinstein, *The Decline of Socialism in America, 1912–1925* (New York, 1967), and Garin Burbank, "The Disruption and Decline of the Oklahoma Socialist Party," *Journal of American Studies*, 7 (Aug., 1973), 133–52.
59. *Advance* (New York), Aug. 2, 1918; *New York Call*, Mar. 23, 1917; *New Age* (Buffalo), Mar. 9, 1918; *Schenectady Citizen*, Aug. 9, 1918; Cook County Executive Committee Minutes, May 17, Oct. 18, 1918.
60. *Socialist News* (Cleveland), Oct. 5, 1918; Minutes of Joint Conference of National Executive Committee and Secretaries, Aug. 10–12, 1918, Chicago, in Socialist Party of America Papers, Duke University; *New York Call*, Aug. 11, 18, Sept. 8, 1918.

Heritage Lost and Regained

"1919 will be known," wrote a correspondent to the women's column of the *Schenectady Citizen*, "as the fatal year to all the illusions by which mankind has been held in bondage."[1] If not that, 1919 did mark the close of a distinct era in the history of American radicalism. Not just faith in the efficacy of political education, but confidence in an eventual triumph—the premises upon which the Socialist movement had been based—faded beyond recognition. The Russian Revolution, the great wave of industrial conflicts in the United States, and the infamous red scare further aided the dismantling of the Socialist movement, such that a calamitous split left two small, warring Communist organizations and a Socialist party reduced to a shadow of its former self. The women's movement suffered a similar fate. It lost both the militancy and the verve that had drawn to it large and diverse sectors of American women, including those from radical movements. The newly created League of Women Voters never gained the political impetus the suffrage societies had enjoyed even during their years of doldrum. The discussions of a proposed Equal Rights Amendment to the Constitution divided longtime activists into hostile camps. And Feminism, once a dynamic force, became narrowly relegated to the individualistic aspirations of professional women. As a break in tradition closed the door to the past, the memory of the Socialist women's movement also faded from view.

This dramatic disjuncture had manifold implications for radical women in the period after 1919. The Socialist veterans, defeated and weary, avoided reflection save for the preservation of sentimental memories of a lost idealistic youth. While union drives and the survival of scattered Socialist institutions kept alive the spirits of some older male leaders and oftentimes translated into stirring memoirs, their female contemporaries rarely commented on the glory of their earlier accomplishments. Nor did the generation of radical women of the 1920s and 1930s preserve the memory of past struggles. In and around the Communist party they shared the prevailing leftist opprobrium toward the entire "reformist" legacy of the Socialist movement, most emphatically including the women's sector and its close relationships with "bourgeois" Feminists.

Once prominent Socialist women spent their remaining years as political ghosts. Some nurtured a sense of purpose, although they lacked the familiar institutional backing. Ida Crouch Hazlett, Caroline Lowe, Lena Morrow Lewis, and Anita Block continued to campaign for the Socialist party during the 1920s. Kate Richards O'Hare found a new dedication; after her imprisonment for anti-war activities, she became an avid prison reformer and senior spiritual advisor to the radical Commonwealth College in Mena, Arkansas. Other women drifted away from political involvements. Theresa Malkiel shifted easily to adult education, while Meta Stern became a reader for the New York Theatre Guild and a local charity activist. Most settled into a well-deserved retirement. Nellie Zeh turned to chicken farming as a means of support and outlet for her remarkable energy; Josephine Conger-Kaneko moved to rural Indiana, where she cared for her aged mother; Luella Roberts Krehbiel followed her actress daughter to Paris and lived the rest of her life abroad. For these as for so many, from turncoat May Wood Simons to loyalist Anna Maley, who died in middle life, the story had simply drawn to a close. Only Meta Stern left a marked trail in an autobiography, *Dear Remembered World* (1947), published a year before her death, but she confined her reminiscences of the Socialist movement to her childhood. Even Lena Morrow Lewis, who spent the last years of her life organizing the library of the Rand School, an institutional remnant of the Socialist past, did not take the opportunity to record her own reflections upon a movement that had sustained her since early adulthood.[2]

The survivors who moved into the Communist camp shed their Socialist past as if it had never existed. Elizabeth Gurley Flynn, always on the fringe of the Socialist party and distant from its women's sector, became the foremost Communist woman leader. Ella Reeve Bloor, who had once urged a "popular front" between the Socialist party and mainstream woman suffrage societies, became enshrined as patron saint of the Communists' own Popular Front, "Mother Bloor" to the next generation. Her children grown, Clara Lemlich Shavelson re-emerged as a living legend of an earlier class struggle. An independent and politically confident widow, Meta Berger also made a brief comeback in the 1930s, toured the Soviet Union, and blessed the Popular Front. Juliet Stuart Poyntz became a foremost Communist trade union leader during the 1920s, but disappeared mysteriously early in the next decade, reputedly spirited away by the Comintern. Thousands of Jewish, Finnish, and Slav women made the transition more quietly; they served the new movement as they had served the old, in strike support activities and in the ever-sustaining web of fraternal institutions. Only Finnish women, geographically and culturally isolated, could mark a straight line between the activities before 1919 and those that followed.[3]

The disjuncture with the past is revealed most clearly in the personage of Rose Pastor Stokes, the Communist image of revolutionary womanhood. Stokes emerged from her origins in the Socialist party as a rare woman leader in the upper echelon of the Communist party in the 1920s. In so doing, she personally obliterated her former stance as a prominent supporter of the Socialist party's women's sector and, indeed, her rebellious participation in the Feminist circle of Heterodoxy in the 1910s and martyrdom for the early birth control movement.

Born to impoverished Jewish parents in Russian Poland in 1879, Rose Pastor immigrated to the United States as a young child. Settling in Cleveland, she helped support her six younger brothers and sisters by working in a cigar factory. In 1903 she moved to New York City to accept an editorial post on a Yiddish newspaper and began to drift into reform circles. In the rarefied atmosphere around the settlement houses she met and betrothed a genteel reformer, the millionaire J. G. Phelps Stokes. Suddenly Rose Pastor Stokes became "the Cinderella of the Sweatshops," a favorite subject of tabloid newspaper copy. In 1906 she and her husband made headlines for a second time by simultaneously joining the Socialist party. As a Socialist she brushed shoulders with international celebrities like Maxim Gorki, conducted agitation for the Inter-Collegiate Socialist Society with Jack London and Upton Sinclair, and even became an avant-garde playwright and translator of the beloved Yiddish poet Morris Rosenfeld. Rose Pastor Stokes had gloriously crossed the bridge from her immigrant, working-class past to the bright world of radical chic and retained her Socialist dedication throughout.[4]

Rose Pastor Stokes played an important part in the women's strikes, although she served as a volunteer for the Socialist women's organizing drive and WTUL functionary rather than trade unionist herself. She spoke frequently to audiences of garment workers during the great shirtwaist makers' strike of 1909–10, and joined campaigns for hotel workers, dressmakers, and other New York unionists. She played a major role in the legal defense campaigns, especially following the unsuccessful Paterson strike of 1913. Her charismatic presence—"rippling brown hair," in the words of an admiring Socialist journalist, and eyes that reputedly shone with the intensity of a Joan of Arc—won the attention of crowds fascinated by her oratory and fairy-tale life.[5]

At the close of the war Rose Pastor Stokes found in Bolshevism an even more consuming dedication. Over the next decade she endured an almost unending persecution for her beliefs. Indicted under the Espionage Act in 1918 for her anti-war statements, put on trial with Eugene Debs, she was prosecuted again in 1922 for participating in the formation of the Communist party. Unswayed, she acted as organizer for the new Workers party (Communist), and served as a delegate to the Comintern's fourth congress, where she became a reporter for the pathbreaking Negro Commission. Along with Juliet Stuart Poyntz, New York union leader Rose Wortis, and a very few other women, Stokes scaled the largely male chain of command to become a Communist leader in her own right.[6]

Stokes had little compunction about attacking any semblance of gender solidarity within the Communist movement. In a 1922 interview she affirmed her indifference to the "purely feminist" and lavished praise instead upon female proletarians who united with "strength and courage in the battle for workers' control of America." She later advised the Comintern to sponsor "Committees of Women" but solely as mechanisms to spread propaganda among working-class women. She denied flatly that there was a "separate woman's problem" and aimed only to "awaken and win to the cause of Communism the masses of proletarian women," for the revolution could not be won without their participation.[7]

Stokes served the Communist movement well. She acted as a street leader for a multitude of Communist causes, her innate enthusiasm caricatured by a critic who described Stokes as a person who could proclaim a revolution for every season. She divorced J. G. Phelps Stokes in 1925, refused to ask for alimony or a financial settlement, and married a promising writer soon to be known as the fiercest axe-wielding polemicist in the Left. She slowed her pace only as her health gave way. Impoverished but a hero to the end, she died in 1933 of breast cancer, which her comrades claimed resulted from a blow of a police officer's club.[8]

From the Communist standpoint the only tragedy in Rose Pastor Stokes's remarkable life was her untimely illness and early death. She seemed to prove that woman could cooperate with man, revolutionary to revolutionary, by casting aside all artificial distinctions. Younger, less prestigious Communist women might experience the situation differently, for the male leadership tended to isolate women as individuals save at the base, upgrade the importance of leaders' wives or companions, but practically shut off the influential positions to women activists. Rose Pastor Stokes did not publicly address this aspect of the movement.[9]

The sisterhood forged earlier by Socialist women did not persist within the Communist movement, and the woman question re-emerged as if it possessed no historic roots in the United States. Neither Elizabeth Cady Stanton nor Frances Willard but Lenin stood as the prophet of women's emancipation; at his side was Clara Zetkin and behind them the familiar trio of Marx, Engels, and Lewis Henry Morgan. Communists cursorily dismissed the contributions of the women's movement as mere expressions of middle-class interest; they rarely referred to the heated discussions carried on by Socialists over the previous fifty years. They refuted the importance of the campaigns for women's emancipation that had pulled Socialists into many activities. Communists regarded the hard-won acquisition of woman suffrage as a minor political advance; questions of sexual liberation they viewed as especially venial, perhaps a plot to shatter the working-class family. Only unequivocally class-conscious events like "women's strikes" remained as major sources of inspiration.

The writings of Lenin thus blessed special work among women, and the International Woman's Secretariat in Moscow directed the formation of the American party's National Woman's Commission formed in 1922. In turn the commission created a United Council of Working Class Women (or Wives), and formed local affiliates such as the Mothers' League of Boston and the Detroit Proletarian Women. Communists even dated the founding of International Woman's Day to 1913 when Bolshevik women first instituted celebrations. And International Woman's Day took on the coloration of a supremely proletarian holiday, with a special section of the party newspaper devoted to the "woman worker" and to the "Mothers of the Proletariat."[10]

Under the tutelage of the Third International, American Communists addressed women (akin to blacks and the foreign-born) as an oppressed sector of the working class. The "vast and fertile . . . mature yet one might say, virgin field for our work," as a correspondent to the Comintern bulletin *Imprecorr* phrased it, had to be cultivated by mobilizing women around economic and political issues, by exerting influence upon existing community and labor organizations, and by creating a leadership cadre attuned to the directives of the party and the needs of the constituency. The Women Workers Progressive League of Cleveland, for example, convened in 1927 "to start work among the working class women in that city, against militarism in the schools, imperialist wars, and for [the] fight against monopolies, against child labor, for the promotion of cooperatives and of trade unionism among women." The *Woman Worker*, an agitational sheet published first by the New York State party and later by the National Woman's Commission, had the same tenor. The message of mobilization seemed written on a blank slate to women who felt commonality with each other only as members of a class and component of the proletarian family.[11]

Because of this stand, Communists salvaged traditions only among the least integrated sectors of the old Socialist movement: the foreign-language federations and the new unions of the 1910s. The early Communist movement drew heavily upon those immigrant groups who had known the lash of Russian czarism and had celebrated the Revolution as a national liberation, no less a promise of Socialism. Lithuanians, Hungarians, Ukrainians, and other groups built upon the fraternal beginnings of the Socialist years in which women had assumed important roles in the fraternal network. Communist Jews and Finns seized the initiative within their already impressive institutions and by dint of energy and commitment directed schools, cooperatives, theaters, and other projects. So, too, especially for the Jewish community, Communist women in the needle trades won considerable respect from the rank-and-file. Others contributed to the desperate strikes against the reduction of wages in the "sick" industries of textiles and coal, to the ardent defense of Sacco and Vanzetti, and to the funds to aid the impoverished and isolated Soviet Union.[12]

Even in the mid-1930s, when the Communist party successfully broadened its program to include "mass work" among women, leaders drew no observable lessons from the agitations conducted earlier by Socialists. Another generation of radical women emerged as labor activists, neighborhood leaders, journalists, and functionaries in the fraternal sector. They occasionally cooperated with middle-class women's groups in struggles for economic and political opportunities. They helped lead housewives in consumer boycotts and union support work, rent strikes, peace campaigns, assaults on racism and fascism. At their peak during World War II, with Communist men at the front and women in the factories, women reached a near numerical parity in the maximum party membership of 80,000. But all this had been achieved within sharp limits. Never did the Communist women's sector gain its own sources of initiative, as much as the Woman's National Committee had claimed within the Socialist party, nor its own independent voice like the *Progressive Woman*, nor its own distinct sensibility. Rarely did any leader convene a public discussion of discrimination within the party ranks, and never did the woman question become a major issue.[13]

In fairness to the Communist movement, it must be admitted that those women who clung to the shrunken Socialist party did no better as a group. Male prerogatives, once challenged, now ruled undisputed again. Half-hearted attempts to reorganize a women's committee suffered repeated defeat. A correspondent to the national office lamented in 1929, "It is very plain that our present plan of enlisting women Socialists . . . is a failure. There are a few women who take pleasure in working in the party locals. They are but few."[14] The survivors of the old days said little; they were unable to explain to young men and women or to themselves the significance of a tradition so badly eroded.

Historical movements are rarely judged solely in the light they cast themselves. During their heyday before World War I, Socialist women believed they summed up a grand historical tradition dating at least to the abolitionist and woman's rights movements and for that reason recorded their own activities as a continuation of earlier struggles. For the next half-century, however, their evidence lay dormant, as a subsequent movement re-evaluated Socialists' accomplishments and failings according to new standards. Only in the 1960s did their legacy have perceived historical significance. Confounded by similar questions about women's position within male-dominated movements, yet another generation of radical women began to return the vanished travelers from obscurity and place them closer to the center of a distinct heritage.

The simultaneous development of the New Left and the women's liberation movement exposed lines of tension buried since 1919. The New Left leadership brushed aside Communist doctrines that had subordinated women's issues: the working class in itself no longer seemed the revolutionary entity; the traditionally male-dominated institutions, trade unions and disciplined leftist parties, appeared unlikely vehicles for mass mobilization. Like the civil rights movement from which it had grown, the New Left sought instead to rally "oppressed peoples" of ghetto slums and rural poverty. As the student cadre grew into a mass campus movement and attention shifted toward the Vietnam War and youth, the old Marxist doctrines fell into exhaustion.

The reassertion of the woman question remained a task for women themselves, for renewed discussions of women's oppression revealed the unwillingness of the male leadership to respond to this issue. The convention of Students for a Democratic Society (SDS) in 1968, for instance, endorsed a series of resolutions including equal pay for equal work, a modest act tantamount to Socialists' endorsement of woman suffrage nearly seventy years before. A larger statement on women's liberation comparable to that demanded for Third World peoples stirred, however, a raucous denunciation similar to what Socialist women had endured when they dared to compare women's oppression with that of the proletariat. Six months later SDS leaders affirmed the centrality of women's liberation to "a socialist revolution in this country." But by December, 1968, radical women were openly attacking "male supremacy" within the movement and beginning to set their own priorities. [15]

Encouraged by this new round of discussion and unbounded by theoretical orthodoxy, numbers of women had already phrased serious questions about the relationship of sex and class oppression. On a practical level they instinctively took up the cause of wage-earning women and sought to bring them into the predominantly middle-class ranks of the movement. Meanwhile, the theoretically minded pored over the classic texts of Marx and Engels and drew fresh insights with the help of Simone de Beauvoir and Herbert Marcuse. Of the younger authors, British socialist Juliet Mitchell, in an essay published in 1966 which later served as the foundation for her book *Women: The Longest Revolution* (1971), offered an especially important contribution. Mitchell presented a structuralist framework to discuss women's status and to predict the timing of their struggle for liberation. Although she employed Marxist terminology, Mitchell issued a strong challenge to orthodox faith. She demonstrated how the question of women's oppression had been extrinsic to classical Socialist theory, and she pinpointed its major shortcomings, what she termed an exaggerated emphasis on economic determinism to the exclusion of other factors like sexuality and biological reproduction.

The presence of a mainstream woman's rights movement also proved significant as its 1910 counterpart to Socialist women. Most New Left women were distanced by age as well as by politics from the National Organization of Women (NOW). But the latter's best-selling manifesto, founder Betty Friedan's *The Feminine Mystique* (1963), surely helped radical women articulate the grievances middle-class women shared against the intellectual and psychological by-products of sex discrimination. And if radical women scorned NOW's goal of integration into the capitalist system, they drew legitimacy from an angry discussion of women's status in American society that spread across the campuses into community life, business, and government. The presence of a well-organized "bourgeois" women's movement also evoked familiar charges from opponents that feminism was the philosophy of "privileged" women and extraneous to the struggles of "genuinely" oppressed peoples. Much like their Socialist forefunners, radical women of the 1960s painfully sorted out the issues and tried to delineate a firm position on their relationship with mainstream women's groups.

Radical women also heatedly discussed their position within the male-dominated New Left organizations. In 1967 they asked if women's liberation should function as a caucus or as an independent movement. This same year a handful of former SDS activists launched a newsletter optimistically entitled *Voice of the Women's Liberation Movement.* By 1968, several groups in Chicago and New York broke with SDS to form their own organizations, while others stayed to carry on the fight for recognition within the student, anti-war, and black power movements. As in the first decade of the century, relationships between these two sectors of radical women became tense and sometimes verged upon open confrontation. By the end of the decade women's liberation comprised a variety of autonomous organizations and sponsored its own magazine, *Women: A Journal of Liberation,* that took up the task, one might say, where the *Progressive Woman* had left off fifty-five years earlier. A separate women's movement with its own goals, tactics, and vocabulary had clearly emerged, but the larger question of the relationship between women's emancipation and the revolutionary struggle grew yet more pressing. What the new generation called "Socialist Feminism" had become a major political issue.

The events of the late 1960s served as the major inspiration for this history of radical antecedents. Other historians had previously recorded the contributions of individual women or had discussed briefly Socialists' confrontation with the woman question; none, however, had been motivated to make the study of Socialist women's collective activities a primary focus. The rise of the women's liberation movement clearly prompted my "discovery" of a larger story yet to be told. Anita Block's "Woman's Sphere" column in the *New York Call,* the proceedings of the Socialist party conventions, and most of all Josephine Conger-Kaneko's *Progressive Woman* (all gathering dust on the library shelves) indicated the existence of a vital Socialist women's movement in the first decades of the twentieth century. Set against the dramatic developments within the New Left, the narrative contours of this history soon began to emerge from the primary sources, and the initial plans for a full-length study took shape.[16]

The mainspring of this study is what historians in the late 1960s called "a search for a usable past." By this phrase they did not mean to imply that history supplies "answers" to present-day questions or "lessons" in a narrow, didactic fashion. Rather, this generation of scholars aspired to locate in tradition a claim to legitimacy and, equally important, self-understanding.

At the turn of the century Socialist women who enjoyed the benefits of tradition established a distinctive presence within their historical epoch. They found shelter from the loneliness of isolation and eccentricity; they achieved subjectivity. In telling their story, I hope to impart that tradition to another generation, and to place within the historical mainstream their undying faith in "the good time coming."

NOTES

1. Lucia N. Oliviere in *Schenectady Citizen*, Dec. 27, 1919.
2. Ida Crouch Hazlett died in 1941; an obituary appeared in the *New Leader* (New York), May 10, 1941. Lena Morrow Lewis resigned from the Socialist party in 1936 but soon thereafter joined the Social Democratic Federation of New York City. She died in 1950. Her papers and scrapbooks at Tamiment Library, New York University, detail her post-1919 activities. Caroline Lowe was admitted to the bar in 1918 and practiced law in Girard, Kans., until her death in 1933; an obituary appeared in the *Girard (Kans.) Press*, May 11, 1933. Anita Block worked for the *New York Call* until it folded in 1923; she became a reader for the New York Theater Guild. She died in 1967; an obituary appeared in the *New York Times*, Dec. 13, 1967. Kate Richards O'Hare died in 1948. David A. Shannon provides a summary of her post-1919 activities in *Notable American Women*, ed. Edward T. James, Janet Wilson James, and Paul S. Boyer, 3 vols. (Cambridge, Mass., 1971), I, 417–20. Theresa Malkiel died in 1948; an obituary appeared in the *New York Times*, Nov. 18, 1948. Meta Stern's obituary appeared in the *New York Times*, Mar. 26, 1948. The post-1919 activities of Nellie Zeh and Josephine Conger-Kaneko are difficult to trace. References to their retirements were found in May Walden Kerr Papers, Box VI, Newberry Library, Chicago. Information of Luella Roberts Krehbiel was provided by Neil Basen, who corresponded with Krehbiel's niece. Krehbiel died in 1933. Anna A. Maley, a victim of the flu epidemic, died in 1918; an obituary appeared in the *Minneapolis Tribune*, Nov. 25, 1918, which was kindly secured by Colette Hyman. May Wood Simons died in 1948. For details of her post-1919 activity, see Kent and Gretchen Kreuter, *An American Dissenter: The Life of Algie Martin Simons, 1870–1950* (Lexington, Ky., 1969), Chs. 9 and 10.
3. Both Gurley Flynn and Bloor left reminiscences of their years in the pre-1919 leftist movements. Elizabeth Gurley Flynn's *The Rebel Girl: An Autobiography* (New York, 1973), first published in 1955, covers her life until 1926 and focuses on her activities in the Industrial Workers of the World. Ella Reeve Bloor, *We Are Many: An Autobiography* (New York, 1940), is divided evenly between her Socialist and Communist years. Paula Scheier, "Clara Lemlich Shavelson: 50 Years on Labor's Front Line," *Jewish Life*, 8 (Nov., 1954), 7–11, discusses Shavelson's activities in the post-1919 period. Meta Berger discusses her latter radical involvements in her unpublished autobiography, Meta Berger Papers, State Historical Society of Wisconsin. Benjamin Stolberg, *Tailor's Progress* (Garden City, N.Y., 1944), 286, alleges Poyntz's mysterious disappearance.
4. Biographical details are available in David A. Shannon's essay in *Notable American Women*, III, 284–86, and Cecyle S. Neidle, *America's Immigrant Women* (New York, 1975), 174–85. See also Stokes's unpublished autobiography, Rose Pastor Stokes Papers, Yale University Library. Stokes's major literary contribution

was a play, *The Woman Who Wouldn't* (New York, 1916). She also edited, along with Helen Frank, *Songs of Labor* (Boston, 1914), a translation of Rosenfeld's poetry.

5. "Rose Pastor Stokes," *Socialist Woman*, 1 (Oct., 1907), 2.
6. Theodore Draper, *Roots of American Communism* (New York, 1957), 193; *The Worker* (New York), Mar. 10, 1923.
7. *The Truth* (Duluth, Minn.), June 23, 1922. An unpublished essay, "Women's Committee," by Rose Pastor Stokes is among her papers at Yale University Library.
8. Samuel Schmalhausen, "These Tragic Comedians," *Modern Quarterly*, 4 (Nov., 1927–Feb., 1928), 220. An obituary by Marguerite Young appeared in the *New Masses*, 8 (June, 1933), 22–23.
9. This situation is vividly portrayed by Vera Buch Weisbord, *A Radical Life* (Bloomington, Ind., 1944), Chs. III-VII.
10. "Woman and the Communist International, Theses Adopted at the Third Congress," *The Communist*, 1 (Nov., 1921), 12–15; N. Lenin, "The Emancipation of Women," reprinted in *The Forge* (Seattle), May 1, 1920; *The Worker*, Mar. 11, 1922.
11. *International Press Correspondence* (*Imprecorr*—the English-language edition published in New York and London), July 6, 1927; see also July 22, May 26, 1926. *The Worker*, Mar. 11, 1922, Woman's Day issue, conveys most accurately the earliest public enunciation of this policy. See also Elsa Jane Dixler, "The Woman Question: Women and the American Communist Party, 1921–1941" (Ph.D. dissertation, Yale University, 1974).
12. See, for example, Al Levine's interview with Fanny Hechtman in *Daily World* (New York), Sept. 28, 1979. *Naisten Viiri* (Superior, Wis.), anniversary issue, July 9, 1976, recounts the transition of the Finnish sector. *Radnick* (Chicago), Aug. 28, 1923, and Sept. 29, 1925, *Chicago Foreign Press Survey*, suggests Communists' policies toward women in one language group.
13. Peggy Dennis, *The Autobiography of an American Communist: A Personal View of a Political Life, 1924–1975* (Westport, Conn., 1977), offers an insightful view of one woman's activities in the 1930s and after. An interview with former International Workers' Order official Nina Goldstein-Wyrob, by Paul M. Buhle in Miami Beach, Fla., Oct., 1978, offers a unique glimpse of women's activities in the fraternal sector; tape recording deposited in the Oral History of the American Left, Tamiment Library, New York University. See also Robert Shaffer, "Women and the Communist Party, USA, 1930–1940," *Socialist Review*, 45 (May-June, 1979), 73–118. The best example of the party perspective on the woman question, especially the Soviet model, is Grace Hutchins, *Women Who Work* (New York, 1934).
14. Report signed by O. C. Kennedy, 1929, in Women and Children File, Socialist Party of America Papers, Perkins Library, Duke University.
15. For an excellent discussion of women's liberation within the New Left, see Sara Evans, *Personal Politics: The Roots of Women's Liberation in the Civil Rights Movement and the New Left* (New York, 1979), Chs. 6–9. For an insightful collection of documents from the early years, see Edith Hoshino Altbach, ed., *From Feminism to Liberation* (Cambridge, Mass., 1980).
16. Written as a seminar paper in graduate school at the University of Wisconsin, "Women and the Socialist Party, 1901–1914," appeared in *Radical America*, 4 (Feb., 1970), 36–55.

Index

Abbott, Wenonah Stevens, 136–37, 139, 151
Abolitionism, 1, 119, 161
ACWA. *See* Amalgamated Clothing Workers of America
Addams, Jane, 189, 228
Adler, Otto, 271
Advance, 204–5
AFL. *See* American Federation of Labor
Alaska Labor News, 165
Alaska Labor Union, 165
Albany, N.Y., 234
Alcott, Louisa May, 50
Allegemeine-Kranken und Sterbe-Kasse, 124–25
Allegheny City, Pa., 7
Allen, Carrie, 192
Amalgamated Clothing Workers of America (ACWA), 196, 204–5
American Federation of Labor (AFL), 71–73, 187, 201, 203
"American" sections (SLP), 20–24 *passim*; 73
American Socialist, 311
Anarchism, 46n63
Anderson, Ind., 112
Anderson, Sherwood, 262
Anneke, Mathilde, 2
Anthony, Susan B.: and Working Women's Society, 54; votes illegally, 61; and the International Council of Women (1888), 66, 67; and Republican party, 68; as mother figure, 293; mentioned, 215, 216
Anti-socialist laws in Germany, 26
"*Appeal* Army," 114
Appeal to Reason, 104, 108, 113, 125, 146, 148, 231, 307, 312
Appeal to the Young, An (Kropotkin), 288
Arbeiter Frauen und Mädchenbund, 34, 38
Arbeiterinnen Versammlung, 34
Arbeter Ring. See Workman's Circle
Arme Teufel, Der, 261
Ashley, Jessie, 258, 276, 278
Association for the Advancement of Women, 3, 65, 76–77, 79

Astoria, Oreg., 303
Avery, Martha Moore, 73–74

Bachofen, Johann J., 250, 251
Baker, Estelle, 255
Ballou, Addie, 78, 141n16
Baltimore, Md., 7, 33, 38, 39, 184
Bar, Russia, 176
Baraboo, Wis., 166
Barnard College, 128
Barnes, J. Mahlon, 165
Barney, Mattie, 117
Barnum, Gertrude, 190
Barton, Clara, 50, 67
"Battle Hymn of the Republic" (Howe), 57
Beauvoir, Simone de, 324
Bebel, August: and *Die Frau und der Sozialismus*, 26–29 *passim*; popular imitators in German-American press, 29, 36; as theorist on woman question, 41, 42; origins of interest in woman question, 47 n70; influences on Socialist women, 180, 274; summarizes *Origins of the Family*, 250; criticized by DeLeon, 251; protests interpretation by *Jewish Daily Forward*, 300; mentioned, 128, 132, 160, 218
Beecher-Tilton Scandal, 61
Belknap, Mont., 118
Bell, Daniel, xviii
Bellamy, Edward, 75, 80, 81, 90, 182, 251
Bellamy Nationalism. *See* Nationalism, Bellamy
Bellanca, August, 205
Bellows, George, 262
Belmont, Alva, 192, 225
Berger, Meta: background and marriage, 129–31; work with NAWSA, 231, 232; joins NWP, 238; post-1919 activities, 319
Berger, Victor, 129–30
Bergson, Henri, 292
Berlin, Germany, 2, 26
Bernstein, Eduard, 29
Bible, 252
Birmingham, England, 71

Birth control campaigns, 249, 268–80
  passim
Birth Control Review, 278
Bismarck, Otto von, 13, 26
Blackwell, Alice Stone, 239
Blatch, Harriot Stanton, 190, 224–25, 239,
  245n80
Blavatsky, Helen P., 78
Block, Anita: on L. M. Lewis, 166; on
  household, 182; on New Morality, 262;
  and birth control campaign, 271, 272,
  273–74, 276, 278; post-1919 activities,
  319; mentioned, 325, 326n2
Bloomington, Ill., 33
Bloor, Ella Reeve, 319
Boffin's Bower, 79
Bogan, Louise, 265
Bohemian-Americans, 30, 185, 311
Bohemian Singing Society, 42
Bolles, Ellen M., 73
Bolshevism, 320
Bonds of Womanhood, The (Cott), xv
Boston, Mass.: and workingwomen's organi-
  zations (1860s), 54; women's clubs in
  Gilded Age, 57–60; WCTU in, 65;
  Socialist Labor party in, 73; Nationalist
  movement in, 77; Socialist women's club
  in, 118; women's garment unions in, 204;
  Socialists introduce suffrage bill in, 229
Boston Nationalist Club, 79, 80
Boudin, Louis, 181
"Bourgeois" suffragists. *See* Middle-class
  women
Bowery, New York city, 15
Boyce, Neith, 258
Branstetter, Winnie: elected to WNC
  (1908), 150; on women's organizations,
  152; woman suffrage activities, 216, 232;
  attacks *Progressive Woman*, 307; men-
  tioned, 310, 311
Brotherhood of Cooperative Common-
  wealth, 136
Brown, Corinne Stubbs: background and
  role in Illinois Woman's Alliance, 71–72;
  in Nationalist movement, 77; at Socialist
  unity conference (1901), 105; chairs
  women's meetings, 138, 149; mentioned,
  151
Brown, John, 42
Brownsville, Brooklyn, N.Y., 278
Bronx, N.Y., 233
Brooklyn, N.Y., 233, 234
Bruere, Mary, 258
Bruere, Robert, 258
Bryan, William Jennings, 91
Buffalo, N.Y., 7, 59

Bullard, Arthur, 258, 264–65
Bund für Mutterschutz und Sexuel Reform,
  270, 271
Burlington, Iowa, 7, 112
Butte, Mont., 239

Caesar's Column (Donnelly), 84
Cairns, Anna S., 81
California: Socialist Labor party women in,
  74; Nationalist movement in, 77–78;
  Socialist women's activities in, 118–20,
  135–40; Lewis's work in, 163; suffrage
  campaign of 1911, 230; Socialist peace
  activities in, 311–12
Calverton, Victor Francis, 262
Campbell, Helen, 90
Camp Unity, 206
Cape Cod, Mass., 258
Carlyle, Thomas, 114
Carnegie Hall, New York City, 200
Carpenter, Edward, 260–61
Cath, Minna, 302–3
Catt, Carrie Chapman, 215, 225, 236, 238
Centennial of 1876, 4
Centralia, Mo., 113
Central Labor Federation of New York, 73,
  177
Chandler, Lucinda, 138
Chicago, Ill.: German-American Socialist
  movement in, 6, 7, 21; German-American Socialist women's activities in, 21,
  32–33, 38, 39, 125; clothing industry in,
  30, 184, 185; M. Livermore's activity in,
  49; WCTU and woman's movement in,
  65; native-born women in Socialist Labor
  party in, 71–73; Nationalist movement
  in, 77; class lines in 1890s in, 91; Socialist women's activities in, 106, 121, 123,
  124, 136, 205, 227, 313; Jewish Socialist
  women's activities in, 124, 297, 299, 300;
  Nellie Zeh's agitation in, 132–33; garment strikes in, 194–96 *passim*; prostitution in, 254, 256; new immigrant
  Socialist women in, 299–302 *passim*;
  women's liberation groups in, 325
Chicago Daily Socialist: women's journalism in, 134; role in garment strike,
  195–96; crusades against prostitution,
  256; mentioned, 146, 147, 149, 166, 195
Chicagoer Arbeiter Zeitung, 29, 38
Chicago Federation of Labor, 195
Chicago Ladies' Branch, 134
Chicago Vice Commission, 256
Chicago Women's Club, 72
Child labor, 220, 322

Children, Socialist, 15, 32, 35, 202, 300, 304

Choirs, Socialist: *Männerchor*, 32; Bohemian Singing Society, 42; German Singing Society, 42; children's, 112, 123; in urban Socialist movement, 122

Christian Socialism, 50, 52, 70, 78, 81, 109, 115–16, 119, 120, 136, 154

Cincinnati, Ohio, 7, 30, 38

Circolo Femminile Socialisme, 299

Civil War; A. Lilienthal's activities during, 2; culmination of moral crusade, 4; as turning point for women, 50–51, 54

Class struggle: women and, 121, 122, 183–84, 240; Second International's position on, 123; in *Progressive Woman*, 148; WNC position on, 152; in relation to woman suffrage, 218; and sex hygiene, 273

Cleveland, Ohio, 59, 125, 205, 276, 320

Cleveland Citizen, 196

Clinton Hall, New York City, 186

Clothing industry: German-American Socialists and, 30, 38; in Chicago (1880s), 72; growth at turn of century, 184–85. *See also* Women's strikes (1909–13)

Club A, New York City, 258

Coffeyville, Kans., 115, 157

Colby, Clara, 117, 142*n*23

Cole, Elsie, 193

Cole, F. C. (Mrs.), 115

Cole, Josephine, 221

Colorado, 215, 275

Columbia, Mo., 114

Columbia University, 206

Coming Nation (Chicago), 307

Coming Nation (Girard), 108, 139, 166

Comintern, 319, 320, 321

Commonwealth College, 319

Communist Manifesto, The (Marx), 6, 9

Communist party: antecedents in German-American Socialist movement, 20; and women, 319–23 *passim*

Comrade, The, 118, 137, 262, 265, 269

Comrade Yetta (Bullard), 264

Comstock, Anthony, 273

Conger-Kaneko, Josephine: poem by, 104; in *Appeal to Reason*, 114–15 *passim*; on women's organizations, 147–48; complains against party, 151; on propaganda, 155; on 1910 party congress, 227; on *Progressive Woman*, 156, 255, 306–7; on abolition of WNC, 310; on World War I, 312; post-1919 activities, 319, 326*n*2; mentioned, 167, 303, 325

Congress, U.S., 30

Constitution, U.S., 68

Consumers' League, Socialist, 205

Conventions, Socialist party: unity conference in 1901, 105; in 1904, 138; in 1908, 149–50; in 1910, 154, 227; emergency, in 1917, 212

Cook, George Cram, 258

Cook County, Ill., 147

Cooperation. *See* Middle-class women

Cooperative Commonwealth, The (Gronlund), 24–25

Cooper Union, New York City, 186, 191

Cott, Nancy F., xv

Crane, Stephen, 263

Crittenton, Charles, 247

Croatian-Americans, 220, 301

Croly, Jane Cunningham, 56–57, 79

Cronoca Sovversiva, 275

Current Affairs Committee, 204

Dall, Caroline H., 55

Dante Alligheri Clubs, 299

Davis, Stuart, 262

Debs, Eugene V.: at St. Louis Socialist meeting (1897), 42; influence on Socialist women, 43, 108–10, 113; propaganda contributions, 155; woman suffrage activities of, 216, 230, 235; on woman question, 242*n*4; birth control activities of, 276, 278; in prison, 279

"Declaration of Purposes" (Populist), 88

DeLeon, Daniel, 177, 251

Delineator, 290

Dell, Floyd: on emancipated women, 266; defends Sangers, 276, 277; on New Morality, 282; on E. Key, 294; on feminine nature, 294; on Feminism, 295; mentioned, 258

Denmark, 270

Descent of Man (Darwin), 156

Detroit, Mich., 7, 21

Detroit Proletarian Women, 322

Dewey, John, 167

Diaz, Abby Morton, 58, 79

Dickens, Charles, 57

Dickenson, Anna, 50

Dietzgen, Joseph, 31

Diggs, Annie L., 83, 84, 88, 91

Disciples of Christ, 247

Discrimination within Socialist movement: San Francisco women protest, 137; against women leaders, 152; discussed in *New York Call*, 305; WNC refuses to recognize, 305–6; O'Hare charges, 308

Doctrine of spheres, xv, 8, 55, 161, 204–5, 267
Dodge, Mabel, 258, 266, 272
"Do-everything policy" (WCTU), 63, 112
Domesticity, 21, 27, 86, 87, 167–68. See also Home
Domestic service, 30, 35
Donnelly, Ignatius, 84, 90, 91, 108, 247, 248
Dorr, Rheta Childe, 190–258
Douai, Adolf: on the family, 8; as Socialist educator, 16, 32, 45n42; testifies at Congressional hearings (1882), 30; influence on Social Democratic Women's Federation, 127
Douglass, Frederick, 5, 67
Dreier, Mary, 191, 228
Dreiser, Theodore, 263
Dresden, Germany, 36
Driftwood, Okla., 311
Dubuque, Iowa, 112
Dues, women's, 147, 172n2
Dunham, Marion Howard: Socialist activity of, 112; on separate organizations, 137–38; background, 141n9; mentioned, 151
Dutcher, Elizabeth, 193
Dvorak, Robert, 195
Dynamic Sociology (Ward), 156

Eastman, Crystal, 258, 295
Eastman, Max, 258, 275, 276, 277, 282
Eddy, Mary Baker, 78
Education: in German-American Socialist movement, 16, 18, 32; in Women's Educational and Industrial Union, 58; in Populist movement, 86–87; in Socialist women's clubs, 111–12; WNC's role in, 154–60 passim; among Italian-American Socialist women, 299. See also Schools, Socialist
Edwards, Albert (pseud.). See Bullard, Arthur
Eight-hour movement, 33, 37, 70
Eleusinian mysteries, 82
Elizabeth, N.J., 127
Elk City, Kans., 115
Elliot, Maud Howe, 77
Ellis, Havelock, 259, 260, 271, 292
Emerson, Ralph Waldo, 114
Emery, Sarah, 83, 84, 88
Employments of Women (Penny), 55
Engels, Frederick: on Socialist Labor party in 1880s, 25–26; writes *Origins of the Family*, 250; cited by Socialists, 254, 270, 274; mentioned, 218, 321, 324

Englevale, Kans., 154
Equality League of Self-Supporting Women, 224
Equal Rights Amendment, 318
Erfurt, Germany, 125
Espionage Act, 320
Etten, Ida Van, 73
Ettor, Joseph, 299
Evansville, Ind., 7

Fabian Socialism, 118
Fales, Imogene, 79, 136–37
Fall River, Mass., 21, 22, 153, 202
Family: German-American Socialists' attitude toward, 8–10 passim; in *The Coöperative Commonwealth*, 24–25; E. Bellamy on, 99n99; and Socialist women, 109–17; F. Engels's interpretation of, 250–51; in birth control campaigns, 280; in E. Key's philosophy, 293; Italian-American Socialists on, 299
Family limitation. See Birth Control
Family Limitation (Sanger), 275
Family wage, 8
Farmers' Alliance. See Populism
Farmer's Wife, 88
Fellowship of the New Life, 260
Feminine Mystique, The (Friedan), 324
Feminism, 288, 290–97 passim, 318
Ferber, Edna, 263
Ferrer School, 258, 299
Finnish-Americans: join woman suffrage campaigns, 234; Socialist women's activity, 302–4; WNC's attitude toward, 311; in Communist party, 319, 322
Finnish-Socialist Federation, 303
First International. See International Workingmen's Association
First Principles (Spencer), 156
Florence Crittenden Mission and Home, 247
Flynn, Elizabeth Gurley: in Lawrence and Paterson strikes, 202–3; in birth control campaign, 276, 277, 278; in Communist party, 319; mentioned, xiii, 288
Foreign-language federations, 298, 322
Forerunner, The, 214
Formalism, 292
Fort Scott, Kans., 154
Forty-eighters, 1, 3
Forum, 290
Frances Willard on Socialism, 108, 170
Franco-Prussian War, 3
Fraternal organizations: among German-American Socialists, 15–17, 32–33, 40, 42; in Patrons of Husbandry, 82; in

Fraternal organizations (*cont.*)
  Socialist party, 107; among Jewish Social-
    ists, 300; in Communist party, 322–23,
    327n13
*Frau in der Vergangenheit, Gegenwart und
  Zukunft, Die* (Bebel), 28
Frau und der Sozialismus, Die (Bebel): on
  the woman question, 26–29 *passim*; in
  relation to *Looking Backward*, 76; in
  Socialist women's education, 157, 180; as
  popularized by Engels, 250; as interpreted
  by *Jewish Daily Forward*, 300
Frauenbünde, 31–40 *passim*
Frauenfrage, 25–31 *passim*, 41
Frauenkränzchen, 15
Frauensection, 17
Frauenvereine: in the 1870s, 17–20 *passim*;
  importance of theory for, 29; rebirth in
  1880s, 33
Frauenversammlung, 17, 33
Free love, 165, 252, 261–62, 265, 299
Freethinkers, 2, 3, 4, 11, 12, 21, 40
Free thought, 1, 36, 38
Freiligrath, Ferdinand, 10
Freud, Sigmund, 259
Friedan, Betty, 324
Friendly Evening Association, 59
"Fuer Frauen," 125, 126
Fund-raising, 16–17

Galena, Kans., 116
Garbutt, Mary Alderman, 119–20, 142n32,
  151
Garment unions: and Italian women, 298;
  and Jewish socialist women, 300. *See also*
  ACWA; ILGWU; UGW
Garrison, William Lloyd, 5
Gay, Bettie, 87
Gellert, Hugo, 262
Gender: as category of analysis, xv; in
  Gilded Age woman's movement, 51, 57;
  in Socialist party, 108, 161, 171, 226; in
  Communist party, 320–21, 322
George, Henry, 128, 248
German-American Socialists: in First Inter-
  national, xii; in women's auxiliaries, xiv;
  and woman question, 1–49 *passim*; in
  trade unions, 1, 6, 8, 24, 38; in urban
  Socialist women's sector, 121–23, 125–31,
  135; in response to Second International,
  123; on woman suffrage, 224, 227, 234;
  on social purity, 249; influence on new
  immigrants, 301; mentioned, 161, 171,
  185, 258, 311
Germania Hall, New York City, 15
German Singing Society, 42

German Social Democracy: influence on
  German-American Socialists, 11–12, 26,
  31, 36, 41; Socialist women's movement
  in, xvi–xvii, 14, 125, 146. *See also* Second International; Zetkin, Clara
German Union for Woman Suffrage, 222
Germany: influence on American women's
  movement. *See* German Social Democ-
  racy; *Bund für Mutterschutz und Sexuel
  Reform*; Second International
Gibson, Lydia, 288
Gilded Age: woman's movement in, 53–69
  passim; separate organizations in, xv, xvi,
  161
Gilman, Charlotte Perkins (Stetson): in
  Socialist Labor party, 74; in Nationalist
  movement, 79; on household, 182; poem
  by, 214; on women's oppression, 251; in
  opposition to E. Key, 294, 324n14
Giovannitti, Arturo, 259, 299
Girard, Kans., 110, 113, 114
Girls' Latin School, 57
Glaspell, Susan, 258, 259, 263
Gleichheit, Die, 125, 303
Goebel, Margaret, 153
Gold, Mike, 262
Golden Age, The, 27, 184, 251
Golden Bottle, The (Donnelly), 84–86, 93
Goldman, Emma, xiii, 276, 278, 279
Gompers, Samuel, 190
Gorki, Maxim, 258, 320
Gotha Congress, Germany: in 1875, 11; in
  1896, 125
"Government as Housekeeping," 219
Grange, The. *See* Patrons of Husbandry
Greenwich Village, New York City, 258,
  266, 280, 294
Greer, Joseph D., M.D., 255, 269
Greie, Emile, 36
Greier-Cramer, Johanna: background, 36; as
  Socialist journalist, 36–37, 38, 39; lec-
  ture tour in 1880s, 38–39, 41; influence
  on Jewish Socialist women, 124; work
  with Social Democratic Women's Federa-
  tion, 125, 126, 127; mentioned, 179
Gronlund, Laurence, 24, 25, 76, 80
Grottkau, Paul, 33
Gutman, Herbert G., xv, xvi

Haeckel, Ernest, 271
Haile, Margaret, 94, 105, 117
Hamburg, Germany, 26
Hapgood, Hutchins: on Jewish women, 185;
  on women's advancement, 266; on femi-
  nine nature, 294–95; mentioned, 258
Harlem, New York City, 233

Hart, Schaffner, and Marx, 194
Hauptman, Carl, 271
Haverhill, Mass., 122–23
Hayes, Eleanor, 202
Haymarket Affair, 37, 72, 73, 74
Haywood, William D., 203, 258, 267, 274
Hazlett, Ida Crouch: background, 214, 241*n*1; on woman suffrage, 214–15, 221, 225; criticizes *New York Call*, 313; post–1919 activities, 241, 319; death, 326*n*2
"Hebe." *See* Stern, Meta
Heine, Heinrich, 10
Henry Street Settlement, 189
Herrick, Robert, 263
Herron, Carrie Rand, 105
Heterodoxy, 291, 296
Hillquit, Morris: history of First International, xiv; on woman suffrage victory, 237; mentioned, 124, 200, 236
Hippodrome, The, New York City, 192
History, materialist conception of. *See* Materialist conception of history
History of Civilization in England (Buckle), 156
History of Socialism in the United States (Hillquit), xiv
Hnetynka, Alberta, 197
Hofmann, Emilie, 105
Holyoke, Mass., 38, 39, 74, 153
Home: in Populist ideology, 87; importance to WCTU, 109; Socialist attitudes toward, 117–18, 134, 158, 167–68; in woman suffrage arguments, 220. *See also* Domesticity
"Home Protection," 63
Homosexuality, 261
Household: and women's labor, 35, 180, 182–83, 209*n*8
House of Bondage (Kauffman), 255–56
Howe, Julia Ward: and New England Women's Club, 57; on women's work, 59; at International Council of Women (1888), 67; in Nationalist movement, 77
Howe, Marie Jenney, 291
Howells, William Dean, 263
Hrdiloka, Mary, 42
Hudson County, N.J., 7, 39, 125
Hull House, 72
Hungarian-Americans, 322
Hurst, Fanny, 263
Husbands: influence on Socialist women, 131–33

Ibsen, Henrik, 258, 267
ILGWU. *See* International Ladies' Garment Workers' Union

Illinois: temperance movement in, 62–63; Socialist women in, 108; presidential suffrage in, 232
Illinois Equal Suffrage Society, 163
Illinois Factory Inspection Act (1893), 72
Illinois Woman's Alliance (IWA), 72–73, 88, 91–92, 188
ILU. *See* International Labor Union
Imprecorr, 322
Indiana, 108
Indianapolis, Ind., 21, 105
Indianapolis Equal Suffrage League, 61
Industrial Conference of 1892, 91
Industrial Workers of the World (IWW): role in Lawrence and Paterson strikes, 202–3; on woman suffrage, 228; appeal to young radicals, 258, 288; in birth control campaigns, 274–77; leaders arrested, 279; Branstetter's attitude toward, 311
Infant Cloak Makers' Union, 176–77
Ingerman, Anna, 126, 127, 226, 271
Intercollegiate Socialist Society, 167, 320
International Association of Machinists, 247
International Council of Women, 53, 66–69 *passim*, 88
International Labor Union (ILU), 22, 24
International Ladies' Garment Workers' Union (ILGWU): and Socialists, 187; and women, 188; during shirtwaist strike, 191–92; and P. Newman, 199; in 1910s, 204–7
International Socialist Review, 146, 147, 166, 276, 279
International Woman's Secretariat, 321
International Woman Suffrage Association, 66
International Women's Day. *See* Woman's Day celebrations
International Workingmen's Association (First International): and women, xiv, xvi, 54*n*34; mentioned, 3, 13, 78
Iowa, 108
Italian-Americans: in garment industry, 185; in garment strikes, 192–94; Socialists on woman suffrage, 220–28; Socialist women's organizations among, 298–99
Italian Socialist Federation, 299
IWA. *See* Illinois Woman's Alliance
IWW. *See* Industrial Workers of the World

Jacobs, Dorothy, 206
Jayne, Marie, 134
Jefferson, Thomas, 42, 219
"Jennie June." *See* Croly, Jane Cunningham
Jersey City Heights, N.J., 127
Jewish Daily Forward, 192, 234, 300

Jewish Socialist Federation, 299
Jews: in garment industry, 30, 185; literature on workingwomen, 178–79; in garment strikes, 194, 196; women in Socialist party, xvi, 123–24, 171, 258, 299–300; in relation to German-American Socialists, 123–24, 297; in Communist party, 319, 322
Jonas, Alexander, 12, 40, 45*n*31
Jones, "Mother" Mary, xiii, 193, 248
Journalism: German-American Socialist, 2–3, 29–31, 125; in *Appeal to Reason*, 113–18; in *Chicago Daily Socialist*, 134; role in organizing women, 138–39; shifts in party, 146; on women in party press (1907), 147; in Yiddish Socialist press, 178–79, 300; during shirtwaist strike, 193, 196–97; during garment strike, 195–96; in garment union press, 204; on woman suffrage, 221; in *Masses*, 262; Finnish-American Socialist women's, 303–4; collapse of *Progressive woman*, 306–7; women's liberation, 325
Juneau, Ala., 165
Juneau Woman's Club, 165
Justice, 204, 206

Kaneko, Kiichi, 147
Kansas: as center of Populist women, 83; Socialist women's activities in, 108, 113, 138, 151; woman suffrage campaign in, 231; Italian-American Socialists in, 299; peace activities in, 311–12
Kansas City, Kans., 247
Kansas City Teachers' Association, 154
Kapital, Das (Marx), 3, 28, 31, 114, 171
Karezza, Ethics of Marriage (Stockham), 269
Kauffman, Reginald, 255
Kautsky, Karl, 29
Kehew, Mary Morton, 189
Kelley, Florence, 225, 228
Kerr, Charles H., 111, 255
Key, Ellen: influence in Europe, 270; Feminist philosophy of, 292–93; in mainstream press, 295; in opposition to C. P. Gilman, 324*n*14
Kishinev, pogrom of 1903, 191
Knights of Labor, 24, 37, 39, 65, 70, 71, 73, 81, 84, 91, 177, 187, 189
Kobrin, Leon, 178
Konikow, Antoinette Bucholz: background, 270–71; in Social Democratic Women's Federation, 126, 127; elected to WNC (1908), 150; on woman suffrage, 224; birth control activities of, 270–72, 276

Kotsch, Georgia, 276, 278
Krehbiel, Luella Roberts: a Socialist party organizer, 113, 138, 141*n*10; on materialist conception of history, 158; post–1919 activities, 319; death, 326*n*2

Labor power, 182
Labor Standard, 21, 22
"Ladies' Branch," 92
Ladies' Federal Labor Union, No. 2703 (LFLU), 71
"Ladies' Night," 122
Lafargue, Paul, 29
Lardner, Ring, 263
Lassalle, Ferdinand, 11, 12, 16, 42
Latvian-American Socialist women, 311
Lavoro, Il, 205, 299
Lawrence, Kans., 112
Lawrence, Mass., 10, 22, 201–2, 228
League of Women Voters, 238, 318
Lease, Mary E., 83, 84, 88, 89, 91
Lee, Algernon, 122
Leiserson Shirtwaist Co., 191
Lemlich, Clara, 191, 199, 319
Lenin, V. I., 6, 321
Lewis, Arthur Morrow, 163
Lewis, Lena Morrow: biography, 162–66 *passim*; on woman suffrage, 216, 221; post–1919 activities, 319; death, 326*n*2; mentioned, 169, 306, 309, 310
Lewis, Sinclair, 258, 263
LFLU. *See* Ladies' Federal Labor Union, No. 2703
Liberator, The, 262, 263
Libin, Zalmon, 178
Libraries, circulating, 112
Liebknecht, Wilhelm, 128
"Lifestyle radicalism," 265–67
Lilienthal, Augusta: background and role in German-American Socialist movement, 1–4, 12; on women's rights, 38, 40, 43; mentioned, 53, 179
Lilienthal, Frederick, 32
Lilienthal, Meta. *See* Stern, Meta
Lincoln, Abraham, 2, 42, 219
Lindsey, Estelle Lawton, 244*n*79
Lippman, Walter, 292
Literature: in German-American Socialist movement, 9–10; in Nationalist movement, 75; *Progressive Woman* recommends, 156; in Yiddish Socialist movement, 178–79; on prostitution, 90; of New Morality, 262–65 *passim*; mentioned, 90
Lithuanian-Americans: WNC attitude toward, 311; in Communist party, 322

Lithuanian Women's Progressive Alliance,
    301–2
"Little Balkans," Kans., 299
Little Falls, N.Y., 202
Livermore, Mary Rice: in Gilded Age
    woman's movement, 49–53 passim, 67,
    68; on WCTU, 62; in Nationalist move-
    ment, 79, 80; endorses Socialism, 121
Lloyd, Henry Demarest, 248
Local 25, ILGWU, 192, 204–7
London, Jack, 258, 320
London, Meyer, 223, 232
Long Island City, N.Y., 127
Looking Backward (Bellamy): plot, 75–76;
    women's opinions of, 79; Willard's reac-
    tion to, 80; influence on Socialist
    women, 108; mentioned, 78, 84, 86
Los Angeles, Calif.: Nationalist movement
    in, 77–78; Socialist women's activities in,
    119–20, 135, 136; woman suffrage cam-
    paign in, 230; anti-prostitution campaign
    in, 256
Lotta de Classe, 298, 299
Love and Marriage (Key), 294
Love's Coming of Age (Carpenter), 260–61
Lowe, Caroline: biography, 173n22; organ-
    izing in Kansas, 1908, 151; as WNC
    organizer, 154–60 passim; on women's
    strikes, 197–98; on woman suffrage, 216;
    post-1919 activities, 319; death, 326n2;
    mentioned, 152, 307
Lowell, Amy, 262
Lowell, Mass., 153
Lower East Side, New York City, 185, 192,
    233
Lutheran church, 302, 303
Lynn, Mass., 153
Lyser, Gustav, 12, 18

McAuliffe, John, 22
McCone, Selma Jokela, 303–4
McCormick, Fannie, 88
McKinley, William, 91
Madden, Okla., 116
Madison Square Garden, New York City,
    203, 237
Magdeburg, Germany, 36
Maggie, A Girl of the Streets (Crane), 263
Mailly, Bertha, 190
Maley, Anna A.: WNC organizer, 152–54;
    in WTUL, 190; in woman suffrage cam-
    paign, 230; death, 319, 326n2
Malkiel, Leon, 177
Malkiel, Theresa Serber: background,
    176–79 passim; in Social Democratic

Women's Federation, 126, 127; on
    women's labor, 184; joins WTUL, 190; in
    garment strikes, 192, 197–98, 199, 200;
    on woman suffrage, 223, 225–26, 233–35;
    peace activities of, 312; post–1919 activi-
    ties, 319; death, 326n2; mentioned, 306,
    309
Manchester, N.H., 7
Männerchor, 32
Man's World, A (Bullard), 264
Marcuse, Herbert, 324
Marcy, Mary, 166
Margolin, Anna, 176
Marot, Helen, 190, 203
Marriage: J. Greie-Cramer on, 39; K.
    O'Hare's, 110; M. Berger's, 129–31; as
    escape from wage labor, 186; K. O'Hare
    on, 246; in Socialist analysis, 250, 252;
    among Jewish free thinkers, 261–62;
    among new intellectuals, 265–66; in E.
    Key's philosophy, 293
"Marseilles," 111
Marx, Karl: on First International, xiv; on
    Lassalleanism, 11; on woman suffrage,
    11–12; opinion of Socialist Labor party
    (1880s), 25–26; on women, 27; economic
    theories of, 181–82; on free love, 252; on
    sex, 270; mentioned, 42, 132, 160, 282,
    321, 324
Marxian Economics: A Popular Introduction
    (Untermann), 180–81
Marxism: in the United States, 171, 323–24
Massachusetts, 229, 232
Massachusetts Woman's Christian Temper-
    ance Union, 62
Masses, The: role among new intellectuals,
    259, 262, 263, 267; defends M. Sanger,
    276
Materialist conception of history: in A.
    Bebel's analysis, 26–29; Socialist women's
    study of, 157–58, 218; on labor, 180–84;
    by F. Engels, 250–51; by E. Carpenter,
    261
Matriarchy, 27, 291. See also Golden Age,
    The
May Days (Taggard), 288
Maynard, Mila Tupper, 168
Megow, Ellen, 195
Membership, Socialist parties: in 1870s, 7,
    21; in 1880s, 24, 38; women's in Socialist
    party (1912), 160; effect of suffrage agita-
    tion on New York City, 235; in 1912, 228;
    new immigrants in Socialist party, 298;
    decline in New York women's, 306; New
    York women's (1918), 313; women's in
    Communist party (1940s), 323

Mena, Ark., 319

Menomenee, Wis., 7

"Merrie England" (Blatchford), 111

Michigan, 302

Middle-class women: in First International,
xiv; German-American Socialists' attitude
toward, 127; Socialists' attitude toward
suffragists, 218; question of cooperation
with suffragists, 222–29 *passim*; Communist attitude toward, 323

Milholland, Inez, 238

Mill, John Stuart, 218

Milwaukee, Wis.: Socialist women's activity
in, 17, 121; home of M. Berger, 129–31;
woman suffrage campaigns in, 231; antiprostitution campaigns in, 256; mentioned, 6, 7, 185

"Milwaukee Idea," 209n18

Minnesota, 302

Minor, Robert, 262

Missouri, 108, 110

Mitchell, Juliet, 324

Modernism, 262

Modern Yiddish Poetry (Imber), 176

Monmouth, Ill., 115

Monmouth College, 162, 164

Monogamy, 284n4

"Monster petition" (1909), 223–24

Montana, 231

Montessori, Maria, 167

Morgan, Anne, 200

Morgan, Elizabeth, 71, 72, 92

Morgan, Lewis Henry, 250, 321

Morgan, Thomas J., 71, 72

Morris, William, 111, 260, 280

Morrisania, N.Y., 127

Motherhood: E. Debs on, 109; K. O'Hare
on, 110; Socialists' attitude toward, 118;
in woman suffrage arguments, 219–20; in
E. Key's philosophy, 292; discussion of in
New York Call, 295; J. Spargo on, 296

Motherhood and the "Bloody Five Laws"
(Stern), 312

Mothers' League of Boston, 322

Mott, Lucretia, 50, 67

Mrs. Herndon's Income (Campbell), 90

Multitude, The, 114

Muscatine, Iowa, 115, 185

National American Woman Suffrage Association (NAWSA): conventions reported by
J. Conger, 114; Lewis's work for, 163;
Hazlett's work for, 215; Socialist cooperation with (1909), 223–24; moves headquarters to New York City, 224; Italian-
American Socialists' attitude toward, 228;
in state woman suffrage campaigns,
229–32; during World War I, 235–38

National Association Opposed to Woman
Suffrage, 237

National Birth Control League, 277, 278–79

National Council of Women, 81, 88

National Educational Committee, 167

National Executive Committee, 147, 152,
166, 223, 274, 289, 308, 309

National Labor Union, 54

National Organization of Women, 324

National Purity Congress, 254

National Rip-Saw, 248, 276, 277, 279, 295

National Socialist Lyceum Bureau, 167

National Woman's Alliance, 88

National Woman's Christian Temperance
Union. *See* Woman's Christian Temperance Union

National Woman's Commission, 321, 322

National Woman's party, 237–38, 296

National Woman Suffrage Association, 66

Nationalism, Bellamy: women's participation in, 77–81 *passim*; influence on
Socialist women, 119, 120; mentioned,
52, 70, 136

Nationalist Woman's Alliance, 77

Natural rights, 218–19, 228

NAWSA. *See* National American Woman
Suffrage Association

Nebraska, 108, 247

Negro Commission, 320

Nelson, Caroline, 276, 277, 278, 280

Neo-Malthusianism, 269–72 *passim*

Neue Zeit, Die (Germany), 29

Neue Zeit, Die (New York), 2–3

Nevada, 231

Newark, N.J., 17, 125

Newark Congress of 1877, 19

New Bedford, Mass., 33, 202

NEWC. *See* New England Women's Club

New England Hospital for Women and
Children, 57

New England Women's Club (NEWC),
57–59, 77, 79

New immigrants: and Socialist party,
297–98; and Socialist women's organizations, 298–304 *passim*; WNC's attitude
toward, 311; in Communist party, 319. *See
also* individual nationalities

New intellectuals: role in Socialist party,
259–68 *passim*; role in birth control campaigns, 268–80 *passim*

New Jersey, 232

New Left, 323–25

Newman, Pauline: in garment unions, 188,

Newman, Pauline (*cont.*)
    199, 206; in WTUL, 189; in woman suf-
    frage campaigns, 223, 234
New Morality: and new intellectuals,
    257–68 *passim*; in birth control cam-
    paigns, 269; and M. Sanger, 272;
    assessed, 279, 283; and Feminism, 290;
    and Communists, 321
New Review, 262, 276, 279
News from Nowhere (Morris), 260, 262
New Testament, 64, 115, 116
New Thought, 114, 115, 120, 141*n*16, 161
New unionism, 187, 204–6
"New Women," 56; 160–69 *passim*
New York, N.Y.: and First International,
    xiv; German-American Socialists in, 1, 7,
    17, 21, 32, 33, 34, 38, 39, 106, 127;
    place of publication of *Die Neue Zeit*, 2;
    clothing industry in, 30, 176, 184, 185,
    187, 204; benevolent activities in, 54;
    women's clubs in Gilded Age, 56–57;
    Socialist women's activities in, 73, 121,
    135–36, 176; Jewish Socialists' activities
    in, 124, 297, 299–300; activities of Social
    Democratic Women's Federation in, 125,
    127; May Day parade (1895), 126; chil-
    dren of Lawrence strikers transported to,
    202; woman suffrage activities in,
    224–25, 233–38; antiprostitution cam-
    paigns, 254, 256; birth control campaigns
    in, 271–72, 276; Feminist activities in,
    290, 291; Socialist peace activities in,
    311–13; women's liberation groups in,
    325
New York Association Opposed to Woman
    Suffrage, 237
New York Call: role of Meta Stern in, 128,
    236, 238; in shirtwaist strike, 193; on sex
    issues, 262, 272–74, 276; on mother-
    hood, 295; on discrimination within
    party, 305; women's column (1919), 313;
    mentioned, 146, 234, 237, 264, 325
New Yorker Volkszeitung: in women's joun-
    alism, 29, 40, 147; on women's labor
    (1882), 30; influence on Social Demo-
    cratic Women's Federation, 125, 126,
    127, 128; on shirtwaist strike, 196
New York Labor Temple, 198
New York Press Club, 57
New York Times, 237
New York Worker, 128
Nietzsche, Friedrich Wilhelm, 258, 260
Northwestern University, 166, 167
"Nude Descending a Staircase" (Duchamp),
    283

Oakland, Calif., 74, 118–19
Oaks, Gladys, 263
Ogden's Grove, Chicago, Ill., 33
O'Hare, Kate Richards: background and
    early activities, 246–48 *passim*; as Social-
    ist propagandist, 110, 155, 253, 255; in
    birth control campaign, 269, 276, 277; as
    F. Crittenton worker, 247, 284*n*3; charges
    discrimination in party, 308; post-1919
    activities, 319; death, 326*n*2
Ohio, 232
Ohio River Valley, 62, 82
Oklahoma, 231, 312
Omaha, Nebr., 34, 111, 112
Oneida, N.Y., 74
Only a Flock of Women (Diaz), 79
Oregon, 163, 229
O'Reilly, Leonora: background and labor
    activity, 189; addresses shirtwaist strikers,
    192; in Socialist party, 199, 200; on
    woman suffrage, 226
Organizations, women's. *See* Women's
    organizations
*Origins of the Family, Private Property and
    the State* (Engels), 250–51
O'Sullivan, Mary Kenney, 189
Ottawa County, Kans., 246
Otto-Walster, August, 6, 10

Pabst Coliseum, New York City, 223
Pack, Emma D., 88
Paine Memorial Hall, Boston, Mass., 118
Panic of 1873, 5, 60
Parlor meetings: in WCTU, 63, 97*n*32; in
    Socialist movement, 110
Parsons, Lucy, xiii
Party, political: in relationship to Socialism,
    6–7
"Party wives," 121, 129
Pasadena, Calif., 155
Passaic, N.J., 202
Paterson, N.J., 16, 185, 228, 275, 320
Patrons of Husbandry: in Illinois, 63, 83;
    ties with WCTU, 64; women's position
    in, 82–83
Peace activities: of Socialist women, 3,
    311–13 *passim*
Pennsylvania, 153
Penny, Virginia, 55
People's Party, 86, 105–6, 119. *See also*
    Populism
"Petticoat pockets," 155
Philadelphia, Pa.: German-American
    Socialist movement in, 7, 17, 19; Social

Philadelphia, Pa. (*cont.*)
  Democratic Women's Federation in, 125;
  growth of shirtwaist trade in, 184; shirt-
  waist strike in, 193–94; garment unions
  in, 204; and Lawrence strike, 202
Phillips, Wendell, 5, 70, 97*n*32
Pike, Violette, 190
Pleasonton, Kans., 154
Plekhanov, Georg, 29
Point Loma, Calif., 78
Poland, 320
Polish-Americans, 185, 201–2
Political democracy: Socialist opinion of,
  220
Ponca, Okla., 117–18
Poole, Ernest, 258
Populism: women's role in, 82–90 *passim*;
  influence on Socialist women, 108, 113,
  115, 116, 247; mentioned, 52, 70, 161.
  See also People's party
Portland, Oreg., 276
Postgate, R. W., xiv
Poyntz, Juliet Stuart, 206–7, 319, 320, 323
Pratt Institute, 189
Preparedness campaigns, 236
Prevey, Marguerite, 150, 151
Progressive party, 228
Progressive reformers, 253–55
Progressive Woman: founded by J. Conger-
  Kaneko, 148; as propaganda, 155; circula-
  tion figures, 156; study lessons printed in,
  157–58; attacked by IWW women, 228;
  suppressed, 255; model for *Toveritar*, 303;
  ceases publication, 306-7; mentioned,
  160, 164, 309, 323, 325
Prohibition party, 65, 105, 225
Proletarka, 301
Propaganda: for women, 138; by WNC,
  155–56, 160; among workingwomen, 186;
  for woman suffrage, 219–20, 223; among
  Italian-American Socialists, 299; in *Jew-
  ish Daily Forward*, 300
Prostitution: antebellum programs, 54; and
  Illinois Woman's Alliance, 72; and Progressive reformers, 253–54; Socialist anal-
  ysis of, 254–56; Socialist campaigns
  against, 256–57; mentioned, 170, 220,
  246, 247, 290, 309. *See also* White
  slavery
Protective Committee, 58
Providence, R.I., 21, 46*n*62, 59, 74, 94
Provincetown Players, 258
Psychoanalysis, 259
Psychopathia Sexualis (Krafft-Ebing), 259
Pullman Strike of 1894, 91

Pure Sociology (Ward), 156
Purvis, Robert, 67

Queens, N.Y., 233
*Question of Workers and Women at the Pres-
  ent Time, The* (Zetkin), 183

"Race suicide," 252, 295
Radnicka Straza, 301
Railroad strike, Southwestern, 33
Rand School, 319
Ranke, Leopold von, 26
Rauh, Ida, 190, 258, 276, 278
Reading, Pa., 185
Reconstruction, 70
"Red scare," 283, 318
Reed, John, 258
Reitzel, Robert, 10, 261
Republican party, 68
Revolutionary Almanac (Havel), 275
Rhine, Alice Hyneman, 21, 69, 73
Ricker, Allen W., 252
Robins, Margaret Dreier, 228
Robinson, Boardman, 262
Robinson, William J., M.D., 271
Rochdale Cooperative Plan, 136
Rochester, N.Y., 30, 184, 185
Rodman, Henrietta, 258
Romanticism: among German-American
  Socialists, 4, 8, 9, 11, 26, 40–41; in A.
  Bebel's analysis, 27; in Gilded Age
  woman's movement, 51–52, 93; in indig-
  enous radical movements, 89; WNC's
  attitude toward, 152; and Socialist
  women, 161, 170; woman as symbol of,
  262
Roosevelt, Theodore, 228, 295
Rose Door, The (Baker), 255
Rosenfeld, Morris, 124, 196, 320
Rovnost Ludu, 301
Ruskin College, 114, 167
Russia, 191, 302
Russian Revolution, 170, 239, 318
Russian Workingman's Club, 177

Sacco, Nicola, 322
St. Louis, Mo.: German-American Social-
  ists in, 6, 7, 15, 17, 42; site of Industrial
  Conference (1892), 91; Socialist activities
  in, 121, 125; garment industry in, 184,
  185
St. Louis Labor, 147
St. Paul, Minn., 35–36, 276
Sample, J. N. (Mrs.), 118
Sandburg, Carl, 262

San Francisco, Calif., 7, 59, 118, 137, 276
Sanger, Margaret: in birth control campaign, 272–79 *passim*; mentioned, 203, 258, 266
Sanger, William, 258, 266
Sanitary Commission, U.S., 50
Sauk County, Wis., 166
Scandinavian Socialist women, 311
Schell, Ada K., 117–18
Schenectady, N.Y., 313
Schenectady Citizen, 318
Schiller, Friedrich, 9
Schneiderman, Rose, 187–89, 199, 226
Schneppe, Charlotte, 127
Schonberg, Mary, 306
Schools, Socialist, 16, 32, 112, 300
Scovell, Georgia, 116
Scudder, Vida, 202
Seattle, Wash., 227, 305
Second International: influence on Socialist women in U.S., 107, 123, 169, 270, 306; resolutions adopted in 1907, 147; on women's organization, 171; on woman suffrage, 222–23; on sexual oppression, 250
Seneca Falls, N.Y., 50, 66, 291
Separate organizations, women's: in Gilded Age, xv; among native-born Socialist women, 107, 110–12, 119, 120; M. Dunham on, 137–38; J. Spargo on, 147; J. Conger-Kaneko on, 148–49, 308–9; M. Stern on, 151; L. M. Lewis on, 164; position of WNC on, 152, 308–9; in Seattle, Wash., 305
Serbian-Americans, 301
Severance, Caroline, 77–78
Sex. *See* Birth control; New Morality; Prostitution; Social purity
"Sexuelfrage, die," 270
Sharp, Mary, 116
Shattinger, Ada, 43
Shavelson, Clara Lemlich. *See* Lemlich, Clara
Shaw, Anna Howard, 215
Shaw, George Bernard, 260, 271
Shirtwaist strike of New York (1909–10), 190–94 *passim*, 225
Sichyns'ky, Irene, 301
Simons, A. M., 166, 167
Simons, May Wood: biography, 166–68 *passim*; elected to WNC (1908), 150; on Socialist theory, 156; described, 168; on woman suffrage, 227; resigns from WNC, 307–8; post-1919 activities, 319, 326n2; mentioned, 212, 310
Sinclair, Upton, 258, 320
Single-tax campaign, 113

Sioux City, Iowa, 112
Sister Carrie (Dreiser), 263
Slavic-Americans: in Chicago garment strike, 194; in Socialist party, 297, 301; women's organizations, xvi, 301, 319
Sloan, John, 234, 262
Slovakian-Americans, 311
Slovenian-Americans, 301
Smith, Anna Ferry, 74, 120
Smith-Rosenberg, Carroll, xv
Social Democracy of America, 113, 136, 177
Social Democratic party of Germany. *See* German Social Democracy
Social Democratic party of Russia, 270
Social Democratic Women's Federation, 125–28 *passim*, 151, 224
Social Ethics, 115
Social Evil. *See* Prostitution; White slavery
Social Evil and the Remedy (Greer), 255
Social Gospel, 64, 68, 115
Socialism and Motherhood (Spargo), 295
Socialist Labor party (SLP): and Newark Conference (1877), 19–20; and "American" sections, 20–24 *passim*; and *Frauenfrage*, 29–31; and *Frauenbund*, 31–40 *passim*; and women reformers, 71–75 *passim*, 92, 106; position on women suffrage, 92, 105, 221; position on women's labor, 92; influence on Socialist women, 113, 119, 121; I. Fales's background in, 316; T. Malkiel's background in, 177; role in labor movement, 186; A. Konikow's background in, 270
Socialist Party of America: founding conference (1901), 105; as successor to indigenous radical movements, 107–21 *passim*; as successor to immigrant radical movements, 121–35 *passim*; women's separate organizations in, 135–40 *passim*; "new women" leaders in, 160–69 *passim*; attitude toward women's labor in, 185–86; support of women's strikes by, 109–204 *passim*; suffrage campaign of, 205, 229–38 *passim*; with regard to new unions, 204–7; theories of woman suffrage, 217–21 *passim*; strategies for woman suffrage, 221–29 *passim*; support of social purity, 249–57 *passim*; attitude toward New Morality, 257–68; role in birth control campaigns, 268–80 *passim*; conflicts of women within, 288–89; with regard to Feminism, 290–97 *passim*; new immigrant women's activity in, 297–304 *passim*; decline of women's leadership in, 505–10 *passim*; peace activities in,

Socialist Party of America (*cont.*)
311–12; post-1919 activities of, 323. *See also* Membership, socialist parties; National Executive Committee; Woman's National Committee
Socialist Trades and Labor Alliance, 177
Socialist Woman. See Progressive Woman
Socialist Women's League of Chicago, 149, 151, 158
Socialist Women's Society of Greater New York, 178
Social purity: supported by Socialists, 249–57 *passim*; mentioned, 58, 109, 110, 138
Social Reform Club, 189
Societies, sick-and-death benefit, 7, 122, 124–25
Society for Ethical Culture, 189
Society of Christian Socialists, 79
Songs, revolutionary, 15, 111, 159
Sorel, Georges, 258
Sorge, Friedrich, xiv
Sorosis, 57, 65
Sorrows of Cupid (O'Hare), 246
Soviet Union, 319, 322
Sozialist, Der, 36, 39
Spargo, John, 147, 262, 295
Spingarn, Joel, 262
Spiritualism, 78, 116, 138
Springfield, Mass., 153
Stahl, Anna, 127
Stanton, Elizabeth Cady, 5, 54, 66–67, 108, 219, 321
Stern, Meta Lilienthal: early life, 128–29; elected to WNC (1908), 150; on separate organizations, 151; analysis of women's history, 183; in WTUL, 190; on shirtwaist strike, 196, 197; on woman suffrage, 216, 223, 226; "Votes for Women" column by, 234, 235; "New Citizens" column by, 238; discusses discrimination within party, 305; peace activities of, 312; post-1919 activities, 319; death, 326n2
Stevens, Alzina Parsons, 22
Stirner, Max, 258
Stockham, Alice B., M.D., 269
Stockholm, Sweden, 292
Stokes, J. G. Phelps, 320, 321
Stokes, Rose Pastor: as Communist leader, 319–21 *passim*; mentioned, 192, 276, 278
Stone, Lucy, 50, 67, 79
Strasser, Adolph, 12
"Strike newsies," 193, 195–96
Strikes: Lawrence, Mass., textile (1877), 10; great railroad (1877), 21; Southwestern railroad (1883), 33; Pullman (1894), 91;

New York cloak makers, 177; in garment industry (1909–1911), 190–201 *passim*; Lawrence, Mass., textile (1912–13), 201–2; Paterson textile (1913), 202–3; effect on woman suffrage campaign, 228; role of Italian-American women in, 299; mentioned, 322
Strindberg, August, 261
Students for a Democratic Society (SDS), 324–25
Stuttgart Conference (1907), 147, 222, 227
Sunrise Club, 290
"Surplus value," 181
Sweden, 270
Symes, Lillian, 259
Syndicalism, 274–75, 288

Taggard, Genevieve, 258–59
Temperance: German-American Socialists' attitude toward, 5; and the Gilded Age woman's movement, 60–69 *passim*; campaigns in Illinois, 62–63; Willard's pronouncements on, 80; Patrons of Husbandry on, 82–83; in woman suffrage campaigns, 232; among Finnish-American Socialists, 303. *See also* Women's Christian Temperance Union
"Temperance ballot," 61
Terre Haute, Ind., 216
Texas, 164
Theater, German-American Socialist, 15–16, 33
Theosophy: in Nationalist movement, 78; influence on Socialist women, 115
Third International, 322. *See also* Communist party
Thomas, Elizabeth H., 105, 231
Thompson, Edward P., xiii
Tingley, Katherine, 78
Todd, Marion, 83, 88
Tokology (Stockham), 269
Tompkins Square Park, 45n31
Toveritar, 303–4
Trades and Labor Assembly, Chicago, 71, 72, 92
Trade unions. *See* individual entries
Trenton, Mo., 114
Trenton, N.J., 185
Tresca, Carlo, 276
Triangle Waist Company, 188, 191
Tridon, Andre, 264
Tufts University, 270
Turnvereine, 2, 32
"Two-arm" labor strategy, 186, 188
Tyomies, 303

UGW. *See* United Garment Workers
Ukraine, 191
Ukrainian-Americans, 322
Uncle Tom's Cabin (Stowe), 75
Union Congress (1876), 13
Union Label Leagues, 122
Union Labor League, 230
Union Signal, 81, 119
Unitarian Church, 120
United Cloth Hat and Cap Makers' Union, 187
United Council of Working Class Women (or Wives), 321
United Garment Workers (UGW), 189, 194–96
United Hebrew Trades of New York, 177
United Mine Workers, 298
United States of America, 7
University of Chicago, 167
University of Chicago Settlement, 166
Untermann, Ernest, 114, 180, 313
Untermeyer, Louis, 262
Uprising of 20,000. *See* Shirtwaist strike of New York (1909–10)
Utopian settlements, 93–94

Valesh, Eva McDonald, 200
Vanguard, 139
Vanzetti, Bartolomeo, 322
Venereal disease, 254
Vickery, Fanny Randolph, 83
Vida Scudder Club, 119
Vietnam War, 324
Vitalism, 292
Voice of the Women's Liberation Movement, 325
Volovich, Sarah, 233
Vorse, Mary Heaton, 258, 263
Vrooman, Walter, 114

Wage Earners' Votes for Women Club, 230
Wallace, Zerelda, 61, 68, 79
Waltham, Mass., 73,
Ward, Frank Lester, 251
War Labor Board, 204
Warren County, Ill., 162
Washington, George, 42
Washington, 230
Was It Gracia's Fault? (Kerr), 255
Wayland, J. A., 113
Wedekind, Frank, 261, 271
WEIU. *See* Women's Educational and Industrial Union
Wells, H. G., 271
Westfield, Mass., 153

West Meriden, Conn., 7
West Point, Okla., 117
West Virginia, 164
Wetherell, Ellen T., 145
What Did Gracia Do? (n.a.), 255
"What Every Mother Should Know" (Sanger), 272–73
White slavery, 74, 253–56 *passim*
Whitman, Walt, 4, 283
Wholesome Woman, The (Greer), 269
Wichita, Kans., 83, 112
Wilcox, Ella Wheeler, 120
Willard, Frances: role in WCTU, 62–68 *passim*; at International Council of Women (1888), 66–68; and Nationalism, 80–81; at 1892 Industrial Conference, 90–91; preaches Socialism, 94, 140n4; influence among Socialist women, 108, 117, 119; Romanticism of, 170; on motherhood, 293; mentioned, 136, 321
William, Morris, 239
William Morris Club, 118
Wilshire, Mary, 149
Wilshire's Magazine, 118
Wilson, Annie, 115
Wilson, J. Stitt, 229
Wilson, Woodrow, 238, 306, 311, 312
Wimmin Ain't Got No Kick (O'Hare), 155
Winfield, Kans., 113
Wisconsin, 229, 231–32
WNC. *See* Woman's National Committee
Woman and Temperance (Willard), 63-64
Woman and the Social Problem (Simons), 167
Woman Citizen, 236
Womanhood: in Gilded Age, xv; German-American Socialists' attitudes toward, 8–11; and Gilded Age woman's movement, 53; in Populist ideology, 84; in indigenous radicalism, 89, 109; J. Conger-Kaneko on, 114, 148; in urban Socialist movement, 134; E. Debs on, 155; among Jewish Socialist women, 179; relation to Feminism, 297; among Slavic Socialists, 301; R. P. Stokes on, 319
Woman Movement, The (Key), 294
Woman question: in First International, xiv; in Germany, xvii; A. Lilienthal on, 1, 40; German-American Socialists on, 1–49 *passim*; in *Looking Backward*, 76; and Socialists, 109, 221, 271; WNC's position on, 152; L. M. Lewis on, 164–65; in *Jewish Daily Forward*, 196; and Communism, 321, 327n13; in the New Left, 324–25
Women Rebel, 275, 277, 278

Woman's Christian Alliance of Lufkin, Tex., 89
Woman's Christian Temperance Union (WCTU): in Gilded Age, 60–69 *passim*; and Socialist Labor party, 74; and Nationalism, 81; and Patrons of Husbandry, 82–83; and Populists, 84, 87; and Socialist women, 112, 115, 116, 119; and L. M. Lewis, 162, 164; and K. R. O'Hare, 247, 248; and women suffrage, 220; mentioned, 72, 136, 170, 230
Woman's Day Celebrations, 223, 233, 313, 322
Woman's Journal, 61, 236
Woman's movement: in the Gilded Age, 53–69 *passim*; and Socialism, 49–94 *passim*; in 20th century, 106
Woman's National Committee (WNC): history (1908–1913), 145–72 *passim*; on woman suffrage, 227; decline, 289; demise of, 304–10 *passim*; failures assessed, 310–13 *passim*; activities during World War I, 311–13; mentioned, 323
Woman's National Progressive League, 149, 151
Woman's National Socialist League. *See* Woman's National Socialist Union
Woman's National Socialist Union, 135–38 *passim*
Woman's Parliament, 120
Woman's Peace party, 312
Woman's Progressive Society of Yonkers, N.Y., 178
Woman's rights movement: German-American Socialists' attitudes toward, 1, 2–3, 11, 18; M. Livermore and, 49; in relation to International Council of Woman, 66–68; E. Key on, 293; mentioned, 2, 224
Woman's Socialist League of Los Angeles, 119
Woman's Socialist Union, Calif., 151, 230
Woman's Socialist Union of Omaha, Nebr., 111
Woman's Tribune, 117
Woman suffrage: advocated by V. Woodhull, xiv; German-American Socialists on, 1, 4, 12, 19; K. Marx on, 11–12; in Germany, 3, 11, 12, 222; Socialist Labor party on, 22, 41, 72, 92; L. Gronlund on, 25; A. Bebel on, 28; M. Livermore's role in, 50; status in Gilded Age, 53, 68; in WCTU, 60, 61–62; F. Willard's efforts in behalf, 63; and Patrons of Husbandry, 83; and Populists, 84–91; among Socialist women, 113, 119, 153, 158; Stuttgart Conference on (1907), 147, 222, 227;

WNC position on, 152; L. M. Lewis on, 163; Socialist campaigns for, 229–39 *passim*; K. R. O'Hare's ties with, 248; in relation to Feminism, 290, 291; among new immigrant Socialists, 301, 304; Communist position on, 321
Woman Suffrage party, 225
Woman under Socialism. *See* Frau und der Sozializmus, Die (Bebel)
Woman Worker, 322
Women: A Journal of Liberation, 325
Women, "fallen." *See* Prostitution
Women: The Longest Revolution (Mitchell), 324
Women and Economics (Gilman), 79
Women's Agitation Committee of Chicago, 195
Women's auxiliaries: in German-American Socialist movement, xvi, 14–20 *passim*, 106–7; in Socialist party, 122–23, 161; in United Mine Workers, 298
Women's clubs: in Gilded Age, 55–60 *passim*; C. Brown's role in, 72; in Los Angeles, 78; M. Lease's role in, 84; Socialist women's, 106, 110–12, 167; Socialist suffrage in New York, 233–35; in Juneau, Ala., 165; Heterodoxy, 296
Women's Educational and Industrial Union (WEIU), 58–59, 79, 189
Women's labor: German-American Socialists' attitude toward, 4, 8, 12, 26; Gotha Congress position on, 11; L. Gronlund's attitude toward, 25; SLP position on, 26, 30, 41, 90; A. Bebel's analysis of, 27; in 1880s, 29–30; in cigar industry, 30; in domestic service, 30, 35; in Gilded Age woman's movement, 53–60 *passim*; in Chicago, 71; Socialist study of, 158; position of Yiddish Socialists on, 178–79; Socialist theory of, 180–84 *passim*; growth in, 184–85, 209n12; in relation to Feminism, 290, 291
Women's liberation, 324, 325
Women's organizations: German-American Socialist (1870s), 14–20 *passim*; German-American Socialist (1880s), 31–40 *passim*; in the Gilded Age, 52–69 *passim*; in SLP (1880s), 70–75 *passim*; in Nationalist movement, 77–78; in Populism, 88–89; Socialist in Midwest and Plains states, 107–18 *passim*; Californian Socialist, 118–20; urban Socialist, 121–35 *passim*; J. Conger-Kaneko on, 148–49; party resolutions (1908), 150; among new immigrant Socialists, 298–304 *passim*; among Feminists, 296; WNC's role in regard to,

Women's organizations (*cont.*)
308–9; in Chicago after World War I, 313;
in Communist party, 321–23. *See also*
Women's auxiliaries; Women's clubs; Sep-
arate organizations; Individual entries
Women's Progressive Society, 124
Women's strikes (1909–1913), 190–201
passim
Women's Trade Union League (WTUL):
Socialist members of, 178, 189–90, 200;
in shirtwaist strike, 192–94 *passim*; in gar-
ment strike, 195; in Lawrence strike, 201;
and woman suffrage, 224, 225; men-
tioned, 199, 203, 207, 208, 297, 320
Women Workers Progressive League of
Cleveland, 322
Woodhull, Victoria C., xiv, 3, 21, 38, 41
Woodward, Okla., 116
Workers' party, 320
"Working Girls' Club," 266
Workingmen's Party of the U.S., 13
Working Women's Protective Union, 54
Working Women's Society of New York, 54,
73, 188, 189
Working Women's Union of Chicago, 22,
23, 71

Workman's Circle (*Arbeter Ring*), 124, 270,
300
Workpeople's College, 303
World War I: M. W. Simons and, 167; and
German-American Socialists, 130; and
labor movement, 203–4; NAWSA activi-
ties during, 236; WNC activities during,
311–13
World War II, 323
Wortis, Rose, 320
Wright, Carroll D., 58
WTUL. *See* Women's Trade Union League
Wyoming, 215

Xenia, Ohio, 82

Yiddish culture, 300. *See also* Jews;
Literature
Yonkers, N.Y., 178, 185
Young, Art, 262

Zeh, Nellie: role in Socialist party, 131–33,
139; regional organizer for WNC, 154;
interprets women's strikes, 197–98; post-
1919 activities, 319, 326*n*2
Zetkin, Clara, xvii, 125, 183, 321

A Note on the Author

Mari Jo Buhle was born in Waukegan, Illinois, and received her B.A. from the University of Illinois (1966). She earned an M.A. from the University of Connecticut (1968) and a Ph.D. from the University of Wisconsin (1974). She is presently an associate professor of American civilization and history at Brown University. Her publications include *The Concise History of Woman Suffrage* (with Paul M. Buhle, University of Illinois Press, 1978) and chapters in several women's history collections, as well as numerous journal articles.